ابر و باد و مه و خورشید و فلک در کارند

تا تو نانی بکف آری و به غفلت نخوری

همه از بهر تو سرگشته و فرمانبردار

شرط انصاف نباشد که تو فرمان نبری

سعدی

CLOUDS, WIND, MOON, SUN, HEAVENS,
ALL ARE BUSY THAT THOU MIGHT ACQUIRE
A BIT OF BREAD, AND EAT IT IN REMEMBRANCE.
FOR THY SAKE ALL CREATION DASHES ABOUT
OBEYING ORDERS—IS IT RIGHT THEN
THAT ONLY THOU SHOULD DISOBEY?

SAADI

Iran
Elements of Destiny
has been created as a companion volume to
Persia
Bridge of Turquoise,
designed and photographed by Roloff Beny.

MOHAMAD MOGHDAM, Editor-in-Chief
JACQUILINE RUDOLPH TOUBA, Editor

HOSSEIN ALI ANVARI
LALEH BAKHTIAR
WILLIAM O. BEEMAN
ALI BOLOUKBASHI
MOHAMMAD HASSAN GANJI
REZA HASHEMIAN
AMIR ABBAS HOVEYDA
E. NADER KHALILI
MOIRA MOSER-KHALILI
NADER AFSHAR NADERI
SAID NEJAND
BAGHER SAROUKHANI
PETER LAMBORN WILSON

Notes to the plates by
MITCHELL CRITES

SHAHRAM KHIAL
Assistant to the Editorial Director

IRAN
ELEMENTS OF DESTINY

Library of Congress
Catalog Card No. 78-53014
ISBN 0-89696-000-5

Printed and bound in England

Designed and photographed by ROLOFF BENY

Editorial direction by
SHAHROKH AMIRARJOMAND

Everest House
Publishers *New York*

MESSAGE FROM HIS IMPERIAL MAJESTY THE SHAHANSHAH ARYAMEHR

Iran today is in the process of a fundamental transformation which not only has a material bearing but also embraces a deep social and spiritual resurgence for Iranian society.

Throughout the country, from north to south and from east to west, an unprecedented creative effort is now taking place. Factories, workshops, roads, ports, airports, urban and rural housing, dams, hospitals, clinics, agricultural centers, forests and parks, educational, cultural, scientific and art museums, sports complexes, and many other vital links one after the other are being formed and brought to serve the interests of the country.

Paralleling this physical advancement, the spiritual and cultural foundations of the modern Iranian society are also being established. This must in a short period of time transform the Iranian nation into one of the dynamic societies of the world through the achievement of political, social and economic democracy, democratic economy, expansion of social justice and education at all levels.

However, in this extensive endeavor, Iran, while looking to its future, is inspired by the genuine and eternal virtues of its civilization. According to these virtues, life, creation, power, health, truth, righteous thinking and all that is symbolic of light and perfection are divine manifestations opposed to destruction, weakness, disease, deceit, bad thought and all the derivatives of darkness and death which are the expressions of evil. A man can only accomplish his true mission through the fulfillment of the creative will of God.

The flourishing economy and industry of the country today and the attainment of the social revolution of the Shah and the People are indications of the firm belief of the Iranian nation in the continuation of a material and spiritual path, which must lead it in a short period of time to an era of great civilization.

In this prodigious effort, all national forces, all talents and virtues, have been mobilized and all the national and international achievements of knowledge, industry and technology have been applied and will continue to be applied. The course of progress in the country will move in an uninterrupted manner until the achievement of the final goal.

The present book, within the limit of its scope and size, is an indication, particularly in its series of expressive photographs, of this national constructive effort in both the material and spiritual aspects. Such a work can familiarize its readers with the evolution of the Iran of today and can assist in the better understanding we have always encouraged. After the publication of the first book, PERSIA—BRIDGE OF TURQUOISE, *which introduced the ancient traditional culture and art of Iran, the compilation of this book, as a sequel, concerned with the Iran of today and of the future, seems useful and indeed essential.*

I consider the realization of this book a positive step, as would be any other initiative that assisted the peoples of the world to learn more about each other and to strengthen friendship and understanding. I wish this book every success and hope it is received warmly by the public.

1

ROLOFF BENY

IRAN

ELEMENTS

OF DESTINY

3

Books designed and photographed by Roloff Beny

AN AEGEAN NOTEBOOK
THE THRONES OF EARTH AND HEAVEN
A TIME OF GODS
PLEASURE OF RUINS
TO EVERY THING THERE IS A SEASON
JAPAN
INDIA
ISLAND-CEYLON
IN ITALY
PERSIA-BRIDGE OF TURQUOISE
IRAN-ELEMENTS OF DESTINY

The design for the Persian title calligraphy of *Iran - Elements of Destiny* (*Iran - Anasor-e-Sarnevesht*) and individual book titles were executed in a variation of *sols* calligraphy by Nasrollah Afjei who also calligraphed the Persian poetry selections in *nasta'liq* form.

TO A COUNTRY AND A CULTURE
AS OLD AS TIME AND AS NEW AS TOMORROW
I DEDICATE THIS BOOK

ROLOFF BENY

Endpapers: Ball bearings at the 1976 Tabriz Trade Fair, Shahgoli Pavilion.

Title page: Ceiling of the Senate building, Tehran.

1 Crest and flag on His Imperial Majesty the Shahanshah's yacht, *Kish,* cruising in the Persian Gulf.

2 Fountains at the entrance to the Shahyad Monument, built to symbolize 2,500 years of Iranian monarchy, Tehran (mirror image).

3 Tiled underarch of the Shahyad Monument.

Overleaf: Silhouetted staircases on an oil storage tank (mirror image).

CONTENTS

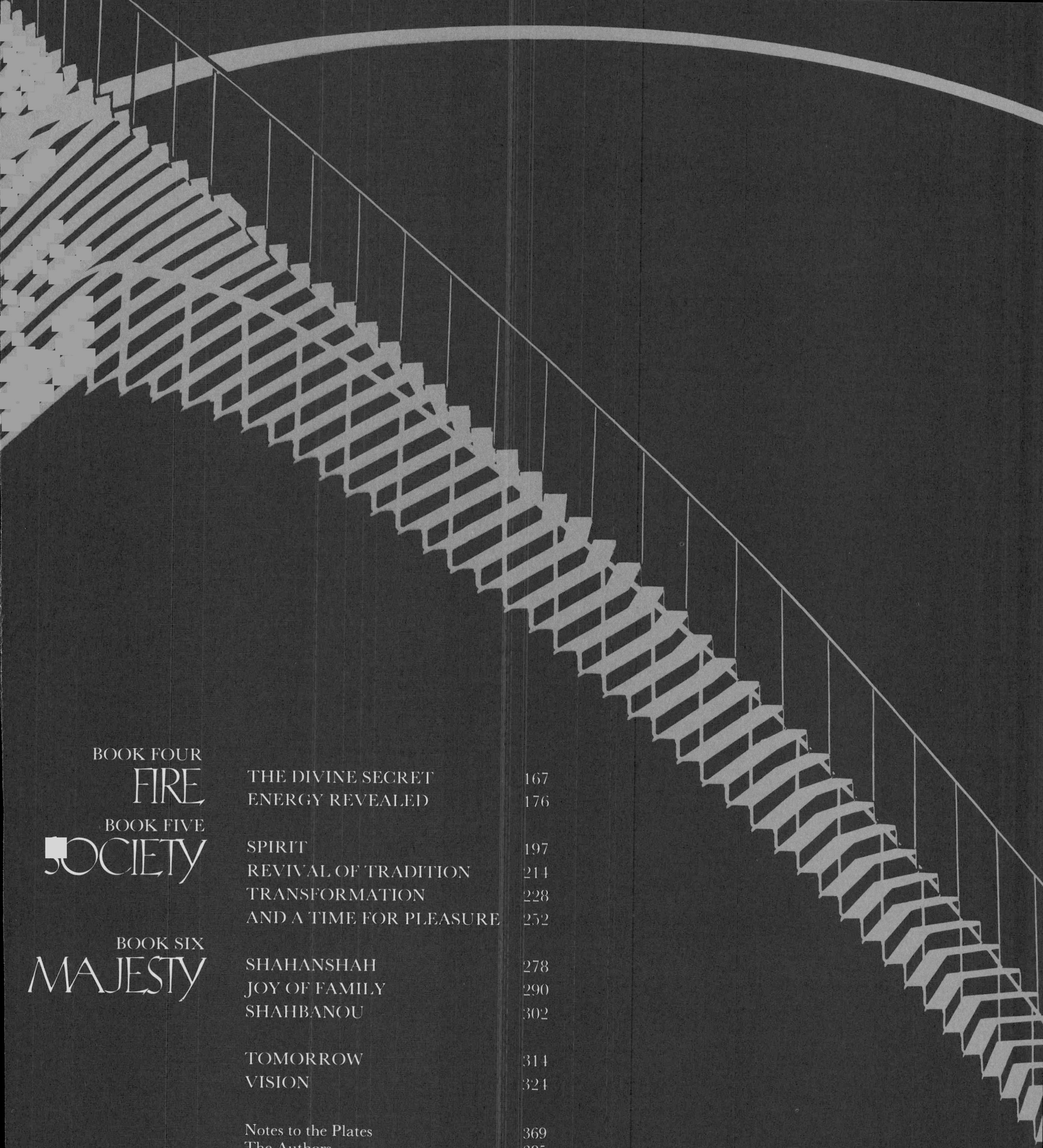

IRAN

U.S.S.R.
Bazargan
Maku
WEST
Farsabad
MOGHAN
Jolfa
Turkey
Khoy
Marand
EAST
TABRIZ
Ardebil
AZARBAYEJAN
REZAIYYEH
Mount Sahand
Miyaneh
Naghadeh
Maragheh
AZARBAYEJAN
ZANJAN
ZANJAN
Saqqez
KORDESTAN
SANANDAJ
HAMEDAN
Qasr-e-Shirin
KERMANSHAHAN
HAMEDAN
KERMANSHAH
Borujerd
LORESTAN
ILAM
KHORRAMABAD
ILAM
Iraq
Dezful
KHUZESTA
AHVAZ
Bandar-e-Shahpur
Khorramshahr
Abadan
Kuwait
Saudi Arabia

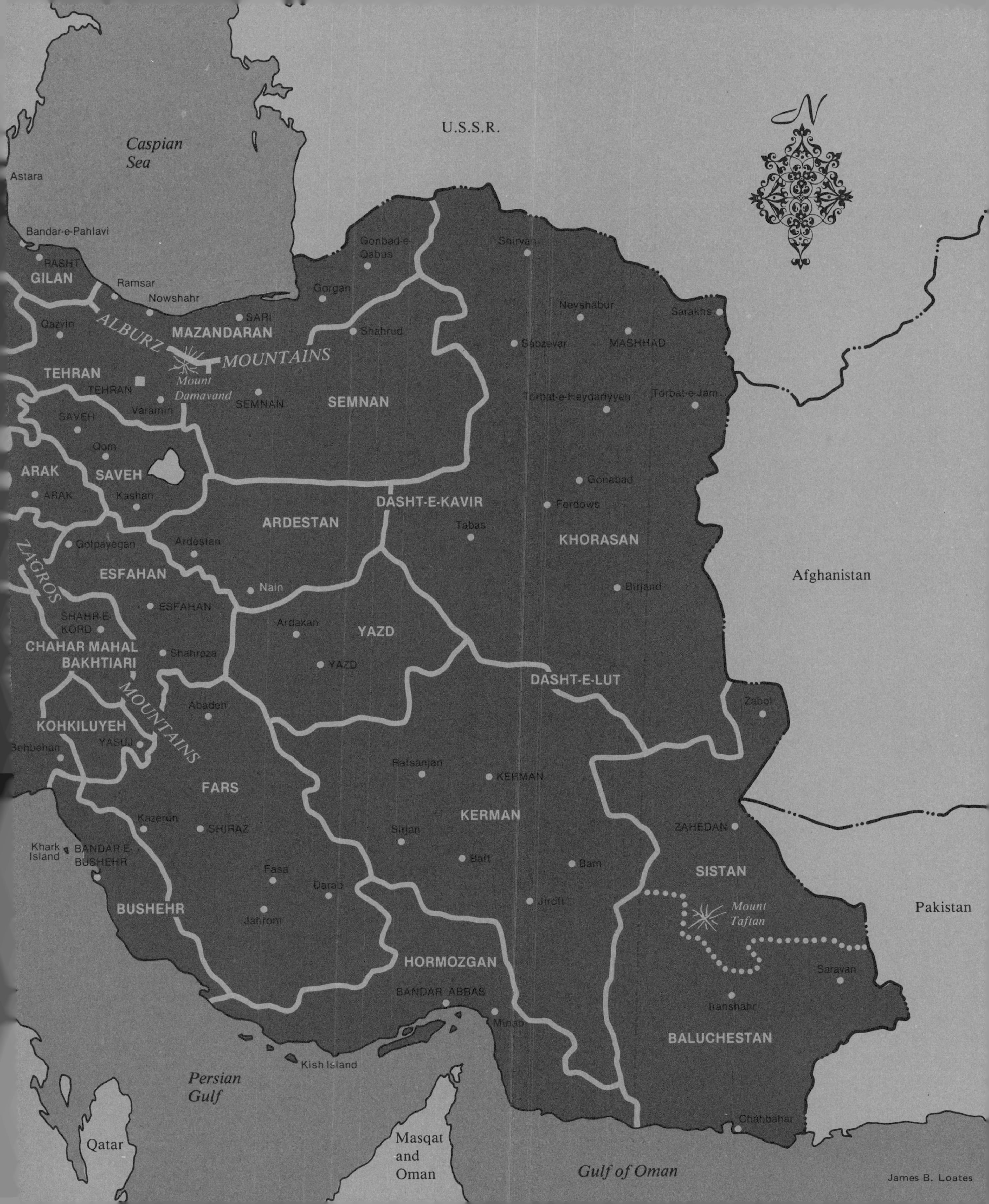

U.S.S.R.
Caspian Sea
Astara
Bandar-e-Pahlavi
RASHT
GILAN
Ramsar
Nowshahr
Qazvin
ALBURZ MOUNTAINS
SARI
MAZANDARAN
Gonbad-e-Qabus
Gorgan
Shahrud
Shirvan
Neyshabur
Sarakhs
Sabzevar
MASHHAD
TEHRAN
TEHRAN
Mount Damavand
Varamin
SEMNAN
SEMNAN
Torbat-e-Heydariyyeh
Torbat-e-Jam
SAVEH
Qom
ARAK
SAVEH
ARAK
Kashan
Gonabad
Ferdows
DASHT-E-KAVIR
ARDESTAN
Tabas
KHORASAN
Ardestan
Golpayegan
ZAGROS MOUNTAINS
ESFAHAN
Nain
Birjand
Afghanistan
ESFAHAN
SHAHR-E-KORD
Ardakan
YAZD
CHAHAR MAHAL BAKHTIARI
Shahreza
YAZD
DASHT-E-LUT
Abadeh
Zabol
KOHKILUYEH
YASUJ
Behbehan
Rafsanjan
KERMAN
FARS
KERMAN
Kazerun
SHIRAZ
Sirjan
ZAHEDAN
Khark Island
BANDAR-E-BUSHEHR
Baft
Bam
SISTAN
Fasa
Darab
Jiroft
Mount Taftan
Pakistan
BUSHEHR
Jahrom
HORMOZGAN
Saravan
BANDAR ABBAS
Iranshahr
Minab
BALUCHESTAN
Kish Island
Persian Gulf
Qatar
Masqat and Oman
Chahbahar
Gulf of Oman
James B. Loates

IRAN–THE ETERNAL LAND

Understanding a nation's geophysical habitat is an essential step toward offering a portrait not only of its past but also of its future, for the relationship established between peoples and natural conditions of life provides the basis of all cultural development. Man creates his own habitat with the means offered him by nature and is, in turn, shaped by his own creation. It is no accident that the turquoise blue of Iran's skies, the burnt brown of its vast deserts, the emerald green of its forests and oases and the wide spectrum of shades offered by its mountains, have always provided the background for its poetry and its painting. The austere majesty of Iran's versatile landscape, the openness of its horizons, the purity of its air and the brightness of its springs, have all contributed to the Iranian people's love of beauty throughout the ages.

Iran has often been described as the land of roses and nightingales. This is because the rose gardens of Shiraz and Esfahan have inspired the imagination of many writers and poets over several centuries. But Iran's flora and fauna are far more versatile than that. This immense plateau, extending from Asia Minor to the Indian Subcontinent, has been and remains one of the world's richest lands in terms of what nature can offer. Iran's foothills have been and remain the abode of hardy and industrious people, while its rich lands were among the earliest to go under cultivation. Iran's mineral wealth, on the other hand, has been tapped in support of civilized communities for many thousands of years, even during that obscure period we call prehistoric. Oil and natural gas deposits were known to its early inhabitants; and abundant building material was used by the people of the plateau as far back as 14,000 years ago, as revealed by archeological excavations in various parts of the country during the past 150 years.

But throughout the ages the Iranian Plateau was a difficult land to settle; it did not yield its wealth easily or readily. It demanded hard work, imagination and collective endeavor. Thus the unique underground water canals, the subterranean aqueducts and the high farmlands of the mountains had to be developed. Life was not easy and thus could not be conducive to sloth and indolence. The extremely cold winters, contrasted with exceptionally hot summers, made it virtually impossible for the people of the land to fall into the blissful lethargy of the kind many other peoples in less diverse climatic conditions have adopted as a way of life. At the same time the distinctly marked springs and autumns offered a respite that in turn gave rise to alternating feelings of joy and evanescence.

The four elements – earth, air, water and fire – played a key role in the Iranian people's conception of nature ever since the dawn of civilization. Each was represented by its own deity in the Iranian mythological pantheon. And when Zoroaster (Zarathustra) formulated his Mazdaean monotheism, the elements retained their particular significance through representation by eternal angels.

Iran, a land of rich natural variety and cultural diversity throughout its long history, developed a distinct national entity of its own. Iran has often been described as the first nation-state created on a large scale. While the Iranian geophysical habitat emphasized uniqueness and individuality, survival demanded unity and cooperation. Nations are, in a sense, the products of collective endeavor and the aspirations of one generation after another. No nation simply happens; it is created with the natural and human means available. Then it is tested for endurance and survival confronting the challenge of progress and weathering moments of adversity. Both require exceptional dedication and heroism that, at each stage of history, are symbolized by a nation's leader.

The non-physical elements in Iran's destiny have, no doubt, reflected the realities of its geophysical habitat as a nation. But civilization begins precisely when man achieves mastery over nature, with which he must, however, strive to live in harmony. In a sense, civilization represents the work done by man on nature, what man adds to or deducts from nature. In going beyond the given conditions of the land, man develops art and science as well as technology and industry. But the main driving force in each civilization, as it advances, remains politico-cultural.

In this context two pivotal elements can be recognized in Iran's long history. The first is the role played by leadership. The second is Iran's ability to develop its natural and human talents in a context of unity without uniformity. Any serious study of Iranian history reveals the startling fact that the presence of an able and dedicated leader could alter the fortunes of the nation and turn decadence and decline into regeneration and progress. The Achaemenian kingdom was an insignificant vassalage of the Medes when Cyrus the Great was crowned its king. Within less than a decade it had become a world empire, excelling not only in the profession of arms and novel modes of administration but also in the projection of new concepts of humanity. Mehrdad the Great, Ardeshir Papakan, Shah Esmail Safavi, Nader Shah Afshar and Reza Shah the Great are among the most outstanding examples of the great leaders the Iranian nation produced in its long history.

The generation to which I belong has witnessed some of the most dramatic moments in Iranian history. It was brought up during the reign of Reza Shah the Great, a reign that witnessed Iran's re-emergence on the world stage. But the same generation witnessed as well the destruction of many high hopes when we were invaded and occupied during World War II. In 1941 when Reza Shah the Great had to leave the country for exile in distant lands, stooping to gather up a handful of the earth of his country to take with him (his poignant last act on Iranian soil), almost everyone expected and was preparing for yet another lengthy period of decadence and decline. Few people believed that within a few decades Iran would reassert herself as a dynamic nation under the leadership of the Shahanshah Aryamehr.

It was on a sweltering day toward the end of the summer that I finally reached Iran after an absence of more than fifteen years. Europe was still fighting its "war of destiny," a conflict that had brought it to the brink of ruin and the looming danger of subjugation. I had lived through the period of the German Army's advance in Europe as a student, a young man of twenty. The last leg of my journey had taken me through the relatively calm Middle East which, in its prolonged torpor, provided a striking contrast with the drama of blood and fire that threatened to assume cosmic proportions. A semi-derelict and badly creaking train had taken me from Syria to Mesopotamia whence I could reach the Iranian frontier.

It was not a particularly happy time to return home. For Iran had been invaded and occupied by the British and Soviet forces despite its neutrality, and was being turned into what was later to be euphemistically labeled "The Bridge of Victory." Entering in the southwestern province of Khuzestan, I began to feel the full impact of the invasion that seemed to have thrown the whole nation off balance. A background of explosive anger provided the setting in which Iran was to suffer the humiliation of occupation with all its destructive consequences for several more years to come. A strange setting for a homecoming, indeed!

Khuzestan had been the birthplace of Iran's independent identity. For Cyrus the Great, the king who established the Achaemenian Empire and gave the Iranian people their special place in history, had been the sovereign of the region between present-day Kerman and the banks of the Shatt al-Arab. Later, under Darius the Great, the city of Susa in northern Khuzestan had become the capital of the empire. Linked through a network of well-paved roads with Persepolis in the east and Athens in the west, the city had been the heart of a great civilization that dominated the ancient world.

I had never visited Khuzestan before my return from foreign lands where my father's diplomatic career and, later, the vagaries of fortune and educational requirements had taken me together with my mother and younger brother, Fereydoun. The unattended farms, dusty cities with their dwarfish mud-houses, the sun-baked plains and the withering palm trees, provided a picture of desolation and sorrow. The fact that most people still wore their traditional black clothes reinforced the funereal atmosphere that enveloped the whole of the province in those days of anger and bitterness.

Continuing our journey toward the uplands of Iran on our way to Tehran, we had to pass through Susa. For years I had longed to see the once great and glorious city. But on arriving I found Susa nothing but a plethora of ruins and memories that bore every mark of history's cruel indifference to civilizations that lose their will to survive. This was no longer a city in any real sense. It was a bitter lesson and a dramatic reminder, manifesting the frailty of human achievements and the elusive goal of civic enterprise. Black tents were pitched where the great palaces had once stood. An inexpressible feeling of loss darkened even the transparent air of the region. The entire region, the granary of the ancient world, had been brought to the brink of famine. Even the sun seemed to be shining oppressively and nights fell with their leaden heaviness on the low horizons. The tall, sizzling flames of blazing gas in the southeastern oil fields continued to burn, providing a sadly symbolic illustration of the Revered Fire of ancient Iran.

I recalled the words of a popular poet who had cried

out, "This mass of ruins cannot be Iran. Where is Iran?" Where, indeed, was Iran? It was only when I repeated the question to myself that I began to see the elements of an answer take shape. Iran was in the hearts of the Iranians. It was in their faith in the destiny of their nation. It was in their proud humility, in their wisdom and generosity.

Over 90 per cent of our people were illiterate in those days. But they still retained a deep awareness of a glorious past together with their unshakable faith in a bright future. Some nations witness the death of their country. Some countries witness the death of their nation, and nothing can bring a nation back to life, while countries can be resurrected and rebuilt. The Iranian culture continued to live. It preserved within its protective embrace the flickering flames that had been left intact by the adverse turn of events. The eternal Fire of the Sadeh continued to burn.

For over a century Iranian intellectuals had debated the question of the path their ancient nation should adopt in order to meet the challenge of the emerging world. Some had advocated a full adoption of the western way of life. Iran had been one of the world's three major powers even in the sixteenth century. But by the beginning of the nineteenth century an entirely different world had come into being around us. This was the world of organized armies with artilleries, of trade and colonialism; a world in which the increasing domination of the machines gave man new productive capacities together with new powers of destruction. Iran had slept through Europe's industrial revolution. It now faced adversaries it could neither understand nor keep at bay. The response of some intellectuals amounted to cultural and moral panic. Some had urged our people to "cast away the past" and seek an admittedly uncertain future in an imposed process of westernization. Others, equally thrown off balance by the multiplicity of phenomena they could not understand, had advocated a full return to the past, a rejection of the world outside and a whole-hearted attempt at recreating a romantic version of the good old days.

Through those decades of storm and stress that witnessed the dismemberment of the country, the Constitutional Revolution and a continuous struggle against the imperialist powers of the day, Iranian nationalism found a new birth. In a sense it had been born in spite of our intellectuals, and the first to sacrifice their lives for Iran had been the hardy warriors of the Zagros and Alborz ranges, brave men who instinctively felt that to sacrifice their identity as Iranian meant a loss of all identity, even individuality. They were neither philosophers nor political scientists. But they had a rich cultural heritage and an intrinsic attachment to their ancestral patrimony, and they demanded a position as the subjects, rather than the objects, of history.

It was only in the 1920s that this rejuvenated nationalism began to rebuild a true nation, a country battered by ravages of imperialism and internal inertia and reaction. The movement had to tackle the tremendous challenge with bare hands. In the early 1920s Iranian nationalism found its leader in the person of a warrior from Mazandaran, Reza Khan. The man who was destined to become the founder of the Pahlavi Dynasty, and was later to be compared with such epoch-making leaders as Ardeshir Papakan, had spent most of his adult life fighting in inaccessible regions of the country. In 1921 when he seized power in Tehran very few people had ever heard of him. But he became a national hero almost instantly. People massed everywhere to express their support for him. They felt as if they had known him for decades. For it was Reza Khan who had told his people that Iran should and could regain its just place in the community of nations. "Today we have nothing," he had told his small number of companions, "but tomorrow our people shall regain their dignity and thus have everything." This simple expression of faith and determination had reverberated throughout the country like a clarion call to regeneration.

Traveling through Khuzestan in those days of dejection and remorse, one could not help remembering the appeal of Reza the Great. One could not forget that before he reunited the country, reaching Khuzestan from Tehran had been possible only through Mesopotamia.

Reza Shah had not formulated his ideas in the manner of a philosopher. He had been a man of action, not much given to philosophical speculation. But a careful study of what he had done could lead his generation and the ones that followed to a clear understanding of Iranian nationalism as he had conceived it. Put in simple terms, he saw the main task of Iranian nationalism as one of modernization without westernization. More than anyone else, he supported and put into effect the idea of mastering western techniques of production and organization. He created a state apparatus and a standing army virtually ex nihilo. He gave the country an effective administration while beginning a series of ambitious attempts at industrialization. In the meantime, however, he made it clear that material progress in itself was nothing but a means to an end. And that end remained the preservation and enrichment of the Iranian culture, the manifestation of our identity. The creation of modern schools and a university, the revival of Persian literature and the new national *prise de conscience* were all the result of a burning desire to preserve the Iranian identity and resume the nation's role as a major contributor to universal cultural endeavors.

Iran's culture has been described as an eternal spring that might disappear from view in times of adversity but would eventually reappear at an unexpected time and place. Its permanence stemmed from its deep moral values that provided for an exceptional spiritual refinement. Contrary to the general trend of western thought that constantly sought the "ideal society," Iranian thinking was primarily concerned with the concept of the "ideal man." One began changing and recreating the world, in order to save or further enrich it, by changing and recreating oneself. The means at man's disposal in that quest were primarily moral and intellectual rather than material. Science was seen as an art whose laws offered extrinsic application without presuming the total exclusion of alternatives. While the West was busy shaping science into a new divinity – a benefactor-cum-tyrant that assumed the role of an invisible Moloch – Iran gave precedence to moral and spiritual values and their finest expressions, literature and the arts. In place of the cold logic of the polemicists, it adopted human wisdom that went beyond the narrow confines of arbitrary semantics.

As early as the Achaemenian era Iran had already developed into a vital cultural link between East and West. It had the unique opportunity of a versatile intercourse with the Hellenistic world and the Mesopotamian and Egyptian civilizations in the West, and the Indian and Chinese worlds in the East. There was a great deal of adoption and imitation. But each idea that was adopted and every form that was imitated were elevated into new modes of thought and artistic expression. The Persians' architechtonic approach to arts as well as socio-political structures made for the creation of new realities on a superior plain. A nation took shape whose members were farmers, poets, soldiers and seekers of the truth all at the same time. Few other nations have been involved in as many wars as the Persians, while still fewer have devoted so much love and energy to the refinement of poetry. Iran began as a bridge between East and West. But a bridge is nothing except a channel for communication. With the rise of Zoroaster and the shaping of the Achaemenian Empire, Iran soon developed into something more than a mere "bridge." It became a vital link in man's cultural and artistic development. Iran evolved from a truly unique experience in the history of mankind.

When I eventually arrived in Tehran I found the capital a scene of sorrow and degradation. There were foreign troops everywhere and rumors spoke of Iran's destiny being shaped in this or that foreign chancery. Evil designs against the nation's integrity were being put together, while the food the nation produced was snatched away from it in order to replenish the supplies of foreign armies fighting in Europe.

During those dark days, a remarkable event took place, one that had escaped the attention of most friends and foes alike.

With the departure of Reza Shah the Great from Iran, the hopes of the Iranian people had been focused on their new Sovereign, Mohammad Reza Shah Pahlavi. The Shahanshah's swearing-in ceremony at the Majles was sure to be a special occasion. But few people had expected it to turn into a spontaneous manifestation of the people's solidarity with their new Sovereign. The occupying forces had done everything to make the occasion as subdued as possible, to the extent that even their respective ambassadors declined the official invitation to attend the swearing-in ceremony. But on the day the Shahanshah rode to Baharestan Square where the Majles is located, the people of Tehran turned out en masse to greet him. Cries of "Long live the Shah!" reverberated throughout the vast square and from there echoed to all the streets and four corners of Tehran. The Sovereign's car was lifted up by the people and carried to the front of the Majles building. The people of Tehran, hungry, brow-beaten and grieved, had nevertheless maintained the enormous courage and hope in the future, represented by this startling show of unity with and support for their new Sovereign.

That event, in all its proud simplicity, marked a truly new phase in Iran's contemporary history. From then on, it was clear that the centuries-old bond of unity between the people and their Sovereign had survived one of its most arduous tests. That day in Baharestan Square shaped contemporary Iran's destiny. It was the beginning of a long struggle for the reassertion of Iran's independence, integrity and national identity. The events that followed are all history: foreign troops were forced to evacuate Iran; the province of Azarbayejan was saved from estrangement from the motherland; foreign-inspired divisive tendencies in several other parts of the country were nipped in the bud; the Iranian army was reconstituted; and the first moves toward achieving full control of the nation's petroleum resources were made.

The Revolution of the Shah and the People, initiated by the Shahanshah, was launched in 1963 with a massive demonstration of solidarity and unity. It is perhaps not necessary to go into detail as far as the achievements of that peaceful and unique revolution are concerned. Present-day Iran is a living testimony to what the Shah-People Revolution has accomplished during the past fourteen years.

Iran, one of the world's five poorest nations in the immediate post-war era, now ranks among the world's top twenty nations with the highest Gross National Product. The number of boys and girls attending school has reached the phenomenal figure of nearly ten million, compared to less than half a million in 1950. The number of students in higher education has increased from 1,200 in 1945 to nearly 200,000 in 1977.

Nearly thirty years after I first arrived in Khuzestan, the Shahanshah was able to state firmly that "those days shall never be repeated." Over thirty years of struggle, perseverance and hard work had made possible that simple expression of faith in the grandeur of an ancient nation. Having survived the cacophony of discord, imposed from without, Iran was now able to speak in a single, united voice: the voice of its Sovereign that remains the expression of national will.

Much has been written about Iran's miraculous economic revival and growth. At times even our friends presume that Iran's rapid economic development has been due solely to rising oil incomes. To be sure, Iran's oil income in 1972 was equal to our country's total income from that source in the preceding sixty years; and oil has sometimes been described as one of the key elements in shaping Iran's destiny. No doubt Iran's oil and natural gas deposits, among the richest in the world, have been and remain of major importance. But it would be simplistic, not to say naïve, to describe rising oil incomes as the nation's sole driving force.

Throughout the sixties, when Iranian oil, together with oil from other OPEC members, was sold at the lowest prices known for nearly half a century, Iran maintained a rate of economic growth that was the fastest in the world.

Much of the nation's modern infrastructure and socio-economic equipment came into being during the same decade. The driving force of the Iranian economy was and remains the far-reaching reforms promulgated by the Shah-People Revolution. It was the termination of the feudal system, the emancipation of women, the creation of opportunities for workers to have a stake in Iranian industries, as well as other revolutionary reforms that made Iran's economic growth and social transformation possible. Without foresight, dedication and a willingness to innovate, no amount of wealth could have made any basic difference.

Furthermore, it was political strength resulting from the revolution that enabled Iran to assume full ownership and control of its oil resources and to seek for its oil more reasonable prices on the world market. Without that basic political strength, Iran would never have been able to challenge the entire edifice of the world's largest and perhaps most influential trade in cooperation with its OPEC partners.

I do not venture to enumerate or render here a detailed account of the achievements and gigantic strides taken by the Iranian nation in the implementation of the Revolution of the Shah and the People. The present book speaks for itself in this regard and gives the reader a vivid insight into what a gifted nation steeped in tradition and history can achieve in the world of today under a dedicated and dynamic leadership.

Iran's destiny is thus shaped by the vision of its leader and the dedication of its people. It is on this basis that Iran is laying the foundations of the Great Civilization, a society based on justice, humanity, equal opportunities, moral and spiritual values, beauty and peace. The aesthetics of Iran's natural habitat should be reflected in its socio-economic setting. And that remains a major objective of the Great Civilization, which could be an Iranian contribution to man's eternal quest for going beyond the dictates of both nature and history. With each step, our people move further away from those days of storm and stress that "shall never be repeated." Iran alone shapes its destiny, in an Iranian context, with Iranian resources.

Amir Abbas Hoveyda

4 Costumed dancers perform during a state visit, Shahyad Monument.

5 A tractor plows through yellow sulphur dunes on Khark Island.

6, 7 Two views of the giant receiving disc at the Asadabad Satellite Station near Hamedan.

8 Flares of escaping natural gas, Ahvaz.

4

9

DAWNS AND DAYS OF THIS MAGIC LAND

If I were given the privilege of starting life again, I would again choose the fine art of creating books, a total art form which combines all the ingredients of creativity. Its visual horizons are unbounded: solid as sculpture, a play enclosed in hard covers, each page acts its appointed role. A book is an opera, a novel, a poem... but its greatest power is as a moveable object, multiple and tactile, which, unlike the painter's single canvas, can be enjoyed in the humblest home or the richest palace in the world. A book of images can be mightier than any weapon—a missile for peace, not destruction. A visual book negates all language barriers—its function is to reveal, if we take the time to see rather than just to look.

I say in my dedication, "To a country and culture as old as time and as new as tomorrow." The responsibility of creating this book is heavy but rewarding to the degree in which it portrays just this.

The subject of both the jacket and plate 175—solar energy—is perhaps as enigmatic as the future. Is it a crystal spider, a space-age Islamic dome, a solar chalice set in a web of concentric energy? This one photograph epitomizes my search for an image, aesthetically abstracted from its basic function—it is pure design. Transcended by its beauty, its power and implications for the future may extend as far as the dreams of science fiction, as far as man's ingenuity can possibly reach.

The book is structured thematically in order to guide the reader through this unfolding country, its past, the seven elements which combine to make the dynamic present possible and a hint of the future. May I ask you to follow me?

I found myself photographing knee-high in sulphur mines on Khark Island, elbow-deep in the grapes of Rezaiyyeh, covered by the moss-green henna in the caves of Yazd, in the middle of three million dollars' worth of radar-guided tractors on the border of Russia at Dasht-e-Moghan, underwater in the Olympic swimming pool of Aryamehr Stadium. I planned photographs while sleeping with ten thousand flamingos, and bundled with a hundred and fifty parachutists in a Hercules transport over the Caspian; while sipping tea in the Star jet piloted by the Crown Prince, and picnicking in fields of wild poppies in Azarbayejan.

My wish is to take the reader with me on this adventure, often in a helicopter hovering over places impossible to view graphically in any other way. Together we explore the fertile Caspian coast and the turquoise crescent of the Persian Gulf, cross vast deserts, wander through dense forests and contemplate the dawns, days and dusks of the four corners of this magic land. As a creative observer, my function is not to lecture or pass judgment but to help those who have little contact with Iran to experience this country through the lens of my camera.

Underneath a matchless carpet of endlessly changing seasons are vast resources only nature can provide. On the surface of this high plateau a new way of life is being woven by the people, guided by the strong sense of destiny and humanistic order emanating from the tireless efforts of the Shahanshah and Shahbanou. I have had the privilege of knowing these two dedicated people for sixteen years. IRAN—ELEMENTS OF DESTINY *was made possible only through their personal direction and profound vision.*

Perhaps my greatest adventure was to be welcomed as I moved throughout the land, to be greeted and helped by people from all walks of life. I acknowledge and will always cherish their many contributions to this book.

Hospitality is legendary in Persia and is considered the first of the virtues. I have found the legend to be true and very much alive today.

Tehran,

9 Brilliant fireworks and massed stadium events celebrate the birthday of the Shahanshah in Tehran.

A GLIMPSE OF HISTORY

This survey of Iranian culture and history from the paleolithic to the Pahlavi spans ten million years of life on this ancient plateau. We move from Iran's prehistory as revealed in the artifacts excavated by archeologists through the semi-legendary epic period described in the Zoroastrian texts and the *Book of Kings*, into the great historic empires of the Achaemenians, the Parthians and the Sasanians. With the advent of Islam, local dynasties emerge followed by the Safavid state with its flowering of arts and architecture, the reigns of Nader Shah, the Zand princes, the Qajar kings and the founding of the present Pahlavi Dynasty, crowned by the White Revolution of His Imperial Majesty Shahanshah Aryamehr, heir to 2,500 years of imperial tradition. Woven into the text are sixteen color images arranged chronologically which highlight magnificent achievements in the art and architecture of each major dynastic period. This brief survey is intended to provide an introduction to the present endeavors of a nation with deep-rooted traditions that has entered an era of modernization and industrialization yet remains a nation determined to preserve its cultural identity.

The Paleolithic

Recent surveys and excavations in Azarbayejan by the Iran National Museum of Natural History have uncovered the remains of extinct forms of animals which roamed this northwestern province more than ten million years ago. Elephants, rhinoceroses, horses and giraffes, as well as hyenas, saber-toothed cats and the many species of antelope and gazelle on which they preyed, had all lived and died near the shores of Lake Rezaiyyeh. Their fossilized remains, still beautifully preserved, are found at a depth of more than 400 meters, and cover an area of more than 1,000 square kilometers.

Not far from the fossil sites, the museum expeditions also located campsites where these animals had been hunted and butchered by prehistoric man. They found primitive stone hand axes, choppers and scrapers made of flint and volcanic rock (see Plate 10), all reminiscent of implements which in other parts of the world had been associated with the remains of the "first true man," *Homo erectus*.

First discovered in Java in 1891, the remains of *Homo erectus* have since been found in east and northwest Africa, western Asia and Europe, and the discovery of his presence in Azarbayejan makes Iran a member of the paleolithic community of the world and expands the horizon of Iranian prehistory to over a million years.

The Neolithic

Stepping down from the paleolithic period to the later Stone Age in Iran, we find at approximately the beginning of the fifth millennium B.C. varieties of pottery, from rough clay to objects that were used for household purposes to delicate painted pottery with varied decorations.

Excavations have uncovered neolithic sites on the coasts of the Persian Gulf, at Susa (see Plate 11), on the plain of Persepolis in the south, at Nehavand in the west, at Sialk in the center, on the plains of Gorgan on the coast of the Caspian, in Khorasan, in the part of northeastern Iran now in Soviet territory, and at other sites. These communities, scattered in the fertile valleys and plains of the plateau, were agricultural, and the main field of artistic activity was polished and painted pottery, some examples of which are extremely refined. In this early period, in most cases decorative conventions had not yet been established. A variety of decorations with symbols of an abstract character have been found. Persepolis figurines were mostly painted with swastikas. Animal designs tended to be realistic. Only later were figurative and abstract motifs combined to create attractive compositions. On rudimentary clay figurines, we find representations of burnt and painted lions, leopards, bears, dogs, oxen, sheep, toads, fishes, snakes and birds, which reveal some of the religious ideas of the age. The close affinity of shapes and designs indicate a homogeneous culture spread over the plateau, with some local differences.

The Copper and Bronze Ages

At the chalcolithic or early Copper Age, we reach a stage when tradition already exists. Figurines of burnt and painted clay and animal figures attain high artistic quality. Toward the middle of the third millennium B.C., with the increasing use of metal, pottery ceases to be the main field of artistic expression. However, the oldest metal vessels adopted shapes that had developed in pottery.

In the region of Lorestan, the remains of an ancient people are found, whose most striking development is the technique of the working of metals, particularly bronze. With the introduction of metal, weapons abound. We have metalwork, in bronze and some in iron, including axes with a variety of forms, swords, daggers with decorative motifs, and theriomorphic ornaments. Predominant among these are stone mace-heads of various shapes and carved animal heads. One such mace in the shape of a bull's head has been immortalized in the *Shahnameh*. This is reputed to have been the weapon with which the great hero-king Feridun brought low the dragon-king Zahak.

Theriomorphic handles became a regular feature of Lorestan bronze vessels. The most popular were ibex, horses, lions, spotted leopards, dogs and some domesticated sheep and cattle, hawks and heraldic eagles.

Many of the Lorestan bronzes were used as harness and trappings for horses and chariots. Cheek-pieces of horse-bits, cast in the shapes of winged horses, ibex, bulls and wild boar, as well as griffins and sphinxes, abound. Many of the horse-bits are of great beauty and extremely ornamental (see Plate 12). Representations of horsemen on seals and bronzes and some iron horse-bits attest to horse-breeding, and the bronze products of the period distinctly present a people with a passion for horsemanship.

Horse-breeding played an important role in Iranian supremacy from the time of the Kassites. These Iranian Kassite tribes from the mountainous highlands of Iran overran the plain of Mesopotamia in the eighteenth century B.C. and established a dynasty that ruled Babylon down to the twelfth century B.C. They bred fine horses and were skillful in the metalsmith's craft, including ironwork.

After the introduction of metal, personal ornaments of gold, silver and precious stones mounted in silver and gold became numerous in Iran. Tombs contain earrings, torques, bracelets, necklaces, pendants, rings in silver, copper, bronze or gold. Iron bracelets are rather rare, but already in the second millennium pearls imported from the Persian Gulf were used as ornaments.

In the Kordestan and Lorestan regions, as well as at other sites, copper, bronze, gold and silver products are found in abundance. They exist in the shape of buckles, plaques and pins with ball-heads, disk-heads and winged or horned animal heads, and sometimes depicting human figures that may have religious significance. Stamp-seals with flat surfaces and negative designs as well as roll-seals appear in this epoch.

Some of the designs and ornaments on these objects and ritual standards depict religious themes; others represent cultic practices described in the *Avesta* and still observed by the Zoroastrians. These include priests carrying bundles of sacred twigs of *barsom* for the *haoma* celebrations. Some iconographic themes and decorative motifs suggest religious beliefs and concepts of a cosmic nature.

More recent discoveries at Amlash, Deylaman and Marlik on the southwestern shore of the Caspian Sea and at Hasanlu near Solduz in Kordestan have yielded art objects of the highest quality decorated predominantly with animal forms. Beautiful masterpieces of the potter's craft have been uncovered, including exquisitely fashioned bulls, stags and bronze horsemen, all full of life and with graceful lines.

Earrings decorated with clusters of miniature gold grapes and pomegranates were found at Marlik and Amlash. From royal tombs at Marlik a number of gold and silver vessels, pieces of jewelry and weapons were excavated. A masterpiece of the goldsmith's craft is the golden goblet from Hasanlu, whose entire surface is adorned with mythological scenes, including human figures whose dress shows close resemblance to both Amlash and Lorestan types.

The Beginning of History

According to the sacred writings of the *Avesta*, the later Pahlavi literature, Ferdowsi's *Shahnameh* or the *Book of Kings* and other sources, Iranian history begins with the semi-legendary dynasty of the Pishdadians, or those of the "Primitive Law." Some of the kings and heroes of this dynasty have their cognate divinities in India.

The first king was Kayumars, or the "Living Mortal," under whose beneficent rule men and beasts thrived. To his successor, King Hushang, the discovery of fire was attributed. He was also the first man to use iron for making implements, and he was credited with the construction of irrigation works. He was succeeded by Tahmures, who vanquished the demons and introduced writing and weaving.

King Jamshid, "the Resplendent Jam," was the first to organize society into four classes: priests, warriors, husbandmen and artisans. During his reign, gold, silver and precious stones were dug out of the earth and used for making ornaments. Wine and sugar from cane were made for the first time. King Jamshid was the first to construct roads and build ships. He also established the festival of New Year's Day (Now-Ruz) on the vernal equinox, which is still celebrated in Iran.

During his long reign, Jam received a divine warning that in three severe winters heavy snowfalls would cover the earth and all creation would be destroyed. But following the divine order, Jam constructed a *var*, or fortress, into which he took the best of men, women, animals, birds and plants to reproduce and replenish the earth after the snows had melted.

Jam's reign was remembered for its great prosperity. But finally, through pride, Jam became a sinner, the "Kingly Glory" left him, and he was defeated and killed by the Dragon-king.

A later king of this dynasty, Feridun, in turn killed the Dragon-king. Feridun is also credited with the discovery of the art of medicine and healing.

In this period, sovereignty descended in the male line and kings ruled by divine favor. Divine Majesty rested upon every king, and gave legitimacy to sovereignty. This symbol of kingship became known under the designation of *Farr-e-Kiyan*, or "Kiyanid Effulgence."

The Kiyanians

With the establishment of the Kiyanid Dynasty in northeastern Iran early in the second millennium, we enter historical ground, although ancient heroes such as Rostam and his family still continue to play their legendary role.

The kings of this dynasty bore the title of *Kavi*, or *Key* in modern Persian, hence the name of the Kiyanid Dynasty. It was under one of the greatest kings of this dynasty, the renowned Key-Khosrow, in the nineteenth century B.C., that Iranian tribes were united. Key-Khosrow is remembered as an ideal king and his court was a forerunner of King Arthur and his Knights of the Round Table, though stories of his life make him more a model for Perceval. He was also the possessor of a cup (the Grail) in which all the marvels of the universe – not only of the "Seven Continents" but also of the planets and stars – could be envisaged.

In his old age, Key-Khosrow, against the pleading of his knights, renounced his crown. After bidding farewell to his knights and exhorting them to continue their good works, he climbed to the peak of a snow-covered mountain and disappeared. According to Zoroastrian tradition, he ascended to heaven and will ultimately return in the company of the Savior Soshyans on the day of Resurrection.

His successor, Key-Lohrasp, was also given to religious seclusion. He too renounced the crown for a hermit's life and left the kingdom to his son, Key-Goshtasp, Kavi Vishtaspa of the *Avesta*, the royal supporter of the prophet Zoroaster or Zarathushtra.

Zoroaster

Two centuries of fermentation of religious thought and mystical seclusion and vision had prepared the way for the fundamental religious reform that was accomplished by the great prophet Zoroaster. Recent research into eastern and western historical traditions and astronomical calculations place Zoroaster's birth date as 1768 B.C. Iranian sources mention dynasties that ruled over Mesopotamia as vassals of the Kiyanid kings. It may well be that movements of the Hyksos westward to Egypt, and of the Kassites to Mesopotamia, were connected with the religious reforms of Zoroaster in northeastern Iran.

Zoroaster's religious and ethical concepts have dominated religious thought in Iran and elsewhere ever since. The concepts include monotheism with Ahura Mazda, or "the Lord of Life and Thought or Wisdom," as the supreme God and Creator, and ethical dualism symbolized by the two Minds, one good and the other evil, that entered the world with the appearance of man and have since struggled one against the other. Zoroaster believed the Good Mind shall at last prevail and annihilate the Evil.

According to Zoroaster, God's will and His plans will be realized only through the endeavors of men who have, by their own free choice, dedicated themselves to Truth and Good Thought. Therefore, his message centers around the idea of the "Kingdom of Ahura Mazda" or "The Good Kingdom," the establishment of which shall be achieved not through sacrificial rites, as had been practiced before, but through Good Thoughts, Good Words, and Good Deeds which will ensure man's salvation in this and in the life to come. He who follows and practices Truth enters heaven which in Zoroaster's concept is the condition of Best Thought; and he who does not enters hell, which is the Worst Existence.

The only outward religious rite that Zoroaster practiced was the circumambulation of fire on the altar as the symbol of Ahura Mazda's light and purity, and a solemn communion meal, an adumbration of things to come in heaven, the blessed dwelling of the Good Mind and of Righteousness.

The Kingdom of Ahura Mazda will be realized through Renovation with the help of Saviors who will strengthen the Good Religion of Mazda. Zoroaster himself prays that may he and those who have accepted his message be those that renovate this existence.

The original teachings of Zoroaster have come down to us only in his seventeen hymns, or *Gathas*, which are the most sacred part of the *Avesta*. The rest of the extant Avestan texts are either later compositions or mainly ancient pre-Zoroastrian pagan hymns and laws reintroduced with a Zoroastrian coloring.

The Medes in the West

The Iranian dynasties of the Kassites ruled western Iran and its extensions in the Mesopotamian plains down to the beginning of the first millennium B.C. Other Iranian tribes had also established their rule in western and northwestern Iran. A branch of the Medes settled in the west in the ninth century B.C. Unification of Iranians in that region with Hamedan as capital was achieved in the eighth century and an extensive kingdom was formed that grew strong enough to capture Nineveh in the following century. Recent excavations are revealing the art and civilization of this Median kingdom that lasted to the middle of the sixth century B.C.

The Persians

Iranians in the southern province of Persia – old *Parsa*, modern *Fars* – had already formed an independent local kingdom in the last decade of the eighth century B.C. under Hakhamanesh, the eponymous ancestor of the Achaemenians. They were, however, reduced to vassalage by the northern Medes until the middle of the sixth century when Cyrus defeated the last Median king and unified the Medes and Persians in one kingdom.

Cyrus the Great was destined to create the first world empire. He conquered Lydia, and the whole of western Asia Minor along with the Ionian cities were subjected. He then moved down the Tigris, subduing the vassal states of Babylonia, and finally took Babylon. He turned his attention to the east, annexing the eastern provinces to his empire, only to fall in battle against the northeastern Iranian Scythians. His body was embalmed and taken to his home province of Fars where his tomb now stands.

Cyrus is remembered as a benevolent conqueror and liberator. Iranian religious beliefs which were basically ethical and universalistic produced a tolerant attitude toward other religions which was exemplified in Cyrus' treatment of conquered peoples to an extent that the Bible describes him as the Lord's Shepherd and Messiah.

On the death of Cyrus, his son and successor Cambyses undertook the conquest of Egypt which was annexed to the empire. At the same time the island of Cyprus was incorporated into the vast empire that extended from the Libyan desert and the river Nile in Egypt to the river Jaxartes in northeastern Iran.

With the passing of the great founder of the empire and the further annexation of Egypt by his son Cambyses, the age of conquests had passed. It was now time to organize and consolidate the vast empire and to maintain its unity. This formidable task was undertaken successfully by Darius the Great.

Although Darius enlarged the empire by annexing the Indian satrapy in the east, and by invading European territory in the west, first subduing the coast of Thrace and then moving northward and crossing the Danube into Scythian territory, his attention was primarily focused on establishing a new order and creating an administrative and legal system for the empire (see Plate 13).

On coming to the throne, Darius found almost all of the provinces of the empire in revolt, including his native Parsa. The story of these revolts and the submission of the rebels was carved by the order of Darius on the rock inscription of Behistun near Kermanshah. His ability and skill is proclaimed by the King of Kings in an inscription at Naqsh-e-Rostam:

> This indeed is my activity: inasmuch as my body has the strength, as battle fighter I am a good battle fighter. . . . Trained am I both with hands and with feet. As a horseman I am a good horseman. As a bowman I am a good bowman both afoot and on horseback. As a spearman I am a good spearman both afoot and on horseback. And the skillfulnesses

which Ahura Mazda has bestowed upon me and I have had the strength to use them – by the favor of Ahura Mazda what has been done by me, I have done with these skillfulnesses which Ahura Mazda has bestowed upon me.

As a statesman and law-giver and administrator of justice and order, which made the "Laws of the Medes and the Persians" a byword of incorruptibility, Darius proclaims in the same inscription:

> Saith Darius the King: By the favor of Ahura Mazda I am of such a sort that I am a friend to right, I am not a friend to wrong. It is not my desire that the weak man should have wrong done to him by the mighty; nor is it my desire that the mighty man should have wrong done to him by the weak.
> What is right, that is my desire. I am not a friend to the man who is a Lie-follower. I am not hot-tempered. What things develop in my anger, I hold firmly under control by my thinking power. I am firmly ruling over my own.
> The man who cooperates, him according to his cooperative action, him thus do I reward. Who does harm, him according to the damage thus I punish. It is not my desire that a man should do harm; nor indeed is it my desire, if he should do harm, he should not be punished.
> What a man says against a man, that does not convince me, until he satisfies the Ordinance of Good Regulations.
> What a man does or performs according to his powers, I am satisfied, and my pleasure is abundant, and I am well satisfied.

With the passing of Darius, his son and successor Xerxes, who did not have the military and administrative abilities of his predecessor, embarked on a policy of alienating the subject peoples. His unsuccessful attempt to invade and subdue the Greek mainland weakened the empire. Under the later Achaemenids, signs of decadence appeared. Revolts in the provinces shattered the empire; and with the domination of Alexander of Macedon in Mesopotamia, the Achaemenian Empire finally collapsed.

Altogether, the Achaemenian Empire contributed two centuries of international prosperity. Maintenance of good roads, protection of sea and land routes and the creation of an efficient mail system combined to increase traffic, and the widespread use of coinage facilitated trade. Agriculture prospered and economic life continued peacefully. All this contributed to stability. This stability was reflected in the imperial art and architecture that gave a cultural unity to the empire, with materials and craftsmen coming from all quarters. The basic feature of Achaemenian architecture was the pillared hall which imparts a sense of lightness and spirituality. The columns in Persepolis still taper upward for some sixty feet.

The religious capital of the empire was Persepolis, where special ceremonies such as the New Year celebrations were held in the royal residences, a compound of sumptuous and solemn buildings (see Plate 14). The imposing entrance to the vast terrace was called "the Portal of All Nations," and was decorated with bas-reliefs of peaceful processions of guards and bearers of offerings from all nations of the empire. The imperial palaces in the administrative capital at Susa were adorned with enameled brick panels, displaying a procession of the imperial archers.

Achaemenian art is characterized by sumptuousness and excellent craftsmanship, especially in metalsmithery. In the minor arts there are impressive metal cups and vases, drinking bowls and drinking horns, ornaments and costume jewelry, weapons in brass, bronze, iron and gold, carved stone bowls, glassware, ivory and inlaid enamel work. Animal-headed armlets and handles, chiefly of goat or ibex, were common. Animal designs, though basically of a symbolic and heraldic nature, also have a tendency toward naturalistic style. Sculptures in the round are in soft stones and lapis lazuli, and small human figures are in gold, silver and bronze.

Tablets from Susa deal with the weaving of colored and embroidered clothes and dresses. Specimens of this textile art are displayed on the garments of the frieze of archers in the palace at Susa. Scythian burials in the Altai region have preserved pieces of Achaemenian carpets with stags and lions interspersed with rosettes.

The Parthians

Parthian history is complicated by the scarcity and obscurity of the surviving evidence. Although the Parthians ruled for half a millennium, their successors, the Sasanians, made every effort, for religious reasons, to obliterate everything connected with Parthian history. According to early historians, they even went so far as to diminish Parthian history by two and a half centuries in order to conceal the religious events that had occurred during the early Parthian period.

10 The recent discovery of animal fossils and paleolithic tools expands the horizon of Iranian prehistory ten million years.

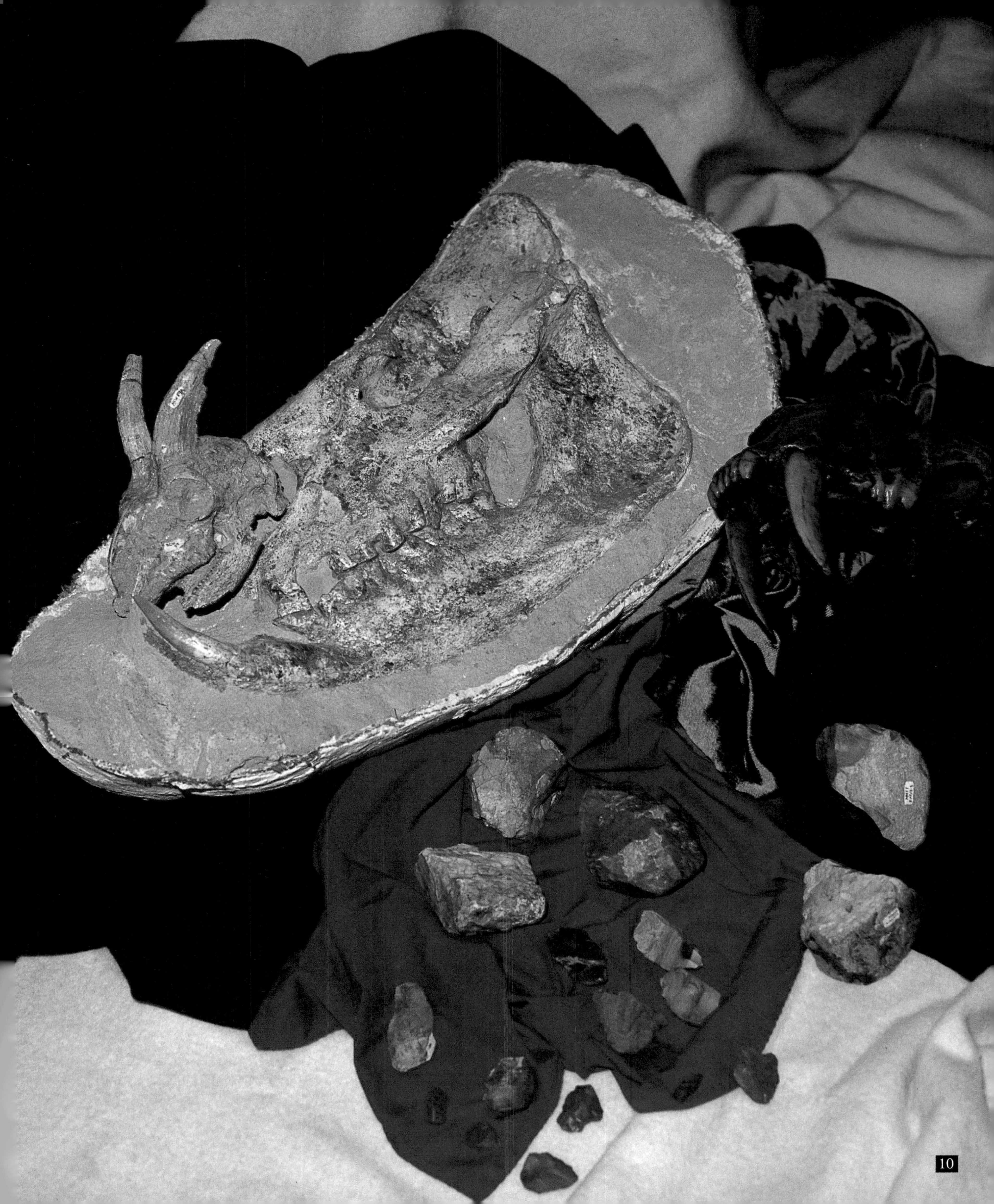

11

The same policy, for the same reasons, was followed by the Roman and Byzantine churches. Although for centuries the Parthians were involved in war or trade with the Roman Empire and shared religious beliefs and practices with them, written documents that have survived are rather scanty, and what has survived may well be termed a Roman Church recension.

But according to Iranian sources, Arshak, or Arsaces, the eponymous founder of the Arsacid dynasty, founded the Parthian kingdom in northeastern Iran fourteen years after the domination of Alexander of Macedon in Mesopotamia and the fall of the Achaemenian Dynasty. In this early period the capital was built on an impregnable mountain site at Dara, not far from Nisa, now in Soviet territory, which served as the royal necropolis and later as the religious capital of the Parthian Empire, in the same way Persepolis had been to the Achaemenian Empire.

According to Iranian historical sources, the birth of the Messiah, or Mithra, the Savior expected by the Zoroastrians, occurred in the fifty-first year of the Arsacids and the sixty-fourth year of Alexander's rule in Babylonia, on the eve of Sunday, the twenty-fifth of December, 272 B.C., a millennium and a half after Zoroaster. This was an event of far-reaching influence for the religious thought and culture of the entire ancient world. According to ancient prophecies and later traditions, Mithra was born from a virgin with the title of Anahita, or Immaculata, who conceived the Savior from the seed of Zoroaster that had been preserved in the waters of Lake Hamun in Sistan. On this site on a small mountain island in the midst of the lake, called Kuh-e-Khajeh or Mountain of the Lord, the Arsacids erected a sacred sanctuary with a royal palace. The Arsacids had adopted the religion of Mithra – the religion that was to embrace the ancient world from the Atlantic to the Pacific within a century after the founder's death or Ascension, as his followers believed. His Ascension occurred in 208 B.C. Parthian coins and documents bear a double date with an interval of sixty-four years, one with the birth of Mithra as a basal point and the other with the Ascension.

In the Parthian homeland, excavations in Nisa, later renamed Mithradatkirt, have brought to light substantial buildings, among them the remains of an imposing mausoleum and a shrine, and documents with inscriptions of the Parthian period. On the holy site of the Mountain of the Lord, paintings of figures and patterns with religious as well as secular scenes decorate the walls and ceilings.

Before long, the Parthian kingdom was transformed into a world empire under Mithridates, who assumed the title of Great King. His dominions stretched from Mesopotamia to Bactria, and a new administrative capital was built at Ctesiphon. Mithraic temples sprang up in western Iran. The largest was at Kangavar, named after Anahita, the Immaculate Virgin Mother of the Lord, situated near Kermanshah on the road to Hamedan. The district itself was called Behestan, Bagestan after Bagh, or Lord, being the special title of the Lord Mithra. Excavations are under way in the terraces of the imposing and elegant ruins of this temple, once considered one of the wonders of the world.

Other Mithraic temples were built in Khuzestan, and in central Iran, where a few tall columns of the temple of Khorheh near present-day Mahallat still stand. In Azarbayejan the temple at Shiz was built on top of an unusual site near a supposedly bottomless, self-feeding lake which flows down the slopes through seven water channels cut into the rock. The Parthian Mithraeum was later transformed to a Zoroastrian fire temple by the Sasanians. In Fars there stood a sanctuary dedicated to Anahita, the Mother of God, whose guardian and priest was the ancestor of the Sasanian kings.

The princes of the desert city of Hatra in upper Mesopotamia, who were vassals of the Parthian kings, embraced Mithraism and built temples and a mausoleum around a huge Mithraic sanctuary. To the west of Hatra at Dura Europos, the ancient Se-deyr or Three Monasteries, Mithraeums richly decorated with wall paintings and ceiling decorations have been excavated. Iconographic figures include Mithra on horseback and priests of the temples and monasteries.

In Armenia, where Parthian princes ruled as local kings, a whole district was dedicated to Anahita. Numerous Mithraic temples were built, and Armenia remained one of the last strongholds of Mithraism. The Parthian kings of Armenia were at the same time priests of Mithra. King Tiridates, as a Magus of Mithra, traveled to Rome where Nero received him in ceremonies of the greatest pomp and placed the crown on his head. Reciprocally Nero was initiated into higher stages of the Mystery and was even addressed as a reincarnation of Mithra.

Armenia, however, was the center of a territorial dispute between the Parthian and Roman empires. They both claimed that the strategically situated kingdom was within their sphere of influence. The struggle

11 Archeologists cutting deep into the ancient mound at Shush have exposed habitation levels millennia old.

over the Armenian throne continued for centuries, and hostilities between the two empires were frequent. In one of the early clashes, the Roman general Crassus, a member of the first triumvirate, crossed the Euphrates but was attacked by a young Parthian general, Suren, who commanded a cavalry force of ten thousand men and a bodyguard of a thousand knights in mail armor. The Roman legionnaires crumbled under the attack of the Parthian cavalry. Finally Crassus and his son met their tragic deaths, and out of his army of forty thousand men, ten thousand escaped, ten thousand were taken prisoner by the Parthians and the rest were killed.

Under the Roman emperor Vespasian the Euphrates was confirmed as the boundary between the two empires. Later, Trajan invaded Armenia and Mesopotamia, but soon after, Parthian counterattacks recovered the lost provinces, and hostilities ceased for half a century.

Meanwhile, extensive trade continued within the Parthian Empire and with neighboring lands. Commodities mentioned in inscriptions include dried fruits, olive oil, salt and other foodstuffs. The luxury trade included perfumes, purple dyes and even bronze statues. Documents tell of land and sea trade with China, involving such articles as exotic animals, gold, silver, precious stones, pearls from the Persian Gulf, perfumes, cloth and rugs.

Agriculture and husbandry formed the backbone of Parthian economics. Sheep, cattle and pigs were raised; cereals, rice, fruits and vegetables were grown. The medical properties of herbs and spices were known. Wine stores and jars have been excavated.

In matters of administration the Achaemenian tradition was maintained, but besides satrapies there were also kingdoms within the empire. The Parthian state was predominantly feudal. At the head of the state stood the king. He sat on a golden throne and slept on a golden couch. His costume was elaborately adorned, and a torque encircled his neck. At the royal banquets bards played music and sang heroic lays. Musical instruments included the lyre, the single and the double pipe and the drum.

The feudal princes ruled in their own domains and had courts on the royal model. The hereditary nature of the powerful feudal princes and sub-kings, however, contributed toward internal instability.

The office of the monarch was not strictly hereditary. Any male of Arsacid lineage from any branch of the family would be acceptable as king, for only to the Arsacid family did the aristocracy show loyalty and obedience. Normally, of course, the king was succeeded by his eldest son. But other arrangements could be made by the Senate that was composed of the vassal princes and the heads of the great noble families, who appointed or confirmed the successor to the throne.

The Parthian army was under the command of the monarch, and the feudal princes had their local armies and joined the king when called upon. The army was composed predominantly of mounted archers. There were light horse-archers as well as the heavily armed cavalry who were armor-plated from head to foot; their great war horses wore iron mail. They used the huge lance and the bow. A well-known Parthian tactic was the feigned retreat and the backward shot over the crupper that gave the West the expression "the Parthian shot."

From the cultural and religious point of view, the Parthian period is of great significance in Iranian history. The spread of Mithraism over the entire territory of the Roman Empire, the hundreds of Mithraeums discovered and excavated in Rome and scattered from Scotland to the fringes of the Sahara Desert, from Spain to the coasts of the Black Sea and all along the Danube; the absorption by Christianity of Mithraic beliefs, rites and practices, ceremonies and festivals, and the spread of Mithraism in the East as far as the eastern confines of China are subjects outside the scope of the present survey. In the sphere of religious art, characteristic scenes of religious processions, the rite of casting incense upon a burner as an offering, and frontal cross-legged sitting posture were among the creations of this period.

Parthian art contributed frontality that soon permeated Roman art. Parthian statuary displays luxurious adornment. The tunics and trousers present subtle patterns of drapery folds, and are covered with jewels. Statues greater than life size were found at Nisa, Shami and elsewhere. The bronze statue found at Shami in the Bakhtiari mountains in west Iran displays an air of great authority (see Plate 16). He wears the Parthian dress, a torque around his neck and daggers at his side. He has a thick, wide moustache. His hair falls to the shoulders, and he wears a diadem similar to that of the Parthian monarch.

12 These bronze Lorestan bridles recall the days when horsemen commonly rode across the Iranian Plateau.

13 Well-preserved Achaemenian rock inscriptions carved on the mountain face at Ganj Nameh near Hamedan.

14 This human-headed bull capital once graced the Tripylon at Persepolis.

14

15

The excavations at Nisa uncovered metal figurines, particularly of Anahita; also terra-cotta figures, glazed pottery, painted glass, marble vases and weapons. A large number of drinking horns of carved ivory bearing figures and embellished with gold and inset stones also came to light.

Parthian architecture was characterized by the use of sun-dried or kiln-baked bricks, with vaults to roof the buildings. A central court, with four *ivans* opening onto it, was a usual pattern. The architectural usages created or developed in the Parthian period were adopted and further refined in the Sasanian period and continued to set the model for the architecture of the Islamic period.

And finally, as evidence of technical skill, a pottery jar from the period was found to contain copper, iron and bitumen, used as a galvanic cell for electroplating silver onto copper.

The Arsacid realm, however, was showing signs of disintegration. The continuing struggle with the Roman Empire exhausted the military power of the Parthians. The appearance of the powerful Kushan kingdom in the east contributed to this exhaustion. The lack of a strong, centralized organization invited internal rebellions. The end was approaching.

After the fall of the Achaemenians, Fars was ruled by a local dynasty within the Parthian Empire. The rebellion which was to overthrow the Arsacids began in this province with the open revolt of Ardeshir, a descendant of Sasan, the eponymous ancestor of the Sasanian Dynasty. Artabanus, the last Parthian king, was defeated in successive encounters and finally killed.

The Sasanians

Ardeshir, king of Fars, having gathered his strength and defeated Artabanus, proclaimed himself King of Kings of Iran. But the defeat of the last Parthian king did not remove all the obstacles that confronted Ardeshir. A coalition was formed by the Parthian king of Armenia, supported by the Scythians and by Rome, with the Kushan king in the east. The coalition, however, was destroyed in a series of battles by the founder of the young, vigorous dynasty, and finally Ardeshir became master of an empire extending from the Euphrates to northeastern Iran.

Ardeshir and his successors had inherited and retained Iranian institutions of the Parthian period, including the feudal system, but a high degree of centralization was introduced into the administration, and the army was forged into a well-disciplined and powerful instrument. This enabled the Sasanians to conduct an active foreign policy and wage war on three fronts: against the Romans in the west, the Kushans and Ephthalites in the east, and the nomads in the north.

Shapur, Ardeshir's successor, after conquering the kingdom of the Kushans, turned to the west and advanced across Syria as far as Antioch. The Roman Emperor Gordian was killed, and his successor, Philip the Arab, made peace, paying a large tribute and ceding Mesopotamia and Armenia to Iran. Fifteen years later the war with Rome was resumed. In a great victory the Emperor Valerian fell into Shapur's hands, and his seventy thousand Roman legionnaires were sent into exile in Iran. Sculptured bas-reliefs on the rocks in Fars commemorate this victory showing the Roman emperor prostrate at Shapur's feet.

During the fourth century the Iranian Empire was in weaker hands. The Kushan kingdom took advantage of the disorder to recover its former power, and northern Mesopotamia and Armenia were lost to the Romans. But Shapur II, following the example of his renowned namesake, conquered the Kushan kingdom and annexed it to Iran as a new province. He then turned to the west and resumed the war against the Romans. With the death of the Emperor Julian on the field of battle, subsequent peace restored the disputed provinces of northern Mesopotamia to Shapur, and Armenia was at last reduced to an Iranian province.

But with the conversion of Constantine and Armenia to Christianity, closer ties between Byzantium and Armenia were developed, with Armenia becoming torn between the pro-Iranian and the pro-Roman factions. As the result of a compromise with Rome, Armenia was partitioned between the two rival empires.

Among the great Sasanian kings, Vahram V, who was brought up in the small vassal state of Hira, west of the Euphrates, became a famous king, renowned for his skills as hunter, poet and musician. Numerous legends grew around his prowess and adventures, and he became a favorite subject of Iranian artists for centuries.

When the Sasanian Dynasty was founded, the concept of the millennium was vigorously alive. Indeed the appearance of Ardeshir and the inauguration of a new era was a millennial act. The year A.D. 232 was the beginning of the twelfth and last millennium in the cycle. It was a millennium and a half after Zoroaster and half a millennium after Mithra. It was also around this time that the Roman Emperor Diocletian, together with the other imperial rulers, dedicated an altar in Carnuntum

15 A Sasanian gilded silver vase.

near Vienna to the "Unvanquished Mithras, the Benefactor of the Empire."

Ardeshir and his ancestors were guardians of a Mithraic temple at Estakhr. Just as the Parthian rise to power had been a millennial act blessed by the epiphany of Mithra, so the founding of the Sasanian Dynasty raised the expectations of the appearance of a savior for the last millennium. Mani, also called Bagh or Lord after Mithra, bore the title of Barkhan, the Iranian equivalent of the Greek Paraclete, whose coming from the west had been foretold. He was born in A.D. 256, during the reign of the last Parthian king. Ten years after, Ardeshir proclaimed himself King of Iran.

Mani proclaimed his message when he was twenty-five years old, during the coronation of Shapur on New Year's Day A.D. 280. Since he was the prophet of the last millennium, he was called "the Seal of the Prophets." According to Mani, the spirit of man was light and his body darkness, and Manichaean ethics centered on the emancipation of the soul from the body. When all light and all souls held prisoner by matter were set free, the earth and the heavens would fall apart, but the Kingdom of Light would endure forever.

The message was in accord with the concept of the Last Millennium and the end of the world. Thus any accumulation of worldly wealth and procreation were incompatible with Manichaean ideals. Hence, Manichaean "elects," who were the highest custodians of the religion, were forbidden to acquire wealth or to marry.

Shapur took a sympathetic interest in Mani and his teachings and extended his protection to this founder of a universal religion that might have succeeded as heir to the religion of Mithra. The faith spread within decades over most of the territories covered by Mithraism, from China to North Africa, Spain and southern France.

Shapur's policy, however, was reversed by his successor. The remnants of the old Zoroastrian priesthood who had lost their prerogatives under the Parthian kings who officially practiced the religion of Mithra were now facing a new menace from Mani and became more active in challenging Mani and his new religion.

Zoroastrianism had deviated from its original teachings by incorporating the ancient Iranian divinities in a new pantheon a century after the death of Zoroaster. Mithraism had, furthermore, impressed itself on the old faith. It was, therefore, a neo-Zoroastrianism that was struggling against Mani.

Manichaeism was denounced in the west by the papacy not only as a dangerous heresy but as detrimental to social life and common human institutions. For similar reasons, the Iranian state condemned the new faith. Shortly after Shapur's death Mani was persecuted and finally put to death during the reign of Vahram. The tragic death of the Prophet and the horrors experienced by his persecuted followers from Spain to Iran are reflected in contemporary hymns and prayers that have survived.

The episode of Mani was over, but the empire was torn by religious strife, and the aftermath was the formation of a social movement that culminated in the Mazdakite revolution of the sixth century. Several years of famine had ravaged the land. Involvement in unsuccessful wars with the Ephthalites in the east and the Huns from the north brought the country to the verge of disaster. The Ephthalites intervened in Iranian domestic affairs, and had a hand in putting Prince Kavad, who had spent his youth among them, on the throne.

It was during the reign of this king that Mazdak proclaimed his revolutionary message, its appeal lying in its call for equality in the distribution of wealth. Kavad had to choose between the powerful nobility and priesthood and the people, the mass of whom followed the Mazdakite movement and demanded far-reaching reforms. Kavad championed the movement and introduced a number of new laws. As the result of a plot, he was deposed and thrown into prison. He escaped and took refuge at the Ephthalite court, then returned with an Ephthalite army and regained his throne.

In the meantime the Mazdakites had instigated uprisings that were marked by excesses. After his restoration, when he nominated his son Khosrow as his successor, Kavad was opposed by the Mazdakite leaders, and he decided to break with them.

At the instigation of the Zoroastrian priesthood during Khosrow's reign, the Mazdakites were overthrown and massacred. Many of those spared were exiled to southwestern Arabia where they formed the nucleus of a revolutionary circle that propagated the ideas and ideals of the movement.

Under Khosrow, the monarchy emerged victorious from the long class struggle. Fundamental reforms were introduced and the empire began once more to grow strong. Khosrow invaded Syria, smashed the Ephthalites, successfully resisted the Huns, annexed Yemen, and invaded Mesopotamia. After a reign of nearly half a century, the old king died. He was idealized as a lover of justice and his reign was a brilliant period for its military and diplomatic triumphs as well as for achievement in art, science and literature.

16 The grandeur of a Parthian prince captured in a larger-than-life bronze statue.

17

Later, under Khosrow II, war was resumed with Byzantium. Armenia was regained. The Iranian army marched across Cappadocia and reached the Bosphorus. The following year Antioch, Damascus and Jerusalem were captured. A few years later Gaza was captured and Egypt invaded. The army then marched up the Nile to the borders of Ethiopia, thus reaching the frontiers of the Achaemenian Empire. In Asia Minor Constantinople was besieged, and the Iranian army was at the same time victorious on the eastern front.

But the new Byzantine Emperor Heraclius launched a vigorous counterattack. In a few years Asia Minor was restored to Byzantium, Armenia was invaded and the Emperor even laid siege to Ctesiphon. Khosrow II was assassinated, and the Sasanian Empire disintegrated into petty states. Within a decade and a half the empire had collapsed. The common people were in utter despair and the land was in turmoil. Conditions were ripe, and the Islamic revolution from southwestern Arabia succeeded in overthrowing the ancient order.

The civilization of the Sasanian Empire was brilliant and its military often omnipotent, but its social structure was corrupt. Nevertheless, the great achievement of the Sasanians was the creation of a stable bureaucracy which provided the link between the provinces and the central authority. This centralization was the foundation of its greatness. Particular attention was paid to the army. There was a rich technical literature dealing with the organization of the army and instructions on the use of cavalry, care of horses and on various aspects of military tactics. The Sasanian administrative system remained a model for future Islamic states.

The national economy continued to be based on agriculture, though trade flourished as in the Parthian period. Textiles, clothing and spices were prevalent commodities. Production improved and expanded, particularly in the silk and glass industries. Through monopolies the state became a producer. It supervised the prices of raw materials and the wages of the workers and the organization of the guilds. Indirect taxes increased the pressure on the people. Official corruption and the social injustice which prevailed drove the people to revolt. There was, however, a more equitable distribution of goods and wealth, thanks to the principles and ideals of the Manichaean religion and Mazdakite movement.

In commerce, Sasanian coinage of silver, copper, and more rarely of gold, circulated over a wide area. The bill of exchange became a legally recognized title-deed, and the banks of the empire used a highly developed system of monetary exchange by writing. Foreign trade was conducted entirely on a monetary basis. The words "bank" and "check" are both of Iranian origin. Commerce was under strict control, and officials inspected the frontier posts and seaports.

Sasanian art so closely succeeded Parthian art that it is often difficult to determine to which period an object belongs. The art of the Parthian period showed a preference for scenes of hunting, banqueting and fighting – themes and features which were later to be so characteristic of the art of Iran in the Sasanian period. Sasanian art radiated over an area from the Atlantic to China. Its influence was particularly great in the West, where it inspired medieval art.

Sasanian toreutic art is represented by plates, cups and bottles of gold, silver and bronze decorated and embossed with a great variety of scenes (see Plate 15). Floral as well as animal and bird motifs, real or fantastic, adorn these objects. The favorite subject is the royal hunt in heraldic style. Other subjects portrayed are investitures, with the king seated on his throne. The banqueting scenes feature dancing girls and musicians similar in conception to those of the rock carvings.

The tradition of rock bas-reliefs continued. In the carvings we find representations of royal investiture, singlehanded combat, victory over the enemy, the hunt, and the king with members of his court or family (see Plate 17).

Comparable with the massive finds of Sasanian coins, thousands of seal-stones and intaglios of the period have been found. Seal-stones served as personal seals. On their miniature surfaces the Iranian craftsmen carved the portraits of their owners, often with their names and titles, but the majority have animal or floral motifs or symbolic designs. Sasanian portraits are found even on silk fabrics that have survived. Portraits of kings and rulers represented on coins, rock carvings, seals, metal vessels and fabrics depicted each ruler with a crown of characteristic shape that was not imitated by his successors.

In architecture the Sasanians carried on the Iranian traditions of the Parthian period. As was noted above, it is not easy to draw a line between art objects of Sasanian and Parthian periods. This is particularly true of monumental bas-reliefs and buildings. Not unlike the policy that was followed in the West where Christian churches were built on the ruins of Mithraeums or Mithraic temples transformed into Christian places of

17 Winter rains momentarily stain the magnificent royal hunt reliefs at Taq-e-Bostan.

worship, Parthian Mithraic temples were transformed during the Sasanian period into fire temples to suit the neo-Zoroastrianism which was established as the official religion of the empire. The obliteration of Parthian inscriptions and the substitution of Sasanian ones in order to destroy the memory of their predecessors and their religion must have been a common policy that was carried on in the Islamic period, as witnessed in the recent excavations under the old Jame Mosque in Esfahan where remains of Parthian-Sasanian ruins and columns were brought to light.

Buildings with well-dressed stones adorned with historical reliefs have been found. Baked and unbaked brick continued in general use, and such buildings were often decorated with sculptured and painted stucco. Common buildings frequently used rubble and plaster in their construction. Temples were vaulted and surmounted by a cupola on a square plan. All these traditions were carried on in the Islamic period.

The four and a half centuries of Sasanian rule represent a dazzling period in Iranian history in which culture and art flourished. It was an age of powerful rulers, scientists, learned scholars and poets. The refinements of life became more evident. Aesthetic tastes were highly developed; music, singing and the arts were cultivated; chess, tennis and polo became popular sports. The court set the fashion in dress, and the gastronomic art was highly elaborated. It was a brilliant society that reflected a culture and luxurious civilization.

The literature that had grown under the Parthians was further developed. Books and tracts appeared in large numbers. A list of such books, covering a wide range of subjects, was given by Nadim, a bookseller in Baghdad under the Caliphs, in his Fehrest or Catalogue, of which few pieces and fragments have survived in the original Pahlavi language.

The Islamic Period

Centuries of war with neighbors on all fronts had sapped the strength of the empire. Internal dissension, revolts of military leaders and feudal lords, court rivalries, despotism and a class war all contributed to the fall of the Sasanian Empire.

Islam was the true heir of Sasanian Iran. The Sasanian administrative machinery remained practically intact during the Damascus and Baghdad Caliphates. The arts, literature, mathematics, astronomy, medicine and chemistry flourished and reached remarkable heights. Not only in Iran but wherever Islam went it carried the forms created by Parthian and Sasanian art and architecture.

The establishment of Modern Persian, or Farsi, as the standard literary language belongs to this period. The ancient Median language of the Avestan texts, and the southern Old Persian of the Achaemenian inscriptions that represented the oldest extant forms of Iranian, gave way to the Middle Iranian Pahlavik of the Parthians and the Parsik of the Sasanians. Modern Persian is a direct descendant of the Sasanian Parsik, with accretions from Parthian Pahlavik and the northern dialects.

The Farsi script, commonly called the Arabic script, was also developed from the "religious script" of the Avestan texts and the Pahlavi script.

The Arabic language, whose grammar was composed and vocabulary compiled by Iranian scholars, became the medium of written communication throughout the Islamic world that extended from Spain and southern France to China, coinciding with territories formerly covered by Manichaeism.

Illustrious Iranian scientists, among them Razi (Rhazes), Kharazmi, Biruni, Ebn-e-Sina (Avicenna) and Omar Khayyam, who also wrote in Farsi, used the Arabic language in their works for wider communication in Islamic lands.

Local Dynasties

With the disintegration of the Caliphate in Baghdad, local dynasties sprang up first in the eastern provinces. Mention must be made of Yaqub, son of Leis, known as Saffar or the "Coppersmith," who rose as a soldier from Sistan. By successive victories he annexed the northeastern provinces and overran the west as far as Fars, ruling an extensive kingdom that remained under the dynasty he founded for half a century, although much diminished in size.

The Caliph in Baghdad who had been defied by Yaqub sent an embassy to remonstrate with him. When the embassy arrived, the great soldier lay dying with a sword by his side and a crust and onions ready to be served for his coarse meal. In this state he received the envoy and sent the following message to the Caliph:

> If I live, the sword shall decide between us; if I conquer, I will do as I please; if thou art victorious, bread and onions are my fare; and neither thou nor fortune can triumph over a man accustomed to such diet.

Another dynasty, the Samanids, named after their

eponymous ancestor, Saman, who rose from Transoxania, ruled for a century and a quarter. They soon extended their domain to other eastern provinces, and later to central Iran. At the Samanid court in Bokhara were gathered a brilliant galaxy of historians, doctors of law, poets and artists. A contemporary writer (tenth century A.D.) writes:

> Bokhara was, under the Samanid rule, the focus of splendor, the shrine of empire, the meeting place of the most unique intellects of the age, the horizon of the literary stars of the world, and the fair of the greatest scholars of the period.

Contemporary with the Samanid Dynasty were the Ziyarids, founded by Mardavij, son of Ziyar. The Ziyarids rose from the Caspian provinces of Tabarestan and Gilan. The dynasty was noted for its devotion to learning. One of his successors was Qabus (A.D. 976-1012), himself an accomplished man of letters and the patron of the great astronomer Biruni, who dedicated to him his famous *Vestiges of Ancient Nations*. His grandson and namesake was the author of the well-known *Qabus-Nameh*, a manual of political conduct and ethics.

Another contemporary dynasty was the Buyid or Deylamite Dynasty, whose founder claimed descent from the Sasanians. This dynasty ruled over central and southern Iran. The Buyid Prince Ahmad, after his conquests in southern Iran and annexation of Khuzestan, entered Baghdad in A.D. 945, where the Caliph perforce welcomed him. The Caliph was later deposed and his successors became puppets in the hands of the Buyid chiefs. It was in this period that Ferdowsi composed his great epic, the *Shahnameh*, or the *Book of Kings*.

The Buyid Dynasty was already in decline when Mahmud of Ghazneh prepared to attack the city of Rey, which during the minority of the last prince of this dynasty was ruled by his mother. When Mahmud sent an envoy to demand her submission, she gave the following reply:

> Had this message been sent in the lifetime of my deceased lord it would have caused serious trouble, but such is no longer the case. I know Soltan Mahmud and am aware that he will never undertake a campaign without weighing all the risks. If he attacks and conquers a weak woman, where is the glory of such an achievement? If he be repulsed, the latest ages will hear of his shame.

The Ghaznavids were a slave dynasty, and their greatest figure was Soltan Mahmud. His successful campaigns in India and his zeal for Islam earned for him the title of "Idol-breaker." He ruled a vast kingdom from Bokhara and Samarkand to Kerman and India.

The Ghaznavids were succeeded in 1037 by the Saljuqs, a more powerful dynasty. Under this dynasty territories stretching from Central Asia to the Mediterranean Sea were united and brought under a single powerful sway. Toghrol, the real founder of the dynasty, was received and blessed by the Caliph in Baghdad. In the ceremony of investiture twin crowns were placed on his head and he was girded with two swords to signify that he was the ruler of the East and the West. A decree was then read, appointing him as Vice-regent and Lord of all Muslims.

His successor, Alp Arsalan, extended the boundaries of the empire and gained Mecca and Medina. In 1071 he defeated a Byzantine army in western Asia Minor and took prisoner the Emperor Diogenes Romanus. This warlike king is chiefly remembered in connection with his famous Prime Minister Nezam-ol-Molk, author of the celebrated *Siyasat-nameh*, or *Treatise on the Art of Government*, who was assassinated by the devotee emissaries of Hasan Sabah, the founder and Grand Master of the Order of Assassins, the "Old Man of the Mountain."

The famous poet, traveler and missionary Naser Khosrow, the eminent mystic theologian Ghazali, and the still more famous astronomer-poet Omar Khayyam belong to this period of Iranian history.

Under Malek Shah, the successor of Alp Arsalan, the Saljuq Empire reached the zenith of its power and prosperity.

Imposing architectural monuments, mainly of a religious nature, come from this period. These include mosques, shrines, religious schools and mausoleums, of which many are in the form of tomb towers of great height with conical domes (see Plate 19). Parthian and Sasanian styles of religious architecture with the square sanctuary chamber crowned by a dome and the barrel-vaulted *ivan* persisted as primary architectural features.

The last important local dynasty was that of the Kharazm-Shahs. The hero of this dynasty was Jalaleddin, who after desperate battles with the Mongol hordes of Changiz Khan in northeastern and eastern Iran finally went to India. There, after a brave counterattack, he jumped into the Indus River and disappeared. Changiz not only forbade arrows to be shot at the hero but held him up to his sons as a model of valor.

After his escape, Jalaleddin returned to Iran where he defeated local pretenders and several Mongol attacks. He even succeeded in subduing Caucasia and defeating the armies of the Caliph. But after making peace with him, the Caliph conferred on him the title of Shahanshah.

However, after a final defeat by the Mongols and another narrow escape, he was killed by a tribesman in 1231.

In the Middle Ages in Europe, Jalaleddin Kharazm-Shah was sometimes identified with the fabulous Prester John who ruled over a rich Christian realm in Central Asia and beyond. His death marked the end of one cycle in the history of Iran.

The Mongol Invasion

According to Iranian computation of the millennia, the year A.D. 1231 was the last of the twelfth millennium and the end of one Great Cycle – in a sense, the end of the world. Thus a cataclysmic act was expected. This was fulfilled by the Mongol invasion. If the Mongols did not bring the world to an end, they certainly concluded an era not only in Iranian history but in world history.

The Mongols had adapted some form of Manichaeism to their shamanistic beliefs and practices. Their religious leaders continued to bear the title of Burkhan, Mani's title (Barkhan), as his successors.

Mani had forbidden men to take the life of any living creature, but that was for the twelfth millennium. Now it was the end of the millennium and Doomsday was at hand. Thus, the appalling devastation wrought by the Mongol hordes was, one may conclude, a religious act. Wherever the Mongols passed, cities and villages were raised to the ground and the population literally exterminated. On the other hand, the millennial convictions of the people must have induced them to submit to destiny.

In 1258, Holagu, grandson of Changiz Khan, marched toward Baghdad with instructions to extinguish the Caliphate. The Caliph surrendered. According to contemporary historians, he was tied up in a sack and either trampled on by horses or beaten to death with clubs. The population of Baghdad was massacred. Thus came about the extinction of the Caliphate more than six centuries after the foundation of Islam. The great poet Sa'di composed a tragic eulogy in which he said the heavens shed tears of blood at the death of the Caliph.

Holagu founded the Il-Khanid Dynasty in Iran. The rulers of this dynasty gradually grew more civilized and became anxious to encourage reconstruction of the buildings destroyed by their ancestors. New architectural monuments rose, especially under Ghazan Khan and Khodabandeh, in which stylistic and decorative trends of the preceding period were maintained and further developed. Many of these great monuments survive. The peak in architectural technique can be found in the tomb of Khodabandeh at Soltaniyyeh, an enormous but graceful octagonal structure surmounted by a dome, twenty-six meters in diameter, the largest and tallest in Iran.

The arts again flourished. Trade was extensively carried on and merchant adventurers, the precursors of Marco Polo, traveled from Europe to the Mongol courts. Marco Polo in his *Book of Travels* describes Iran as "a great country which was in old times very illustrious and powerful, but now the Tartars have wasted and destroyed it." He continues: "In the cities there are traders and artisans who live by their labor and crafts, weaving cloths of gold and silk stuffs of sundry kinds. They have plenty of cotton produced in the country, and abundance of wheat, barley, millet, panick, and wine, with fruits of all kinds."

With the disintegration of Il-Khanid rule, petty local dynasties of short duration ruled across the country until the end of the fourteenth century.

Tamerlane

Timur the Lame, known as Tamerlane, was aptly called the World Conqueror by his official historian. He invaded territories stretching from Moscow to India, overran Iran, Mesopotamia and Syria, defeated and captured Soltan Bayazid of Turkey, conquered Caucasia and laid waste many districts that had previously escaped Mongol devastation.

The great mystic poet and seer, Hafez, Master of Shiraz, who was a contemporary of Tamerlane, exclaimed of the devastations of the Mongols and Timur:

> From the poisonous winds that blew over the rose-garden,
> It is strange and a wonder that the color of the rose and the scent of jasmine still remain.

There is a story that when Shiraz opened its gates to the World Conqueror, Tamerlane sent for Hafez and said to him:

> I have subdued with this sword the greater part of the earth; I have depopulated a vast number of cities and provinces in order to increase the glory and wealth of Samarkand and Bokhara, the places

18 Ceramic treasures of the early Muslim period on display at the Glassware Museum in Tehran.

19

of my residence and the seat of my empire; yet thou, an insignificant individual, hast pretended to give away both Samarkand and Bokhara as the price of a little black mole on a pretty face, for thou hast said in one of thy verses –

"If that fair maiden of Shiraz would accept my love, I would give for the dark mole which adorns her cheek Samarkand and Bokhara."

The poet replied: "Alas! O Prince, it is this prodigality which is the cause of the misery in which you see me." The repartee delighted Tamerlane so much that he treated the poet with kindness and generosity.

Tamerlane died in 1405 and was buried in a domed mausoleum at Samarkand. The cenotaph consists of a block of black jade, believed to be the largest in the world.

The court of Timur's son, Shahrokh, who reigned for nearly half a century with Harat as his capital, was famous for its splendor and attracted men of learning and science. Shahrokh's wife, Gowhar-Shad, built the magnificent mosque at Mashhad with its exquisite tile-work.

His son Ologh Beg was also a patron of science, and the celebrated astronomical tables were dedicated to him.

The Timurid Dynasty lasted for nearly a century and a half. Splendid buildings survive from this period (see Plate 20). The art of bookmaking with magnificent bindings and illuminations remains unsurpassed. The famous miniature painter Behzad and the school of painting created in Harat belong to this culture.

The Safavid Dynasty

The local dynasties of the Black Sheep and the White Sheep in northwestern Iran and Mesopotamia and the Sheybanis of Transoxania were all subdued by Shah Esmail, the founder of the Safavid dynasty. A youth of fourteen when he ascended the throne of Iran in 1501, he was not only a brave soldier but also a great leader of men and was worshiped by his subjects as a saint and head of the religious organization.

The Mongols had at least done one great service in the extinction of the Sunnite Caliphate of Baghdad: they made it easy for the Safavid Shahs to establish the Shiite doctrines as the national religion of Iran.

Shah Esmail, although suffering a defeat at the hands of the Ottoman Soltan Salim, was victorious in successive campaigns. He united Iran from Caucasia to the Persian Gulf and from Mesopotamia to India and Central Asia, and ushered in a new era in the history of Iran.

During the reign of his successor Tahmasp, after several Ottoman aggressions under Soleyman the Magnificent, hostilities between the two states ended in a treaty of peace.

Hostilities had again broken out between the two states in 1587 when Shah Abbas the Great ascended the throne. He wisely ceded the western provinces of Iran to the Ottomans and concluded peace with them in order to concentrate his resources in the east. The Uzbaks who raided the eastern provinces and even took the sacred city of Mashhad, carrying off the treasures of the shrine and massacring its inhabitants, were finally defeated in 1597, and their annual raids ceased for many years to come.

The victory over the Uzbaks was once more gained shortly after a millennial event. It was during the Muslim year 1000 (A.D. 1591) that Shah Abbas, fearing the danger predicted by astrologers, vacated his throne. A certain Yusof was crowned and surrounded with royal state. On the fourth day he was put to death, and Abbas reascended the throne on a propitious day with promises of a long and glorious reign. The millennium was also the occasion of the propagation of Noqtavi doctrines in Iran and the proclamation of the Religion of Universal Peace by the great Akbar, emperor of India.

Shah Abbas then turned his attention to the reorganization of the army and substituted the tribal contingents for a cavalry and infantry that were administered by the crown. He invited members of all tribes to enroll as "Friends of the Shah." The Sherley brothers from England were instrumental in modernizing the army and in encouraging Shah Abbas to form an alliance with Europeans against the Ottoman Empire.

In 1602 Shah Abbas took the field against the Ottomans and defeated them. The Shah thus regained the northwestern and western provinces.

The fame of Shah Abbas does not rest only on his military exploits. His genius for administration, his consolidation of the various tribes, and the improvement of communications throughout the empire add to his fame as a great ruler.

He made the city of Esfahan his capital and lavishly adorned it. The complex of magnificent buildings around the large Royal Square in the heart of the city, which also served as the royal polo ground, is still preserved. The royal mosques, with their graceful and per-

19 Saljuq tomb towers at Kharraqan preserve some of the finest examples of medieval brickwork in Iran.

fect proportions, contain exquisite tilework and superb calligraphic decorations. The royal palace of Chehel Sotun or "Forty Columns" is decorated with splendid frescoes. The best of the world-famous carpets date from this period, with a variety of beautiful floral and geometric designs (see Plate 21). Safavid miniature paintings and calligraphic art remain unsurpassed. Textiles of the highest quality with delicate colors and designs are among the most delightful products of this art.

The days of great poetry had passed, but works of famous theologians and historians survive from this period.

With the death of Shah Abbas came the decline of the Safavid Dynasty that ruled Iran for more than two centuries. Chardin, the great French traveler, wrote: "When this great prince ceased to live, Iran ceased to prosper."

After Shah Abbas no able monarch sat on the throne of the Safavids. The Ottoman Turks under Soltan Morad captured Hamedan, and three years later Baghdad was subdued.

The last king of this dynasty, Shah Soltan Hoseyn, a feeble monarch given to piety and meekness, was unconscious of the approaching doom. Afghan bands under Mahmud, after several unsuccessful attempts, finally received the surrender of the Shah and the throne and entered Esfahan in triumph.

Nader Shah

Tahmasp Mirza, the son and heir of the last Safavid monarch, left Esfahan before its fall. He tried to raise an army in vain. Meanwhile the northwestern provinces were occupied by the Ottomans, and Peter the Great of Russia had captured Baku and occupied the Caspian province of Gilan. Tahmasp, unable to meet the invaders in the field, made a bid for the support of Peter against the Afghans and agreed to cede the Caucasian and Caspian provinces to Peter. The treaty was never realized.

In 1724, negotiations between the Ottomans and Russia culminated in an agreement for the partition of the north and northwestern provinces of Iran. Russia had already occupied part of her portion. It remained for the Ottomans to make good the possession of their share. In a short time they rounded off their conquests until the whole of western Iran was in their hands.

Meanwhile the Afghan Ashraf had succeeded Mahmud and occupied himself in consolidating his power. It was under these circumstances that Nader Qoli, destined to ascend the throne of Iran as a great conqueror, joined Tahmasp in his court in the Caspian province of Mazandaran.

Nader was appointed Commander-in-Chief of the army. In his first successful campaign he took Khorasan and Harat from the Afghans, on which occasion the title of Tahmasp Qoli Khan was conferred on him.

Ashraf, realizing the danger that was impending, marched to Khorasan where he was defeated by Nader. A second defeat north of Esfahan made the Afghans prepare for flight.

Hailed as deliverer of Iran, Nader was joined by hundreds of men and entered Esfahan in triumph. He then pursued the Afghans to Shiraz. Ashraf was killed in flight by a Baluchi Khan, ending Afghan rule in Iran.

After the Afghans had been uprooted, Nader turned his attention to the Ottomans. His first campaign was successful and he gained the western provinces. Tahmasp, jealous of his general, took the field in person, was defeated, lost all that Nader had won back, and made a humiliating treaty with the Ottoman Soltan.

The defeat of Tahmasp afforded Nader the pretext he had hitherto lacked. He protested against the treaty, then marched to Esfahan and upbraided Tahmasp. He sent him prisoner to Khorasan, put a son of Tahmasp on the throne and proclaimed himself regent.

He was defeated in his first attempt to take Baghdad, but in a second attempt he routed the Turkish army. Another brilliant victory gave Nader the northern provinces in Caucasia.

Meanwhile, the Russians evacuated Gilan, and the Caspian provinces were restored in 1732. Three years later Baku surrendered to Nader.

On the death of the infant Shah, Nader invited leading Iranian officials to celebrate the New Year's Day on the plain of Moghan in Azarbayejan, and exhorted them to choose a worthy Shah from among the princes. He was then unanimously requested to protect Iran and to ascend the vacant throne. After refusing for a month, he responded at last to the prayers of the assembly. The crown was placed on his head in 1736, and Nader Shah, in pomp and splendor in a magnificent hall, seated on a jewel-encrusted throne, received the homage of his grateful subjects.

20 Fragment of a luster-ware tile that once adorned the prayer niche in the Jame Mosque at Qom.

21 Woven arabesques surround the central lion medallion of this outstanding sixteenth-century carpet.

22 Glittering emerald and diamond headdress ornament from the time of Nader Shah in the Crown Jewels Collection.

21

22

The ambitious conqueror then turned to the east and, subduing Afghanistan, entered India and took Peshawar. He crossed the Indus and swiftly marched across the Punjab to face the Moghol Emperor Mohamad Shah. The emperor was defeated and Nader marched in triumph into Delhi, where he was entertained in the most sumptuous fashion by the emperor who handed over to him the amassed wealth of his ancestors, including the celebrated Peacock Throne. In this fortunate expedition Nader had won the fabulous wealth of India and with it enduring fame (see Plate 22). He allowed the emperor to remain on the throne, but he recovered all the provinces west of the Indus which had once formed part of the Iranian Empire.

After successfully adding Bokhara and Khiveh to his list of conquests, he proceeded to Mashhad to celebrate his victories. Nader was now at the zenith of his fame. His empire stretched from the Oxus to the Persian Gulf and from Mesopotamia to the Indus.

In the last years of his reign, Nader Shah turned into a tyrant, and there was almost a general rebellion against him. He was finally assassinated at the hands of one of his own tribesmen.

The Zand Dynasty

With the death of Nader Shah, rebel leaders and pretenders to the throne rose on every side. Of these, Karim Khan of the Lor tribe, who had served Nader as a soldier, became the sole ruler of southern Iran, and by his kindliness, generosity and justice won the hearts of his subjects. After several defeats at the hands of the Qajar chief and the Afghans, the final victory lay with the popular Zand chief.

Karim Khan, who ruled Iran from 1750 to 1779, refused to assume the title of Shah, and termed himself "Representative of the Peasants." It is interesting to note that Karim Khan's attitude in this respect preceded the French Revolution by three decades.

Karim Khan's only expedition outside Iran was against the city of Basra which was taken. He had given Iran two decades of rest, and when he died at a great age he was deeply mourned.

He held Shiraz as his capital, and the fine buildings in the city, especially the graceful and clean Vakil Bazaar, were all erected by him. The architecture and paintings of the Zand period have a special touch of pleasing delicacy and grace (see Plate 23).

23 This webbed stucco dome inside the Dowlatabad Gardens in Yazd expresses the genius of Zand architecture.

Upon the death of Karim Khan, rivalries and ambitions, family feuds and assassinations weakened the Zand family. The long struggle for power between the Zands and the Qajars was renewed and ended in the victory of the Qajars.

The Qajar Dynasty

Lotf-ali Khan, the last ruler of the short-lived Zand Dynasty, was a brilliant soldier and skilled leader. After several desperate attempts, though, he was defeated by his rival Aga Mohamad Khan, the founder of the Qajar Dynasty. Lotf-ali tried to escape, but fell into the hands of his foe. The gallant hero was blinded and suffered other indignities, and was at last sent to Tehran where he was strangled.

Aga Mohamad Khan's first military exploit was the successful invasion of Georgia and Armenia. Upon his return from this expedition he was crowned in 1796. He then marched into Khorasan whose petty rulers capitulated without any resistance.

In 1799 he went on a second expedition to Georgia, and after a successful raid was assassinated by his personal servants. This Eunuch-Shah was cruel; but by courage, patience, judgment and insight, he succeeded in winning the crown and in once more uniting Iran.

He was succeeded by his nephew Fath-ali Shah, the last Shah in the grand old style. Napoleon made overtures to the Shah for an alliance against Russia to which the Shah responded favorably, at the same time declaring his assistance in case the French intended to invade India.

Meanwhile Russia had annexed Georgia. This angered the Shah. Hostility erupted and several campaigns that followed ended in disaster, with Iran losing the provinces north of the Aras River.

During the reign of Nasereddin Shah who was crowned in 1848, and under the direction of his Chief Minister Mirza Taqi Khan Amir Kabir, administrative and financial reforms were carried out. But these reforms were resented by many, including the powerful Queen mother. Although the young Shah at first supported Amir Kabir loyally, and even gave him his own sister in marriage, Amir Kabir was at last ordered to retire and after two months was executed.

The occupation of Harat by the Iranian army in 1856 prompted a declaration of war by Britain. Hostilities in the Persian Gulf finally ended in the evacuation of Harat.

Meanwhile Russia had advanced in Central Asia and was a growing menace to Iran. Anglo-Russian rivalry became more acute as the years went by, and friction grew.

Nasereddin's reign was the beginning of modernization in Iran. He ruled for nearly fifty years, and was assassinated in 1896.

Under his successor's reign, a revolutionary movement resulted in constitutional government being granted by the Shah in 1906.

An almost immediate attempt to overthrow the constitution was repulsed. Meanwhile, in 1907 Britain and Russia agreed to end their rivalries, which had enveloped Iran.

World War I brought new calamities to Iran. Ottoman and Russian forces were engaged in the northern and western provinces, while the British occupied the south. In 1919 an Anglo-Iranian agreement was submitted by the British, virtually placing Iran under British influence. This agreement was never ratified by the Iranian parliament.

Some innovations occurred in the field of art and architecture during the Qajar period. Iranian artists had hitherto been occupied mainly with illustrating manuscripts with miniatures and illuminations. Oil painting, although introduced at the beginning of the seventeenth century, began to flourish under the Qajars. The term "Qajar" is particularly associated with painted lacquer work, portraits and pictures of dancing girls or musicians. Painted enamel, lacquer book bindings and pen boxes are products of this period (see Plate 24).

Developments in prose writing – particularly historiography – also occurred. Fath-ali Shah was a great patron of painting and the long reign of Nasereddin Shah permitted a new flowering of literature.

The Pahlavi Dynasty

After a period of apathy, stagnation and foreign influence, the coup d'état of Reza Khan once again ushered in a new era. Reza Khan marched to Tehran and seized the government in 1921. He was appointed Minister of War, and in 1925, Prime Minister.

Soltan Ahmad Shah, the last king of the Qajar Dynasty, was a weak ruler who spent most of his days in Europe. He was deposed by a National Constituent Assembly and Reza Khan was offered the crown. The coronation took place in 1926.

Reza Shah spent most of the early years in office working on restoring order throughout the country. The stability and security that he established permitted him to launch fundamental reforms in all directions.

Reza Shah had a passion for reviving the ancient glories of Iran. In 1934 he launched the celebration on an international scale of the millenary of Ferdowsi, the great epic poet. The revival of the ancient solar calendar and month names to replace the lunar calendar, and the establishment of the Iranian Academy for purging the Farsi language, are further testimonies of his attachment to Iranian traditions.

The abolition of the veil in 1936 led to the emancipation of Iranian women and was a step toward the many social reforms that followed.

Reza Shah organized the army along modern lines and formed the nucleus of an air force and a navy. In short, he changed the face of the country.

In World War II, although neutrality had been declared, Iran was invaded by American and British forces from the south and the Soviets from the north. Reza Shah abdicated in favor of his son and went into exile where he died. His people, however, gratefully remembered what he had accomplished for the country; and parliament, in gratitude, gave him the deserved title of "the Great."

His recently published diaries throw new light on the character and ideals of Reza Shah the Great.

The fiftieth anniversary of the establishment of the Pahlavi Dynasty was celebrated in 1976. In the productive years of the reign of His Imperial Majesty the Shahanshah Aryamehr, great strides were taken toward the realization of what His Majesty has named the Great Civilization.

The Shahanshah, conscious of his international obligations and determined to preserve the integrity of Iran, has tried to establish Iranian independence on the basis of political, economic and social stability. To guarantee the realization of these goals, the steady build-up of the armed forces has not been neglected.

In 1962 the Shahanshah launched the White Revolution, or the Revolution of the Shah and the People. In a referendum on the original six-point program of reforms, he received the massive support of the people. Other points were later added to cover the entire spectrum of economic and social affairs. The program included, first of all, drastic land reform to ameliorate the condition of the rural population; the nationalization of natural resources, including forests and water; co-ownership and profit-sharing of laborers in industry; extension of literacy and health facilities, and educational reforms including provision of free education.

24 Detail from a glowing lacquer-ware box in the Negarestan Museum's collection of Qajar art.

24

Due to the interest and encouragement of Her Imperial Majesty the Shahbanou Farah, special attention has been given to cultural matters and revival of arts and crafts, and the restoration of old monuments.

The ceremony of coronation was postponed so that it could be celebrated when the country had reached a stage of reconstruction worthy of the endeavors of the people of Iran led by their far-sighted Monarch and Leader.

Four years after the coronation, in 1970, at a magnificent gathering of heads of state, the largest ever assembled in one place, the 2,500th Anniversary of the Founding of the Achaemenian Empire was celebrated in all its splendor at Persepolis.

At the majestic and solemn ceremony before the tomb of Cyrus the Great, among other remarks, His Imperial Majesty addressed the following statement to the founder of the Achaemenian Empire:

> After the passage of twenty-five centuries, the Iranian flag is flying today as triumphantly as it flew in thy glorious age. The name of Iran today invokes as much respect throughout the world as it did in thy days. Today, as in thy age, Iran bears the message of liberty and the love of mankind in a troubled world, and is the guardian of the loftiest human aspirations. The torch thou kindled has for 2,500 years never died in spite of the storms of history. Today, it casts its light upon this land more brightly than ever and, as in thy time, its brilliance spreads far beyond the boundaries of Iran.

Herodotus concludes his *History* with the following:

> Artembares instructed the Persians in a design which they took from him and led before Cyrus; this was its purport: "Seeing that Zeus grants lordship to the Persian people, and to you, Cyrus, among them, by bringing Astyages low, let us now remove out of the little and rugged land that we possess and take to ourselves one that is better. There be many such on our borders, and many further distant; if we take one of these we shall have more reasons for renown. It is but reasonable that a ruling people should act thus; for *when shall we have a fairer occasion than now*, when we are lords of so many men and of all Asia?" Cyrus heard them, and found naught to marvel at in their design; "Do so," said he, "but if you do, make ready to be no longer rulers, but subjects. Soft lands breed soft men, wondrous fruits of the earth and valiant warriors grow not from the same soil." Thereat the Persians saw that Cyrus reasoned better than they, and they departed from before him, choosing rather to be rulers on a barren mountainside than slaves in tilled valleys.

No Iranian now aspires to rule other lands and peoples. Fortunately the rugged land and barren mountains cover vast resources of oil and minerals. Only through knowledge and hard work the people of this land may achieve the establishment of a vigorous, integrated society which is the goal of the National Revival.

"WHEN SHALL WE HAVE A FAIRER OCCASION THAN NOW?"

Mohamad Moghdam

CHRONOLOGY

Pishdadians	Third millennium B.C.
Kiyanians	End of the third millennium to the middle of the second millennium B.C.
Zoroaster	1768-1691 B.C.
Medes	Eighth to seventh century B.C.
Achaemenians	Seventh to fourth century B.C.
Parthians	Fourth century B.C. to third century A.D.
Mithra	272-208 B.C.
Sasanians	Third to seventh century A.D.
Mani	A.D. 256-315
Local dynasties- Islamic period	Seventh to thirteenth century A.D.
Mongol invasion	Thirteenth century A.D.
Safavid Dynasty	1501-1722
Nader Shah	1736-1747
Zand Dynasty	1747-1787
Qajar Dynasty	1787-1925
Founding of the Pahlavi Dynasty	1925
The White Revolution	1962
2,500th Anniversary of the Founding of the Achaemenian Empire by Cyrus the Great	1970
Celebration of the 50th Anniversary of the Pahlavi Dynasty	1976-1977

25 A golden cameo of the Shahanshah crowns the Staircase of History inside the Shahyad Monument's new audio-visual theater.

BOOK ONE

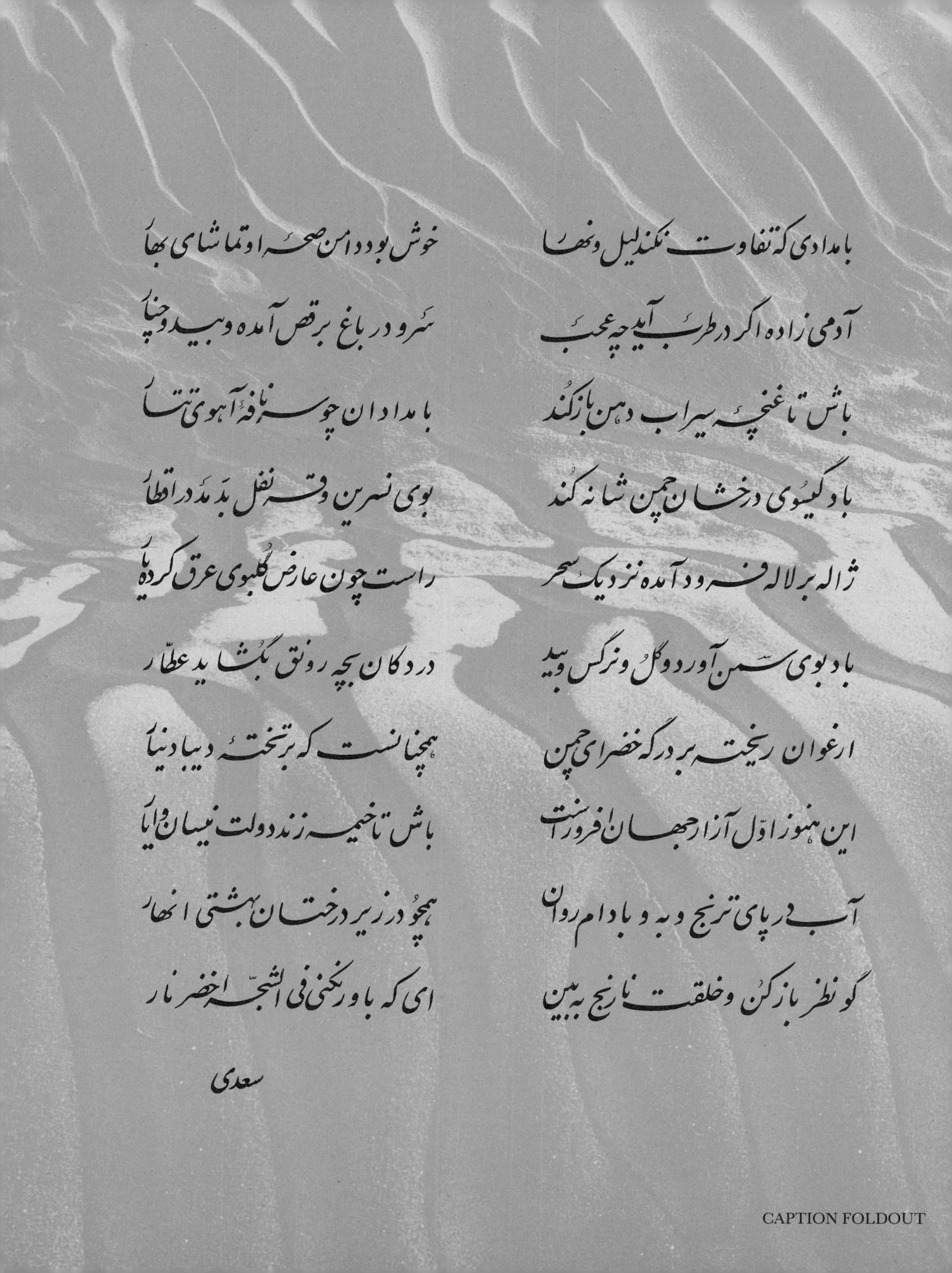

بامدادی که تفاوت نکند لیل و نهار　　خوش بود دامن صحرا و تماشای بهار

آدمی‌زاده اگر در طرب آید چه عجب　　سرو در باغ برقص آمده و بید و چنار

باش تا غنچهٔ سیراب دهن باز کند　　بامدادان چو سر نافهٔ آهوی تتار

باد گیسوی درختان چمن شانه کند　　بوی نسرین و قرنفل بدمد در اقطار

ژاله بر لاله فرود آمده نزدیک سحر　　راست چون عارض گلبوی عرق کردهٔ یار

باد بوی سمن آورد و گل و نرگس و بید　　در دکان بچه رونق بگشاید عطّار

ارغوان ریخته بر درگه خضرای چمن　　همچنانست که بر تختهٔ دیبا دینار

این هنوز اوّل آزار جهان افروزست　　باش تا خیمه زند دولت نیسان و ایار

آب در پای ترنج و به و بادام روان　　همچو در زیر درختان بهشتی انهار

گو نظر باز کن و خلقت نارنج ببین　　ای که باور نکنی فی الشجر الاخضر نار

سعدی

CAPTION FOLDOUT

 For notes to these plates, see pages 371 to 374

CONTOUR AND PROFILE

26 Aerial view of the austerely beautiful Baluchestan terrain.

27- A montage of images showing
38 the wide variety of natural landscapes found within the borders of Iran.

27 Mount Ararat.
28 Rice paddies, Mazandaran.
29 Dasht-e-Kavir desert.
30 Winter at Soltaniyyeh.
31 Mount Sahand, East Azarbayejan.
32 Mount Taftan, Baluchestan.
33 Snowbound village, Alborz Mountains.
34 Mount Damavand.
35 Karaj tree farm.
36 Alborz Mountain pass.
37 Hormoz Island, Persian Gulf.
38 Kandovan village, East Azarbayejan.

39 Erosion patterns fan out across the rust-red Khuzestan Plain northeast of Ahvaz.

40- Spring and summer flowers
44 blooming in formal gardens and in the wild.

40 Aryamehr Botanical Gardens, Tehran.
41 Tulips in north Tehran garden.
42 Spring flowering trees.
43 Pelican in Tabas garden.
44 Wild thistle, Persepolis.

45 Alpine meadows in the upper Alborz Mountains near Bandar-e-Pahlavi.

PATTERNS OF INDUSTRY

46 Freshly thrown clay pots bathed in sunlight at the pottery village of Lalejin near Hamedan.

47- Patterns of Iranian industry
66 and transporation.

47 Symbol of the Fiftieth Year of the Pahlavi Dynasty.
48 Oil storage tanks, Shiraz.
49 Steel pipes.
50 General Motors of Iran.
51 Harvesting sugarcane, Haft Tappeh.
52 Forestry machinery, Gilan.
53 Iron display.
54 Dyed wool, Yazd.
55 Pars Paper Company, Haft Tappeh.
56 Karun Sugarcane Project, Shushtar.
57 Heavy machinery.
58 Aluminum pots in local bazaar.
59 Brass rice cookers.
60 Wheel of progress.
61 Sarcheshmeh Copper Complex.
62 Atomic Energy Reactor, Bushehr.
63 Motorcycle store.
64 Decorated truck.
65 Lar Valley Tunnel.
66 Rails, Ahvaz Train Station.

67 Painters candy-stripe two soaring smokestacks at the Sarcheshmeh Copper Complex near Kerman.

68 Abstract design formed by stacked water pipes.

69 Rolled steel strip produced by Krupp and photographed in Tehran's Park-e-Shafagh.

70, Two views of the enormous
71 Arya Cement Plant under construction in Esfahan Province.

72 Pulp and paper mill being built on the edge of the thick Caspian forest in Gilan.

73 Mulch-spraying tractors stabilize drifting sand dunes surrounding Ahvaz.

74 Grapes ready for processing into wine and other products at the Pakdis Winery, Rezaiyyeh.

75- A sampling of the cultivated
95 fruits, vegetables and animal husbandry from all parts of Iran.

75 Sheep, Pars Meat Packing Plant.
76 Tree farm, Shahrud.
77 Dasht-e-Morghab agro-industry.
78 Watermelons, Tabriz bazaar.
79 Palm frond basket, Baluchestan.
80 Aerial view of farm, Gilan.
81 Fertilized date palm.
82 Citrus orchard, Jiroft.
83 Sliced melon, Rezaiyyeh bazaar.
84 Date palm oasis, Baluchestan.
85 Wheat fields, Dasht-e-Morghab.
86 Banquet table, Tehran.
87 Banana blossom, Ahvaz.
88 Banana plant, Chahbahar.
89 Tea bushes, Caspian.
90 Statue in fountain, Gilan.
91 Cutting sugarcane, Haft Tappeh.
92 Ripe pistachios, Khorasan.
93 Lemon blossoms, Mazandaran.
94 Pear tree, Rezaiyyeh.
95 Cherry orchard, Tehran.

96 This bronze statue at the entrance to the Ministry of Agriculture and Rural Development in Tehran pays tribute to the Iranian farming family.

EARTH

EARTH

CONTOUR AND PROFILE

That morning when night and day
	are finally equal, what pleasure
to watch the lawn's skirt
	sweep the Spring.
No wonder men are happy: the cypress
	even the willow and sycamore dance.
Just wait: the rosebud will purse its lips
	wait: wind will comb the
tresses of trees and the incense of wild rose
	and carnations will burn
The last frost dawn-descended on the
	tulip's face: beads of sweat
on the beloved's attar-washed cheeks.
	The rill that washes the feet of the
orange and almond trees: water of paradise.
	Saadi: open your eyes and study the orange:
	Don't you believe green trees may hide
		an interior fire?

Saadi

◁ Pattern of frost on desert dunes.

CONTOUR AND PROFILE

Geological History

Geologists believe that at some distant past in the earth's history, namely during the late Paleozoic eras some 250 million years ago, cycles of mobility were initiated which resulted in the establishment of the framework of surface structures of our planet. By that time the supercontinents of Gondwanaland and Laurentia (two gigantic land masses from which all the mainlands of the continents have supposedly been derived) had been assembled. In Mesozoic times (225 to 65 million years ago) the supercontinents in question broke up when the continental framework so formed drifted apart and the widening spaces between them were filled by extensive seas in which crustal materials of oceanic type were deposited. One of the major depressions so formed was the Thetys Sea that extended right across the Old World as a continuation of the present Mediterranean. According to geologists, it was in this sea that the belt of the Alpine Himalayan mountain system, which today runs from West Europe to the Indian Ocean and within which Iran is situated, was first developed.

The initial major mountain-building disturbances of the Alpine Himalayan system took place in the late Cretaceous times (approximately 70 million years ago) when some of the Zagros chains were born. The disturbances were concentrated in the internal zones of the system where extensive marine deposition was brought to an end in the Tertiary era during which the important folding took place, creating the Alborz Mountains. By the Miocene period (26 to 7 million years ago) the major structural patterns had been built up and regional elevation had led to the expulsion of the sea from the great part of the land that separated the folded areas. Subsequent vertical movements, seven million years ago to recent times, rejuvenated the mountain belts with consequent intensification of erosion and deposition. Concurrent with these vertical movements, the effects of which are still felt in the seismic areas of Iran, climatic fluctuations resulted in the drying up of the inland seas and the appearance of the interior deserts. It was thus that the Iranian Plateau came into existence and provided the habitat for the local people and culture.

27

28

29

30

31

32

33

34

35

36

37

38

40

41

42

43

44

Physical Background

The vast continent of Asia consists of peninsulas in the south, mountains in the middle and plains in the north. Most of southwest Asia, including Iran, lies within the western extremities of the Asian mountain system which tapers in two important places – namely, the Pamirs and the Armenian knots. Between these two lies a great plateau, long known to geographers as the Iranian Plateau, and occupied by the states of Iran and its eastern neighbor, Afghanistan. Geographically this plateau extends from 44 to 74 degrees east longitude and from 25 to 38 degrees north latitude.

The Iranian Plateau is divided into two unequal parts by a series of broken highlands that run almost along the line of 60 degrees east longitude and coincide with the political boundary between Iran and Afghanistan. A glance at the relief map of Iran would reveal the plateau and mountainous nature of the country, with the mountains concentrated mainly in the northern and western sections where they form continuous and almost unbroken belts. In the east, the highlands are broken and appear more like isolated uplands rather than chains of mountains.

Another striking feature of the relief of Iran is the almost complete absence of lowland plains, especially along the seas that lie to the north (the Caspian Sea) and to the south (the Persian Gulf and the Sea of Oman). This is particularly the case in the north of the country where the plains of the Caspian Sea average a width of no more than 50 kilometers. The only exception to the rule is found in the low delta plain of Karun at the mouth of the Persian Gulf, which finds its physical continuance in the Mesopotamian lowlands to the west.

Mountain Systems

In Iran there are two major mountain systems with different characteristics. These are the Alborz, running almost from west to east, and the Zagros, extending from northwest to southeast. The two systems meet at the Armenian Knot or the great mountain junction of Armenia to the northwest of Iran. From here the two systems branch off in such a way as to form a rim of higher ground along the northern and western peripheries.

The first of the two systems, the Alborz, forms a continuous wall along northern Iran from Mount Ararat in the northwest to Sarakhs in the northeast of the country.

In Azarbayejan this system is represented by Ghara Dagh which runs parallel to the Aras River that separates Iran from the U.S.S.R. At its eastern extremities, this range joins an independent chain known as the Talesh Mountains which extend in a north-south direction, parallel to and not very far from the southwestern shores of the Caspian. After taking a right turn to the east, due south of the city of Rasht, the Talesh Mountains end at Manjil Gap. It is here that the Alborz proper begins as a mighty system which encircles the southern Caspian Sea and continues eastward to the highlands of northern Khorasan. The whole system consists of a relatively narrow series of folds with extremely steep ridges and with a number of summits exceeding 3,000 meters in elevation. Within the Alborz system and some 50 kilometers to the northeast of Tehran lies the magnificent volcanic dome of Mount Damavand, the highest and most prominent peak in the entire country, reaching an elevation of 5,678 meters above sea level.

The parallel ranges of the Alborz unite to the southeast of the Caspian Sea to form Shah-Kuh, due north of Shahrud city, after which they branch off again in the form of Ala-Dagh, Binalud and Hezar Masjed, constituting the highands of northern Khorasan. Beyond the eastern borders of Iran, the Alborz system joins the Hindu Kush mountains of northern Afghanistan which in turn join the Himalayas at the Pamir junction.

The Zagros Mountains begin at Ararat and run southward as an unbroken and impenetrable wall of mountain no less than 400 kilometers in width. They attain heights of over 4,000 meters and therefore influence the climate of Iran, which in turn exerts a strong influence on the life of the Iranian community. Among the prominent peaks included in this portion of the Zagros Mountains are Shotoran-Kuh, Kabir-Kuh, Shahin-Kuh, and Zard-Kuh, ranging from 3,700 to 4,700 meters in height.

In western Iran, the Zagros Mountains embrace West Azarbayejan, Kordestan, Lorestan, Bakhtiari and parts of Khuzestan – providing some of the most fertile and populous plains and basins, among which are Kermanshah, Mahidasht, Khorramabad, Borujerd and Nahavand.

Before reaching Khuzestan, the Zagros range assumes a southeasterly direction and runs through the two southern provinces of Fars and Kerman. These provinces have peaks over 3,500 meters high with fertile and prosperous plains and basins. Further east in Baluchestan, the Zagros tend to concentrate near the coast, preventing all maritime influence of the southern seas from penetrating the interior of the plateau.

Beginning south of Azarbayejan and running parallel with the main Zagros system, there is a series of broken mountains that, for lack of a better name, have been termed the Central or Interior Mountains of Iran. Running almost uninterrupted for 1,000 kilometers between Azarbayejan in the northwest and Baluchestan in the southeast, this series, with peaks that exceed 4,400 meters, forms a prominent feature of Iran. It separates some fertile and relatively well-populated valleys and basins like Esfahan and Sirjan from the desolate and sparsely peopled deserts of the interior.

Other topographical features of Iran include the semi-active, triple-peaked volcanic cone of Mount Taftan which stands 4,043 meters high in Baluchestan, the eastern highlands in Bajestan, and the Qayenat uplands of middle and southern Khorasan.

Drainage

From this description of the topography, it may be noted that the encircling mountains give a basin-like character to Iran despite the fact that it has become known as a plateau.

The rivers of Iran flow into the Caspian Sea, the Persian Gulf and the Sea of

Oman, Lake Rezaiyyeh and the Sistan Depression, as well as into the country's interior.

The interior of Iran covers an area of 900,000 square kilometers and is the driest part of the country. Nevertheless, during the short rainy season, the river-beds are flooded and torrential currents of short duration rush down toward the internal basins and salt wastes into which they eventually disappear. In this season, heavy erosion occurs and produces extensive gravel slopes and fans all along the foothills. It is on such foothill gravel slopes that most Iranian villages and cities – including Tehran, the capital – are built.

Of the rivers flowing south from the Alborz Mountains, the two most important are the Karaj and the Jajerud, some 40 kilometers to the west and east of Tehran respectively. Their waters are used extensively for agriculture. As well, the city of Tehran, with a population of over four million, depends on these rivers for its water supply. An important river of the interior of Iran is the Zayandeh-Rud, which rises in the Zard-Kuh in the Zagros range, and follows an easterly course into the fertile and prosperous basin of Esfahan where it brings life to one of the most populous districts of central Iran. Its waters are used to the last drop and it is only in very rainy years that some reach the Gavkhuni swamp into which the river is eventually lost.

The streams that drain some 350,000 square kilometers of Iranian territory into the Persian Gulf and the Sea of Oman diminish in importance from the northwest to the southeast. The western slopes of the Zagros are among the relatively well-watered parts of Iran and they pour their waters into great rivers that, after passing through tortuous but picturesque valleys, join the Tigris and the Arvand-Rud before reaching the Persian Gulf. The most important river of Iran, and the only one navigable to small commercial vessels, is the Karun which starts in the Zard-Kuh, where a distance of only a few miles separates it from the inland-flowing Zayandeh-Rud. In fact, the Karun River has recently been partly diverted into the Zayandeh-Rud's channel. In its northern sections, the Karun runs a tortuous course through deep valleys and gorges. It is in one of these gorges that the greatest hydro-electric and irrigation project in Iran, the Mohammad Reza Shah Dam, has been built to irrigate the fertile Khuzestan Plain at the mouth of the Persian Gulf. Following the coast of the Persian Gulf and the Sea of Oman southeastward, practically no river of importance is encountered. Aridity prevails everywhere.

The Caspian littoral is a narrow coastal plain with an average width of about 50 kilometers, uncovered by the gradual retreat of the sea, which at one time extended as far as the very foot of the Alborz Mountains. Numerous rivers festoon the northern foothills but they invariably cover only small distances before reaching the sea. There are, however, four rivers of considerable importance flowing into the Caspian Sea. The Aras or Araxes is the longest. It rises in the heart of Anatolia and has a total length of 3,000 kilometers. The Sefid-Rud has its source in Kordestan, far to the southwest of the Caspian. After flowing east and then north up to Mianeh, and southeast to Manjil, it heads for the Caspian in a northwest direction. The Atrak and Gorgan rivers both rise from the northern highlands of Khorasan and after flowing for some distance reach the fertile plain of Gorgan where their waters are being used to irrigate this agriculturally rich district.

In eastern Iran there is another important hydrographic unit known as the Hamun Lake, or the Sistan Depression. Within Iran, the basin includes no more than 100,000 square kilometers, but it drains almost the whole of Afghanistan. There is one major river system in the whole basin and that is the Hirmand which rises in the mountains of the Hindu Kush in Afghanistan. During the rainy season, the Hirmand receives a number of tributaries; but in other months of the year, not unlike the Nile, it runs for hundreds of kilometers through dry and parched deserts, with the result that in dry years it has hardly anything to offer its delta that lies within the Iranian territory. Yet it is a bountiful river that brings life to the fertile plain of Sistan, where its waters are now received more regularly because of international treaty arrangements between the two countries.

The last hydrographic unit and the least in area (40,000 square kilometers) is Lake Rezaiyyeh in the northwest of Iran. The largest permanent saltwater body in Iran, this lake receives fourteen small rivers from all sides. Although at an elevation of 1,200 meters above sea level, this lake is drying up rapidly due to excessive evaporation and its exteme shallowness. It has an average depth of about five meters and its waters are brackish enough to preclude any kind of life.

Flora and Fauna

Out of the total land surface of Iran, roughly 180,000 square kilometers, or more than 10 percent, is covered by forests. The densest and most intensive forests of a subtropical variety are to be found all along the northern slopes of the Alborz Mountains facing the Caspian Sea from which the necessary moisture is received. Most of the northern forest area, covering some 3,400,000 hectares, consists of industrial hardwood, including elm, oak, walnut, medlar, box, alder and similar types of trees. The forests of the high Zagros Mountains are less dense and cover much more area, some 10,000,000 hectares; with most of the trees being elm, oak, wild pistachio and the like. Other forested sections of the country include the higher hills of northern Khorasan, Fars, Kerman and Baluchestan where pistachio, fig and tamarisk are the predominant varieties.

As one leaves the higher elevations and approaches the interior from all directions, the vegetation rapidly gives way to steppe varieties, creating a ring around the more interior desert type.

Iran is a land of plentiful fruit, with grapes, figs, apricots, cherries, plums, apples, peaches, and dates being exported, primarily to Europe. The date palm grows in Iran as far north as Tabas, and the olive, a typical Mediterranean plant, thrives in the Sefid-Rud valley in the Alborz Mountains and particularly in the Rudbar and Manjil areas.

Iran has a much richer animal life than one might expect. Among the mammals, some species, such as the lion and tiger, are probably extinct; others, like the well-known zebra or the wild ass of the interior, appear to be approaching a similar fate. Apart from these, other animals that exist in a wild state in certain areas include varieties of deer, ibex, mouflon, leopard, lynx, bear, hyena, wolf, jackal, fox, hog, badger, hare, porcupine, polecat, weasel and marten. In addition, Iran boasts of an indigenous cat with a world-wide reputation and is famous for the breeding of donkeys, mules and horses. In fact, as far back as Achaemenian times, there was mention of the pride Iranians had in their horses.

More than 400 species of birds are known in Iran, among which are the pheasant, partridge, woodcock, flamingo, pelican and many smaller birds such as the famous nightingale of Persian literature. The Caspian Sea has a large variety of fishes such as salmon, herring and sturgeon which is the source of the best caviar in the world. The southern seas of Iran contain a far richer variety and amount of fish as well as shrimps and oysters, the exploitation of which has assumed importance in recent years.

Mohammad Hassan Ganji

WESTERN RED SHEEP
Ovis ammon gmelini

EARTH

PATTERNS OF INDUSTRY

Resources and Their Development

At the present time, land, water, climate, energy and manpower are regarded as the basic resources available to mankind. The first four correspond to the four elements which the ancients considered to be the main components of their universe. Water, climate and energy will be explored later, and now we shall concentrate on certain aspects of the land of Iran which have provided a favorable setting for the development of the country.

The "earth formation," as expressed in this volume, implies ways in which the land has been put to use over the ages and the present patterns of land utilization in this country. The uses of land will be referred to briefly under four major headings – namely, Agriculture and Forestry, Mining and Industry, Transportation, and Urban Development.

Agriculture and Forestry

According to one definition, "Agriculture covers man's productive efforts to make use of and, where possible, to accelerate and improve the natural genetic or growth processes of plant and animal life, to the end that these processes will yield the vegetable and animal products desired by man." This definition of agriculture implies that man must live in permanent settlements and in constant touch with nature, on which agriculture depends. In this sense, agriculture in Iran dates back to the early days of civilization.

Over the centuries that separate present-day Iran from the time that the original dwellers of the Iranian Plateau first learned to sow seeds, agriculture has developed to such an extent that it has become the backbone of Iranian society. It has been a way of life by which more than 90 percent of the Iranian population have made their living until almost a few decades ago. During that period an ingenious irrigation system – namely, the *qanat* – was developed, implements were discovered, seeds were selected, cross-breedings of plants were effected, water laws were laid down, and land management methods were designed. All these had a share in creating the long-lasting agricultural society of Iran that defied all unfavorable events, whether natural or human, and persisted as the basic element in Iranian population until the present generation. The traditional agriculture which evolved not only made Iran self-sufficient but produced a surplus of certain products. In addition, the traditional agriculture was responsible for forming the cultural and social organization of the country.

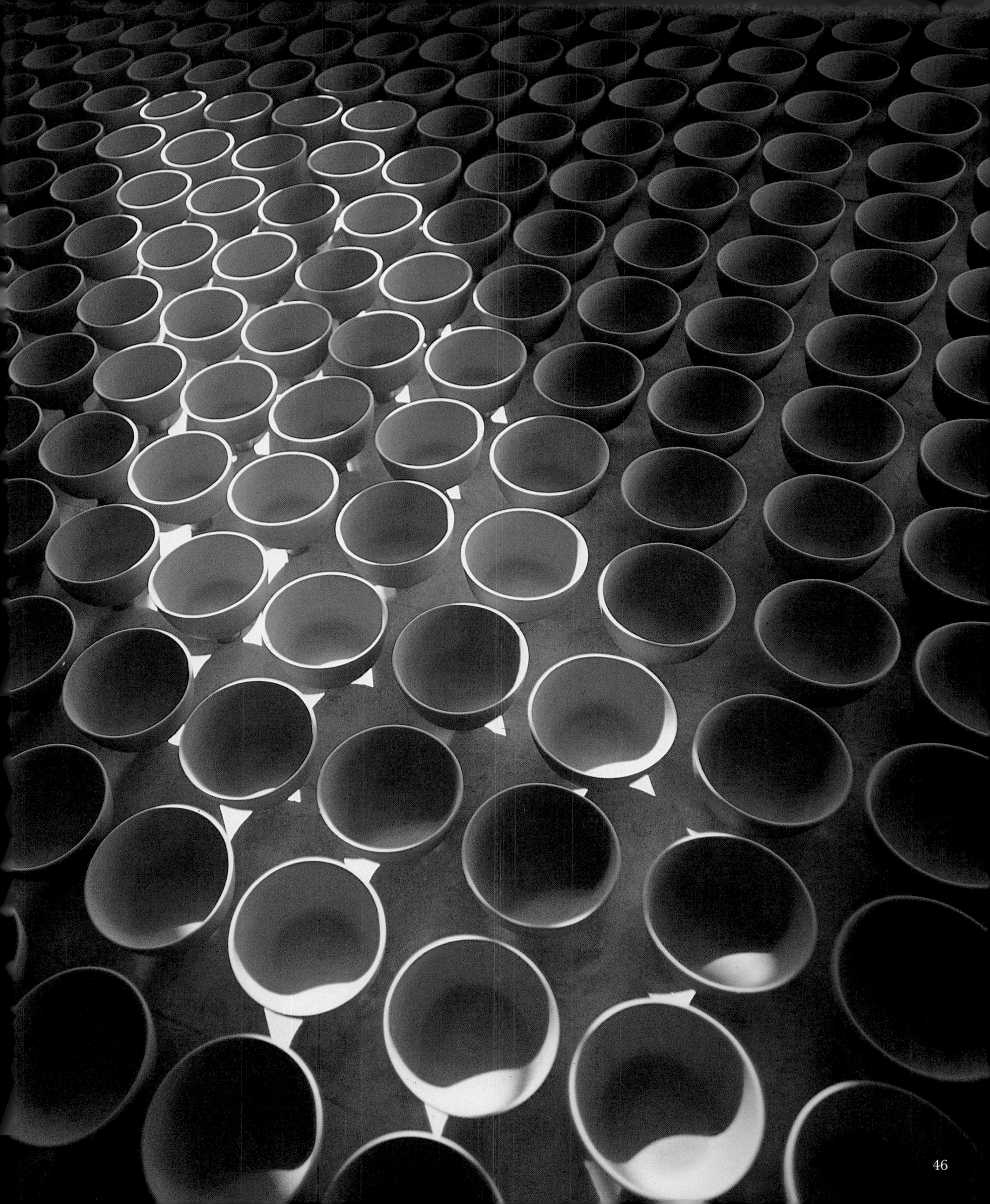

47

48

49

50

51

52

53

54

55

56

57

58

59

60

61

62

63

64

65

66

In modern times the impact of western civilization, the increase in population, the improved standard of living, the expansion of urban life, and the introduction of improved methods of nutrition and health care, have made traditional agriculture incapable of meeting Iran's requirements. Agriculture had to be revolutionized, and this was accomplished in the following ways: Agricultural education was taken to the villages where the bulk of the agricultural population lived. Modern methods in cultivation, seed selection and crop conservation were introduced. And most important of all, measures were taken to introduce land reform through legal channels.

As a consequence of all these efforts over the past two decades, Iran's agriculture is now entering a modern phase characterized by scientific know-how, technical equipment, progressive social systems and cooperative methods of production and consumption. Land reform was introduced in Iran in 1962 as part of the first stage of a number of progressive measures known as the Revolution of the Shah and the People.

Recently, an awareness of the rapid rate of increase in population, in comparison to the noticeable food shortage in the world market, has shifted attention to agriculture and resulted in more investment being made in agricultural activities.

Today the main objective of Iran's agricultural policy is to bring the country to a self-sufficient level by merging a number of smaller villages into "agricultural poles" which would result in lower costs per unit of production and more services to the agricultural population. According to available information, there are 65,180 villages in Iran, of which 26,000 have fewer than fifty households each and another 20,000 have fewer than ten households each. It is considered logical to have at least 20,000 smaller villages merged into larger ones.

In 1975 the total arable lands of Iran were estimated to be 17,294,000 hectares, of which 35 percent were under irrigation and the remaining 65 percent under dry farming. The more important agricultural products were:

Wheat	4,700,000 tons
Barley	863,000 tons
Rice	1,310,000 tons
Sugarbeet	4,300,000 tons
Oil seeds	79,000 tons
Potatoes	533,000 tons
Onions	305,000 tons
Beans	210,000 tons
Tea (green)	96,000 tons
Cotton	715,000 tons
Soya beans	35,000 tons

It is estimated that Iran has a total of 18 million hectares of forest and another 100 million hectares of various kinds of pasture. The forest belt of the Caspian Sea, although no more than 3,400,000 hectares, or 18.8 percent of the total area, is by far the most productive of all forested parts of the country. The output of wood from the Caspian Sea forests is estimated at half a million cubic meters annually.

The use of minerals, particularly metals, dates back to the early days of recorded history. Knowledge of metals and control over their supplies have been major factors in determining the course of history. Thus, countries and peoples with long historical records must be credited with having access to adequate quantities of metals for making their war materials and armaments.

Because of their usefulness, beauty or scarcity, metals, particularly the precious ones, have always aroused the cupidity of man; and because of their durability, they have encouraged the accumulation of wealth beyond current needs and thus promoted an interest in private property and wealth.

As a resource of nature, minerals have certain peculiarities that should be borne in mind in any analysis of their importance. Compared with the resources of agriculture, minerals are highly localized and their availability is limited. Due to their hidden nature discovery has been largely a matter of chance, especially in ancient times. Minerals are exhaustible, and therefore their continuous exploitation often produces difficult problems.

In analyzing the part played by minerals in the development of Iran, the above attributes of minerals should be taken into account and attention given to historical circumstances. Some minerals, such as copper, have been used in Iran for at least 4,000 years. Numerous primitive foundries have been unearthed by archeologists, and copper articles of Iranian origin are found in many important museums. The rich literature of Iran – and particularly the *Shahnameh* of Ferdowsi, which dates back ten centuries – gives detailed accounts of battlefields where the quality of swords and other metal weapons are beautifully described. Hundreds of books on alchemy are other indications of the mastery of Iranian artists and scientists in various fields of metallurgy.

Geological studies made over the past fifty years by oil prospectors, and recently by researchers of the Geological Institute of Iran, have all proved that apart from oil Iran possesses extensive and varied mineral resources. The subsurface riches of Iran are under the control of laws and regulations enforced by government ministries and organizations, such as the Industrial and Mining Bank of Iran. Created in 1959, this is a resource credit bank for all kinds of mining and industrial enterprises. Statistics in the 1976 Iran Almanac reveal that between 1940 and 1975 some 10,603 mining permits were issued by government authorities. In 1975 no less than 505 non-metallic and 55 metallic mines were in full operation, employing 38,304 and 8,078 miners respectively. In 1974 Iran's export of metal ores totaled 729,825 tons valued at 2,186 billion rials.

In 1974 the government decided to invest 10 billion rials in Iran's largest iron ore mines of Golgohar, 320 kilometers north of Bandar Abbas. These mines are believed to have reserves amounting to 200 million tons, and the ore is to be directed exclusively to the National Iranian Steel Company complex near Esfahan. Previously copper was mined mainly in Anarak, Zanjan and Abbasabad. Then in 1974 it was announced that two rich new fields had been discovered at Zahedan and Sarcheshmeh near Kerman with 100 and 200 million tons of reserves respectively. These discoveries bring the total known copper reserves of Iran to one billion tons. During the Sixth Plan some 100 billion rials are to be invested in Sarcheshmeh, which is expected to have an annual capacity of 160,000 tons.

69

70

71

Coal was formerly believed to be limited to the Alborz area, but in 1974 fresh fields of extensive wealth were reportedly discovered in the Kerman, Bojnurd and Shahpasand regions. In most of these, exploitation has already begun with the aim of meeting local requirements. Other minerals mined and exported to the world market are chromite, uranium, turquoise, zinc, lead and sulphur.

A few decades ago, it was realized that because of unfavorable natural conditions, and because of its considerable sub-surface riches, Iran could no longer depend entirely on its agricultural resources. The national economy underwent a shift, aimed at transforming the country into an industrial nation, one that would exploit its mineral wealth more efficiently and extensively. Great success has been achieved in the implementation of this policy, with the result that present-day Iran produces not only a major part of its own manufacturing requirements but is rapidly approaching the stage when its manufactured goods will find their way to the world market.

After World War II, industrialization gained momentum. Many spinning and weaving factories, ranging from cotton to wool and silk, were set up in various parts of the country. This was followed by the creation of food-processing plants such as flour mills, sugar plants, canning factories and tea-packing plants. Many new industries were introduced, including footwear, rubber, plastics, metal-works, vehicle assembly and production, radio and television, machine and tool-making. By far the most important industrial development of Iran during this period was the formation of the National Iranian Steel Company located near Esfahan. This huge plant began operation in 1973, when it produced 400,000 tons of cast iron and around 250,000 tons of steel. The annual capacity of this plant is to expand from two to four million tons in 1980 and probably to six million by 1983. Another drastic step in the industrialization of the country has been the large investment in petrochemicals, which is destined to become the fulcrum of Iranian industry. Initiated in the mid-sixties in the oil-rich district of Khuzestan, the Iran Fertilizer Company presently consists of four plants operated by the National Petrochemical Company. It is anticipated that by 1983 this company will be one of the world's leading producers of petrochemicals, with an estimated investment of $12,000 million.

Transportation

The road-building tradition of Iran goes back to the early days of the first kingdoms. The well-known Achaemenian Royal Road, linking Susa to Sardis in Asia Minor, dates from the sixth century B.C. Ever since then, and until the discovery of sea routes between Europe and the Far East, the country remained a center of routes linking East and West. The fabled Silk Road of the Middle Ages ran through Iran. During the later Middle Ages, the road system of Iran fell into a state of decay which cost the country a great deal by pushing it into seclusion.

In exploring the surface transportation in Iran, the geographical circumstances should be considered. Iran is a vast country consisting mainly of plateaus, mountains and deserts. Distances between centers of population are great and the topography complex, making road building extremely difficult.

Modern road-building efforts began in the early twentieth century and have continued to the present, but progress has been slow and the network is still far from complete. During the past decade serious efforts have been made to connect villages with provincial centers, all of which are now linked with Tehran, the real hub of the country. In 1975 Iran had 60,000 kilometers of main highways and 10,000 of secondary roads.

In 1938 the first Trans-Iranian railway came into operation, linking the Caspian Sea and the Persian Gulf. This railway was built without any outside financial help; and from this spine of railroad communication, secondary lines branched out to all corners of the country to produce the present network that in 1974 totaled 5,229 kilometers. The Railway Administration of Iran handles more than 4,000,000 passengers and 70,000,000 tons of cargo annually.

Iran has practically no internal waterways, but its external marine transportation has been increasing at a phenomenal rate. Presently the southern ports of Khorramshahr, Bandar Shahpur, Bandar Abbas, Bushehr and Chahbahar have an annual capacity of roughly five million tons but there are plans to increase this figure to about 60 million tons.

The state-owned Arya Shipping Company was created in the late sixties with an operating fleet of six ships having a total tonnage of approximately 70,000. There are plans to expand this fleet to sixty ships over the next five years. Similarly, the National Iranian Tanker Company, presently maintaining a fleet of seven vessels with a total tonnage of 670,000, plans corresponding expansion.

Until the early sixties Iran was served by most international airlines without any restrictions. In 1962 the Iran National Airlines Corporation, known internationally as Iran Air and locally as HOMA, was created with a small capital and a few four-engine planes. Good management and generous government support have now made Iran Air one of the leading international airlines, commanding a fleet of fourteen Boeings in service, with four more on order. It operates within a worldwide network serving twenty-two countries on four continents. It is also responsible for all national flights. In 1975 the company flew 2,100,000 passengers of which 600,000 were international travelers. Iran now has seventeen airports in operation and there are plans to build three new ones as well as to remodel some of the existing ones. The Tehran-Mehrabad Air Terminal, designed over twenty years ago, has proved to be inadequate to handle present-day traffic although it has been expanded greatly. Plans have been made for a new international airport to be built 40 kilometers south of the capital at a cost of nearly one billion rials ($143 million). Work on this airport is underway and it is expected to begin operation in 1980. The new Tehran International Airport will have a capacity of ten million passengers annually by 1990 and fifteen million by the year 2000.

Urban Development

Urbanism is deeply rooted in Iranian civilization. Remains of compact settlements that go far beyond the normal village size have been discovered all over the Iranian Plateau, especially in the Karun flood plain in the southwest and also on the foothill alluvial plains of the various mountain ranges. Accounts of the ancient cities of Susa, Hagmatana (modern Hamedan), Hekatompylos (modern Damghan) and Persepolis, and descriptions in travel books of cities existing during the Middle Ages, such as Rey, have all indicated the continuity of city life over the plateau and the important part that cities have played in giving shape to the history and personality of the Iranian people.

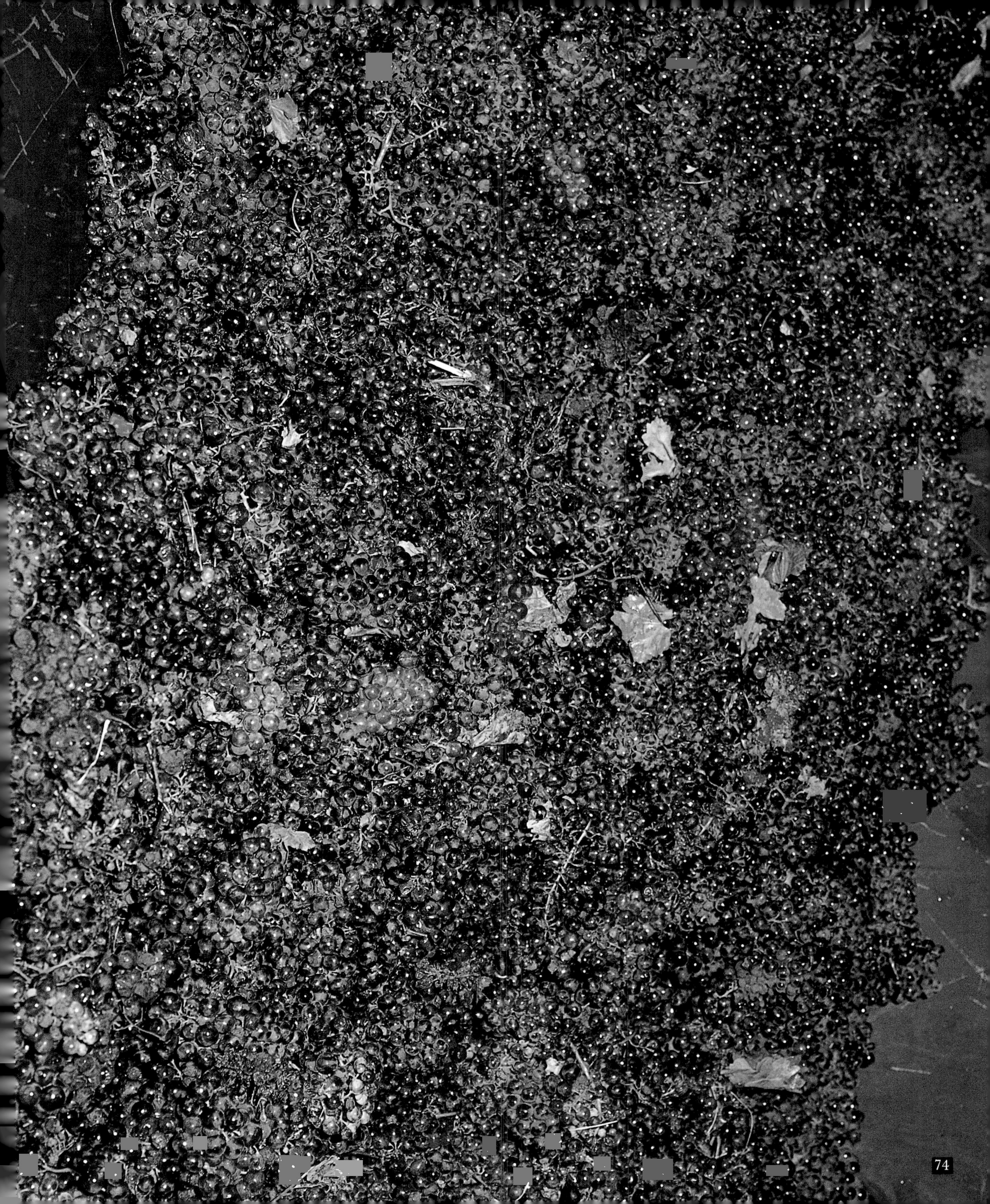

75

76

77

78

79

80

84

81

82

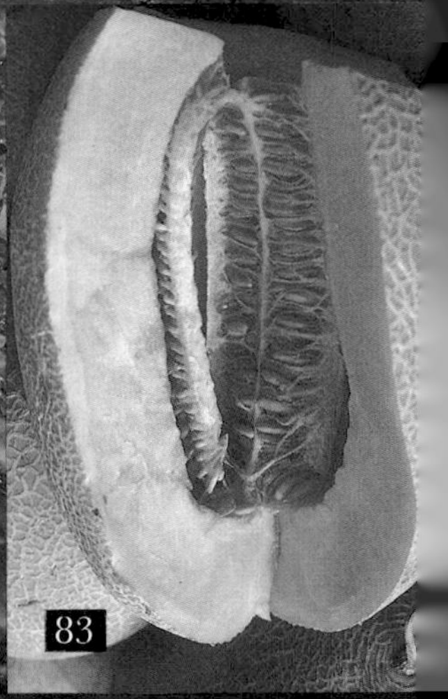

83

85

86

87

88

91

89

90

92

95

93

94

In modern times, and especially after the industrial revolution of eighteenth-century Europe and America, town-dwelling has assumed particular importance.

Topography and water availability can be considered the main determining factors, not only in shaping human habitation and settlements of Iran but also in forming the character of peoples and their social conditions. The deep gorges of Iran, the unnavigable rivers, the empty and impenetrable deserts and the high snow-covered mountains resulted in a tendency for human settlements to be isolated from each other. The population became concentrated around the peripheries of the dry interior open spaces, along the foothills, in the inter-mountain plains or in the occasional oasis in the desert region.

Village settlements vary according to their geographical environment. Kashan is an example of a town of the plains. It is built on a rectangular pattern. The houses of Kerend, a terraced settlement of the mountains, are built from mud and straw or bricks and stones. Rasht, on the shore of the Caspian Sea, features a predominance of two-story wooden houses.

In spite of their large size, however, most pre-twentieth-century towns of Iran were, in reality, no more than expanded villages which reflected their geographical environment. With the advance of urbanism and the rapid increase in population, towns had to be remodeled and fresh patterns superimposed on old textures. The transition from old to new, especially at such a rapid rate, created inevitable difficulties. The larger the size of the city, of course, the greater the difficulties have been.

Tehran, with a population of more than four million, is a typical outgrown village of the foothill type. It is situated at an elevation of 1,200 meters in the foothills of the Alborz Mountains. Tehran's supremacy dates back to 1788 when it was chosen as the capital. To begin with, its location at the fringe of the fertile plain of Varamin, its command over the foothill highways, its proximity to the agriculturally rich Caspian coastal plains, all contributed to its choice as the national capital. It had a population of nearly half a million when World War II broke out and it has continued to increase in size and, correspondingly, in the magnitude of its problems. These include chronic water shortage, service inadequacies, high cost of living, traffic congestion and air pollution.

Esfahan is now considered the second-largest city of Iran and its history as a continuously inhabited site goes back further than 1000 B.C. It is situated in the fertile plain of the Zayandeh-Rud and enjoys an abundance of water, rich soil and the resultant agricultural prosperity. Esfahan owes its historical importance to its geographical position as a nodal point commanding all the main traffic arteries of the country. A highly industrialized city, it was called the Manchester of Iran, even before the National Iranian Steel Company was built nearby.

Scores of other Iranian towns, each with its unique character, could be mentioned. These would include Tabriz, a historical center; Mashhad, a religious center; Shiraz, noted for its contribution to literature and the arts; and Abadan, the headquarters of Iran's petroleum industry.

Mohammad Hassan Ganji

BOOK TWO

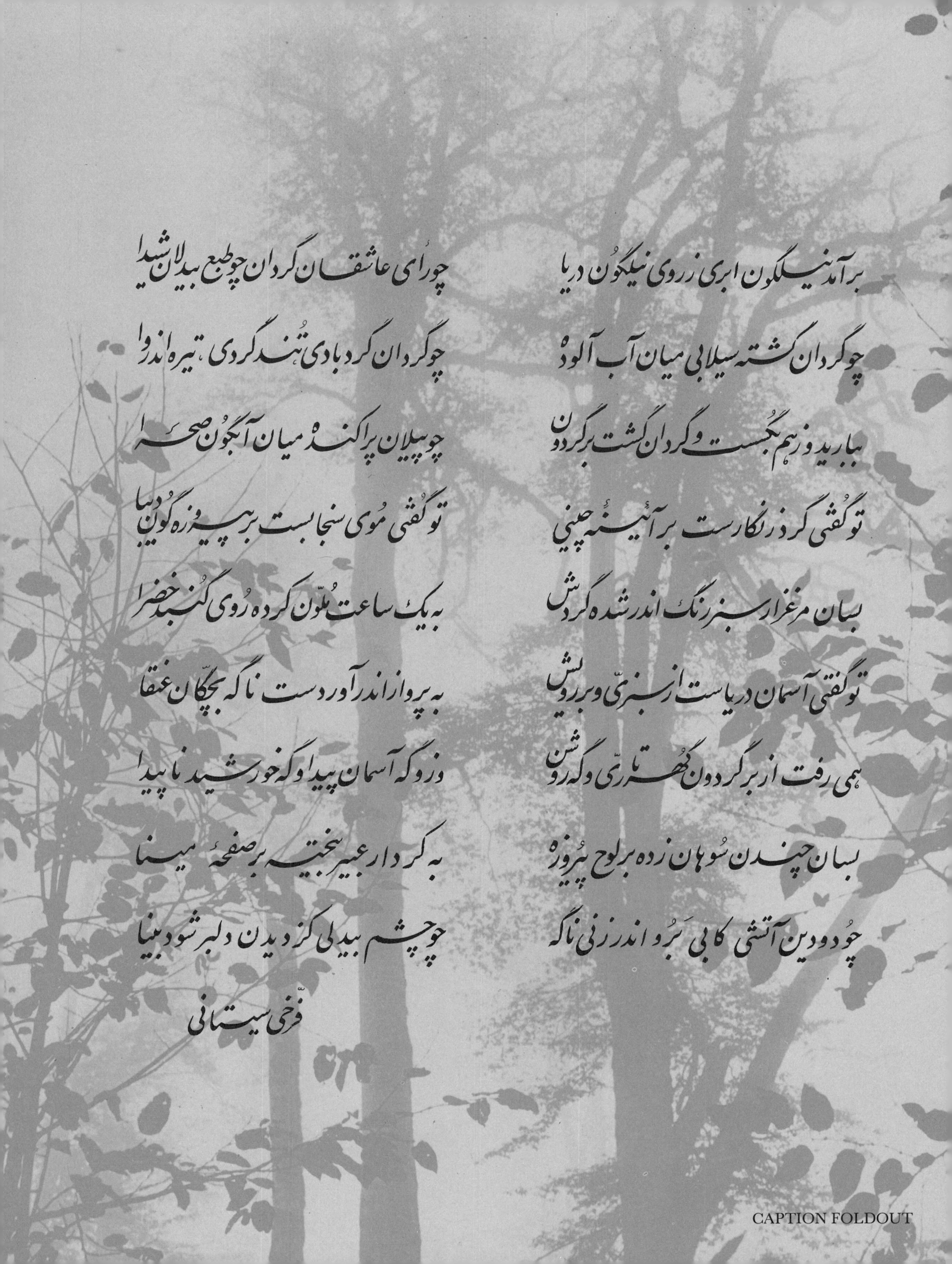

برآمد نیلگون ابری ز روی نیلگون دریا   چو رای عاشقان گردان چو طبع بیدلان شیدا

چو گردان گشته سیلابی میان آب آلوده   چو گردان گرد بادی تند گردی تیره اندر وا

ببارید وز هم بگسست و گردان گشت بر گردون   چو پیلان پراکنده میان آبگون صحرا

تو گفتی گرد زنگارست بر آیینهٔ چینی   تو گفتی موی سنجابست بر پیروزه گون دیبا

بسان مرغزار سبز رنگ اندر شده گردش   به یک ساعت ملوّن کرده روی گنبد خضرا

تو گفتی آسمان دریاست از سبزی و بر رویش   به پرواز اندر آوردست ناگه بچگان عنقا

همی رفت از بر گردون گهی تاری و گه روشن   وزو گه آسمان پیدا و گه خورشید ناپیدا

بسان چندن سوهان زده بر لوح پیروزه   به کردار عبیر بیخته بر صفحهٔ مینا

چو دود دین آتشی کابی برو اندر زنی ناگه   چو چشم بیدلی کز دیدن دلبر شود بینا

فرخی سیستانی

CAPTION FOLDOUT

Captions for plates 97 to 125 AIR For notes to these plates, see pages 374 to 375

DAWN, DAY AND DUSK

97 A solitary gull flies above Mount Damavand.

98 Golden fruit and crystal raindrops depict the agricultural riches of Iran at the Sixth of Bahman Museum, Tehran.

99 A flock of high-flying birds above the Persian Gulf at sunrise.

100 Giant receivers and antennae of the microwave station etched against orange flares surrounding Ahvaz.

101 The serenity of an autumn sunset from an island in Lake Rezaiyyeh.

102 Clouds and wind surround motorcyclists on a quiet country road near Shahrud.

SPACE, SOUND AND TIME

103 Helicopter display at the Pahlavi Dynasty Exhibition, Tehran.

104-110 Images of developing Iranian military and civil aviation.

- 104 Imperial Iranian Special Forces parachuting, Bandar-e-Pahlavi.
- 105 Acrojet pilot, Tabriz.
- 106 Control panel of Iran Air 747.
- 107 Parachutists, Bandar-e-Pahlavi.
- 108 Air Force helicopter pilot.
- 109 F-4 fighter pilot.
- 110 Parachute landing, Bandar-e-Pahlavi.

111 This modern sculpture, a symbol of the liberating spirit of air, glitters within the central dome at the Kish Island Airport.

112 Flying in precision formation, the Golden Crown Acrojet Team performs over Tabriz.

113-115 Three abstract views of an Iran Air 747 photographed at Mehrabad International Airport, Tehran.

116 Shahanshahi Park at sunset with the central offices and studios of National Iranian Radio and Television (NIRT) on the hillside above.

117-124 A montage of the wide-ranging activities of National Iranian Radio and Television (NIRT) throughout Iran.

- 117 NIRT station, Bandar Abbas.
- 118 Pars National Ballet, Tehran studio.
- 119 Musical program, Tehran.
- 120 Dance performance, Tehran.
- 121 NIRT buildings, Tehran.
- 122 The Shahbanou at NIRT, Tehran.
- 123 Annual Now-Ruz broadcast.
- 124 NIRT crew at Rey.

125 Flags of contributing nations at the annual Tehran trade fair.

AIR

AIR

DAWN, DAY AND DUSK

THE CLOUD

sapphire, lifted, loomed from the sapphire face
of the sea, shifting, changing as a lover's
breast
enraptured as the moods of a lover
whirled like a slow tornado over oily ocean
twisted like a maelstrom
shattering itself to shreds
spiraled majestic showers
over the horizon, shadows
like herds of startled elephants
lumbering here
there
in the midst
of a watercolor
wilderness
You said
it's like dust on a china mirror
you said
squirrel's fluff ruffed on turquoise brocade
a whole green meadow
turning hourly on an axis
wide as heaven
greening the underside
of the cosmic
upturned bowl
you said
the sky has become
an ocean for greenness
and across its wide waves
a sudden flight
of young phoenixes
our cloud
rippling, ripping across the sphere
now dark now light
—a fleck of sky—
sun
lost to sight
iron filings spilled on a turquoise binding
ambergris sifted on an emerald page
smoldering fire
—a splash of water—
roiling smoke
a lover
spies his beloved
the clouds clear
from before his eyes

Farrokhi

◁ Morning mist veils the Caspian forest.

DAWN, DAY AND DUSK

Of all the natural elements that make up the human environment, climate is by far the most important. Climate is an important factor influencing not only the daily life of people but also their history and culture.

Physically, climate is an important agent responsible for forming the shape of the earth surface upon which man lives. Deep gorges in the mountains, flat flood plains with their rich soil, deserts with their moving sand dunes, rivers and lakes, forests and pastures and scores of other features of the geographical landscape are all the result of climatic action.

Historically, climate has been related to the formation of civilizations in past centuries, and also to the shaping of cultural patterns. A study of the basic religious beliefs of the Iranians, their moral codes, folklore, literature and arts, provides some examples of the close relationship that exists between all these aspects of the Iranian culture and the climate that has prevailed over the Iranian Plateau since the early days of its occupation.

Scientifically, it is impossible to discuss fully the climate within the bounds of the political borders of any country, however large it may be. This is because the atmosphere of our planet is in permanent motion and often travels in gigantic masses covering thousands of square kilometers and extending to heights of more than ten kilometers. Such air masses, having the characteristics of their place of origin, exert tremendous influence in shaping the weather and climate of the areas of the earth over which they travel. It is no wonder that we are often warned by the meteorologists of the expected changes in our weather conditions due to heat waves from Africa, precipitation from the Atlantic Ocean or cold winds from Siberia.

It is not only the air masses that make up the climate of Iran. Other geographical factors play an equally important part.

Latitudinally, Iran is situated approximately between 25 and 40 degrees North in a belt of descending airs and trade winds. Being in the middle latitude, Iran has clear-cut seasons with sharp changes from winter cold to summer heat. This has had a great influence on the life of Iranians. The regular changes in the sun's elevation and in the duration of day and night struck the minds of early thinkers of Iran to such a degree that the solstices and the equinoxes were recognized in the calendar system on which all agricultural activities were based. The social consequences still hold a strong grip on Iranians. This is shown in the annual celebration of Now-Ruz (New Year), Yalda (winter solstice) and other important days that indicate a fundamental change in the sun's position.

It has already been indicated that Iran is a mountainous country with a plateau nature. The lowest parts are the coasts of the Caspian Sea where certain portions are below sea level. The highest point is Mount Damavand with an elevation of 5,678 meters. Between these two extremes lies the bulk of the territory of Iran, with an average altitude of some 1,500 meters. This means that, under normal conditions, the amount of heat energy received by virtue of Iran's latitudinal position is lowered considerably due to its elevation. The mountainous nature of Iran and the resultant lowering of temperature at higher levels have affected the life of Iranians in a number of ways. The different seasonal growing times between low plains and high mountains for instance have produced favorable conditions for transhumance or the tribal way of life. Similarly, the cooler higher levels have attracted populations, with the result that most Iranians – with the exception of those in the Caspian coastal towns – live at elevations exceeding 1,000 meters.

In a dry country like Iran rainfall is regarded as an important life-giving gift of the natural environment. Yet the proximity of oceans and other large bodies of water is considered a decisive climatic element, and Iran is situated between the Caspian Sea on the north and the Persian Gulf and the Sea of Oman on the south. Besides, it is not very far from the Mediterranean, the Red Sea and, above all, the Indian Ocean, all of which exert a certain influence on the climate of the country.

The alignment of mountain ranges is also an important factor in producing rainfall. Since rain is produced when the moisture in the atmosphere is cooled for some reason or other, and mountains are responsible for such cooling, these two mountain ranges of Iran play an eminent part in the life of this country by producing rain on their windward side and aridity on their leeward side. The Alborz range is an example, with one observing dense forests and bountiful agricultural land on the windward, seafacing side, while on the leeward side aridity is the prevailing factor.

Apart from the Caspian coastal areas, most of the rainfall of Iran results from Mediterranean depressions that travel across the country in the cooler half of the year. These same rain-bearing currents travel further north in the summer months, resulting in dry summers for Iran.

Situated at the heart of the Eastern Hemisphere, Iran's climate is influenced by air masses flowing over it from all directions. In the cooler half of the year, the climate is dominated by moist and relatively warm air from the west, especially the Mediterranean Sea, and cold and dry air from the heart of Asia, especially Siberia. In the warmer half, hot, dry air from Africa and warm, moist air from the Indian Ocean exert a similar influence. Such outside elements, combined with the varied features of the Iranian landscape, create a complexity in the climate of the country that defies simple classification.

Air masses may move unnoticed. They never appear like normal winds which are considered the immediate result of motion in the atmosphere. They are recognized by the meteorologists only by means of qualities such as pressure, temperature and humidity. Therefore, they should not be mistaken for the winds which blow normally from the northeast or northwest over the Iranian Plateau throughout the year. The juxtaposition of plains and mountains, the wide expanses of empty deserts, the extensive mountain belts, valleys and other geographical factors, produce local winds of many types and qualities such as the forceful winds of Manjil in the Alborz and the winds of the well-known "120 Days" in Sistan.

Bearing in mind that in Iran most of the higher lands and mountains are concentrated in the northern, northwestern and western parts of the country, while the interior consists of lower and more level lands, the colder parts of Iran are obviously in the north and west, and the warmer sections in the center and south of the country. Such relative statements do not, however, reveal the actual state of temperature distribution.

Except for the coastal areas of the Caspian Sea that show maritime conditions, January is Iran's coldest month. The average temperature in this month varies from 20 centigrade in the south along the coasts of the Persian Gulf to -3 centigrade in the higher levels of the northeast. During this month, in Hamedan, Ardabil and Bostanabad temperatures lower than -30 centigrade have been recorded. The mean January temperature of Tehran is around 3 centigrade, but occasionally temperatures as low as -15 centigrade have been experienced in the capital. In the Caspian coastal area, where the effect of the sea produces pockets of warm air, February is the coldest month. But all along the coast sub-zero temperatures are of rare occurrence.

With March, there is a sudden rise in temperature all over the country. In the south of Iran the heat is so intense that crops are harvested in April and temperatures of around 40 C. are recorded. July is the hottest month except in the Caspian and some mountainous areas. Monthly averages of 30 C. are quite common to most of the interior where the thermometer may reach well over 40 C. In Tehran, for instance, 43 C. has been recorded. The hottest parts of the country during the summer are the flat and low-lying plains of Khuzestan and the cavity of Jazmurian in Baluchestan, where a record high of 53 C. has been recorded.

Taking into account all aspects of temperature distribution, it can be said that normally the temperature decreases over Iran from southeast to northwest and from south to north. The Zagros highlands form a continuous belt of lower temperatures all the way from Shiraz to Azarbayejan where the country's most severe winters are experienced.

Temperature ranges are great in all parts of Iran with the exception of the coastal areas that come under maritime influences. Cool nights following hot days make life comfortable in the central and hotter parts of the country. Here it often happens that day temperatures of over 40 C. fall to less than 20 C. at night. Over the whole country, the difference between the highest and the lowest temperatures is no less than 88 degrees C. It is this high range of temperature that has led some climatologists to describe the general climate of the country as having strong "continental" aspects.

Due to the dryness of the atmosphere and the clear skies that are characteristic of Iran, high temperatures can easily be tolerated as long as one is not exposed to the direct rays of the sun. Therefore, it has been a deep-rooted tradition for people to shun daytime travel during the summer months.

Iran is situated in a dry belt extending all the way from West Africa to the heart of Asia. However, of all the lands included in this belt, Iran is probably environmentally the most fortunate because of its high altitude, its closeness to the sea, and its high mountains so laid down that they help form precipitation.

Unlike the rest of Iran that receives rainfall in the winter months and in small amounts, the coastal plains to the south of the Caspian Sea receive rain in considerable amounts throughout most of the year. This is due to a number of factors such as the high mountains, the moist air of the Caspian and the prevalent winds. In this part of Iran rain occurs in almost every month of the year, although autumn is regarded as the rainiest season. The amount of annual precipitation decreases from west to east. According to existing records, Bandar-e-Pahlavi, to the southwest of the Caspian Sea, receives on the average a little less than two meters of annual rainfall, but this amount decreases as one goes east until it drops to around half a meter in the Gorgan plain southeast of the Caspian.

Over the rest of Iran rainfall decreases from north to south and from west to east, so that the northwestern province of Azarbayejan becomes the wettest and the southeastern province of Baluchestan the driest area, with the exception of the central desert areas where aridity prevails throughout the year. The windward slopes of the Zagros and the uplands of Azarbayejan are the best-watered portions, receiving from 35 centimeters in the southern sections to over 50 centimeters in the north. The higher levels of the Alborz and the northeastern province of Khorasan receive about 40 centimeters, which is far from adequate. Over the rest of Iran the amount of precipitation decreases to such an extent that some interior desert areas show records of less than five centimeters with some years of practically no rainfall at all.

Whatever the amount of rain over the plateau, it falls in the cooler half of the year and particularly in the winter, known as the rainy season. Except for the spring thundershowers, most of the rain that falls is of a cyclonic type that starts gradually and is long lasting. Nevertheless, the number of rainy days are few and in Tehran they hardly reach thirty in a year. Especially on higher and mountainous grounds, precipitation falls in the form of snow, which is valued by the agricultural people of the plains, for they depend on it for their water supply.

With the passing of the spring equinox, or the Iranian New Year, rainfall decreases, but sometimes torrential downpours occur after severe thunderstorms. Rain of this nature often produces damage in urban areas and heavy soil erosion in rural areas. Nevertheless, these storms fill reservoirs that provide water for both city dwellers and agricultural villagers. By May summer is in full swing and rainfall becomes scarce over the plateau. Most people in the smaller communities can spend their nights outdoors without any fear of rain. The scarcity of summer rain, combined with clear, cloudless skies, has made outdoor life prevalent, and this has influenced the folklore and cultural traditions of Iranians. Similarly, the unreliability of rainfall, which is common to all dry lands of the world, combined with the dependence of life on water supply, has also played a part in shaping the history and civilization of the Iranian people.

Mohammad Hassan Ganji

AIR

SPACE, SOUND AND TIME

The beautiful Iranian sky with its innumerable stars has witnessed galaxies of lovers and provided the source of inspiration for a great many of this land's poets during past millennia.

Wise men have been astonished by the magnitude of this eternal manifestation of creation, trying perhaps in vain to find a way to the secrets of the universe. The glory of the sky has had an effect on Iranian civilization and culture, which includes vast treasures of Persian poetry renowned throughout the world.

The sky, poetically called the "blue dome," has been compared to ultimate beauty and glory; the moon and the sun to the gleaming beauty of the beloved; the northeasterly wind "Bad-e-Saba" to the beloved's messenger; the new moon to the curve of the beloved's eyebrows; the breeze to the beloved's aroma; and thunder to a sudden strike of love. Mars, Jupiter, Venus and the Pleiades all have been treated metaphorically and referred to as fairies and angels inhabiting heavenly castles. The infinite cycle of day and night, the break of day, the glorious morning dawn and its exhilarating breeze, are but a few of the images freely used in Persian literature.

While poets and writers have been inspired by the stars and the sky, scientists, astronomers, astrologers and mathematicians have concentrated their efforts on studying space and the movements of heavenly bodies. This was connected to the belief that Man's destiny is determined by the motion of heavenly bodies.

It is known that Iranians were interested in astronomy from ancient times. There is evidence they utilized their knowledge of astronomy in their early methods of agriculture by studying various motions and forces of the sun, moon and stars acting upon the earth. It was then that the first Prime Meridian was chosen, passing through the town of Zabol in the province of Sistan. At that time Sistan was called "Nimruz," meaning meridian.

The Sasanian period was marked by a compilation of astronomical observations in the form of a book called *Zij-e-Shahriaran*, or the Royal Astronomical Tables, in which the astronomical phenomena known at the time were recorded.

Great scholars, astronomers and astrologers, such as Kharazmi, Biruni, Khazeni and Omar Khayyam, were instrumental in discovering and promoting astronomical phenomena and developing mathematical disciplines.

DANGER
KEEP AWAY
SH-3D
8-2311

104

105

106

107

108

109

110

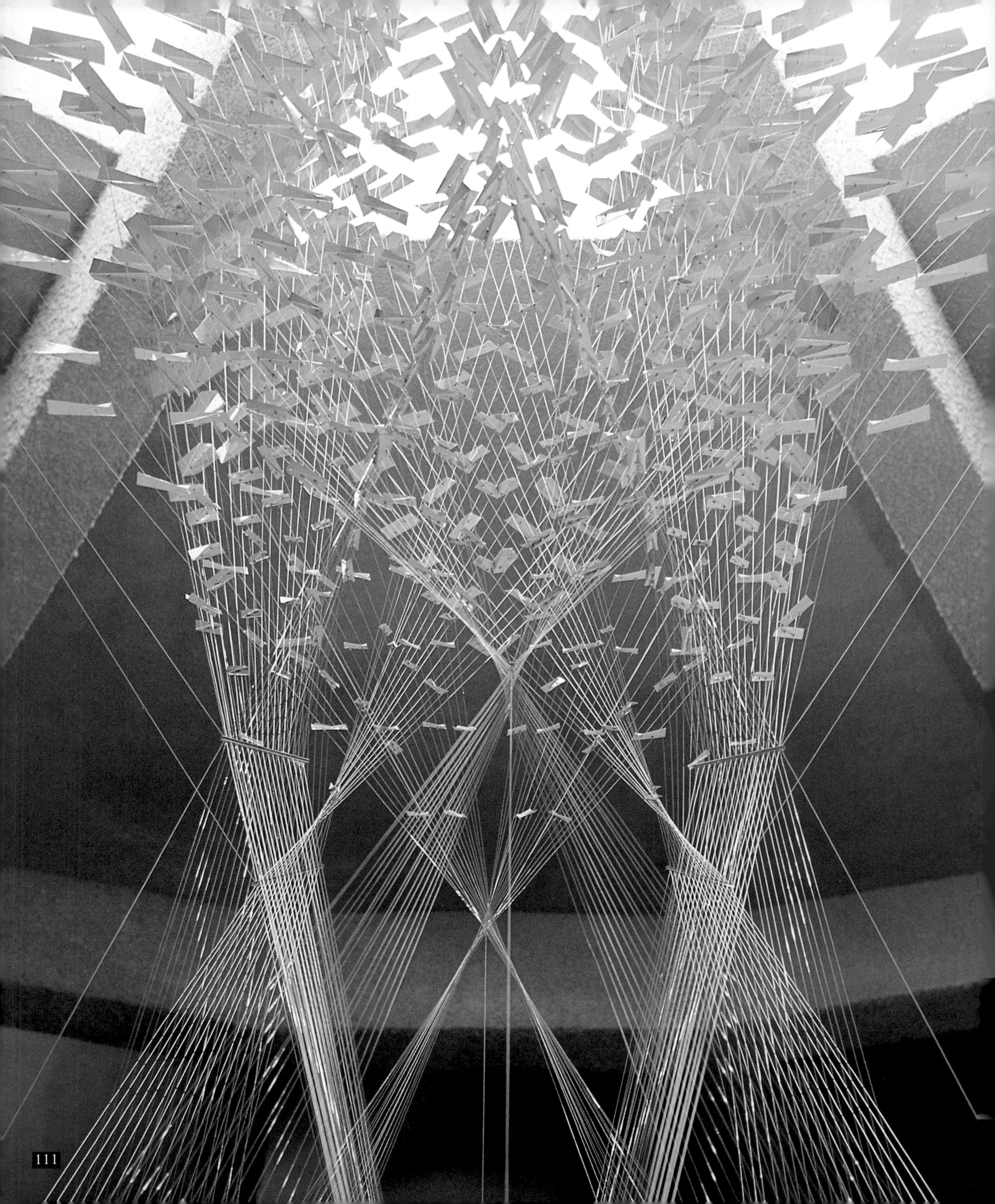

113

114

115

The famous observatory of Maragheh, a town in northwest Iran, was used between A.D. 641-657 by the great scientist Khajeh Nasireddin Tusi, known as the "Ostad-ol-Bashar," meaning master of men. He also prepared a comprehensive book of astronomical tables. The Samarkand observatory was modeled on the technical specifications of the observatory in Maragheh. The building of the Samarkand observatory was the result of a cooperative effort made by a number of scholars and mathematicians. These included Ghiyaseddin Jamshid Kashani, Moineddin Kashi and Moulana Ghazi-zadeh, who compiled another book, *Zij-e-Jadid-e-Shahi*, or the New Royal Book of Tables, published in Samarkand. This book was considered important enough to be translated into English, published by Oxford University in 1665 and subsequently translated into other European languages.

Tycho Brahe, the Danish astronomer who laid the foundation for the first European observatory on Hveen Island, modeled many of the instruments used in this observatory on Maragheh's equipment.

The fascination with astronomy has not ceased. In the past it attracted Iranian scholars and mathematicians to places like Samarkand and Maragheh; now their descendants are engaged in various research centers such as the Geophysics Institute of Tehran University and the well-equipped observatories of Shiraz and Tabriz. At present three stellar telescopes are being installed at Azarabadgan University in Tabriz. The observatory at Pahlavi University in Shiraz is equipped with a 50 cm. stellar telescope for photometrical studies.

Since it was established fifteen years ago, the Geophysics Institute of Tehran University has made spectacular progress in studies of space physics and other geophysical subjects. Now it is considered the center of space science in Iran. The institute has a solar observatory with a 15 cm. telescope of the coudé refractor type including such accessories as are used in photospheric observation and chromospheric studies.

The Cosmic Ray Station of the Geophysics Institute of Tehran University is in possession of eighteen neutron monitors of the NM64 type. Observations and measurements of ozone are carried out with the Dobson spectrograph and its ancillaries, while investigation of the ionosphere with Satellite Tracking Methods is also carried on here.

Meteorology as a scientific subject is not new in Iran. Astronomers were involved in weather-forecasting in ancient times. Anvari, an Iranian poet and scientist of the thirteenth century, forecast weather and wind courses, sometimes making mistakes and exposing himself to the mockery of his contemporaries. At present, however, this branch of science plays a vital role in Iran. There is a well-organized, nation-wide network of meteorological stations entrusted with various duties ranging from weather-forecasting to rain-making. This network within the Meteorological Organization of Iran was founded twenty years ago and already employs more than one thousand persons. The main function is to compile meteorological data required by the Civil aviation organization, the Iranian Air Force, the Port and Shipping Organization and the marine authorities. In addition, continuous weather forecasts for the entire country are communicated locally and abroad. Experimental studies of methods of adjusting climatic conditions are conducted with the application of various systems, such as cloud-seeding and rain-making. Extended studies are conducted in meteorological fields, such as investigation of the climates of the Lut Desert, the Persian Gulf and the Sea of Oman, analysis of the precipitation of river basins in Iran, investigation of winds, storms and the jet stream over Iran during various seasons, preparation of climate maps, computation of potential evapotranspiration, and investigation of the influence of atmospheric conditions on air pollution.

The Meteorological Organization of Iran has also installed receiving antennae and telepicture equipment for obtaining photographs from meteorological satellites and improving forecast quality.

The science dealing with space and atmosphere was developed to a certain extent in ancient Iran and is now pursued with the use of modern technology. The concept of traveling in space and covering long distances in a short time was visualized as well.

There are numerous references to flying carpets in Iranian mythology. For instance, Jamshid's throne could fly. Jamshid, a semi-legendary king of Iran, commanded the wind's course and by subjugating demons and genies was able to travel in space. Ferdowsi, the great epic poet, narrated a fascinating story in his *Book of Kings* about Kavus, a king of the Kiyanid Dynasty:

> Once Kavus Shah had conquered the civilized world of his time, and established peace and prosperity and order, he embarked upon the conquest of space. On his command, a number of hawks were bred and reared until they were fully grown. He then ordered the construction of a special throne, to which four of these hawks were chained. Having been kept hungry for days, the hawks were ferociously eager to fly in search of food. Thus, Kavus Shah sat on his throne and soon the hawks flew him high into the sky, where he was about to realize his dream of space conquest.

Other stories about human flight appear in ancient sources. This ancient aspiration of mankind has finally been realized, and now aircraft actually perform the legendary role of the flying throne or carpet.

Traveling by air is a comparatively recent event in modern Iran, and the pace of its development has been rapid. The building of airports throughout the country, the establishment of air control networks and the founding of the Iran National Airlines Corporation (Iran Air) are some of the activities in this field.

The Civil aviation organization, with thirty years of experience, is responsible for the operation of airports in Iran. There are three large international airports, twenty-two secondary and many small airfields all over Iran. Prominent airlines run regular services between Iran and most major cities in the world, and Tehran is already a center for international flights.

The total area of Iran is covered by radio and 70 percent by television. National Iranian Radio and Television (NIRT) is one of the most active organizations in the country.

Iran's first radio transmitter was installed in 1940 with a total power of 22 kilowatts. By 1967 the number of transmitters had increased to 31 with a total power of 620 kw., and grew rapidly over a considerable area, to reach 68 transmitters with more than 9000 kw. power by 1975.

These short- and medium-wave transmitters now make the voice of Iran audible all over the country, in half of Europe and all the regions in Asia and Africa. Iran now has 30 radio stations producing and broadcasting more than 450 hours of various programs daily, including news and comments, features and plays and varieties of popular and classical music. It is estimated that more than 7 million receiver sets are in use all over the country.

The expansion of television networks has also been considerable. By 1971 there were nine production and transmission stations in Iran. Six new stations have since become operational. There are now 15 production studios in 34 transmission stations. As well, there are 120 centers for relay transmitters and booster stations to improve the quality of sound and pictures.

In 1967 television reached about 2.1 million persons, while by 1975, 21.5 million people were receiving television programs, including 13.5 million urban viewers and 8 million rural viewers.

Presently the average daily television transmission from 15 main centers in Iran is over 100 hours per day, including news, general events, plays, arts, science, educational, cultural and music programs, as well as full-length feature films.

Efforts are being made to bring the whole country under TV's umbrella. There are more than 3 million TV sets in private homes and this number is increasing by 350 thousand sets annually.

Since 1976 NIRT has transmitted color pictures, but this is limited to Tehran. In addition, Tehran viewers may enjoy black-and-white programs on three channels, one being an international channel broadcast in English.

The Open University of Iran and the Ministry of Education have cooperated with NIRT in planning and producing a series of educational programs. These regular features are valuable audio-visual aids to general education.

Iran, a country where the ruins of historic communication towers are still visible in its vast open spaces, is now moving into the new era by equipping itself with modern telecommunication technology, and is becoming the communication center between the Far East and the West. Telecommunications in Iran are sponsored by the Ministry of Post, Telephone and Telegraph and by an organization called the Telecommunication Company of Iran (TCI).

The first semi-automatic local telephone exchange was put into service in Tehran in 1927 with an initial capacity of 2,000 subscribers. Today the local network in Iran is a combination of manual and automatic equipment, consisting of 98 exchanges serving 56 cities and 709,000 subscribers. During the next ten years an extensive switching system expansion program will result in provision of dial service to approximately 5 million subscribers in all areas of the country. Some of these services have already been put into operation. New, computer-controlled, electronic switching systems will be installed to provide a full range of features for the most sophisticated user.

Installation of a microwave system started in 1964. Today's network includes 20,500 kilometers of microwave lines and 696 stations, providing adequate interurban telephone and television coverage throughout the major cities of the country. Expansion of existing microwave links to full capacity and installation of a large number of new microwave radio routes are planned to provide for interconnection of the expanded switching network and for other telecommunication needs such as private-line circuits and data. Both existing analogue transmission and newer digital transmission are being considered for use in the transmission facilities network.

The transmission network expansion plan for the next ten years also includes a domestic satellite system to provide for a variety of needs, including television distribution, educational television, diverse routing and telephone service to remote villages. This system will employ the latest satellite technology available.

The first earth station was inaugurated at Asadabad, near Hamedan, in 1969, permitting Iran to exchange telephone and telegraph services of high reliability with other countries of the Western Hemisphere via a communication satellite over the Atlantic Ocean. The commanding feature of the earth station is a 30-meter diameter antenna and a satellite circuit of 192 voice channels and capability for transmission of color television programs. A second antenna with similar characteristics went into service in 1975, linking Iran with the Eastern Hemisphere via a 252-channel communications satellite over the Indian Ocean. Furthermore, work is under way to provide fully automatic dialing.

In line with the objective of industrial independence, the Iranian Telecommunication Manufacturing Company (ITMC) has made a major contribution to the development of the telephone network. The annual production of the plant is approximately 80,000 line units, with an ultimate capacity of 120,000 line units. Telephone growth is projected to exceed the capacity of the ITMC plant in future years. Additional switching capacity will be provided using electronic computer-controlled switching equipment. In the light of these plans, the Iranian Telecommunication Manufacturing Company is presently evaluating a proposal to establish local manufacturing facilities for the latest computer-controlled digital time division switching systems. Iran's continuing requirements for telephone exchange equipment can thus be covered to a great extent by local manufacture.

A second manufacturing facility became operational in 1973. The plant manufactures items relating to microwave, UHF systems and their associated multiplex equipment as well as 3-12 channel carrier systems.

Iran is presently manufacturing a large variety of electronic and telecommunications equipment and is expanding its manufacturing capacity to meet the total national requirement for these materials.

The existence of the microwave network as well as other new technological developments has greatly modernized telegraph facilities in Iran. Today 200 cities are equipped with teletype or teleprinter equipment. The telex and gentex network consists of an automatic system serving over 2,000 terminals. By the end of 1974 a 6,000-line center was operational and fully equipped with computer facilities. This is being expanded at present to 8,500 lines.

Air pollution is an enormous problem of industrialized nations, and Iran is no exception. With the rapid growth of industry in Iran, certain preventive measures are being taken by various organizations. The Material and Energy Research Center, affiliated with the Aryamehr University of Technology, as well as other interested concerns, are engaged in carrying out research programs in this field.

117

118

119

120

121

122

123

124

Iran can be proud of having fostered many great scientists, philosophers and particularly mathematicians. Today there are young mathematicians who follow in their forebears' footsteps with the help of computers.

Significant strides have been taken in recent years toward more extensive computer use. Computers are being used in scientific data processing, management information systems, teaching and research.

Many organizations in the public sector have large computer systems, in particular the Plan and Budget Organization, the National Iranian Oil Company, the National Iranian Gas Company, the Iran Statistics Center, the Ministry of Agriculture and Natural Resources, the Ministry of Science and Higher Education, the Ministry of Education, the Central Bank of Iran, the National Bank of Iran, the Imperial Armed Forces and many institutions of higher education.

Among the privately owned industrial firms and government corporations, there are many which have in-house computer facilities or can avail themselves of a computer system via remote job entry terminals. Several institutions of higher education offer computer training. The largest educational and training center in this area is the College of Planning and Computer Application which was founded in 1973. In 1976 it had an enrollment of 1,100 students, offering a four-year program in computer science, systems analysis and related fields.

The computer is the best means at present of calculating many terrestrial problems of man. It is also an instrument which has enabled man to uncover many secrets of the universe. With the help of computer technology, it is possible to calculate the smallest fractions, relating either to human activities or the motions of the solar system on which the reckoning of our calendar also depends. But it is astonishing how in ancient times complicated calculations of the Iranian calendar were done with high accuracy by mathematicians and astronomers without the aid of computers.

During the Sasanian period the Iranian calendar was based on the solar year. Our early ancestors reckoned 365 days as the official year, dividing it into 12 months. Each month consisted of 30 days, and the remaining 5 days were added to the end of a particular month, usually Esfand (February/March) or Aban (October/November). Because the official year was shorter than the solar year, the difference was made up by calling a bisextile year after every 120 years. The bisextile year had 13 instead of 12 months.

The Iranian months which have been prevalent since Sasanian times are: Farvardin, Ordibehesht, Khordad, Tir, Mordad, Shahrivar, Mehr, Aban, Azar, Dey, Bahman and Esfand. They were named after the protecting angel of the month. In the same manner, each day of the month had its particular name.

At present the first six months in the Iranian calendar have 31 days each, the next five have 30 each, leaving 29 days for the twelfth month or 30 every four years.

The first day of the year falls on the first day of spring, usually March 21, called Now-Ruz, and this day is celebrated all over Iran and in some neighboring countries.

The present calendar of Iran reckons the year 1977 as 2535/2536, with the founding of the Achaemenian Empire as its basal point.

Hossein Ali Anvari

BOOK THREE

WATER

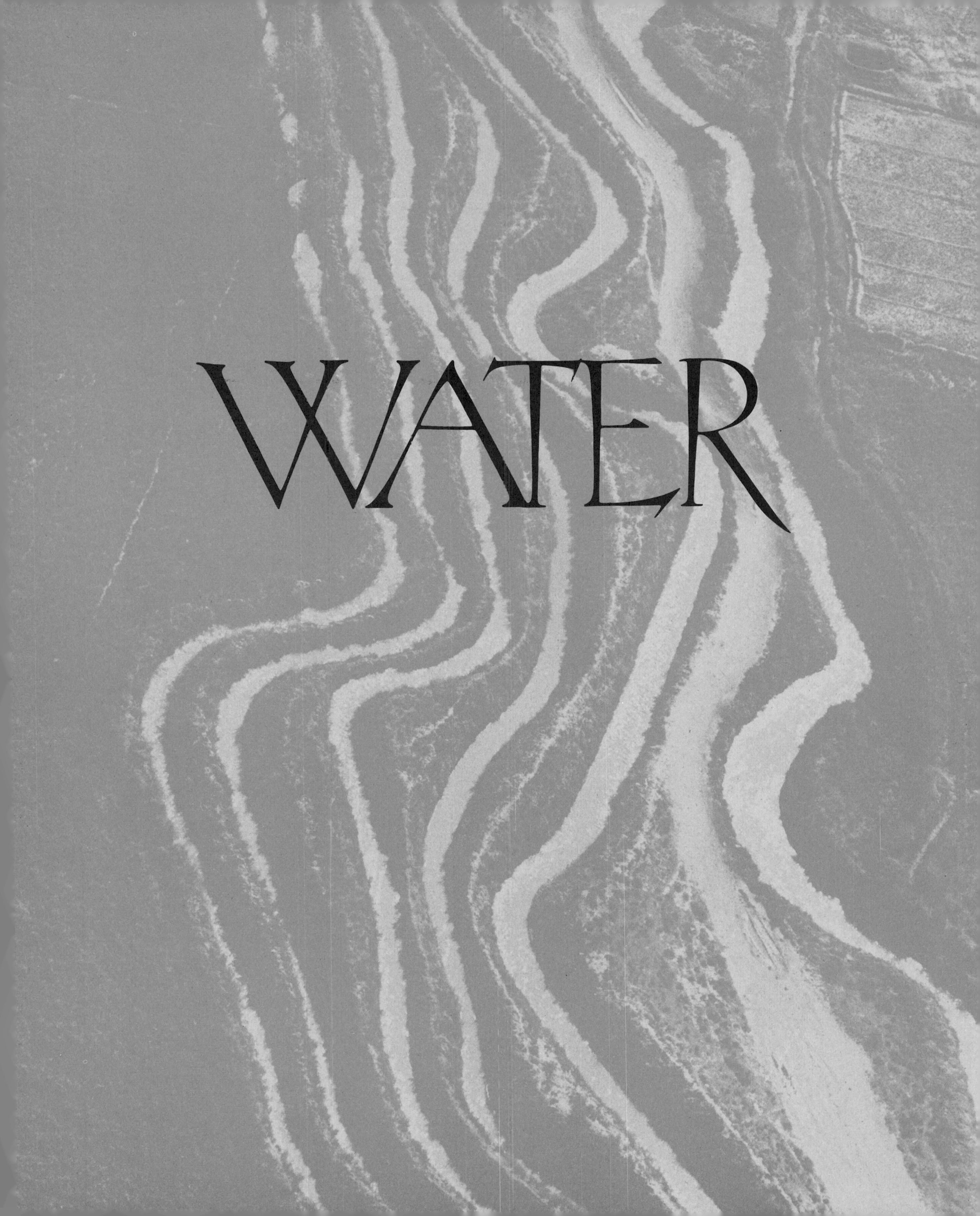

CAPTION FOLDOUT

آب

WATER

GIFT FROM HEAVEN

Gold sun
sparks
over
dawn frost
crystal
by crystal
diamonds
or submarine
goldfish
and the sun
jumps
over
the waves

Nima Yushij

◁ Aerial view of irrigation canals near Tabriz.

GIFT FROM HEAVEN

Since most of Iran is located in a zone which is relatively arid, the proper utilization of water resources has been a main problem which has caused severe limitations on the country's economic development. This problem led Shahanshah Aryamehr to give the following guidance to the national water planners. "We should admit that proper utilization of land and water has been and still is the main problem in the country. It is difficult to find a parallel elsewhere in the world as to the efforts made and the difficulties overcome. While Iran covers 165 million hectares, at the present time the main factor which severely limits the agricultural and industrial development of the land is water. It is imperative that each Iranian understands the importance of water. For this reason the country's water resources have been nationalized."

Precipitation in the foothills of the Alborz and Zagros mountain ranges is generally sufficient, and in the Talesh region on the Caspian Coast, it is about two meters per year. However, the annual rainfall in the country as a whole is meager, averaging only about 250 millimeters. The total yearly rainfall with respect to the surface area is about one-third of the world average and less than half of the average precipitation on the surface area of the Asian continent. The lowest amount of precipitation occurs in the catchment areas of the plateau region, where the average is about 140 millimeters and sometimes less than 50 millimeters in some locations such as in the Salt Desert and Lut Desert areas.

The uneven distribution of precipitation, which forms the main source of water in Iran, is due to relief features. The two mountain ranges, the Alborz range located in the north and the Zagros range situated in the south and west, severely limit the circulation of moisture-laden clouds. During the growing season three-quarters of the already-meager precipitation evaporates before reaching the ground.

Iran can be divided into the following six main catchment zones:

(1) The Persian Gulf Catchment Zone, constituting 25 percent of the area;
(2) The Caspian Sea Catchment Zone, covering 12 percent of the area;
(3) The Lake Rezaiyyeh Catchment Zone, covering 3 percent of the area;
(4) The Central Iran River System Catchment Zone, covering about 50 percent of the area and further subdividing into seven sub-catchments;
(5) The Hamun Lake and the related River Catchment Zone, located in the Irano-Afghan border area, of which the Iranian part constitutes about 7 percent of the Iranian land mass; and
(6) The Eastern and Northeastern Rivers Catchment Zone, the waters of which flow toward the Qareh Qom Desert (U.S.S.R. side).

In general, the average amount of water contributed by the rainfall each year to the Iranian land mass is more than 400 billion cubic meters. About 70 percent of the precipitation returns to the atmosphere as a result of evaporation and evapotranspiration. Twenty-five percent of the infiltrated water is being utilized for irrigation and domestic purposes, and the remaining 75 percent flows out to

the lakes or the sea. As a result, Iran lacks green or wet stretches of land. In central Iran the excessive rate of evaporation consumes 32.5 percent of the total rainfall. In the Caspian Sea catchment zone, with 12 percent of the Iranian area only, about 22.5 percent of the precipitation leaves the land surface annually due to a relatively low evaporation rate.

The presence of fossil water, which has remained in place for decades, trapped and unextracted, is now known. To this category may be added mineral and thermal waters, which emerge in the vicinity of inactive volcanoes. Qualitatively, these waters are significant, although they are of little importance for agricultural use. They are found in Azarbayejan, at Mahallat and near Mount Damavand, but are sparsely distributed in other parts of the country.

For domestic, agricultural or industrial use, the brackish or saline water of Iran does not appear to be of much importance in its present state. It does, however, contribute significantly to the formation of rain clouds by evaporation.

The main saltwater areas are the Persian Gulf, the Caspian Sea and Lake Rezaiyyeh. The Persian Gulf is located in southern Iran and covers an area of 251,226 square kilometers, and is bordered by the Iranian coast and the Sea of Oman on the east and by Saudi Arabia and the United Arab Emirates on the south and west. The length of the Persian Gulf, from Abadan to the Strait of Hormoz, is more than 1,200 kilometers. The Persian Gulf was created by organic activity during the Tertiary period. The same activity was also responsible for the formation of the Zagros range in southwest Iran. Being an international gateway, the Persian Gulf has had special geographic significance since historical times. The chemical composition of the Persian Gulf water is similar to ocean water. It is rather shallow, being less than 100 meters deep in the deepest part while at the entrance it is only 36 meters deep.

The Caspian Sea, located between Iran and the U.S.S.R., is the largest landlocked water body in the world. Its perimeter is 6,380 kilometers, out of which the southern 992 kilometers, between Astara in the west to Hoseynqoli Bay in the east, is located in Iran, the rest being situated in the U.S.S.R. The total area occupied by this vast lake is about 424,300 square kilometers. The Caspian Sea, which is presently receding and losing its depth at the rate of 10 centimeters a year, is important for its fisheries and caviar industry. It is also a haven for tourists.

Lake Rezaiyyeh is next in size and its physical and chemical characteristics are very different from the Caspian Sea. It is located near Rezaiyyeh, at a general elevation of 1,275 meters above sea level. The total area occupied by Lake Rezaiyyeh is about 5,000 square kilometers. The maximum depth in the northern part is seven meters, but in the southern part it is about 15 meters. Lake Rezaiyyeh is one of the saltiest lakes of the world which means that only hard-shelled animals can thrive in it. The dissolved salts are in the vicinity of 300 to 400 grams per liter, with seasonal fluctuations. Although little life can survive within its brackish waters, one of the natural beauties of Lake Rezaiyyeh is the annual summer migration of graceful flamingoes who come to feed and nest along the lakeshore and on small islands in the lake.

Said Nejand

The Gold Bowl of Ninth Century B.C. Hasanlu

Southwest of Lake Rezaiyyeh stands the ancient site of Hasanlu. In the early first millennium B.C. there was a thriving community here. Farmers and artisans lived in the outer town, while on the citadel royalty graced a fortified complex of palaces. These kings were wealthy; they commanded the agricultural resources of the fertile Solduz Valley— fertile because of an abundance of water.

Wealth, however, creates greed. Toward the end of the ninth century an enemy sacked and destroyed the city in a hurricane of fire. In 1958 archeologists discovered the now-famous gold bowl of Hasanlu clutched in the hands of a soldier who had died in the crash and tumble of falling mud brick while the town burned around him.

Today that bowl remains an artistic puzzle. Do we see here iconographic borrowings from the neighboring peoples? Or is this perhaps a purely Iranian work, depicting episodes from the Iranian national legend? Opinion is divided.

These arguments aside, look at the upper register of figures on the bowl and remember the fertility of the Solduz Valley. Three deities ride toward the

right, the most important being the winged god in the chariot pulled by a bull. From the bull's mouth a never-ending stream of water gushes forth with such volume and force that it creates a bubbling pool. Facing the water god are three worshipers. One bears a cup, the other two bring sheep for sacrifice. The focus of the whole scene is water—the life-giving water which comes from properly worshiped gods.

Local artists or craftsmen using borrowed motifs, the people who made this bowl knew the Iranian landscape. They had experienced its heat and desiccation; they appreciated the need for water. From water, spreading over the land, comes life. Life through water is a gift from heaven.

T. Cuyler Young, Jr.

The main pavilion of the Bagh-e-Fin (Coste).
Engraving from *Persian Gardens and Garden Pavilions* by Donald N. Wilber, copyright © 1962 by Charles E. Tuttle Company, Japan.

"Such beauty as arises from shade and the purling of water is all that the Persian requires."

Lord Curzon.

In Iran, the most precious element has always been water. Though in the Caspian provinces rainfall is abundant, and the mountains are densely forested, over much of the plateau there is insufficient rain to support agriculture without irrigation.

To a large extent, therefore, Iran is dependent on the winter snows, trapped in the numerous mountain ranges and released gradually during the spring and summer months. The life-giving water thus produced would evaporate long before it could reach the towns and villages in the plains, had not the Iranians in ancient times devised a system of qanats, or underground water channels, which bring water to fields and habitations sometimes as much as fifty miles away.

The contrast between the desert and the town is striking; in the words of the English traveler, Gertrude Bell: "A little water and the desert breaks into flower, bowers of cool shade spring up in the midst of dust and glare, radiant stretches of soft color gleam in that gray expanse."

Iranians have always designed gardens not only to delight the eye but also to enchant the ear with the sound of running water.

"Under the broad thick leaves of the plane-trees tiny streams murmur, fountains splash with a fragrant sweet sound, white-rose bushes drop their fragrant petals into tanks, lying deep and still like patches of concentrated shadow."

Gertrude Bell

Kings and commoners alike have adorned their gardens with fountains, cascades and ornamental ponds, and Hafez could not imagine that the beauty of the streams and meadows of his native Shiraz could be excelled even in paradise.

The themes of water and gardens recur in Persian paintings and are depicted in many Persian carpets:

"Golden skies and silver water, black-green cypresses against white-blossoming trees, the autumn foliage of the spreading plane, clustered figures in raiment of scarlet, crimson and azure, diaper tiles and dainty frescoes, bright gardens behind slender fences of cinnabar-red: these together compose the gayest of all possible symphonies."

A. Upham Pope

Roger M. Savory

Sources of quotations:

Lord Curzon, quoted by V. Sackville West, *Persian Gardens*, in *Legacy of Persia* (ed. A. J. Arberry), Oxford, 1953, p. 286.
Gertrude Bell, *Persian Pictures*, London, Ernest Benn Ltd., 1928, p. 36.
A. Upham Pope, *An Introduction to Persian Art since the seventh century A.D.*, London, 1930, p. 109.

آب

WATER

CHANNELS OF POWER

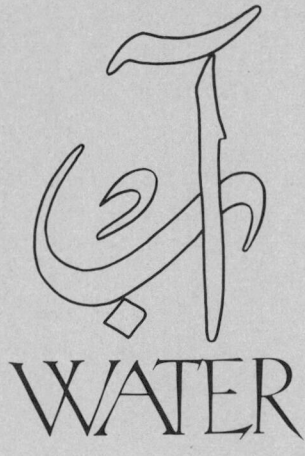

Fresh Water Utilization

During the past fifteen years, Iran has followed a sound policy of water management. At present four billion cubic meters of water per year is being harnessed from the flood waters of Iranian rivers by the Shahbanou Farah Dam and Mohammad Reza Shah Dam for agricultural and city supplies.

Utilization of fresh water resources for agricultural, industrial and domestic use was first started in the reign of Reza Shah the Great. At that time a department was created to supervise the construction of several diversion dams. This was accelerated during the reign of Shahanshah Aryamehr. Toward the end of the Third Development Plan, the nationalization of water resources was declared. This started a new phase of water management where optimum use of additional fresh water resources and correct consumption practices were emphasized. The excellent results based upon the last several years of work in this field are evident today and are expected to develop further in the future.

During the past fifty years, thirty large dams and diversion dams including twelve multipurpose dams were constructed. Twenty-eight of the thirty dams were built during the reign of Shahanshah Aryamehr. The twelve multipurpose reservoir dams were built in the last fifteen years.

The largest multipurpose reservoir dam is the Mohammad Reza Shah Pahlavi Dam in Khuzestan, which is situated on the Dez River. This dam is capable of irrigating more than 100,000 hectares of agricultural land. It also serves to protect the land from the annual floods of the Karun River, floods that created much havoc before the completion of this dam. The power-generating capacity of this dam is 520,000 kilowatts which produce 2,200 kilowatts per hour annually.

Other reservoir dams serving Iran are the Shahbanou Farah Dam at Manjil, the Aras Dam at Qezel Qeshlaq, the Shah Abbas Kabir Dam on the Zayendeh Rud near Esfahan, the Dariush Kabir Dam near Shiraz, the Kurosh Kabir Dam at southeast Bokan, the Shahpur Avval Dam at Mahabad, the Amir Kabir Dam at Karaj, the Farahnaz Pahlavi Dam at Latiyan, the Voshmgir Dam at Gorgan, the Shah Esmail Dam at Golpayegan, and the Shahnaz Pahlavi Dam at Hamedan. With the completion of these twelve multipurpose reservoir dams, all of which are presently in use, about 14 billion cubic meters of water will be harnessed. In addition to irrigating 760,000 hectares of agricultural land, these dams also provide water to cities, towns and industrial units. The total hydro-electric power generated is in the range of 804 megawatts.

Parallel to this, the groundwater resources have not been forgotten. About 18 billion cubic meters of groundwater is being pumped annually from the existing wells and *qanats* located on the alluvial plains of Iran.

The amount of water being harnessed in this country today is much more than was previously available to Iranians. Using the most advanced methods, it has become possible to overcome the natural drawback of the topography that results in uneven distribution of water resources. However, demand is higher than in the past and water consumption is increasing daily due to growth in general. As a result, six reservoir dams are currently under construction, including the Reza Shah Kabir Dam, the Minab Dam, the Jiroft Dam, the Lar Dam, the Qeshlaq Dam and the Pishin Dam. Other dams under study are the Nader Shah Dam, the Saveh Dam, the Khoda Afarin Dam and the Baho Dam.

In addition, further development of surface water and groundwater resources will continue. The sedimentary carbonate formations of the Zagros and Alborz ranges are currently under study. The present and future policy of the country as the Shahanshah has declared is "... to use the last possible drop of water from the very core of rocks or streambeds and utilize it for domestic, agricultural and industrial purposes for the betterment and prosperity of Iran."

History of the Water Resource System Management

Since ancient times Iranians have given special attention to water problems and pioneered the building of structures for the storage and conveyance of water. This is evident from the writings of the ancient Iranian scientist and philosopher Karaji, who lived more than 1,000 years ago. He expounded scientific principles on the storage and movement of sub-surface water and the extraction of groundwater. He writes: "Despite the presence of mountain ranges, plains, reliefs, the earth is round. God has created the earth as the center of the universe and the earth revolves around its center till eternity. The earth by itself is very small. The sun with its heat takes the lighter part of the water and converts it into air. Conversion of air to water takes place in the cold days of the cold places, and water to air in the warm days in the warm places. This is continuous and cyclic and is useful in rehabilitating the land."

About the formation of water and rainfall, Karaji states: "God, in water, has created such a wonder that it fills all the fractures and veins, and the excess part flows out to sea. Therefore, the main source of water should be snow and rain and the change of water to air and air to water."

Karaji's discussion of the causes of precipitation and formation of water resources is in conformity with present knowledge of the water cycle in nature. He also wrote about the construction of dams and *qanats*. On earth dam construction, he wrote that the canal is to be covered by a layer of clay. The clay should be slightly moist at all times. For compacting the soil or preparing the clay layer, herds of sheep or animals should pass over it so that their hooves compress the underlying soil. Modern methods of dam construction are similar, although animals are no longer used for this purpose, their place having been taken by the compaction machine.

Qanats, a method of utilizing groundwater, were pioneered in Iran and later adopted in other parts of the world. The *qanat* is an extension of a horizontal underground channel, a long gently sloping drainage tunnel which conveys the water a distance of several kilometers. In the past Iranians constructed *qanats* along the seepage line and all the loosened soil was piled in one place. It was therefore impossible to continue after a few meters of digging, and a new solution was necessary. The Iranians solved the problem by digging wells in such a way on the *qanat* line that the earth from the lateral channel could be brought to the surface from the next well (vertical shaft) without the necessity of carrying it a long distance. The extracted soil was piled near the well openings. This solution allowed the surface water to infiltrate the *qanats*, and prevented the tunnel or the *qanat* openings from clogging. These piles of earth along the *qanat* openings give an interesting aerial view and provide a clear picture of their extension on the land.

The depth of the wells connecting a *qanat* system varies, from almost nothing at the point of water outflow to the "mother well" at the beginning which is several hundred meters deep. The deepest mother well in Iran is about 400 meters. Distance between the wells generally ranges from 20 to 50 meters. The lateral tunnel has a dimension of 60 x 120 centimeters, requiring the builder to dig the connection tunnel either by sitting or crawling. The length of the *qanat* varies according to natural conditions. This is also dependent on the slope of the land and depth of the mother well. The longest *qanat* existing in Iran has a distance of about 70 kilometers near Gonabad in the Khorasan province. The number of existing *qanats*, although still not completely known, is decreasing for many reasons. Due to the high cost of labor, maintenance expense has become prohibitive. Further, the present high rate of deep well drillings and consequent groundwater offtake is causing the groundwater level to decline in many areas with the *qanats* drying up.

There are about 50,000 *qanats* in Iran and if 7,000 meters is considered as the average *qanat* length, the total is about 350,000 kilometers, a distance equal to that between the earth and the moon. The total outflow of water from existing *qanats* is estimated to be nearly 6 billion cubic meters per year, mainly used for agricultural purposes. Half of this amount flows out unused since its continuous flow cannot be controlled especially in the season when agricultural activity is at its minimum. This is wasteful, and even if their repair were not costly, *qanats* are no longer economical. Thus, the descendants of the pioneers in the field of water irrigation are developing new and better techniques for serving the needs of modern Iran.

Plans are in progress for new projects on water recycling in major towns, suppression of evaporation from the water surfaces in large reservoirs and desalination schemes for coastal towns and seaports in the Caspian Sea and Persian Gulf areas. In some cases, projects are already under construction. These efforts are all being made with the objective of improving irrigation and water supply in Iran.

Said Nejand

134

135

136

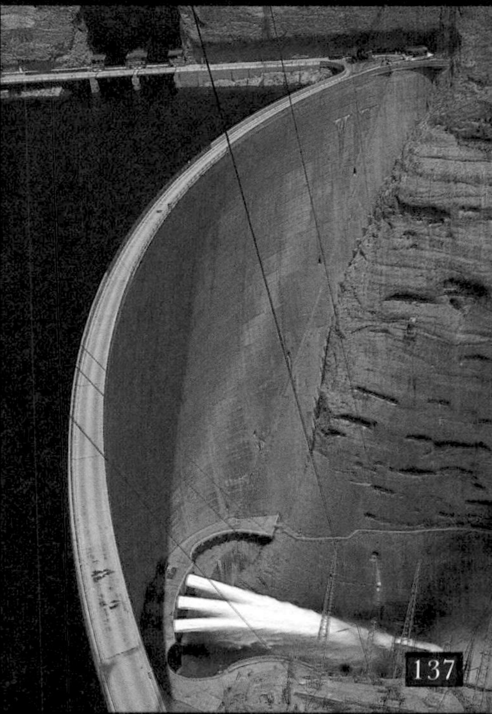
137

138

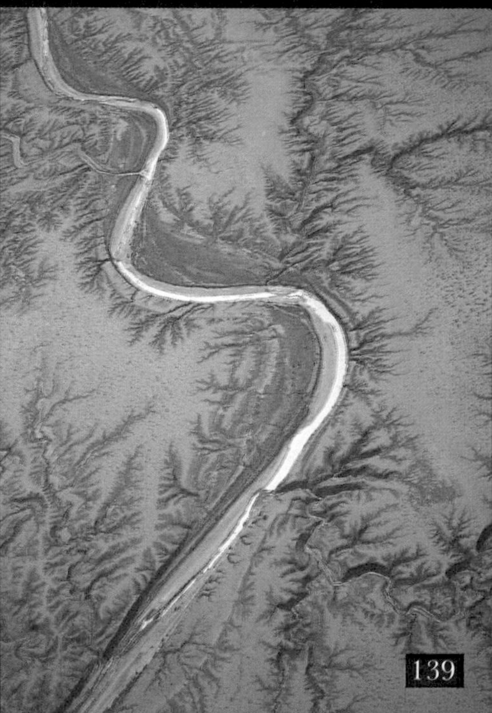
139

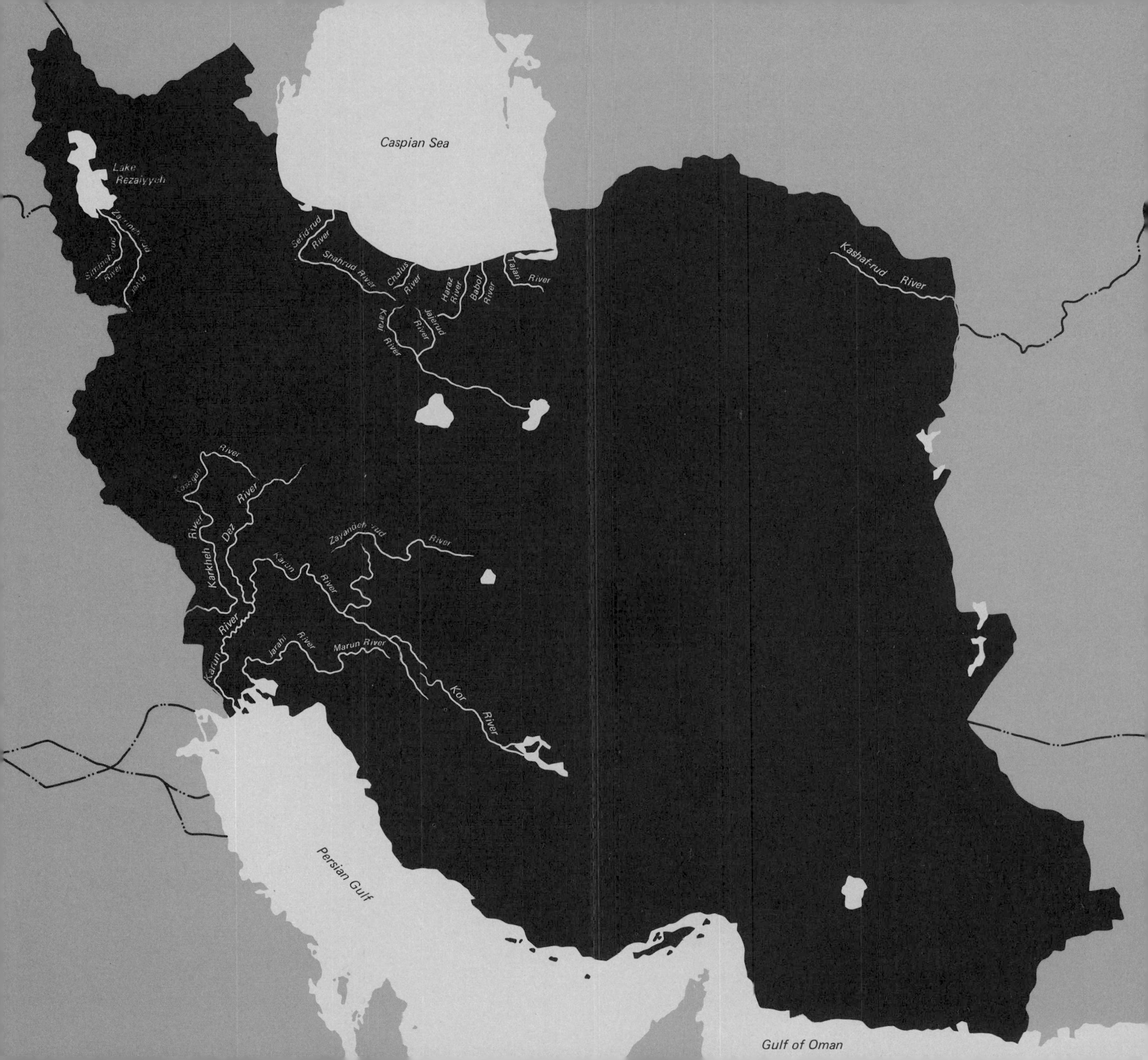

Caspian Sea
Lake
Rezaiyyeh
Zarrineh-rud
River
Simineh-rud
River
Sefid-rud
River
Shahrud River
Chalus
River
Haraz
River
Babol
River
Tajan
River
Jajarud
River
Karaj
River
Kashaf-rud
River
Kashgan
River
Dez
River
Karkheh
River
Zayandeh-rud
River
Karun
River
Karun
River
Jarahi
River
Marun River
Kor
River
Persian Gulf
Gulf of Oman

Shipping and Navigation

Shipping and navigation as well as management of water resources have played an important role in Iran since ancient times. Although a detailed history of Iranian shipping does not exist, there is evidence of this preoccupation. The Achaemenian king, Darius the Great, commanded that a canal be dug in the Suez area in Egypt, and the inscription discovered there attests to his keen interest in navigation and sea routes within the Achaemenian Empire. The presence of an Iranian navy is also reported in stories describing the invasion of Xerxes on the Greek mainland.

During the Parthian period, sea trade among Iran, India and China flourished and continued to be encouraged by the Sasanian monarchs who established regular commercial sea routes with key bases located along the Persian Gulf coast. Iranian vessels reached the ports of Ceylon, where Chinese silks and other precious goods were acquired and transported to the thriving Persian Gulf markets. In the sixth century A.D., south Arabia was invaded by the Iranian navy.

During the early Islamic period, the large and prosperous port of Siraf on the Persian Gulf coast, located between Bandar Abbas and Bandar-e-Bushehr near the present-day village of Bandar-e-Taheri, was active in commercial activities between the Persian Gulf, India and beyond, serving as the western terminus for Iranian and foreign ships. Recent excavations at Siraf dramatically reveal the prosperity of this port city in Sasanian and early Islamic times.

Linguistic clues also provide evidence of the far-reaching sea routes covered by Iranian sailors and merchant ships. The names of Malabar and Zangebar (Zanzibar), for example, located on opposite ends of the Indian Ocean, are Iranian in origin. The Persian word "bar" means coast, and Malabar, the coast of the Malays. Zangebar is the coast of the Zangs or the black people.

During Saljuq times and later, this activity diminished considerably, until it was revived by the Safavid ruler, Shah Abbas the Great, and by the Afsharid, Nader Shah. After Nader Shah, Iranian shipping lost much of its influence, and it became almost extinct during the Qajar period. However, in the Pahlavi Dynasty, shipping and navigation have been given new life and have developed along world standards.

Commercial Ports

During the present reign, Iranian seaports have regained their importance. Among the more developed ones is Khark, which has become a primary port for the export of petroleum. Here a 500,000-ton vessel can easily be handled. Other commercial ports include Bandar Abbas, Bandar-e-Shahpur, Khorramshahr, Abadan and Bushehr in the south, and Bandar-e-Pahlavi and Nowshahr in the north.

The total capacity of these ports is realistically estimated at five million tons; but in view of three shifts, operating day and night (in the southern ports), eleven million tons are actually handled – which is indicative of Iran's determination to progress. The most effective port at present is considered to be Khorramshahr. It has thirteen jetties, four of which have been added during the past year. Also, extensive projects are under way, the most impressive of which is the construction of a port located fifteen kilometers from Bandar Abbas. Trading in these ports is expected to be so vast as to have been unimaginable ten years ago.

The Shipbuilding Industry

The extraordinary progress in shipping during the early reign of the Shahanshah Aryamehr also influenced the development of the shipbuilding industry in the Persian Gulf, both for the Imperial Navy and commercial vessels. A company dealing with the shipbuilding industry, capable of constructing vessels up to 20,000 tons, has been formed. It is also equipped to deal with repairs and to build commercial vessels and oil tankers up to 500,000 tons. In addition to fulfilling domestic requirements, it will serve as a repair center for incoming ships and tankers. Located twenty-seven kilometers west of Bandar Abbas, it has the capacity to repair and service one hundred large ships and one hundred and forty small vessels, as well as to build six vessels. With the expectation that it will expand in the future, this is an indication of the rapid growth of the shipping industry.

The Imperial Iranian Navy

Following World War II and the political vicissitudes, the Imperial Iranian Navy has once more been strengthened.

During the early phase of its development, the Imperial Navy lacked a properly trained cadre. For this reason, the first training ship, the *Karsak,* with thirty-two trainees, was commissioned in 1948. Due to lack of proper accommodation, the trainees used the living facilities of the naval ship *Simorgh.* The Imperial Navy continued to grow rapidly, and the ships *Babr* and *Palang* were added to the existing fleet. These two vessels bore the names of earlier Imperial ships sunk in action during World War II. The first voyage of the *Babr,* with an Iranian crew, was between Khorramshahr and Bandar Abbas. On reaching their destination, the crew were warmly welcomed by the local population.

The Imperial Navy's acquisition of large and powerful ships, along with trained personnel familiar with the most advanced techniques of navigation and defense, resulted in Iran's complete control over its ocean frontiers.

Said Nejand

142

143

144

146

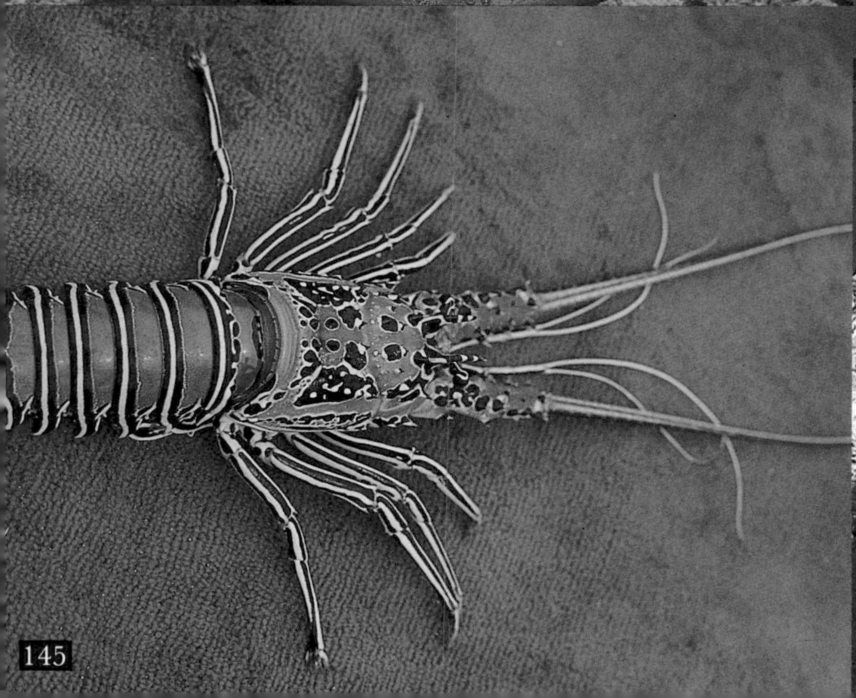
145

147

148

149

150

151

152

153

154

The Battle of the Genius of Rain with the Demon of Drought

The command of the rains was in the hands of the dog star, Tishtrya, or Sirius. In the sacred *Avesta,* Tishtrya is pictured as a youth with shining eyes, tall in stature and powerful. Quick and clever, he flies about bathed in a self-generated light. Devotees made sacrifices to him to bring rain, and the *Avesta* contains many prayers such as this:

> We sacrifice unto Tishtrya, the bright and glorious star for whom long flocks and herds and men looking forward to him and deceived in their hopes:
>
> "When shall we see him rise up, the bright and glorious star Tishtrya? When will the springs run with waves as thick as a horse's size and still thicker? Or will they never come?
>
> ". . . We sacrifice unto Tishtrya
> We sacrifice unto the rains of Tishtrya
> We sacrifice unto the first star; we sacrifice
> unto the rains of the first star."

Tishtrya was sacred to the fourth month, Tir, the modern form of the name, and protected the earth during this time. He assembled the clouds during this month and commanded rain from them, bringing water to the dry, thirsty land; turning the trees and grass green; causing flowers and fruits to bud and bloom, and the rivers and streams to fill and swell with water, making the land of Iran fruitful.

According to the *Avesta,* the Genius of Rain appears in three different guises during the month of Tir. In the first ten nights he appears as a beautiful tall youth with shining eyes; in the second ten nights, as a powerful bull with golden horns; and in the third ten nights, as a white horse with golden ears and a golden bridle. As it rains, all the earth's vermin and evil creatures were said to be eliminated and the earth made clean.

> We sacrifice unto Tishtrya, the bright and glorious star, that afflicts the Parikas (evil spirits), that vexes the Parikas, who, in the shape of worm-stars, fly between the earth and the heavens, in the sea Vouru-Kasha, the powerful sea, the large-sized, deep sea of salt waters. He goes to its lake in the shape of a horse, in a holy shape; and down there he makes the waters boil over, and the winds flow above powerfully all around.

> Then Satavaesa makes those waters flow down to the seven Karshvars of the earth, and when he has arrived down there, he stands, beautiful, spreading ease and joy on the fertile countries (thinking in himself): How shall the countries of the Aryas grow fertile?

The Demon of Drought is called Apaosha in the *Avesta,* and was constantly at war with Tishtrya. Apaosha imprisoned the waters, keeping them away from men. Ancient Iranians, whenever they were faced with drought, came before Tishtrya and made offerings and sacrifices to him. With prayers and entreaties they would ask him for rain. Tishtrya would hear their pleas, accept their offerings, and in his incarnation as a white horse with golden ears would sweep down from the heavens to the sea and obtain water for the people.

Once Apaosha, obeying the orders of Ahriman, the principle of evil, sprang to attack Tishtrya in the form of a terrifying black steed with short black ears, mane and tail. The Genius of Rain and the Demon of Drought fought for three days and nights beside the sea. Apaosha was the victor and turned Tishtrya back from the water. Tishtrya stormed into the presence of Ahura Mazda, complaining and swearing, and told him of his loss. He warned him that now that he had suffered loss at the hands of the demon, the people would no longer offer prayers to Ahura Mazda.

The people heard the complaint of Tishtrya and made renewed offerings to him. Strengthened by these offerings, he once again descended from the heavens to the shore of the sea. The demon encountered him and they fought together until noon.

> The bright and glorious Tishtrya proves stronger than the Daeva (demon) Apaosha, and he overcomes him. Then he goes from the sea Vouru-Kasha as far as a Hathra's length: "Hail!" cries the bright and glorious Tishtrya. "Hail unto me, O Ahura Mazda! Hail unto you, O waters and plants! Hail, O law of the worshipers of Mazda! Hail will it be unto you, O lands! The life of the waters will flow down unrestrained to the big-seeded cornfields, to the small-seeded pasture-fields, and to the whole of the material world!"
>
> Then the bright and glorious Tishtrya goes back down to the sea Vouru-Kasha ... He makes the sea boil up and down; he makes the sea flow this and that way: all the shores of the sea Vouru-Kasha are boiling over, all the middle of it is boiling over.
>
> And the bright and glorious Tishtrya rises up from the sea ... and vapors rise up above Mount Su-hindu that stands in the middle of the sea Vouru-Kasha ... Then the wind blows the clouds forward, bearing the waters of fertility, so that the friendly showers spread wide over, they spread helpingly and friendly over the seven Karshvars (lands).

AVESTA
Tir Yasht

Saith Darius the King: "I am a Persian and I gave order to dig this canal from a river by name Nile which flows in Egypt, to the sea which goes from Persia. Afterward this canal was dug thus as I had ordered, and ships went from Egypt through this canal to Persia thus as was my desire."

Suez Inscription of Darius the Great

BOOK FOUR

FIRE

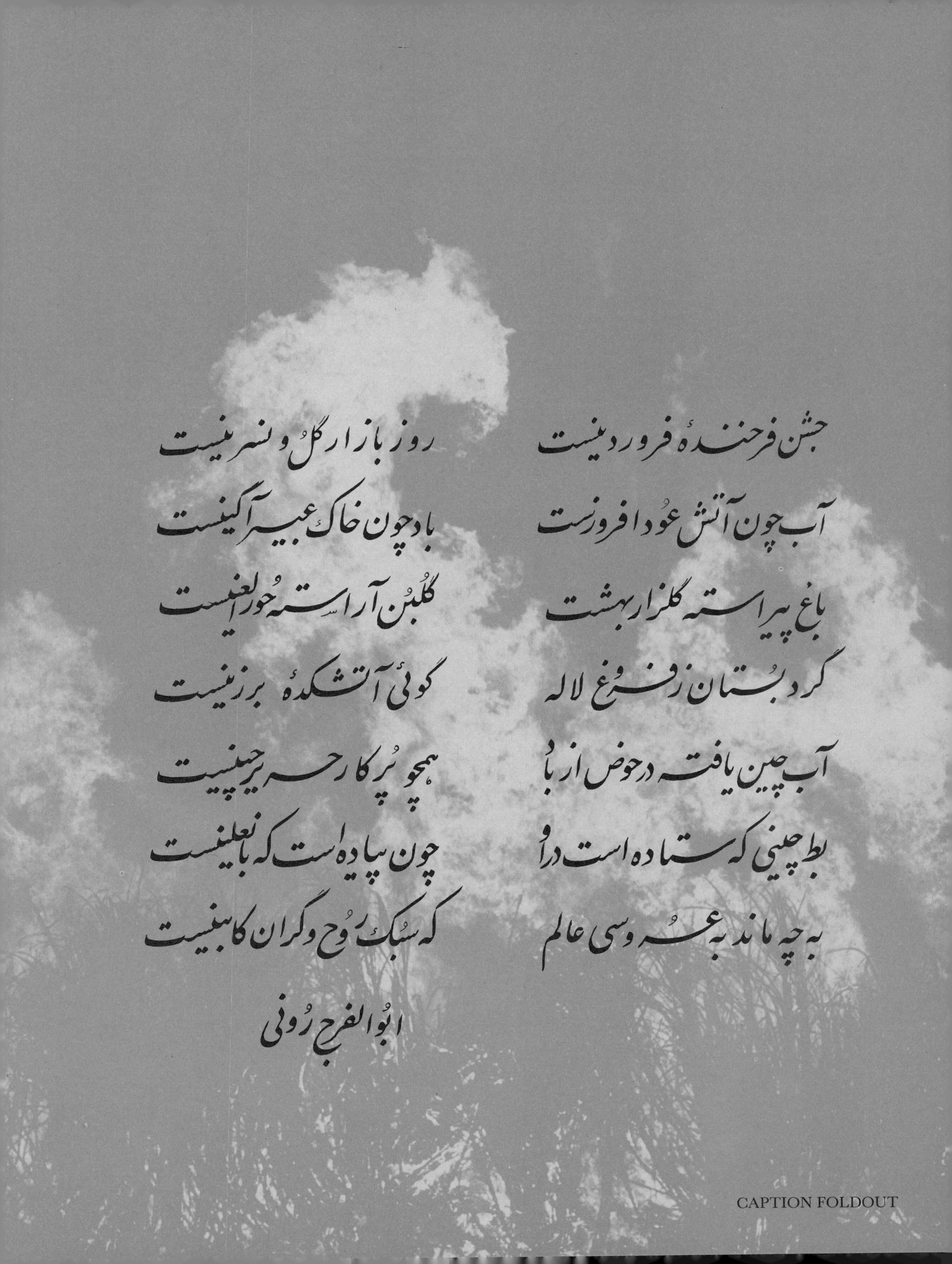

جشن فرخندهٔ فروردینست — روز بازار گل و نسرینست

آب چون آتش عود افروزست — باد چون خاک عبیر آگینست

باغ پیراسته گلزار بهشت — گلبن آراسته حورالعینست

گرد بستان ز فروغ لاله — گوئی آتشکدهٔ برزینست

آب چین یافته در حوض از باد — همچو پرگار حریر چینیست

بط چینی که ستاده است در او — چون پیاده است که با نعلینست

به چه ماند به عروسی عالم — که سبک روح و گران کابینست

ابوالفرج رونی

CAPTION FOLDOUT

FIRE آتش

THE DIVINE SECRET

Festival of the Equinox: market-day
for the rose and the wild rose;

Water: fire that smolders with incense
Wind: earth mingled with ambergris.

The garden: rose-bed of Paradise
each rose painted with fairy cosmetics.

The fountain: water wrinkled by the wind
like an expensive China silk.

So bright around the garden; is it not
the very fire temple of Borzin? . . .

Abolfaraj Runi

◁ Sugarcane burning at Haft Tappeh.

THE DIVINE SECRET

"Tis the flame of Love that fired me," Jalaleddin Rumi, the thirteenth-century Iranian mystic, tells us in his famous *Masnavi.* The concept of fire as the symbol of love has inspired Iranians to develop profound philosophical ideas and create incomparable poetry. Fire has always played a predominant role in the lives of the Iranian people.

A swift form of energy present in all things as consuming inner heat, fire has a penetrating and transformative presence which is communicated to all who approach it, activating a certain receptivity. By doing so, fire turns all things into its own likeness. It is said that when a candle is lit, its flame effaces the essential quality of the candle. As Joneyd, the mystic, expressed it:

> When a moth threw itself into a fire
>   it was consumed.
> The moth dying said, "I am fire,"
>   but the words were from the tongue of the flame.

Fire penetrates all substances and, by doing so, cleanses and purifies them, thereby transforming the substance to its own level of energy.

Fire came to be held sacred by early man on the Iranian Plateau, and if one were to return to this vision of the world, one would see that fire has not changed since the beginning of time. What was sacred then is still sacred. What has diminished is the depth of seeing.

Traditional cosmologies developed around the concept of the fire of love, for it is through a cosmic love that one has for a form lower than itself that the other actually comes into existence. "The attraction of love holds together the sun and the shadow," said a poet. It is the dominance of love in the universe that fires the motion of the stars and planets.

It is said that love is the astrolabe of the mysteries of God. Nasafi, a thirteenth-century mystic philosopher, expressed the order in the universe as follows:

> All things in the world of existence are on a journey to attain to their goal, and man too is on a journey. But the goal of man is maturity and freedom. The motive for the traveling of all these things is love. Oh, dear friend, the seed of all plants and the sperm of all animals is filled with love, indeed all the parts of the world of existence are drunk with love, for if there were no love, the sphere would not turn, the plants would not grow, the animals would not be born. All are full of love for themselves, strive to behold themselves, desire to see themselves as they really are and to disclose the beloved to the eyes of the lover.

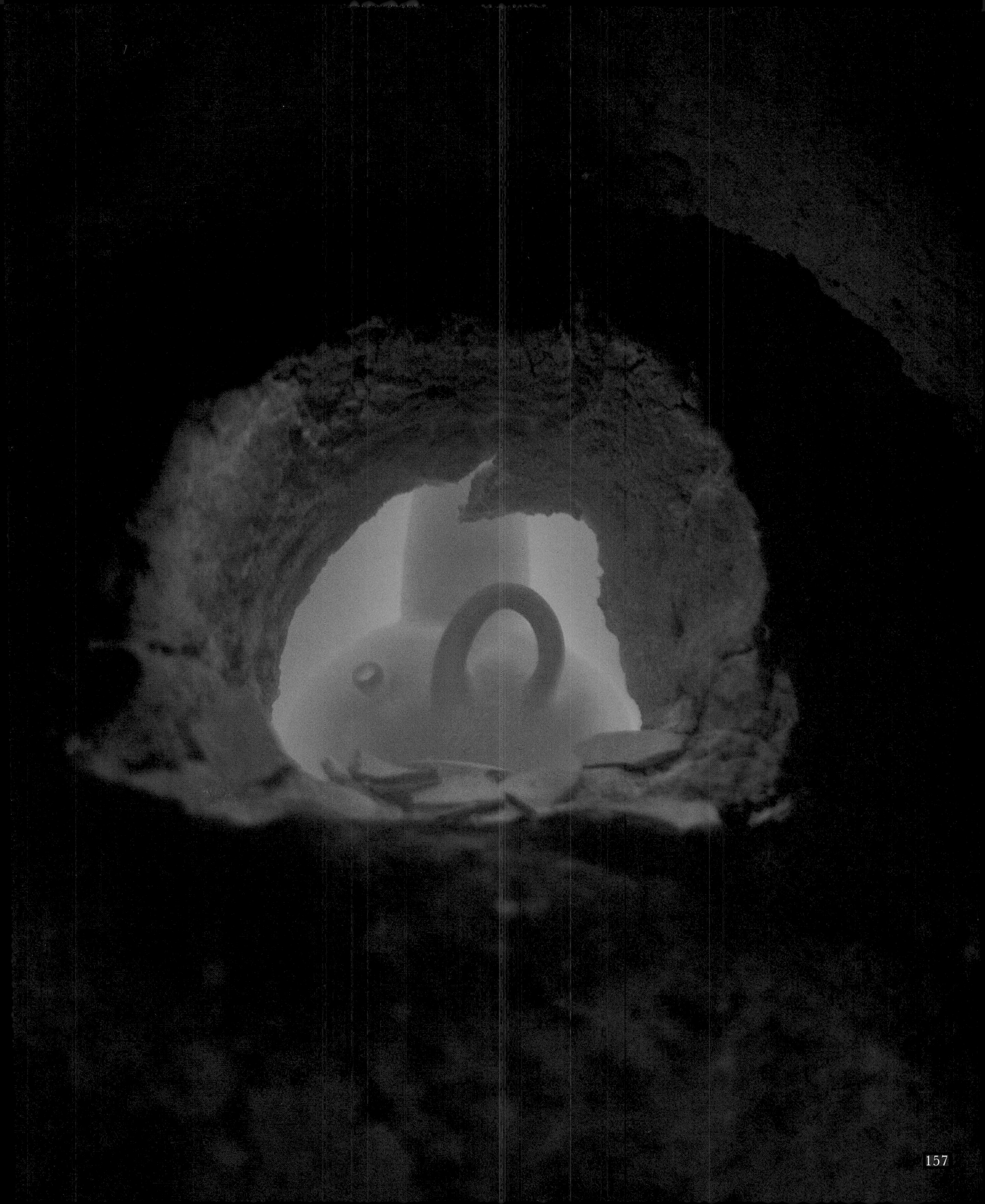

According to the traditional cosmologies which developed on the Iranian Plateau, the sun and other planets occupy the upper world, the world of intelligences. Their intermixture and intermingling of energies are all gathered in the sphere of the moon and it is the moon which serves as the place of descent to the earth of the four elements. Fire occupies the highest sphere because it is the lightest.

In Avestic cults, the Fire of Life is seen as vitality. It is a fire which is to be fed every day with the purest of foods, and vigilance is required to maintain it. Essentially, the Fire of Life is a product of the vital processes which are to be nourished within an organism with natural foods to bring about human vitality. Fire, at the same time that it is energy-giving, is also energy-consuming and in a constant state of decline. Something has to be added in order to sustain it and herein lies the role of man who becomes responsible for the sustaining effort.

In the creation of the world according to Zoroastrian traditions, fire is the last of the created elements and yet it permeates all the others. The brilliance of fire comes from the Endless Light and it is fire which is the origin of the seed of man and bull. Fire is truth, the male and active principle at work in all things.

In Iran today we see traditions relating to the sacredness of fire remaining from these earliest times. The last Wednesday of the year is observed by a special ritual of purification performed by jumping over fire while chanting "My yellowness to you, your redness to me" – that is, your vitality to me and my ills to you.

Iran still finds itself rich in fire-producing natural resources. Oil, the black gold which is stored in the treasuries of the earth, serves mankind in the march toward a better quality of life. Known as "nature's savings account toward one day becoming a star," the wealth of this resource has only recently been considered. Today the Shahanshah Aryamehr has emphasized the need for other sources of energy so that this natural resource is not misused.

It is this direction and guidance which mankind tends to forget in over-extending its needs to the detriment of nature – for fire, its causes and effects, is but a created thing. Through its expression, light is made manifest.

Within the traditional world view, each individually created form is a symbol reflecting a level higher than itself as one moves from the world of matter and physical creation toward the subtle and the world of ideas.

Symbols in the traditional perspective are guides and incentives and the invocation of symbols serves as a form of remembrance of the higher state of being. The remembrance is not incidental but rather essential, for the symbol itself is but a reflection of a higher reality. By analogy one can compare the shadow and the object which casts the shadow to a symbol and the invisible form which casts it.

> Verily God disdaineth not to cite a symbol even a gnat or something smaller. (*Quran,* II,20).

As Iranian genius developed over the centuries, so did the higher levels of the concept of fire take stronger hold. Fire speaks through light. Light is hidden in the potentiality of fire and it is light which is expressed to us in fire.

There were two types of people described by fire and light in relation to the created world. The Companion of Fire is one who reaches a stage where desires and error are negated and thereby the self is negated because fire consumes the thing in question and then consumes itself. The Companion of Light is one who has reached a stage where he has found eternal life, for light bestows being.

Other traditional expressions for the relationship of fire and light as they relate to the faith of the Muslim is seen in the following concepts: Knowlege of Certainty, Eye of Certainty and Truth of Certainty. Conceiving of fire as truth, the Knowledge of Certainty belongs to one whose knowledge of fire comes from having heard fire described – for instance, those who heard the words of Moses concerning the Burning Bush. The Eye of Certainty belongs to one whose knowledge of fire comes from seeing the light of the flames. Truth of Certainty belongs to one whose knowledge of fire comes from having been burned and consumed in it.

The growth of the concept and its many levels of interpretation are expressed in a story from Rumi's *Masnavi*:

> A priest brought an idol and placed it next to a funeral pyre. Whoever refused to bow before the idol was thrown into the fire. As it would be, a woman and her child were about to pass the idol. When she refused to bow before the idol, the priest threw her child into the blazing fire. The woman, terrified, was about to recant her faith when the child, amidst the flames, cried out, "I am not dead. Come in, Mother. I am happy here although I am in the midst of the fire. Fire is a spell that binds the eye for the sake of screening the truth. In reality, it is Divine Compassion which has appeared from the world of the Unseen. Come in, Mother," the child called again. "Come and see the evidence of God so that you might behold the delight of God's elect. Come in," she continued, "and see water that has the semblance of fire; come away from a world which is really fire and only has the semblance of water. Come in and see the mysteries of Abraham who in fire found cypress and jasmine. I saw only death at the time of my birth from you; great was my dread of separation from you. But when I was born, I escaped from the narrow prison of the womb into a world of pleasant air and beautiful color. Now," the child continued, "I deem the earthly world to be like the womb, since in this fire I have seen such peace: in this fire I have seen a world wherein every atom possesses the life-giving breath of Jesus. It is a world apparently existent but it has no permanence. Come in, Mother," the child beseeched, "by the right of motherhood; see how this fire has no fierceness. Come in, Mother, for felicity is come; come; come in, Mother, do not let fortune slip from thy hand. You have seen the power of the priest, now come and see the power of the grace of God. It is only out of pity that I call you here for, indeed, my rapture is such that I care not for you. Come in and call the others as well for the King has spread out a feast within the fire. O true believers," the child called out, "come in, all of you: other than this sweetness, all is torment. Oh, come in, all of you, like moths; come into this fortune which has a hundred springtimes."
>
> As the child cried amidst the multitude, the souls of the people were filled with awe. After that, men and women alike, beside themselves, cast themselves into the fire, without custodian, without being dragged, for the love of the friend, because from Him is the sweetening of every bitterness.

> Finally the king's guards were holding back the people, saying, "Do not enter the fire!" The priest, covered with shame and dismay, became sorry and sick at heart because the faith of the people had grown more ardent, more loving and more willing to suffer the mortification of the body. Thanks be to God, the devil's plot caught him in its toils. Thanks be to God, the devil saw himself disgraced. The shame he had been inflicting upon the believers was all accumulated upon the visage of the priest. He who was busy rending the garment of honor and integrity of the people found his own garment rent while they remained unhurt.

This story illustrates the fire of love and faith and in passing refers us to this world which is seemingly light though in reality, in comparison to the world the child had entered, it is darkness.

Darkness and light are pairs of created forms most often expressed in Iranian philosophy and literature. Natural and immediate self-expressions of a root experience of truth, the Iranian view sees light as that which brings all things to birth and darkness as the potential of this creative spirit. It is essentially a play between light and dark – everything and nothing; but, paradoxically, this reverses itself in the invisible world. For then the world as we see it is all darkness and shadow, nothingness in comparison to the light which resides in the world beyond forms.

The world beyond forms holds a dilemma before man, as expressed by the tenth-century Iranian theologian and mystic Ghazali:

> The difficulty of knowing God is therefore due to brightness; He is so bright that men's hearts have not the strength to perceive it. There is nothing brighter than the sun, for through it all things become manifest; yet if the sun did not go down by night, or if it were not veiled by reason of the shadow, no one would realize that there is such a thing as light on the face of the earth. Seeing nothing but colors, they would say that nothing more exists. However, they have not realized that light is a thing outside colors, the colors becoming manifest through it; they have comprehended light through its opposite . . . He is hidden by His very brightness.

Fire, love, faith, light – simple words with profound implications when one searches out their physical properties, their psychic forms and spiritual meaning. It is no wonder that Iran today finds itself blessed with such traditions.

Laleh Bakhtiar

FIRE آتش ENERGY REVEALED

The story of man may be told in the way he has learned to control and convert various types of energy. The history of cultural, economic and technological development is, in effect, the history of the interaction between man and his environment, and without energy such interaction would not have been possible.

At some stage of prehistory man first learned to use fire. He used it to prepare his food and heat his home. In the centuries that followed, he developed ways to harness fire as well as wind and water. In some regions, wood fire was used in the manufacture of bricks, which proved to be a vast improvement over the sun-drying technique previously practiced. Around the thirtieth century B.C., wood was burned in the process of turning limestone into mortar, and in the production of glazed and enameled pottery.

As far back as the twenty-fifth century B.C., crude oil was used in the west and southwest of Iran for heating and illumination. Petroleum and some of its compounds were also used for painting, waterproofing and as mortar.

Energy and fuel played a predominant role in the development of Iranian civilization, both in technology and art; in the manufacture of metal objects, ceramics and glassware. Other technological innovations of cultural and artistic importance ranged from the building of windmills to the production of steel.

As travel became more widespread, many Iranian cultural and technological developments were introduced to the West, resulting in further developments which led to the industrial revolution.

The industrial revolution resulted in a demand for more efficient fuels. Coal was initially used, but it was soon realized that oil had many advantages, including its clean burning, the lack of ashes and the reduction in air pollution. Oil was also easier to extract, transport and handle; and the variety of compounds and by-products could be utilized. Oil soon became an essential element for a technology-based society and its consumption continued to increase rapidly.

In the present age of technology, the demand for oil is still growing. The consumption of oil rose from 26 percent of the total world energy in 1937, to 59 percent in 1960, and to 68 percent in 1975, reaching the phenomenal amount of about 89 million barrels per day.

Iran has taken a leading role in the supply of this commodity to the world industrial market. It is now exporting over five million barrels of oil per day, being the second-largest oil-exporting country in the world. Iran has about 10 percent of the world's total reserves of oil, mostly located in the southwestern part of the country in the states of Khuzestan, Fars and along the shores of the Persian Gulf.

٢٠٣٣
٢٠٣١

These and other factors have given Iran leadership status in setting the oil policy. Iran's effect on international dealings has been well recognized, especially in connection with the recent energy crisis.

The oil policy is, however, a purely economic one. It is a projection of the need to increase revenues from the oil sector for the timely implementation of Iran's development programs and to sustain the country's economic growth.

The modern history of oil in Iran goes back to 1908 when Iran became the first country in the East to establish its own oil industry. In that year, oil sprang from a 1,100-foot well at Masjed-e-Soleyman to an altitude of fifty feet above the drilling tower. This was just the beginning of the vast development of a nationwide industry, and it was followed by many important events, such as the nationalization of the oil industry in 1951, the foundation of the National Iranian Oil Company (NIOC), and the acquisition of full control over oil production and pricing. NIOC is now one of the largest companies in the world, operating on an international basis, and is in charge of the entire operation: refining, transportation and distribution of oil. With its staff of 42,000, NIOC is involved in the production of oil from over 350 wells, amounting to about 6.5 million barrels of crude oil per day. A large portion of it is pumped through thousands of kilometers of pipes to the huge export loading bases in the Persian Gulf and Khark Island, and it is shipped to the international market with an Iranian fleet having the capacity of nearly 1.3 million tons. The company has also established a widespread network of pipelines and pumping stations for transporting and distributing various oil products throughout the country. At the moment there are four oil refineries and one distillery station in operation and more are to be established in the near future, which will produce a variety of oil by-products amounting to 7,000 barrels per day.

The National Iranian Oil Company has also invested in the construction of oil refineries and in the refinery projects in other countries. Furthermore, plans have been launched to increase NIOC refineries and distribution operations abroad.

Iran's oil industry produced over one-quarter of the Gross National Product (GNP) and contributed about half of the national budget in the year 1975.

Despite the affluence the oil industry has brought to the country, it cannot be depended on indefinitely. The oil supply can be depleted very fast, even in a period less than a generation. On the other hand, as with any other natural resource, oil belongs to the entire nation, including future generations. Investing oil revenues in industries that ensure future income is the best means of safe-guarding the share of future generations in this natural wealth. For this reason, Iran has sought to diversify its economy into a multi-sector infrastructure by channeling oil revenues into development programs and industrialization. This will also raise the nation's standard of living to the level of a developed society. The five-year development plans, four of which have already been completed, have resulted in the expansion of various sectors, including agriculture, industry and mining. The Fifth Development Plan has turned its attention appreciably to social-welfare projects. As a result of the drastic shift in the price of oil in 1973, the Fifth Development Plan could no longer meet the needs of Iran's changing society, either in its objectives and programs, or in its guidelines and policies. Therefore, basic steps for the revision of the plan were taken in 1974.

In the revised version of the plan, some of the limitations were removed due to the increase in oil revenues. The new Fifth Plan provides for total fixed investments of 4,634 billion rials. Of this, the public sector will account for 66 percent and the private sector for the remainder. The total fixed investment by the public sector amounts to 2,619 billion rials, which the government will invest directly, and a further 445 billion rials of investment which will be used by state-owned public enterprises. Not reflected in this figure is the sum of 471.8 billion rials set aside for current needs, as against fixed development expenditures, and a further 229 billion rials that will be transferred from the public to the private sector through the banking system in the form of loans.

Iran's policy in developing its technology and industry is based on a desire for permanent progress. It must therefore seek the latest achievements in technology. The crucial and most sensitive factor is the choice to make in this regard, and also the procedure to adopt for such a transfer of technology. Iran will have to be selective and employ methods which suit local needs and possibilities. Furthermore, in regard to the technology transfer, the aim should not be to acquire technology merely by importing machines, equipment and skills. The policy is to develop Iran's national technology on the basis of the country's natural and human resources in order to meet its cultural and social needs.

Iran's recent movement into modern economic development can be divided into two phases. The first stage, going back to the fifties, was a period of building dams, roads and railroads, in which investment in public and private enterprise received the highest priority. Such investments provided the first building-blocks for the developing country. The second stage, which started in the early sixties, was a period of establishing an industrial base designed to change the traditional image of the nation's economy. It was in this phase that the industrialization process spread to different regions of the country, and nationwide industries such as steel, copper, petrochemicals, motor vehicles and agricultural machinery were established.

Iran has experienced a rapid growth in her economy over the past decade. The average growth rate of the Gross National Product has been about 16 percent per annum, and Per Capita Income (PCI) has now reached 110 thousand rials.

Iran is now verging on self-sufficiency in the production of consumer goods. Some examples are air conditioners, gas stoves, television and radio sets, refrigerators, water heaters, electric bulbs and appliances, telephone receivers, tires and tubes, canned fruit and vegetables, paints, vegetable oil, detergents, cotton and nylon yarn and textiles, cigarettes and footwear. However, at this stage emphasis is shifting from consumer goods to capital goods and heavy industry. Special importance is being attached to the development of hydrocarbons (chemicals and petrochemicals) and the steel industry. The development of agriculturally based industries (to increase food production and raise rural incomes) and consumer and durable goods industries is also being encouraged in the Fifth Plan. The plan is paying considerable attention to the industries that are regarded as necessary for meeting educational requirements. The total fixed investment in the industrial sector in the course of Iran's Fifth Plan has been projected at 780 billion rials, public investment accounting for 277 billion rials, and 503 billion rials for private investment.

Iran had to import all her steel until the large Aryamehr steel mill near Esfahan started operating in 1973. Although development of its steel industry began as early as 1930, and construction of a plant was started near Karaj, World War II interrupted shipment of the equipment. Finally in 1966 a contract was signed for the installation of the first steel mill near Esfahan, with a capacity of 4 million tons.

Today this steel mill forms the core of a large industrial complex that stretches as far as Kerman. In Esfahan there are about a dozen large production units. The most important is the blast furnace with a capacity of 1,033 cubic meters producing 1,600 tons of cast iron daily. Work is now in progress on the second blast furnace with an even larger capacity, which would raise production to 1.9 million tons annually. By 1980 the total capacity of the plant in Esfahan will be further increased to 4 million tons, and to 6 million tons in 1983. At present, the steel production units in Esfahan consist of two converters and a casting unit, which overall produce 550,000 tons of steel annually as primary materials for the rolling mills. Other machinery is also provided for the production of steel rods, steel bands, angle iron, channels, profiles, rails, reinforcement bars and rolled steel.

The National Iranian Steel Industries Corporation is another industrial complex. Its five steel mills, with a total capacity of 10 million tons of steel per year, will be going into full operation over the next four years. Such steel mills use direct reduction (gas) processing, and the construction of the first plant situated in Ahvaz is almost completed. Initially, this plant will produce 2.5 million tons of sponge iron and 1.5 million tons of steel per year. The construction of the second plant, which will produce some 3 million tons of steel per year, is already under way in Bandar Abbas. This is the first plant to produce both cold and hot rolled steel sheets, and 40 percent of its production has been earmarked for export. The next direct reduction (gas) steel mill is being planned at Esfahan, with an annual capacity of 1.2 million tons, and most of its products will be for structural use. The fourth mill, to be established at Kangan, will produce 2.5 million tons of sheets and ingots mainly for export. The National Iranian Steel Industries Corporation is also jointly involved in the construction and operation of a plant which will annually produce some 220,000 tons of special steel to be used for steel parts, tools and springs.

The coal for the Aryamehr steel mill is provided by the Ravar mines near Kerman, Neyshabur in Khorasan and several mines in the Alborz Mountains. The mill obtains its iron ore mostly from the Cheghart mines at Bafq, which have an estimated iron-ore reserve of nearly 150 million tons. However, National Iranian plants are to be supplied with iron ore from the Golgohar mines close to Sirjan – which have an estimated iron-ore reserve of nearly 200 million tons and will be able to supply some five million tons of ore a year.

Iran's petrochemical activity started in 1961 with the installation of a modest-sized plant for the manufacture of fertilizer at Marvdasht, near the city of Shiraz. In 1975 the National Petrochemical Company had five main petrochemical complexes producing close to one and a half million tons annually of ammonia, phosphate, fertilizers, soda ash and nitric and sulphuric acid.

The decision to move ahead rapidly with the development of Iran's petrochemical industry is a result of a conviction that the real value of oil does not lie in its use as a primary source of energy. Currently less than five percent of the world's hydrocarbons are employed as petrochemical raw materials.

Iran recently reached a joint agreement with some foreign investors on financing of a giant petrochemical complex plant at Bandar Shahpur. Under the agreement, Iran and the other parties will contribute some 140 billion rials in the form of equal participation in the project. Besides other industrial activities, this project, to be owned and operated on a 50-50 basis, represents a major step toward the realization of Iran's intention of rechanneling her oil resources into petrochemicals.

Some 19,000 persons are expected to participate in the construction of the Bushehr Petrochemical installation, and over 3,500 technicians will be involved in its operation. The complex will be composed of three separate divisions. The first unit will produce sodium chloride using 400,000 tons of salt annually extracted from the Persian Gulf. The second unit is a crack unit for the production of olefins, including ethylene and propylene, and the third unit will produce aromatics.

For the implementation of this project and the accommodation of construction, technical and support crews, the National Petrochemical Company has laid plans for the construction of a city of 50,000 inhabitants, as well as the expansion of railroad facilities, airports, schools, hospitals and recreation facilities. In preparation for such a project, the National Petrochemical Company has also launched a special training program to meet the needs for specialized skills and technicians. A major bottleneck in this respect – as in other highly sophisticated technologies – is the lack of sufficient infrastructure.

Iran started motor vehicle assembly some ten years ago with initial delivery of 7,000 cars a year. During the past decade an appreciable amount of expansion and improvement has occurred in the industry. Iran assembled and/or manufactured 115,000 motor vehicles during 1975-76. The Iran National Plant produced 60 percent of Iran's total automobile products. The rest was produced during the same period by General Motors, Jeep, Morattab, Citröen, Zamyad, Iran Kaveh, Leyland Motors, Mazda and Khodrowsazan.

Another important development in industrialization was the creation of the Industrial Development and Renovation Organization of Iran in 1967. This organization was to act as the coordinator of government participation in all phases of industry. By 1976, 89 companies were under their auspices.

During 1975-76 the Tabriz tractor assembly plant delivered about 10,000 tractors, and production will be increased 80 percent by 1980. These tractors range from 40 to 80 horsepower and will serve the country's agricultural projects which are in need of some 120,000 units.

The Tabriz machine tool plant is engaged in the production of drilling equipment, water pumps and electric pumps, with a capacity of 80,000 tons per year. An expansion project is under way to produce diesel engines, presses, lift trucks, compressors, corundum and special tools. The Arak Machine Manufacturing Company manufactures boilers, mine wagons, transport equipment and pressure tanks with an annual capacity of about 30,000 tons.

165

166

167

168

169

170

Due to the developments that are taking place, Iran has adopted an energy policy which, on the one hand, is to satisfy the ever-increasing demands for energy use and, on the other, to direct the energy demand of the country into appropriate channels with regard to national resources and future demands. Efforts are under way for the development of a twenty-year master energy plan which provides for:

(1) reduced dependence on crude oil as a source of fuel, and increased dependence on natural gas, particularly as a replacement for middle distillate crude products;
(2) rapid installation of large nuclear stations;
(3) maximum tapping of hydroelectric potential;
(4) rapid development in the use of solar energy and other non-conventional energy sources;
(5) increased emphasis on research and development in areas concerning energy technology; and
(6) increased efficiency in energy resource utilization.

However, a short-term energy plan calls for the rapid expansion of nationwide power-generating capacity through the installation of nuclear and hydroelectric facilities. During the Fifth Development Plan the total electricity-generation capacity is in the range of five thousand megawatts, with hydro sources providing 30 percent; steam, about 35 percent; and gas turbines, 25 percent. The estimation of electrical energy consumption for the Eighth Plan, which is to begin in 1988, is in the range of 34,000 megawatts, scheduled to be generally available from nuclear plants, hydro sources, steam and gas, turbines and other sources.

Besides expansion of electrical power generation, the installation of widespread transmission lines and distribution facilities is under way. The purpose is not only to provide sufficient electricity for the industrial sector and the conventional energy consumers in the cities, but also to feed almost every village and small rural community in the country through a nationwide grid system.

Iran's rapid economic growth is due mainly to industrial expansion. Such growth requires guaranteed sources of energy with rapidly increasing capability to keep up with rising energy consumption. Energy from oil can no longer be the ultimate solution. An end is almost in sight to the continuous growth of oil production in Iran, as well as in other countries in the area, and by 1985 oil production from present reserves is unlikely to keep pace with world demand. In addition, with trends in Iran's policy to reserve oil primarily for export or for use as the feedstock of her petrochemical industries, some other forms of energy must be sought.

One such source of energy is nuclear power. The decision to initiate a large-scale nuclear program was made in March 1974. Some months later Iran's Atomic Energy Organization was set up and commissioned to plan and implement all projects related to peaceful uses of nuclear energy. The organization is now in the process of installing four pressurized water reactors. The first two units at Bushehr, each with a generating capacity of 1,200 megawatts, are scheduled for 1981 and 1982; and the last two units, each with 900 megawatts, are due for 1983 and 1984. Locating the reactors has been a primary concern for Iran. The reasons are numerous. Nuclear reactors require a substantial amount of water for cooling purposes. Each 1,200-megawatt unit, for example, requires about 200,000 cubic meters of water every hour. Thus, reactors cannot be situated in Iran's arid zone. Another consideration is the availability of sufficient port facilities to unload the massive reactors, and appropriate overland or water routes for transportation of the equipment to the installation sites. Population density, earthquake frequency and intensity are other main conditions that need to be studied to determine locations with minimum hazards. On the basis of these considerations, sites have been selected along the Persian Gulf, the Caspian Sea and the Karun River. In addition, for reactors themselves, measures must be taken to gain access to adequate and ensured sources of uranium, as well as uranium-enrichment plants. Besides the agreements with some foreign countries calling for joint exploratory activities in search of atomic fuel in those areas, and for joint ownership in uranium-enrichment factories, the search for uranium deposits in Iran is also in progress.

With Iran's oil-production capacity almost leveling off, energy developments are now increasingly being centered on natural gas. Iran's rich natural gas reserves place her second in the world, according to existing data. Gas plays a major role in economic expansion, for domestic and industrial consumption as well as the manufacture of petrochemicals, with sizable quantities for export both by pipeline and in the form of liquefied gas.

Most of the associated gas, unavoidably produced in conjunction with crude oil, is flared, but Iran has tried to utilize this valuable form of energy. In 1970 flaring in Iran as a whole was reduced to 60 percent of the total 95 million cubic meters of associated gas produced. By 1980, it is hoped that nearly all the gas produced will be used in one form or another. Recently some huge gas fields were discovered in Iran. The National Iranian Gas Company, as a subsidiary of the National Iranian Oil Company, estimates total associated and non-associated gas reserves at 9 to 20 trillion cubic meters, of which some 3 to 10 trillion cubic meters are located offshore in the Persian Gulf.

Iran's first major gas project was the construction of the Iranian gas trunkline to the Soviet Union, which was connected in 1970. About 2.3 million cubic meters was exported and this has been increased to about 35 million cubic meters. This pipeline also provides gas for cities along its route. In the final stage of the project, which is nearing completion, the capacity will be raised to 53 million cubic meters, allowing about 20 million cubic meters for internal consumption. At the same time, domestic consumption of natural gas is provided by liquefied gas produced at the various oil refineries. This is expected to increase from 221,000 tons in 1973 and 322,000 tons in 1975 to 540,000 tons in 1979.

Gas is processed in the Agha Jari, Marun and Ahvaz oil fields, where natural gas liquids are first extracted and piped to the Bandar Mahshahr refinery for separation into some 35,000 barrels per day of propane, butane and natural gasoline for export. The lean gas from the recovery units is sent to the Bid Boland gas refinery for cleaning and pumping the gas into the trunkline. Associated gas is also being used as feedstock for the petrochemical industry. The petrochemical plant at Shiraz uses about half a million cubic meters of gas per day coming from the Gachsaran oil field, and the petrochemical unit in Abadan uses 300,000 cubic meters of gas as feedstock. The Bandar Shapur plant, on the other hand, is estimated to utilize some 7 million cubic meters of gas mainly from the Masjed-e-

Soleyman oil field; and 5 million cubic meters of associated gas is being used by the Khark Chemical Company, which is a 50-50 joint venture between the National Petrochemical Company and foreign investors.

The ultimate source of energy available to man is the sun, the huge thermonuclear furnace that supplies the earth with heat and light. Our food and fuel supplies have been made possible by the sun through the photosynthetic combination of water and atmospheric carbon dioxide in growing plants. The remains of plants and animals – which themselves are fed with plants buried in swamps and seas millions of years ago – were transferred into the fossil fuels: coal, oil and natural gas. Man has developed the capacity to use such forms of energy. His cultural and economic achievements have been due mainly to vast industrial developments made possible by cheap and abounding fossil fuels. The limited sources of fuel and the growth of world population have created an imbalance in regard to fuel energy. The stored supplies of fossilized fuels will soon be consumed and plans must be made to develop substitutes.

Solar energy requires neither transportation of fuel nor distribution of electricity because it can be produced in small electrical converters wherever the electricity is to be used for heating and cooling. The use of sunlight directly to heat water and air, and indirectly to heat and cool houses, food and water, has long been practiced in Iran. Drastic variation in the climate, especially in the dry and hot regions in the south and southeast of Iran, is reflected in the architecture in those regions. The city of Yazd is a typical example, with wind towers standing on roofs, providing conditioned circulation of air by channeling the desirable flow. The air-circulation system in the bazaar at Yazd is designed to render a favorable and natural flow of air.

In a worldwide effort for modern utilization of the sun as an ultimate and lasting source of energy, Iran is doing its share. As a vast country with an abundance of sunlight, it is trying to develop the relevant technology within the next twenty years. Research centers have been established to make full use of solar energy in all its applications – heating, cooling, providing mechanical and electrical energy – and to facilitate local and regional needs and possibilities. The Solar Energy Laboratory at Pahlavi University and the Materials and Energy Research Center (MERC) are the two major research and development centers. MERC is involved in providing a base in Iran from which the latest technological advancements in solar energy may be evaluated, their potential benefits for Iran quantified, and Iranian research and development on this vital project undertaken. The main demands for solar energy are in the areas of domestic heating and cooling (including cooking, drying and refrigeration), industrial utilization of high-temperature heat, electricity generation (direct and indirect) and fuel for transportation. The aim is to design a system compatible with the climatic, social and economic conditions of the country.

Reza Hashemian

BOOK FIVE

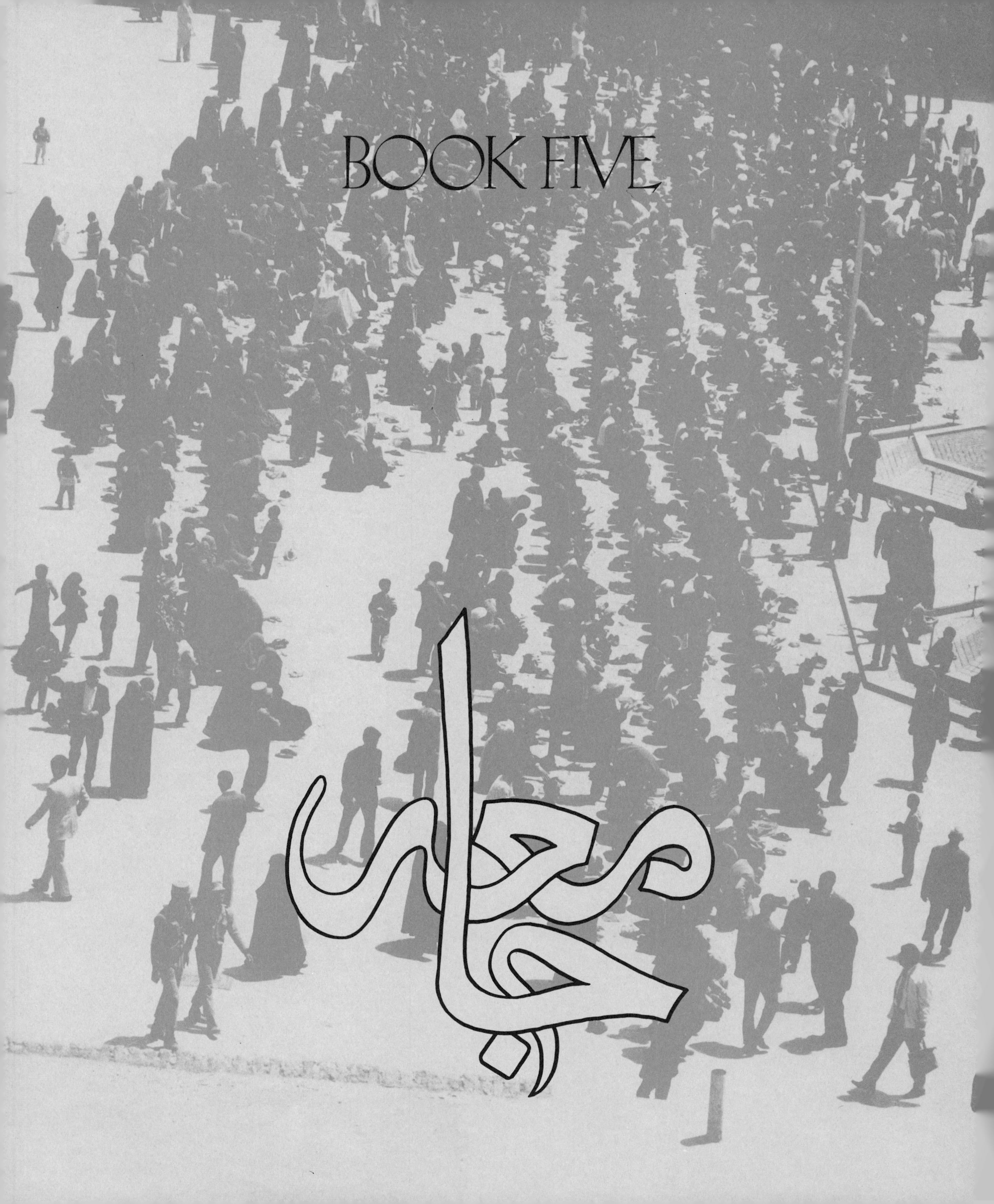

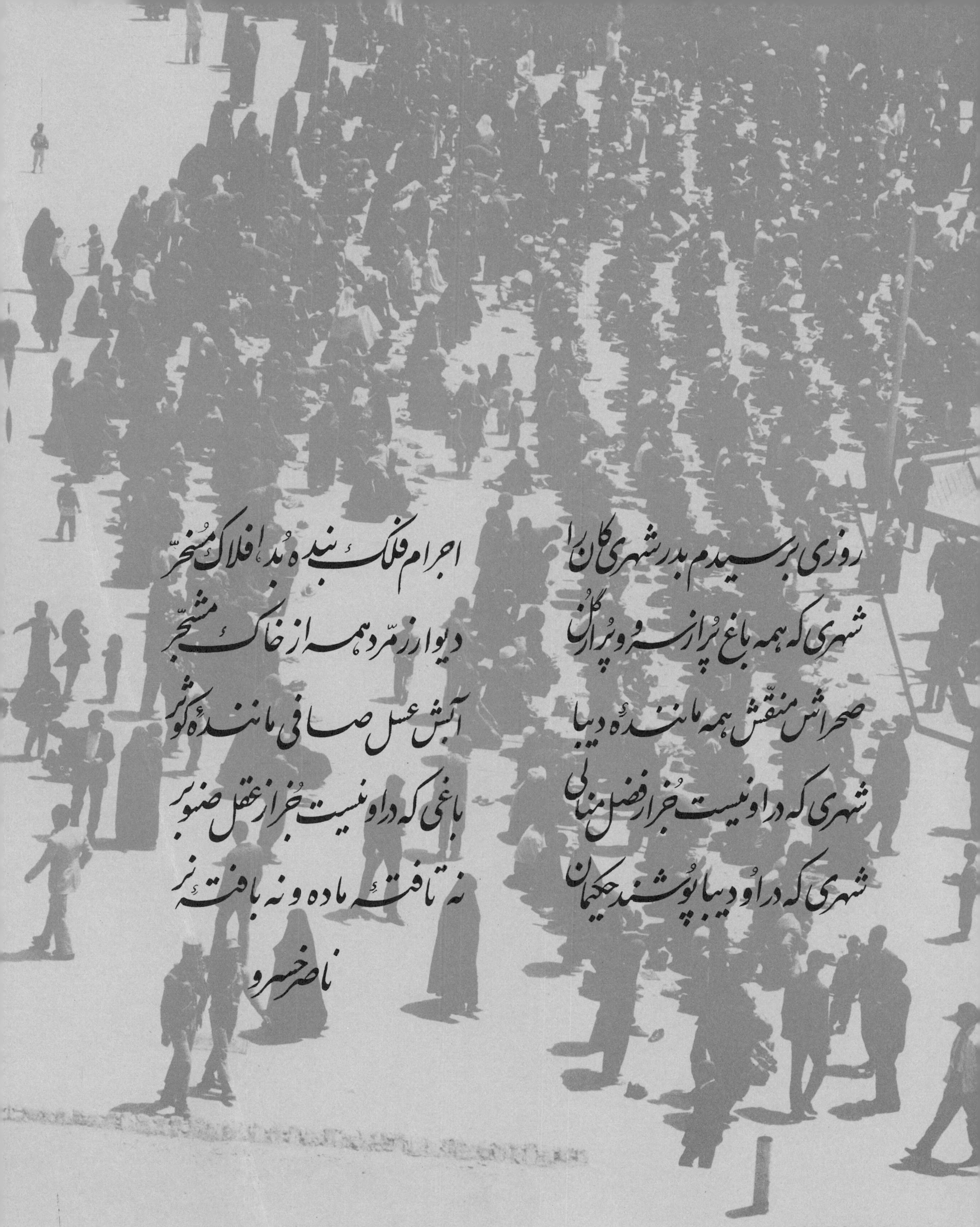

روزی برسیدم بدر شهری کان را — اجرام فلک بنده بُد افلاک مسخّر
شهری که همه باغ پُر از سرو و پُر از گُل — دیوار ز مرّد همه از خاک مشجّر
صحراش منقّش همه مانندهٔ دیبا — آبش عسل صافی مانندهٔ کوثر
شهری که در او نیست جُز از فضل منالی — باغی که در او نیست جُز از عقل صنوبر
شهری که در او دیبا پوشند حکیمان — نه تافتهٔ ماده و نه بافتهٔ نر

ناصر خسرو

CAPTION FOLDOUT

 For notes to these plates, see pages 378 to 384

SPIRIT

176 Misty dawn light filters through a tree on the road to Ganj Nameh.

177 A young man prays in the garden of the Ebrahim Khan Madreseh, Kerman.

178 A mullah crosses a tiled courtyard at the shrine of Emam Reza, Mashhad.

179 Ritual metal standard and other regalia of the *tazieh* (passion play) in an exhibition held at Shiraz.

180 Moving performance of the *tazieh* of Hazrat Abbas.

181 A Zoroastrian priest reverently tends the sacred fire in the Yazd Fire Sanctuary.

182-185 Four images of Iran's rich Armenian heritage.

- 182 Qara Kilise, Church of Saint Thaddeus, near Maku.
- 183 Archmandrite Ashjian, Old Savior's Cathedral, New Jolfa, Esfahan.
- 184 Holy Mass celebrated at the Old Savior's Cathedral.
- 185 Tree-of-life in stone, Qara Kilise.

186 An ancient *Torah* inside the shrine of Queen Esther at Hamedan.

REVIVAL OF TRADITION

187 Tribal students dancing in the desert near their tent schools.

188 Light filters through stained-glass windows of a restored Safavid palace transformed into a museum at Qazvin.

189 A traditional storyteller entrances visitors to the Caravanserai Moshir at Shiraz.

190 Aerial view of the holy shrine of Emam Reza at Mashhad, showing extensive reconstruction of the entire shrine area.

191-202 A series of images showing the rich variety of traditional artistic and cultural expressions being revived and restored in Iran.

- 191 Tehran Rug Society exhibition.
- 192 Restoration of a Safavid bath, Esfahan.
- 193 Nineteenth-century house under repair, Tabas.
- 194 Bronze sculpture, Darius Hotel, Persepolis.
- 195 Modern statue from an ancient theme, Aryamehr Sports Complex, Tehran.
- 196 Wandering darvish, Esfahan.
- 197 Play rehearsal for the Tus Festival.
- 198 Traditional musicians in period costume.
- 199 Ministry of Culture and Art dance troupe.
- 200 Musicians, First Annual Festival of Popular Traditions, Esfahan.
- 201 Imperial Iranian Academy of Philosophy, Tehran.
- 202 Tomb of Ebn-e-Sina, Hamedan.

203 Restoration of the Hasht Behesht, a fabulous Safavid palace in Esfahan.

204 The poignant story of Farhad and Shirin cast in bronze outside the elegant tiled walls of Tehran's City Theater.

205 View across the gardens of the luxurious Shah Abbas Hotel in Esfahan, a restored caravanserai.

TRANSFORMATION

206 Aerial view of the Shahyad Circle, a green island at the western entrance to Tehran.

207-221 From department stores to a newspaper press—scenes of daily life in Iran.

- 207 Fruit and vegetable market.
- 208 Rudaki Hall banquet.
- 209 Shahanshahi Park.
- 210 Cloth shop window.
- 211 Gold chains hanging in a Yazd shop.
- 212 Teahouse.
- 213 Furniture store.
- 214 Fruit-juice stall.
- 215 Pars Department Store.
- 216 Rastakhiz Party congress.
- 217 Ecbatana housing development.
- 218 Diplomatic party.
- 219 Senate building.
- 220 Etelaat press.
- 221 Hyatt Regency Hotel near Chalus.

222-228 A frieze of new stadiums and the symmetry of massed stadium events.

- 222 Aryamehr Stadium, Tehran.
- 223 Farah Stadium, Tehran.
- 224-227 Celebrations for the birthday of the Shahanshah, Tehran.
- 228 Workers from the Paykan Automobile Factory.

229 Aerial view of the University of Tehran in the center of the capital.

230 New Hyatt Hotel, Tehran.

231 Rapidly expanding west Tehran.

232 Headquarters of the Rastakhiz Party, Tehran.

233-239 Tehran Museum of Contemporary Art—a dramatic new architectural form, and scenes from the opening of the museum.

240 Children photographed at a delightful recreational and camping center in the Niavaran section of north Tehran.

241-245 Scenes from the festivities of Azarbayejan Day and the Coronation.

AND A TIME FOR PLEASURE

SOCIETY

SOCIETY

SPIRIT

. . . Then one day I reached those city gates
where angels are servants, where planets and stars are slaves,
A garden of roses and pines girded round with walls
of emerald and jasper trees, set
in a desert of gold-embroidered silk, its springs
sweet as honey, the river of paradise;
a city which only Virtue can aspire
to reach, a city whose cypresses are like
the blades of Intellect, a city whose sages
wear brocaded robes woven of silk . . .

Naser Khosrow

◁ Pilgrims at the shrine of Emam Reza, Mashhad.

SPIRIT

As an aspect of the spirit pervading Iranian society, interfusion and the concept of unity upon which it is based serves as a process linking man to man. From this viewpoint Iranian society accepts the possibility of the multiplicity of forms whether expressions of the spirit or expressions of ethnic groups which form the total society.

The principle of interfusion occurs the moment when differentiation and distinction between self and non-self disappears. The interfusion which takes place at that moment is part of a larger concept known as *hamdami* – "breathing together," "con-spiration," or simply sympathy. It is a concept which applies to all of nature.

Hamdami is a state of being beyond form. It relates to the world of feeling and, as an aspect of the spirit of Iranian society, it eludes description, for it is the mystery which binds forms one to another. It is an expression for that which exists inwardly within all things.

The idea of mystery helps to explain the concept which can only be realized through an intellectual attitude where one opens oneself to essential reality. This attitude is not receptivity but pure act. Through spiritual acts, if performed in the presence of Divine Grace, one comes to know the world beyond form. But the concept only blossoms forth when all distinctions between self and non-self have been eliminated and then one becomes the mystery itself.

This mystery, this sympathetic "breathing together," is behind the idea of brotherhood, for when distinction and differentiation exist multiplicity prevails and one only comes to know the differences. Unity lies in sameness and the ability to realize sameness only occurs when an attitude of *hamdami* is present.

Hamdami is the sympathy which exists between all things. This sympathy can be perceived in two ways. The first is a motion of expansion from one's self to the selves of others. It is to move from egocentric consciousness to the consciousness of one's fellow man. An individual in this state expands his love in graduated quantities.

The second method, known as ontological experience, involves an identification and interfusion between the One and the many, of man and the universe.

The first is a measuring out of love and sympathy and this creates relations of nearness and remoteness. It is a rational type of sympathy.

The second method revolves around the primary source of love, the secret root and spirit of all love and compassion. It is a feeling which is arrived at intuitively but with it one realizes the essence of a thing and this realization is to have *hamdami*.

Mankind lives in the world of multiplicities in which the tendency is strongly toward retaining the multiplicities, the distinctions. The force of unity is hidden in the world of forms and requires active participation in order to be revealed, for an integration and interfusion to occur. When the hidden order is emphasized, it becomes the binding force between multiple centers and forms.

Islam, with its emphasis on the oneness of God – "There is no god if it be not God" – is open to all forms as long as the basic unity is not compromised.

Iran has played an important role in the development of Islamic civilization, at the same time integrating many aspects of its pre-Islamic past into Islam's universal perspective. By retaining their own identity, the Iranians were able to create a cultural center within Islam. One of the most important aspects of Islam is brotherhood and the flourishing of other cultural centers would but add to the brotherhood of mankind.

Within the Islamic viewpoint, it is a certain attitude toward brotherhood which essentially relates to society as a whole.

This attitude was expressed by the Prophet when he said: "Wilt thou then force men to believe when belief can come only from God?" Once a group of Christians visited the Prophet and he invited them to conduct their services in the mosque for "it is a place consecrated to God." In his charter to the people of Medina when he fled there from Mecca, it is reiterated: "The Jews ... and all others domiciled in Yathrib (Medina) shall . . . practice their religion as freely as the Muslims."

Islam sees its message as the reiteration of the message of Abraham which was to return to the Unity of God.

The Jewish people have a long and continuous history on the Iranian Plateau as well. This goes back to the time of Cyrus the Great who freed the Jews from Babylonian captivity, from whence they returned to Jerusalem to rebuild the temple. Darius paid for their religious rites from his treasury. The successor to Darius, Artaxerxes I, gave gifts and vessels for the temple ritual in Jerusalem to Ezra when he was leaving with 1,500 Jews.

In the Book of Ezra it is written:

> From the days of our fathers to this day we have been in great guilt ... we are bondmen, yet our God has not forsaken us in our bondage, but has extended to us his steadfast love before the kings of Persia, to grant us some reviving to set up the house of our God, to repair its ruins and to give us protection in Judea and Jerusalem.

Two active shrines sacred to Iran's Jewish community are the tombs of the Prophet Daniel at Shush, ancient Susa, and of Queen Esther, Jewish wife of an Achaemenian king, and her foster father Mordecai, at Hamedan.

At this time in Iran, the Achaemenian kings were followers of Zoroaster although it was not until some seven hundred years later that the Zoroastrian religion became the official religion of Iran, which it remained until the seventh century A.D. and the advent of Islam.

Within Zoroastrianism, the central concept which concerns society as a whole is its ethical principles. In Mazdaism, as it is also called, the choice is twofold. A Gathic passage tells us:

> The two primordial Minds that were heard as Twins are the Excellent and the Evil, in thoughts, words and deeds; and in between these two the wise, not the foolish, have made their choice . . . And when these two Minds met, they first established Life and Non-Life and that, at the end, the worst existence would be that of the followers of the Lie and the best spiritual life would be that of the followers of the Truth. Between these two Minds, the followers of the Lie choose the acting of the Worst One, but the Most Holy Spirit, who covers himself with the firm stones of heaven as his robes, chooses the Truth, and those who desired to satisfy Ahura Mazda through righteous actions did the same.

Within the Zoroastrian world view, fire was a gift to mankind from Ahura Mazda, the Supreme One. It symbolized a precious offering through which one could realize the nature and essence of the Wise Lord.

Priests initiated according to ancient ritual still keep the sacred fires fed as they follow strict rules in performing their duties. Boys are invested with a sacred shirt (the *sudra*), and the sacred thread (the *kusti*), a three-ply cord, worn as a girdle symbolizing good thought, good words and good deeds.

During Sasanian times other religions took root, although Zoroastrianism remained the official religion.

The Nestorian Christians were expelled from the West and sought refuge in Iran. They were free to establish schools and centers throughout the country.

Within Christianity and the special forms which persisted in Iran, there are basically two groups which have had almost two thousand years of history in this cultural climate: the Nestorians of the East Syriac church and the Armenians, who at an early date took up the form of the Gregorian church.

The Nestorians resemble the Orthodox church more closely than the Roman Catholic in both doctrine and ritual. Their priests marry and they grant the Pope a primacy of honor only. The liturgical language is Syriac; and although they do not decorate their churches to the extent of other Orthodox groups, they place special emphasis upon the cross. Their seven sacraments differ from other Christians in that they combine baptism and confirmation and omit unction. Instead, they make a sacrament of the crossing of oneself, a particular one being the holy leaven. This leaven is used in making bread and it originates from the leaven at the Last Supper.

The head of the church is known as the Patriarch of the East. Perhaps their most important distinction from other Christian groups is their denial that the Virgin Mary is the Mother of God although they place her in great honor.

The Armenians represent an independent Christian church although it too is closer to the Orthodox church than the Roman Catholic. It differs from the Orthodox church in certain rituals as, for example, the use of unleavened bread at mass. The priests are allowed to marry and the mass is performed in Armenian.

In the sixteenth century, during the time of the Safavid kings, the official religion of Iran became the Shi'ite sect of Islam. It is in the context of Shi'ism that Iran thrives as the culture continues to express both joy and sorrow.

The expression of cultural sorrow comes once a year during the month of Moharram at the time of the martyrdom of Emam Hoseyn. Based upon the moon calendar, the seasons change from year to year. It is a time for realizing fully the tragedy of mankind in the paradox of being near to and, at the same time, separate from God. The observance of the martyrdom is marked by passion plays *(tazieh)* throughout the country.

The concept of the future savior is another important aspect of Iranian life. It is believed that the Twelfth Emam went into occultation and will return at the end of the world. The birthday of the Twelfth Emam is marked with joy and happiness throughout the country.

Shrines located all over Iran are important places of pilgrimage. Tombs of Shi'ite Emams, their descendants or Sufi saints, range from a small, domed chamber in some remote area of the country to the holiest center for pilgrimage, the shrine of the Eighth Emam, Emam Reza, in Mashhad. This shrine is connected to a school for the education of religious leaders as well as a library and museum. Mosques serve as gathering places, and in large cities they are found within the bazaar, the center of the daily life of the people. Larger mosques serve an educational function by providing centers of learning. Villages and small towns use the mosque space itself for this purpose.

Each large city also contains a Khaneqah or Sufi center where prayers, invocation and special dances are performed, for in the Islamic tradition, knowledge is to be gleaned from books as well as from interaction with people.

The most important rituals of the Iranians are the same as their Muslim neighbors though they differ in some details. To the Muslim there are five pillars to follow, saying, "There is no god but God" and "Mohammad is the Prophet of God"; daily prayers, fasting, pilgrimage and remitting the special religious tax.

The spirit lives within this context of Iranian society, and although it assumes many forms, it is the mystery which binds divergent cultures and religions into a totality of peoples. Within this view of mystery lies the principle of *hamdami* as a force existing within all things. The word *hamdami* was first used by Jalaleddin Rumi in the twelfth century A.D.

> To speak the same tongue is a kinship and affinity; a man (when he is) with those in whom he cannot confide is like a prisoner in chains.
>
> Oh, many are the Indians and Turks who speak the same tongue; oh, many the pair of Turks that are as strangers (to each other).
>
> Therefore the tongue of mutual understanding is different indeed: to be one in heart is better than to be one in tongue.

Laleh Bakhtiar

Surely, when I contemplate my own body, I see that it is beyond my power to make it grow or shrink, to ward off evil from it or attract to it the good; then do I know that my body has a Maker, and I acknowledge Him. But indeed I have seen the celestial spheres turn through His power, and the appearance of clouds, the whirling of the winds, the procession of sun, moon and stars. I have seen His wondrous and perfectly made waymarks, and this has made me testify that creation has a Creator, One Who Determines, One Who Produces.

Emam Reza

This I ask you, O Lord, answer me truly:
Who set the Earth in its place below, and the sky
among the clouds that it should not fall?
Who made the waters and the plants?
Who yoked the two steeds to wind and clouds?
Who, O Wise One, created the Good Mind?

Hymns of Zoroaster
AVESTA
Yasna 44:4

The Black Church, Qara Kilise, of Saint Thaddeus in Azarbayejan, is the principal religious shrine for the world's Armenian Christians, visited by thousands of pilgrims each year. Its history is closely bound up with that of the Parthian and Sasanian dynasties of Iran as well as the lives of the two central Armenian religious patriarchs: Saint Thaddeus and Saint Gregory, the Illuminator, credited with the Christianizing of Armenia.

According to tradition, an early Armenian king, Agbar, who lived during the time of Christ, suffered from a dread disease. On hearing of the miracles performed by Jesus Christ, he sent envoys to invite him to Armenia. Jesus sent Thaddeus, supposed to have been another name for Jude, the brother of Saint James, who cured and converted Agbar. Under Agbar's successor, Thaddeus was martyred and buried on the plains of Ardaz in Azarbayejan.

The Elevation, which is when the priest raises the Chalice in the eyes of the congregation, brings to mind the Ascension of Christ into heaven to "sit with the Father," as the prayer of Elevation indicates. It shows the highest point of the upward procession of the life of the soul.

The priest turns to the congregation and raises the sacrament in the sight of the people and says aloud, "In holiness let us taste of the holy and precious body and blood of our Lord and Savior Jesus Christ, who, having come down from heaven, is distributed amongst us."

From the Divine Liturgy of the Armenian Church

182

183

184

185

Now in Shushan the palace there was a certain Jew, whose name was Mordecai, the son of Jair, the son of Shimei, the son of Kish, a Benjamite;

Who had been carried away from Jerusalem with the captivity which had been carried away with Jeconiah, king of Judah, whom Nebuchadnezzar, the king of Babylon, had carried away.

And he brought up Hadassah, that is, Esther, his uncle's daughter: for she had neither father nor mother, and the maid was fair and beautiful; whom Mordecai, when her father and mother were dead, took for his own daughter.

So it came to pass, when the king's commandment and his decree was heard, and when many maidens were gathered together unto Shushan the palace, to the custody of Hegai, that Esther was brought also unto the king's house, to the custody of Hegai, keeper of the women....

So Esther was taken unto King Ahasuerus into his house royal in the tenth month, which is the month Tebeth, in the seventh year of his reign.

And the king loved Esther above all the women, and she obtained grace and favor in his sight more than all the virgins; so that he set the royal crown upon her head, and made her queen instead of Vashti.

Then the king made a great feast unto all his princes and his servants, even Esther's feast; and he made a release to the provinces, and gave gifts, according to the state of the king.

BOOK OF ESTHER
Chapter II, Verses 4-8, 16-18

SOCIETY

REVIVAL OF TRADITION

Traditions have remained strong on the Iranian Plateau throughout its long history. Despite war, strife, floods and earthquakes, the character of these traditions has persisted, surviving often in a hidden form only to be rediscovered and explored by later generations. Iran now finds itself rediscovering its past, which was necessitated by the rapid development toward modernization. For a time the present consumed the energies of the people, but now that the country is well on its way toward industrialization, traditions are being revived.

In the awakening and rediscovery of these traditions one faces the question, "What is tradition?" It defies easy definition for it is a process which forms part of a cultural continuity expressed through new methods and in a conscious search for its roots. Tradition is the vitalizing principle that exists within the life of the people, allowing the past to merge with the present and the future. It can be expressed by an act as simple as greeting another, while at the same time it is a complex of attitudes, beliefs, and conventions.

Traditions are rooted in the eternal principles beyond man. They relate to feelings transmitted through knowledge as well as art forms, for it is tradition which advances symbols and ideas within a culture. When one consciously or unconsciously encounters traditions and their symbolic expression, movement occurs which often leads to inspiration in all its forms. Symbolic forms of a tradition can just as well lead to meditation, dreaming, waiting and lingering, which correspond to memory, learning and wisdom.

Traditions have a stabilizing quality when they relate to quantitative time; when they speak to the creative spirit, they speak qualitatively. They are continually changing and within each change a new and different quality is assumed, but the principle remains constant.

Tradition relates to both will and conception. In the first instance, it centers on the intellectual ordering process which concerns society and the universe. In conception, it accepts the seed and allows it to grow. As the seed grows, it waits; it awaits the boiling, baking, germination and ripening until the process is completed; it awaits the birth of the fruit. It is in this state that symbolic forms are concerned with realization and birth.

Both aspects of tradition demand expression, and one must seek both will and conception in order to produce a new form. As one seeks to revive old traditions, new traditions take their place alongside them. In the state of continual change, the permanent must be sought so that order is preserved. There must be an exchange between past and present, will and conception, the revival of tradition and the acceptance of new expressions of those traditions.

191

192

193

194

195

196

197

198

199

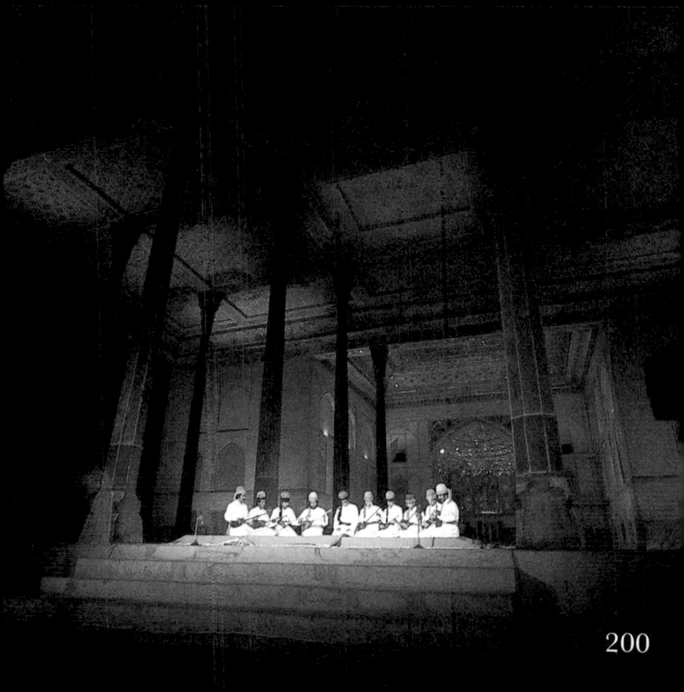
200

201

202

It is with this in mind that the revival of tradition flourishes in Iran, for without the understanding of the past, how can one know the present? When ignored, the cultural tree becomes barren, for the spirit is lost and the roots are not nourished.

The complementary aspect of tradition operates at three levels: physical, psychic and spiritual. At each level the resolution is in the form of an exchange. At the physical level, there is an exchange of sacrifice; at the psychic level, an exchange of symbols; and at the spiritual level, there is a transfer of principles so that what is usually termed "either/or" essentially becomes "and."

In the Iranian view, one not only appreciates the gateway – for example, in its physical presence – but also its non-being as passage through it. This exchange of being and non-being, positive and negative, is at the very foundation of both Iranian thought and art.

The circle is a universal symbol of heaven; the square, a symbol of earth. The use of these two forms in Iranian architecture, from a simple domed room to the space of the great Shah Mosque in Esfahan, reveals the concept of exchange. The square base is uplifted through the use of the circular dome, and the circular dome rests on the square base. The exchange is sacrifice of the totality of one or the other. The two unite to form aspects of both.

If the revival of traditions as forms existing in the past can unite with the present, expression of the great traditions of Iranian culture will once again flourish.

Classical Iranian Music

Historically, Iranian music has served as the basis for certain musical forms which were to develop from the Indian subcontinent in the east to the Arabian peninsula and as far as Spain in the west. These are forms capable of remarkable expansion of expression.

Classical music in modern Iran has a particular character which can be seen in instruments such as the *tar* and the *setar*. The first means string and the other means three strings. The *tar* is a double-bellied lute with a long neck and six strings. It is played with a metal plectrum. It is used as both a solo instrument and as an accompaniment for singers. The *setar* is smaller, pear-shaped and has four strings. It is most often used as a solo instrument.

The *santur* is also very popular. A dulcimer, it is played with sticks. It most often has four strings in eighteen groups tuned in unison with a range of two and a half octaves.

When listening to classical Iranian music, one cannot forget the *ney* or reed flute. Pressed against the teeth, it has a lonely, burning tone which one can recall long after the last note has been played.

Two more instruments should be mentioned – the *kamancheh* and the *tombak*. The *kamancheh* is a small instrument most often with four strings. The *tombak* is a goblet drum.

Traditional Iranian music is based mostly on improvization within a given mode. There are seven major modes called *dastgah*, and five minor modes called *avaz*. Both have a special repertory of melodic ideas called *gusheh*.

An exchange within the arts of Iran appears most distinctly in the use of music as a religious accompaniment to poetry and dance. Musical modes are written in a circle divided into sections, and each section is identified with a color.

The exchange between permanence and change can perhaps best be seen in a musician's relationship to an established mode. The musician gives free range to his imagination, using his voice or instrument in such a way that a new work of art is created even though written by another without ever letting the mode be lost.

The *zurkhaneh* or "house of strength" is another example of exchange. A drummer sits on a tiger skin chanting poetry while men dance or wrestle.

Men sing at work and women hum while weaving. Masons sing as they pass bricks from hand to hand. Such workers are usually paid more, for productivity increases by such means.

Traditional Storytellers

The art of storytelling in Iran relates mainly to the recitation of the *Book of Kings* or *Shahnameh*, written in the tenth century A.D. by Ferdowsi. The poem tells the legends and historical narratives of Iran from the beginning of time until the seventh century A.D. when it became a Muslim country.

The *Book of Kings* has become a national legend. Written in 60,000 couplets, it took forty years to compose. The stories of the epic heroes in this great poem still live on within the Iranian culture. Every year a festival is held in Tus near Mashhad where traditional storytellers from all parts of Iran compete in this art.

Architecture

An awakening of traditional architecture is occurring in Iran. Faced with the onrush of new techniques and methods of building, a revival of past forms has become essential. Cities and towns are expanding at a rapid pace and only by the preservation of traditional architecture will new generations gain insight into their heritage.

A city was traditionally planned along the main route of the bazaar which wove naturally through an area depending upon available land. It often extended from city gate to city gate. Within this main branch were shops, caravanserais and bath houses. The needs of both residents and travelers were met in this central line of the city. The bazaar also served as the social, political and religious center of the city.

Iran is actively pursuing the renovation of architectural forms. Palaces are being restored and becoming available to the public as museums. Bath houses are being transformed; and isolated domed structures, where desert water was collected and kept cool, are being changed into theaters. Caravanserais, which served the traveler, are being restored for the same purpose, and the natural atmosphere proves to be more desirable than many hotels.

The most permanent feature of Iranian architecture is the garden. It is a symbol of Paradise and reflects the basic Iranian attitude toward life – the world is thereby excluded and the family cherished and protected. The land demands constant effort in order to be productive, so every flower and tree is valuable.

Traditional Philosophy

In the world of ideas, we encounter the strong revival of traditional philosophy. The establishment of the Imperial Iranian Academy of Philosophy, sponsored by Her Majesty, made possible a forum for the exchange of ideas. Iranians may come to know their vast heritage of philosophical works as well as the philosophies of other civilizations. With an awareness of their philosophical roots, they will be able to contribute new branches to the wealth of ideas so much a part of the nation.

The Iranians developed what came to be known as "Oriental Philosophy," a philosophy oriented to light. In the twelfth century A.D., Yahya Sohrewardi, in the light of the revelation of Islam, synthesized the previous philosophies of the Magi, Manichaeans and Mithraists. He also referred to Plato and Hermes in his great masterpiece, *The Wisdom of Illumination*, where he tells us:

> Although before the composition of this book I composed several summary treatises on Aristotelian philosophy, this book differs from them and has a method peculiar to itself. All of its material has not been assembled by thought and reasoning; rather, intellectual intuition, contemplation and ascetic practices have played a large role in it. Since our sayings have not come by means of rational demonstration but by inner vision and contemplation, they cannot be destroyed by the doubts and temptations of the skeptics. Whoever is a traveler on the road to truth is my companion and aid on this path. The procedure of the master of philosophy and *emam* of wisdom, the Divine Plato, was the same, and the sages who preceded Plato in time like Hermes, the father of philosophy, followed the same path. Since sages of the past, because of the ignorance of the masses, expressed their sayings in secret symbols, the refutations which have been made against them have concerned the exterior of these sayings, not their real intentions. And the illuminative wisdom, whose foundation and basis are the two principles of light and darkness as established by the Iranian sages like Jamasp, Farshadshur and Buzarjomehr, is among these hidden, secret symbols.

Conclusion

The revival of tradition in Iran continues. We have taken a glimpse at music, storytelling, architecture and the world of ideas, which the creative spirit is challenged to explore. The Iranian language should also be mentioned, as great strides have been taken toward strengthening it. The language which has survived through so many centuries of change now faces the challenge of western scientific information. The Iranian language, so rich in poetic and literary expressions, must now expand from within to be able to hold the new bodies of scientific expression. The Iranian language has been found to have great elasticity and it is within this framework that the effort at revival is directed.

Laleh Bakhtiar

SOCIETY TRANSFORMATION

It is far beyond the scope of this essay to deal with the entire history of Iran. However, Iranian society cannot be understood without an analysis of certain structural features of its long history, which may provide insight for a better appreciation of the present.

Iran, called the cradle of human civilization, represents a unique case in the history of mankind. As Arthur Upham Pope records, "Agriculture, metallurgy and the initial religious and philosophical ideas as well as the art of writing and the science of numbers and astrology and mathematics originated in the lands that today we call Middle East, and the origin of many of these cultural elements is in the plateau of Iran."

In the course of its long history, Iran has achieved much, but has suffered greatly as well. At times the borders of the Iranian empire reached the banks of the Rivers Sind and Jaxartes in the east and the shores of the Black Sea and the blue waters of the Nile in the west.

On more than one occasion the name of Iran as an independent nation would have been erased from the face of history if the defensive mechanisms of the society had not functioned on time. The assault of Alexander the Macedonian (fourth century B.C.), the advent of the Muslims (seventh century A.D.), the invasion of the Mongols (thirteenth century) and last, but not least, the interferences of foreign powers in the internal affairs of the country in the nineteenth and the first quarter of the twentieth century, could each have completely changed the destiny of the Iranian people. Iran not only survived the disasters but each calamity resulted in the enrichment of its culture and reinforcement of its structural cohesion.

In fact, such a remarkable recuperative vitality of Iranian society has always puzzled the scholars of society and history. How could a society undergo these ascents and descents for over twenty-five hundred years and still retain its independence, identity and cultural authenticity?

By briefly analyzing certain structural features of this society throughout history, an attempt has been made here to uncover some of the defensive mechanisms of Iranian society and its dynamic recuperative power.

Emphasis is placed on the social organization of Iran at two levels: group relations and social order. To understand the potential solidarity or conflict within the society, group structure and intergroup relations are analyzed. To appreciate the distinctive and interwoven patterns of the Iranian social organization, an attempt is made to deal with the social order.

The recorded history of Iran, both through the findings of archeologists and the works of historians, endorses the hypothesis of the existence of a tripartite society prevailing on the Iranian Plateau.

As early as the third millennium B.C., in this part of the ancient world, urban life developed alongside the pastoral tribes and the peasant community. They were in steady osmotic interaction. Such interacting social systems were positively adaptive in the face of the physical and human environment of the plateau.

In fact, through thousands of years, the inhabitants of the Iranian Plateau had to cope with the diversified nature that characterizes the plateau as well as with the adjacent cultures of Mesopotamia which were, for centuries, incorporated into the Iranian Empire. Out of such adaptation, Iranian society developed with certain institutionalized forms of organization and intrinsic defensive mechanisms. Thus, Iran was not only able to maintain its existence throughout its fluctuating history but also to contribute to the enrichment of human civilization.

The Tribes

Experts in animal tending, the tribes with their cohesive social structures were scattered throughout the country. However, they dwelt mostly in mountains, creating inaccessible and quasi-autonomous entities. Although impenetrable to alien elements, the tribesmen were not only in constant contact with villagers and urban dwellers but always represented in the Iranian army, consequently interacting with peoples and cultures outside Iranian territories proper.

According to Herodotus, in the army of Xerxes (fifth century B.C.) the tribes made up one-tenth of the cavalry. It was the Parthian Dynasty (third century B.C.), originally from an Iranian tribe, who drove the Seleucids out of the country. The Qezel-bash tribes, later called the Shahsavan, constituted the main body of the Safavid (1500-1736) army which put an end to the last Mongol chieftainships in Iran and obstinately barred the borders of the society to the Ottoman Empire. Nader Shah (1736-1747), who chased out the enemies and thus regained the independence of Iran before conquering India, was from the Afshar tribe and enjoyed the support of the tribal communities. Karim Khan Zand (1750-1779) was raised in a Lori tribe. The founder of the Qajar Dynasty was also a tribal chief.

Contrary to the view of many western anthropologists, the Iranian tribes were neither primitive nor did they constitute a closed community. In fact, they were closed only to the penetration of alien elements but they were open in regard to active participation in defending the independence of their global society and in playing an important role in the achievement of victories throughout Iran's history.

Even Islam, which so rapidly spread throughout urban life in Iran, long afterwards penetrated into the Iranian tribes. The Mongols who invaded the country in the thirteenth century also never integrated the Iranian tribes who arduously preserved their traditions, their dialects and their identity.

However, as much as the tribes had constituted a eufunctional defensive mechanism for such a long period of time, they later became dysfunctional and anachronous.

The Villages

Spanning thousands of years, the village community had been composed mostly of individuals belonging to a single lineage; that is, the village members were all relatives claiming to be descendants of a fictitious or a real ancestor. Such a non-segmented social structure contributed greatly to the cohesiveness of the village community, safeguarding it from alien elements in rural areas. Patrilineality and the practice of patrilocal marriages refuted the intrusion of any ethnic and linguistic elements which attempted to penetrate the village community, guaranteeing rural cultural authenticity.

On the other hand, great numbers of the rural population, due to repeated foreign invasions, had to gradually move into the interior of the country, settling in the arid zones which were not attractive to enemies. The scarcity of water in these central parts of the plateau resulted in the invention by the peasants, long before the Christian era, of a most genuine and unique device – the *qanat*. This device was used for conveying water through deep underground canals from the foothills to the most arid zones. Thus, the arid areas, which were made habitable by the genius of Iranian peasants, created another obstacle for aliens incapable of maintaining such refined techniques.

The relationship between peasants and urban dwellers was that of the dominated and the dominant. From the Achaemenian period, 2,500 years ago, to the implementation of the land reform law in 1962, the land tenure system had not changed structurally. Most of the peasants did not own the land but worked for the landlords and obtained a share of the agricultural produce, as little as one-fifth if not less.

However, village life in Iran must not be considered as only defensive in nature. Throughout history, the villagers proved themselves capable of organizing great movements which directly or indirectly helped in upholding independence. Many great scientists, philosophers and poets of world renown also emerged from village life.

The Cities

Urban life, the cradle of Iranian creativity, almost always enjoyed a flourishing development. However, cities constituted the most vulnerable components of the society. Cities were the first targets of all attacks, thus the main milieu of conflicts and contacts.

Within urban life a highly refined civilization developed whose reflections permeated the political borders of Iran, creating cultural interaction with adjacent civilizations. Furthermore, the vast territories governed by Iranians for over a thousand years resulted in the development of a sophisticated and effective administration.

Under the Achaemenian Empire the conquered peoples and lands were organized into locally independent *satrapies* (provinces) along lines of nationality. Within the empire lived a wide range of ethnic and religious groups who were allowed to freely follow their own cults. Good roads were maintained, and no historian of ancient civilization has neglected to express his admiration for the administrative ability of the Iranians.

207

208

209

210

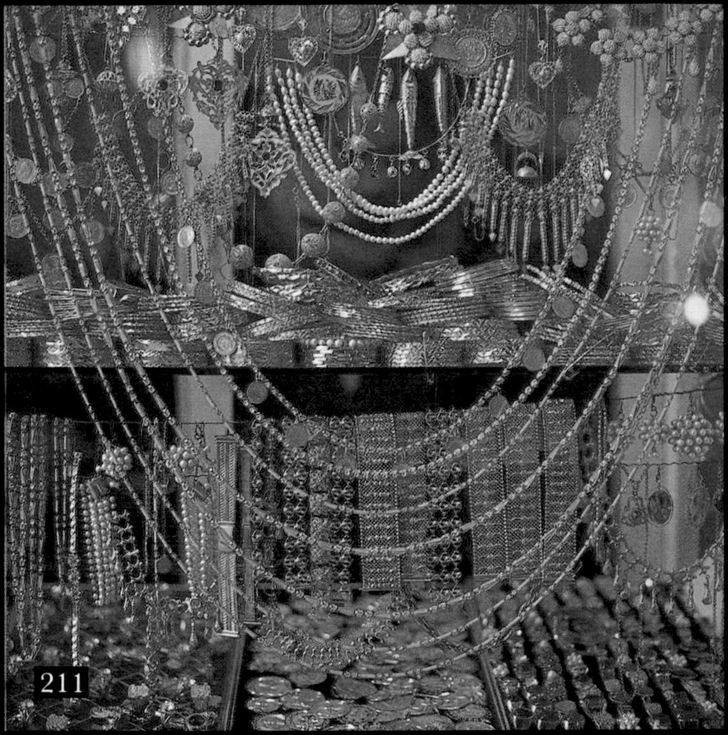

211

212

213

214

215

216

217

218

219

220

221

222

223

224

225

226

227

228

To rule over such a vast and diversified territory, the Iranians required great skill and a large administrative set-up. Therefore, any invader also had to work through the existing effective administrative devices. Thus, they had to obtain the collaboration of the Iranians, resulting in the enemy becoming the prey in the labyrinth of Iranian administration and adopting their behavior patterns, consequently merging into Iranian society.

Two defensive mechanisms in urban life served not only to maintain the independence of the society but also functioned to assimilate both invaders and Iranians who came in contact with the cities. First was the exceedingly developed civilization which was always superior to that of the enemy; second was the unparalleled administrative set-up which characterized the glory of Iranian empires.

Under the Sasanian Empire not only the military achievements of Iran deserve a great deal of consideration but also the development of architecture, astronomy, pharmacological knowledge, medicine, and especially trade. Jundishapur, the most important medical center, was built during the reign of this dynasty. The Silk Road served as the most important bridge for trade between East and West. Iranian merchants had reached both the Chinese and the Roman empires. These merchants, however, were not only the bearers of goods but also the propagators of Iranian culture.

The highly developed pre-Islamic urban life of the cities expanded more and more with the advent of Islam; and for centuries Iranian cities became the centers for the diffusion of science, literature and the Muslim religion.

The Institution of Kingship

The network of social interaction in every society is articulated within institutionalized channels that are coordinated in a characteristic and unique manner. For Iran one such pattern of integration has found its most direct expression in the institution of kingship.

Such a configuration of social systems, so positively adaptive to nature and man, could neither develop nor be maintained without parallel development of an institution which could integrate the components into a working unity and perform the function of leadership. In Iran this has been from time immemorial the institution of kingship.

Within the traditions inherent in this institution, scientists, philosophers and poets enjoyed equal protection, thus enabling them to advance the Iranian civilization to its zenith.

It has also been within the institution of kingship that the most important political unity has been achieved, however heterogeneous the components of the Iranian society might have been.

Within the Achaemenian Empire lived a vast range of peoples from many origins. The inscription on the tomb of Darius at Naqsh-e-Rostam reads as follows:

> By the favor of Ahura Mazda these are the countries which I seized outside of Pars: I ruled over them; they bore tribute to me; what was said to them by me, that they did; my law – that held them firm; Media, Khwaja, Parthia, Aria, Bactria, Sogdiana, Chorasmia, Drangiana, Arachosia, Sattagydia, Gan-

dara, Sind, Haoma-growing Scythians, Scythians with pointed caps, Babylonia, Assyria, Arabia, Egypt, Armenia, Cappadocia, Sardis, Ionia, Scythians who are across the sea, Skudra, Petasus-wearing Ionians, Libyans, Ethiopians, men of Maka, Carians.

The pattern of maintaining and controlling such a great empire required a combination of local autonomy with centralized authority and responsibility.

Such a coherent tripartite social structure, which through thousands of years had efficiently functioned to reject alien elements and maintain the cultural continuity of Iran, became dysfunctional at a certain historical conjuncture.

In the West, beginning with the renaissance and continuing into the eighteenth century, the industrial revolution was in the process of fermentation. The accumulation of knowledge was sufficiently developed to produce the basic ingredients of a new form of technology based on scientific research.

This industrial period of eighteenth-century Europe coincided with one of the most chaotic periods in the history of Iran. The country had become an enclave surrounded by numerous enemies.

On the west the Ottomans had reached the height of their territorial expansion. On the north the Russians, building on the scientific foundations laid by Peter the Great, were becoming stronger and expanding southward. And on the northeast the Uzbaks were infiltrating Iran.

In Iran itself the once thriving Safavid state was withering under its last weak rulers. The country had become so defenseless that in 1722 a group of ten thousand bandits invaded Iranian territory and conquered the capital, Esfahan.

Nader Shah, the Zands, and Aqa Mohammad Khan, who reigned over Iran from 1726 to 1797, effectively utilized the tribal forces in order to drive the enemies out of Iran and maintain the boundaries of the country. However, they were too intensely preoccupied with defending the society to take full notice of changes occurring at the same time in Europe.

In the nineteenth century the West was rapidly developing its industry and forming modern nationwide organizations and institutions necessary for the growth of such industrialization.

It was during this time, however, that Iran was being ruled by the weak Qajar Dynasty.

The key strategic position of Iran, on the one hand, and the extreme weakness of the Qajar rulers, on the other, made Iran the center of conflicts and conspiracy for foreign powers. The interference of these powers in the internal affairs of Iran had reached a point where the central government virtually lost control.

The tribes could not combat the modern weapons of the enemies. Nevertheless, if they had been well utilized, they may have been able to confront invasions and maintain the territory which was overrun and captured under the Qajar Dynasty. But the government was incapable of either mobilizing the defensive mechanisms of the country or adopting western science and technology.

The discovery of oil in southern Iran in the early twentieth century increased the interest and consequently the direct interference of foreign powers. Even the tribes, once so important for maintaining independence, were penetrated by foreign powers, thus forming the nuclei for turmoil and factioning within the society. The peasants, over-exploited by absentee landlords, were incapable of providing any assistance in preventing this conjuncture. The administrative network, so effective in the past, gradually weakened and finally reached its decadence under the Qajars, and the country was now in full decline.

The Qajar Dynasty was incapable of fulfilling the responsibilities required of the institution of kingship.

It was in the midst of this turbulent political milieu that Reza Khan, a military officer from a modest rural family, organized the famous coup d'état of 1920 against the central government which was composed of incompetent nobles. This coup completely transformed Iranian destiny.

Reza Shah the Great, who was officially crowned in 1926 but who ruled the country from 1921 when he was designated as Minister of War and Commander-in-Chief of the army, found himself faced with a turbulent society. In the south Sheykh Khazal claimed independence, and the Iranian tribes of the western and southern areas also constituted autonomous entities. In addition, the foreign powers supported any movement which would serve to weaken the central authority.

The first imperative task was therefore the establishment of order, both political and social. This was achieved through a planned campaign against individual entities claiming autonomy and through the utilization of a modernized army. The tribes were disarmed, rebels dissipated, and a nationwide state of order was implemented.

Reza Shah the Great initiated many modern institutions which should have guaranteed the continued progress of Iran. This progress was discontinued, however, when World War II extended into the country.

The occupation of Iran by the Allied Armed Forces during the war, and the political movements supported by foreign powers, once again brought about turmoil and disorder, with consequences that lasted more than a decade.

The then-existing patterns of the land tenure system which were based on the one hand on large land ownership, and on the other on the presence of the unchanged tribal structure which – although under the control of the armed forces had practically hindered the establishment of nationwide modern institutions – did not correspond either with the aspirations of the nation or the prerequisites of rapid technological change.

A radical change seemed imperative if Iran was to renew its past glory. Changes were needed that would lead to technological progress.

It was time to develop an institutional structure capable of absorbing the various social and economic changes inherent in nationwide industrialization.

The vast majority of the Iranian population, approximately 80 percent, still lived in rural areas. The rate of illiteracy found among these people was well over 80 percent, with the illiteracy rate for women actually over 90 percent. Any effective action had to embrace this rural majority of the population.

The tribal system still resisted any form of change introduced by the central government, whether it was educational, medical or economic. In order to exploit not only the land but the peasants and their offspring, large landowners created obstacles which denied the peasants educational attainment. The overriding concern of the landlords was greater agricultural productivity, which could be achieved only with further exploitation of the peasants. Thus, every peasant – man, woman and child – labored continuously in order to enrich the absentee landlord.

It would have been impossible for Iranian society to penetrate into the era of modern technology as long as there was a continuation of either the existing tribal system or the landlord-subject structure found in rural areas. Thus, it was essential that action be taken toward fundamental structural change. These changes were initiated with land reform.

The idea of land reform was launched in 1962 by His Imperial Majesty the Shahanshah Aryamehr. The conception of land reform, however, must be traced much further back than this nationwide implementation. In 1951 Shahanshah decreed that over two thousand villages belonging to the Crown estates be given to the peasants.

The implementation of the land reform law, endorsed in a referendum by the nation, deserves special attention. While important literature on Iranian land reform does exist, its impact on the ancient tribal structures has been overlooked.

Land reform was initially intended to distribute land among peasants and thus remove landlords who owned several and, in certain cases, hundreds of villages. However, once implemented, the distribution of land was also extended into tribal communities.

According to tribal tradition, the chief "khan" of a tribe was considered by the state, as well as his subjects, to be the traditional owner of the tribal territory, including the tribesmen, their animals and whatever was cultivated. The tribe was viewed as a political unit under the control of the chief in that the government agents and even the armed forces considered the chief to be responsible for maintaining peace and order within the tribe.

Through the implementation of land reform, the tribal chief, like his subjects, received a piece of land. His legal ownership of this new parcel of land relinquished his claim on tribal territories. Thus, the whole tribal structure, which had existed since the beginnings of Iranian society, collapsed once and for all. At the same time the thousand-year land tenure system in the rural areas was uprooted. Consequently, the society was prepared for the harmonious absorption of nationwide modern organizations and institutions.

The social, economic and political achievements of Iranian society in the past fifty years – and especially during the last fifteen years, that is, after land reform – are too all-encompassing to be dealt with in these pages.

Political stability now reigns over the society with a population exceeding 33 million, of which approximately one-half live in rural areas. Nationwide institutions, such as compulsory education, justice and public health, have penetrated into the most remote corners of Iran. Widespread mass media have provided the opportunity for every citizen to be aware of what is occurring in Iran as well as in other parts of the world.

Horizontal and, more importantly, vertical mobility have created the psychology of civil equality regardless of the social class to which the individual belongs.

The economy is now thriving, propelling the society toward a new greatness, with every individual Iranian constituting a defensive mechanism under the leadership of the institution of kingship.

Nader Afshar Naderi

229

230

231

232

233

234

235

236

237

238

239

The Farah Pahlavi Social and Educational Association

The Farah Pahlavi Social and Educational Association was founded in 1953 by decree of His Majesty the Shahanshah and it has since established itself as an organization dedicated to children and adolescents bereft of parental care.

Her Majesty the Shahbanou has served as High Patron of the association since 1960, with Madame Farideh Diba acting as her deputy. Benevolent Iranian women have volunteered their time and resources to ensure the success of its many programs.

In its early years the association served as a general welfare center, but its programs are now channeled toward aiding orphaned children, those of large, low-income families, and children of poor single parents unable to support them. Every opportunity is given these children to develop and realize their potential.

The association's first boarding schools were established in Tehran in 1960 and 1961. There are now eighty establishments, providing care for 8,600 children throughout the country. In addition to the twenty-four boarding schools where children are maintained through high school, there are day care centers, kindergarten and elementary schools and boarding facilities for young workers.

Two holiday camps for children from seven to eighteen have been particularly successful. Since their inception only a few years ago, the Niavaran camp in the mountains and the Shahsavar camp by the sea have accommodated over twelve thousand children and youths in 21-day sessions.

In recent years the association has turned to the sponsorship of training centers designed to meet special educational needs. The Farah Choir School offers special training for musically gifted youngsters chosen from applicants throughout the country. The Sohrab Vocational School is involved in training students for specialized technical work in electricity, metal technology, construction and mechanics.

Through its Educator Training College, degrees are granted to individuals specializing in training children; and the Nursery Training School grants a diploma in nursery and child care and helps to provide workers for the child care facilities of the association.

Poster Art in Iran

Sadegh Barirani

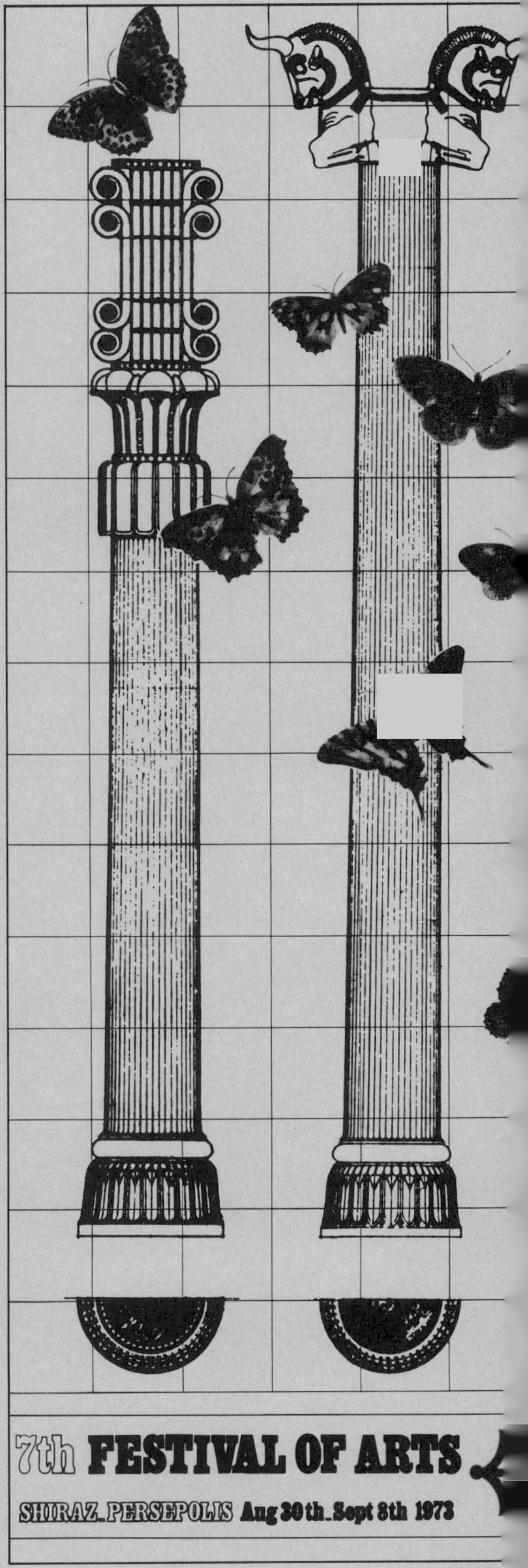

Fereydoun Ave

The poster as an art form has not been given appropriate recognition in Iran, even though posters have been one of the few artistic mediums freely exposed outside museum walls. The consequence of their public display is highly significant, for they have contributed to the development of artistic tastes among the urban population. Due to the proliferation of poster art, the Iranian graphic artist has rapidly established himself as an integral element within the artistic community.

Kamran Diba

هشتمین جشنواره
سینمای آزاد ایران
باهمکاری رادیوتلویزیون ملی ایران
سینما سینه موند
۱۵ تا ۲۰ مهر ۲۵۳۵ تهران
8TH FESTIVAL OF CINEMA-YE-AZAD IRAN
2ND INTERNATIONAL FESTIVAL OF SUPER 8
فدراسیون جهانی سوپرهشت وسینمای آزاد ایران برگزار می‌کنند
دومین جشنواره جهانی سوپرهشت
ORGANIZED BY INTERNATIONAL FEDERATION OF CINEMA SUPER 8 AND CINEMA-YE-AZAD IRAN
INCOOPERATION WITH NIRT
TEHRAN-7-12 OCTOBER 1976 CINEMA CINEMONDE

Ghobad Shiva

Poster Art in Iran

For the graphic arts in Iran, whose history reaches back to the second half of the nineteenth century, the wall ad or poster is a new feature. In the past, our graphic arts were comprised chiefly of calligraphy, book illustration, signage, caricature and illumination. These elements formed the pillars of our graphic arts.

About fifty years ago, the first movie posters the size of cinema billboards were designed and produced by the Soruri brothers, Mushekh and Napoleon, who had immigrated to Iran from Armenia. Later, Frederick Talberg, an émigré from Sweden, took the lead in poster design, particularly in advertising. Despite such activities, the poster did not play a significant role for the culture as a whole, largely because of the lack of printing machines for producing large posters.

After August 25, 1941, during the Second World War, the situation began to alter. The Azarbayejan Theater of Tabriz, various theaters in Tehran and finally merchandisers and political organizations began to use the poster as an effective means for publicizing information. From this time on, the poster was taken seriously in our culture, especially since it coincided with the founding of the College of Fine Arts at Tehran University, which offered a class in "Decorative Composition," with poster design a subject under discussion.

Because the pioneer teachers and designers of this medium were trained in the European tradition, the outcome was pervaded by a Western spirit. For example, the works of the Soruris or Talberg had a clear Russian derivation; and since the professor of the Decorative Composition class of the College of Fine Arts was a Frenchwoman, university students (some of whom later figured among our graphic artists) were inevitably influenced by such designers as Cassandre, Charles Lepot, Herbert Lubin and Bernard Villemot. But the strongest impact was left by the Soruris, Talberg and their followers.

After 1942 the trend toward new directions started because a number of students had graduated from the College of Fine Arts and were attempting to present new views and experiments. At this time, there were three basic classifications of poster art:

1. Cinema posters. These were usually large, single advertisements, 8 x 3 meters, painted with oils on canvas and posted at the entrance of the cinema. These posters were called "Plakate" after the German word for posters. Whatever tendency could be perceived in cinema posters was the result of the impact upon our graphic artists by American and Indian designers. The best known and strongest film-poster artist was Ejaghian.

2. Political posters. These were derived from the political posters of the Second World War, especially the Russian variety. Such styles continued until recently when, under the influence of a new trend in our graphics, they took a different direction. Most political posters were created by Mohsen Davallu, who had a highly individual approach.

3. Commercial posters. The development of these posters has been primarily affected by popular taste, even though occasional European influences were evident. The best of this group came from Mohammad Bahrami, whose special style in illustrations had a strong impact on other designers.

The new wave in poster-making originated in the works of a few people such as Hushang Kazemi, Sadegh Barirani and this writer. Kazemi is the first graphic artist to have had formal schooling in this field. After completing his studies at the Ecole des Arts Decoratifs in Paris, he came to Iran and helped to organize the School of Decorative Arts for the Ministry of Culture and Fine Arts, where a special program for graphic arts was instituted. The first posters of the new period were generally printed in limited editions of 50 to 300 for art exhibitions or amateur theatrical groups.

During the 1960s and 1970s, the opportunities offered by several government agencies such as the Center for the Intellectual Development of Children and Young Adults, and later the National Iranian Radio and Television and the Ministry of Culture and Fine Arts, allowed designers and artists to give shape to the graphic arts as they exist today.

In the search for new directions, Iranian poster-makers have welcomed the influences of various international sources—Polish, German, American and Swiss. But it is pleasing to note the recent tendency of the Iranian artist toward introspection and self-expression, as he attempts to build upon the foundations of his own cultural heritage.

Morteza Momayez

From the catalogue for the exhibition *Poster Art in Iran*, October 14, 1977, at the Tehran Museum of Contemporary Art in affiliation with the Shahbanou Farah Foundation.

241

242

243

244

246

247

248

249

250

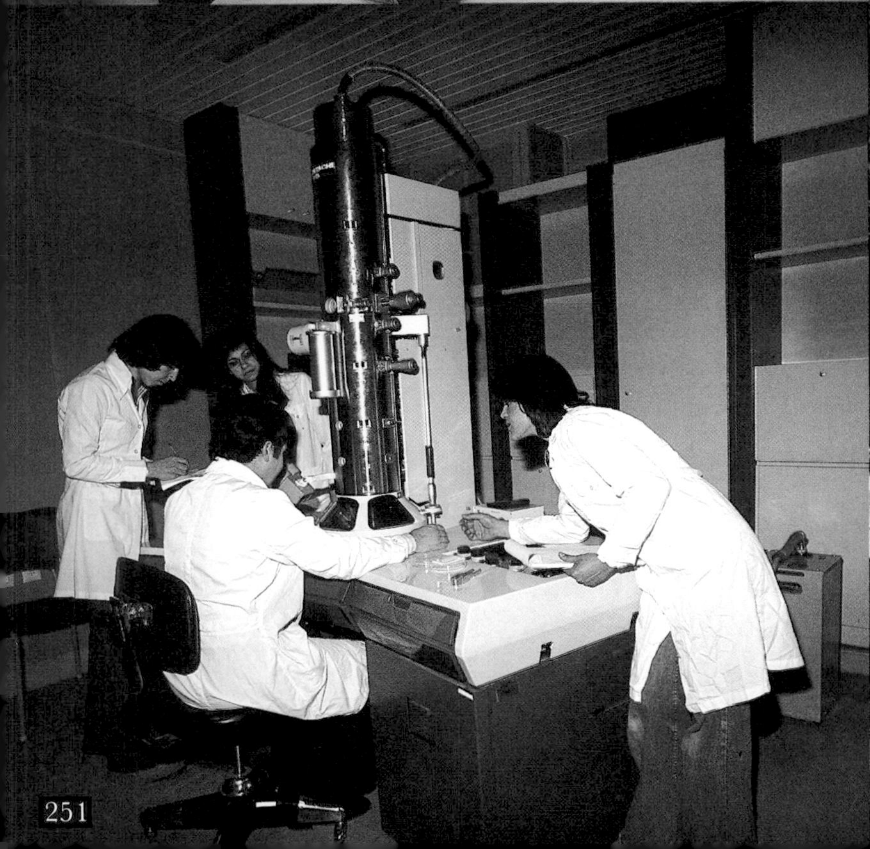

251

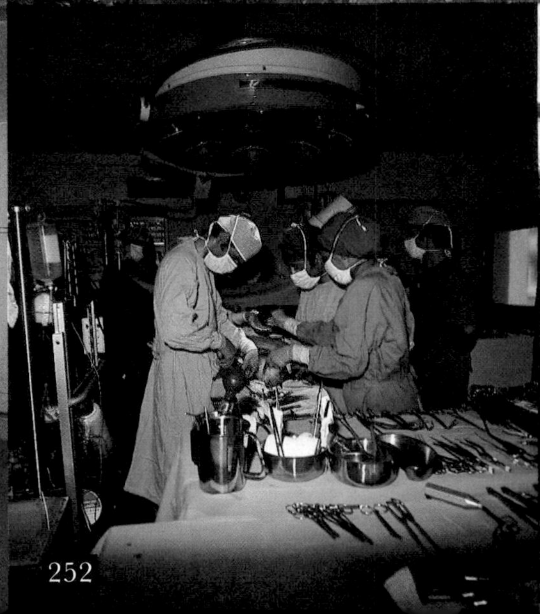

252

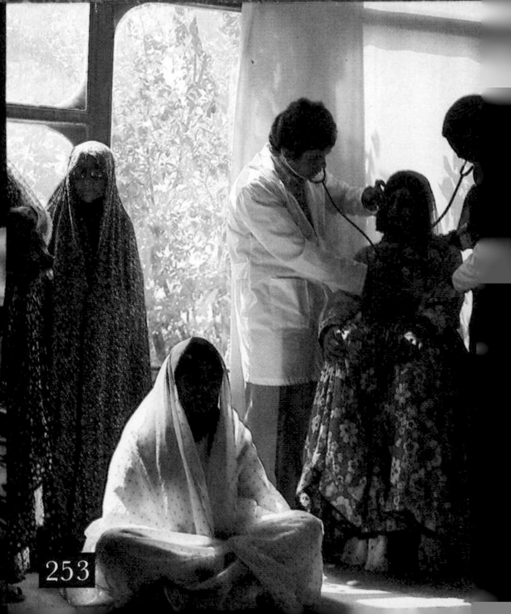

253

254

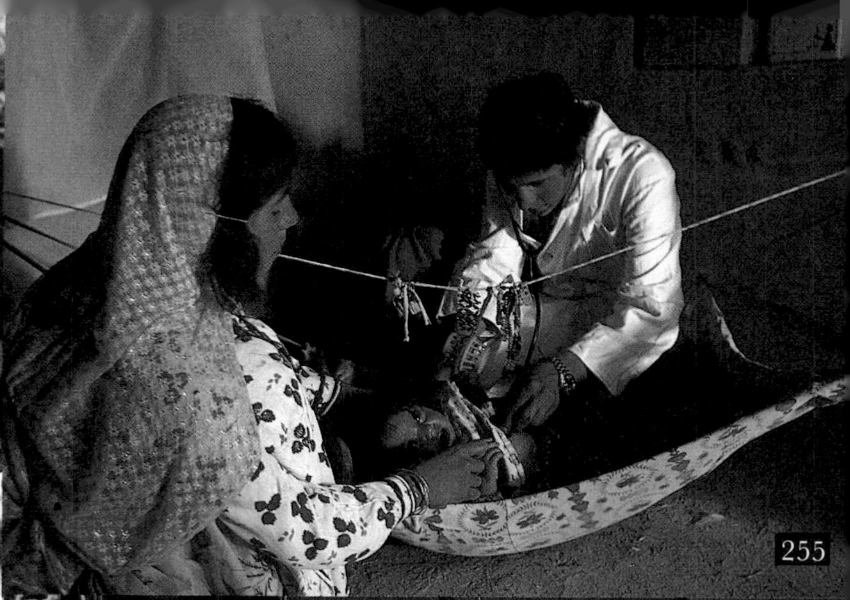

255

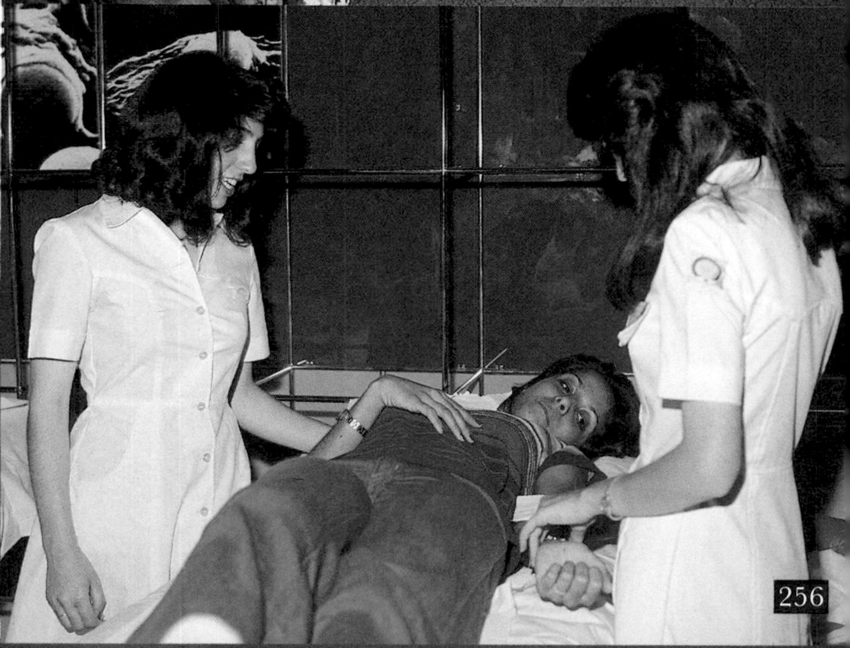

256

257

258

259

260

261

262

263

264

265

266

Arched portico of the new
railway station at Mashhad

SOCIETY

AND A TIME FOR PLEASURE

Joy in Iran takes many forms. It is earthy and sensual as a lavish banquet, light and ephemeral as a song on the wind, full of the blare and fire of a parade, and cool and calm as a poem recited beside a mountain pool.

The wellsprings of joy lie in tradition, which connects men with each other, with nature, and with the spiritual forces which give meaning to life. For Iranians that sudden warming of the soul which signals joy comes when these connections are made. Then that joy finds expression in exuberance, laughter, the sweetness of contemplation, and even the happy release of tears.

The means for joy are many and varied. Some are simple and personal – having a child curl up at one's side, sitting with friends and talking over endless glasses of tea, or picnicking with the family in a garden of fruit trees. Some have more formal artistic expression in poetry, music, literature and traditional performance. Others reflect organization for the pleasure of all—traditional holiday celebrations, national observances, weddings and festivals. And still others offer the engagement and energy of games, sports and vigorous physical activity.

Joy in Music and Poetry

Music, songs and poetry are blended with every aspect of Iranian life. Iranians demonstrate their artistic character in these areas everywhere, at all times, in every occupation and activity.

For example, one sees itinerant peddlers advertising their fruits, vegetables and melons with poetry and song in order to attract customers and lull them into buying. There is pleasure here both for the artist and his public. One seller of *zal-zalak,* a small fruit resembling a cherry, cries:

Zal zal-zalak e
Rostam-e zal zal-zalak e

Zal was the father of the legendary hero Rostam, who was noted for his mighty stature. Thus the caller is noting the size of his wares through a literary reference. A possible translation might be:

Here are Zal zal-zalak
Here are the Rostam of Zal-zalak

Another example comes from the sellers of roasted ears of maize:

Shir balal o shur balal
Shire -ye Quchani balal
Barre-ye beryani balal

Milk ears and salty ears
Milk of Quchan ears
Charcoal-grilled lamb ears

The seller of corn, with an astute sense of both the commercial and the artistic, knows that both the milk products of Quchan in the province of Khorasan and the taste of fresh-grilled lamb are excellent. He weaves both of these into references to the milky juice of the maize and to the fact that the ears are being charcoal grilled too.

Poetry and music in Iran have always been mixed. Recitation of poetry is common in all sectors of Iranian society. Poetry is sung as often as it is recited, either with or without the accompaniment of musical instruments. Music and poetry provide a powerful connection between the outer secular life of the everyday world and the inner life of the spirit and the emotions. It is perhaps for this reason that Iranians are able to express themselves best through these media, and have consequently produced over the ages some of the finest poetry the world has ever known.

Poetry finds its best expression in the rich, complex fabric of traditional Iranian classical music. Penetrating yet almost ethereal in nature, this musical tradition was once almost lost, but has enjoyed an unprecedented renaissance in the last twenty years. Each traditional mode taps a particular emotion, and as the vocalist and instrumentalists weave their tapestry of sound, their listeners are engulfed in a siren-song of longing, passion and sorrow arising from the beauty of the music. Suddenly the mood changes, and the ensemble strikes a lively rhythmic dance raising the company to the heights of hilarity while the poetry exhorts:

Shad zi ba siyah cheshman shad
Ke jahan nist joz fesaneh o bad

Live happy, happy with your black-eyed one
The world's just stories and the wind when all is done

(*Rudaki*)

From every home and shop and on every street, music and poetry fill the air. Even in the most remote areas of Iran, in villages and tribal areas, the sound of traditional instruments carries the news of celebration for miles. Today, in addition to traditional music, the sound of the popular singers of the day is also heard via the mass-media network which now covers the country. One knows that the electronic revolution has truly arrived when watching the men and women of Gilan transplanting rice shoots in the fields and alternating traditional work songs with popular music from the radio and tape recorder.

Joy in Nature

Iran is traditionally a rural society. Thus fields, streams, sun and open air hold a special place in the Iranian heart. Nature can give pain as well as pleasure, and the management of both good and bad aspects of the elements has been an organizing principle of Iranian life since ancient times. Engagement with nature is a process which produces joy in many forms.

The deities of ancient Iran were largely associated with the elements and their manifestations. Consequently the major festivals of the ancient Iranian world revolved around the processes of nature.

Mehr was the name of the ancient Iranian god of the sun. In the fall of the year ancient Iranians held a celebration called Mehrgan. In the time of Cyrus and Darius the Great the rulers of Iran received the first fruits of the harvest at the festival of Mehrgan. At this time they wore their most brilliant clothing and drank wine. At the time of Mahmzud of Ghazna, the best products of all the craft guilds were added to the offerings.

The use of fire and lights in public celebrations is widespread. Fire was conceived to be the son and tangible earthly symbol of Ahura Mazda, the chief of the heavenly world and the principle of good. Even today oaths are sworn on fires, fireplaces, lamplight and the light of Salman, the saintly Iranian companion of the prophet Mohammed. Thus lights, fire and fireworks enhance public celebrations by providing an additional spiritual dimension to the festivities.

The middle of winter when nights are the coldest is the occasion for one of the oldest of Iranian festivals, the fire festival Sadeh. The epic poet Ferdowsi traces the origin of this festival back to a legendary prehistoric ruler, Hushang. On this night, fires are still lit on the roofs of homes everywhere throughout Iran. In ancient times people spread the fires by tying flaming thorns to the feet of birds and loosing them to set fire to the bushes of the plains. The fires of Sadeh drive away the cold of winter and signal the short period of time left before Now-Ruz, the joyous celebration of the New Year.

Shi'a Muslims in Iran celebrate the birthdays of prominent historical religious figures such as the prophet Mohammed, his heir, Ali, and the Twelfth Emam, Mahdi. Other joyful religious occasions such as the day of Mohammed's succession are also celebrated. In honor of these events the people decorate streets, houses and bazaars with lamps, carpets and religious pictures. On these days the shops and industries of the cities are closed. In the public squares, where the people gather to celebrate, fires are lit, and fireworks add to the occasion.

National holidays are celebrated with lights, fires and colorful displays as well. One of the happiest national holidays is the birthday of His Majesty, the Shahanshah, on the fourth of the month Aban. On the night before, the streets of all the cities and government buildings are decorated with lights and national flags. In the principal squares of the cities, fireworks displays are arranged and military bands in their flashing uniforms fill the air with bright, stirring music.

On the fourth of Aban itself, stadium events are held in which the royal family participate. Classical Iranian athletic exercises, light gymnastics, contests and sports events alternate with colorful full-dress revues of military personnel and civil employees. The day's festivities are then capped by fireworks displays in the evening.

268

269

270

271

272

273

274

275

276

277

278

279

Water too has special significance for Iranians. Because most of the land is dry, the ancient deities that controlled the water were greatly honored. Anahita, goddess of water, was tall, handsome and fearless. Her slim waist, white arms and fulsome breast from which flowed milk symbolic of birth and life, made her a special protector of women. Temples honoring Anahita were built throughout Iran, beside streams, rivers and waterfalls, and were especially favored for contemplation and pilgrimage.

Anahita's companion in the ancient pantheon was Tishtar, or Tir, god of rain. According to legend, the fourth month of the year was sacred to him. During that month he assembled the clouds and commanded rain to fall, bringing water to the dry, thirsty land, turning the trees and grass green. He caused the flowers and fruits to bud and bloom, and the rivers and streams to fill and swell with water. In ancient times and even today among Zoroastrians a festival called Tirgan is held in honor of Tir. According to legend, in ancient times there was no rain for an entire year. The people came together on the day of Tirgan and prayed until rain came. When the rain fell the people joyfully sprayed each other with water and held a grateful festival in commemoration of the day. The festival held this form down through the centuries, and on Tirgan people would gather to dance, sing and spray each other with water.

Even today the rain does not always fall. In rural Iran people still practice rain ceremonies which hearken back to appeals to Tir. In Khorasan a small doll is made, called Talu, and this verse is recited to it:

The flowers are withered, Talu
Springtime has come now, Talu
Now, by God, make the rain come
Now, without end, make the rain come
Make endless the barley and wheat
Make the staff of the shepherd bear sheep
Make the spade of the farmer bear wheat
The barley and wheat in the dust
Are withering and dying of thirst
The tulips, wild and red
Are groaning and crying from thirst

In the villages of Borazjan, in the south of Iran, a man dresses to resemble a goat in a felt shepherd's cloak, straw hat with two wooden horns sticking out, and bells hanging from his neck. Called *galeen,* which means "bride," he whitens his face with flour and is led through the streets by a rope. Singing children and youths accompany him through the streets while people spray water on him and his companions from the rooftops of their houses amid much laughter and shouting.

Gifts are given to the *galeen* and his followers by the people. When all the gifts have been collected the *galeen* distributes them to his companions. However, he places a stone among the gifts. Whoever receives the stone is made to promise that rain will come in two weeks; otherwise his companions will come in a body and strike him, again amid much laughter and joking. If in two weeks rain does not come, the one receiving the stone will again be assailed by his companions, and he must make a second promise of rain. This continues until rain finally comes. The *galeen* is outwardly the symbol for Anahita, and the one receiving the stone takes the role of Tir, with whom men also plead for rain.

It is perhaps because Iran has been a country thirsty for water for so many centuries that this element is revered so widely. Every Iranian home, no matter how small, will have a pool of some sort in the courtyard where children can play, clothes can be washed, and water can be obtained for sprinkling the floor before sweeping or for a cooling foot-bath. On Fridays families leave home to take their noon meal out in the open. Any small stream of water becomes a magnet for the picnickers; indeed such streams, as in the days of the worship of Anahita, often become the sites of religious shrines and other pilgrimage spots.

The two great bodies of water that border Iran on the north and south are no less of an attraction. With improvement in transportation, holiday makers, both royalty and common people alike, flock in droves to enjoy the cool Caspian waters in the summer. In recent years the Persian Gulf has likewise become a winter resort and is now crowded with vacationers during the cool months. New man-made lakes throughout the country offer still more opportunities for water recreation.

Joy in Society

One of the greatest sources of pleasure for Iranians is other Iranians. What joy there is in Iran in socializing, being with other people, talking, walking, arguing, bargaining, boasting, flattering, joking, sympathizing, complaining, exaggerating and, above all, crying and laughing!

At the center of all is the joy that arises from the family. Iranian families are close-knit, extended and loyal. It is often said that when two people marry it is really their families that are marrying. A man has binding claims on his brother's wife's cousins and vice versa. He can drop in on them unannounced and stay as long as he likes as a welcome guest. For this reason, great care is taken to make certain of an elaborate network of compatibilities at the time of marriage.

Children, of course, are the chief source of pleasure in any family. Iranian children are notable for their sweet temper and good public behavior. They are clever, active and traditionally loyal to their parents and siblings. Small children learn social graces early and will be quick to offer guests sweets and fruit before they take any for themselves, just as their elders would do. The mother is the protector and defender of her children, and the lengths to which an Iranian mother will go in order to shield her children from harm are legendary. The poet Iraj Mirza writes of a son who is urged to kill his own mother by his jealous sweetheart. He does the awful deed and is bringing his mother's heart to show the girl, when his foot strikes a stone. His mother's heart then cries out, "Woe is me! My son has hurt his foot!"

The world outside of the family is alive with intricate networks of social relations cemented with fine-tuned rituals of social behavior. Every individual in Iran has his own special status in relation to others, and his speech, bodily attitudes and actions all reflect his position at the moment. A postal clerk is deferential to the postmaster, but he is a king among the letter carriers. And the system can be played to one's advantage. Oh the pleasure in being able to flatter one's superior into granting a favor! Oh the joy in knowing that there is always someone somewhere, no matter who one is, who will consider it his duty to attend to one's needs!

But there are friends as well, intimate friends of undying loyalty who share life completely, and whose chief desire is to render absolute service to each other. The intensity of such relationships is so great that often only the family structure can bear it. Thus strong friendships often occur between cousins, brothers-in-law or sisters-in-law. If two from separate families become particularly close, a religious vow may be taken which creates a kinship tie.

Intimate social life is symbolized by the dinner cloth. In traditional homes the cloth is spread on the floor for all meals, with family and guests seated cross-legged all around, the oldest and most respected at the head. Iranian food should be fresh for each meal, and its loving preparation goes on for three or four hours before mealtime. The cuisine is elegant – a balance of tastes, textures and colors. At the center are the twin staples – rice and fresh-baked unleavened bread. The rice may be a savory pilau full of fruits, nuts or cooked vegetables; or it may be fluffy, white, tender chelow – steamed and crowned with a crisp brown crust of fried rice from the bottom of the steaming pan. Around the dinner cloth is an array of meat and vegetable stews to eat with the rice, simmered with delicate spices to a rich goodness. A stew of lamb, squash and eggplant sits next to lamb and quince; still another of yellow peas, potatoes and meat peeks out from another corner. Kebabs, stuffed vegetables, chicken and delicate egg-vegetable dishes may also be set off by fresh greens, cheese, yogurt, pickles, and always in every season, fresh fruit and melon to begin and end the meal.

Happy is the guest in such a setting! After the meal and endless glasses of tea, the dinner cloth is removed and all stretch out on the carpeted floor to doze and digest the food. Then on awakening there is more tea, conversation, perhaps a game of backgammon or a leisurely walk. Anyone invited for a meal is likely to be urged to spend the night. Extra mattresses and bedding seem to appear inexhaustibly to accommodate any and all who need them. Guests are considered a gift from heaven in Iran, and nothing is spared for their comfort. Indeed, the host derives perhaps more pleasure than his guests in knowing that they are comfortable and happy.

In the traditional Iranian city the bazaar is the center of all social and commercial life. At one end stands the city's principal mosque, and the bazaar trails away from it like the backbone of a great vital organism. Strung out on all sides of the bazaar are bathhouses, barber shops, small mosques and religious schools, restaurants and teahouses. The merchants of the bazaar use their shops as social gathering places as well as commercial establishments; and small boys carrying tea, sherbets and ices for visitors to the shops can be seen bustling here and there among the shoppers.

Of all the social institutions in the traditional city, perhaps the most important is the teahouse. It is a place where people from all social strata come together to while away spare time, sitting, talking, drinking tea, smoking water pipes and playing chess or backgammon. It may also be a place to transact business, and often has served as the meeting place for different craft guilds.

The teahouse is a bastion of oral tradition as well, for it is the place where the professional storyteller can be found. Most often the *naqqal,* as he is called, narrates the great epic of Ferdowsi, the *Shahnameh,* or *Book of Kings.* The epic is narrated in its entirety, a small section at a time throughout the year. The performance of the *naqqal* is not merely a recitation. He retells the classic stories, taking on the roles of the characters and punctuating important sections with actual quotations from Ferdowsi.

The long nights of winter and Ramazan, the Islamic month of fasting, are traditionally the times when Iranian teahouses are full and active. On these evenings every teahouse takes on a special atmosphere. Especially in Ramazan, after the breaking of the fast at sundown, the teahouses remain open until dawn and are lively all night with special games and activities. For the *naqqal* the height of his performance comes with the narration of the battle between the hero Rostam and his own son, Sohrab, whom he unwittingly kills. When the *naqqal* reaches this point in the *Shahnameh,* he refuses to continue until he receives substantial gratuities from his audience.

Another institution of the traditional city is the *zurkhaneh,* or house of strength. Iranians from ancient times have been conscious of the importance of a strong and healthy body as a key to mental and spiritual strength. The strongest men in any community have always been revered. But even more is expected of them. By virtue of their physical power, they are expected to be pure and altruistic in their use of that power – to serve as protectors of the community and its mores. These men, often referred to as *pahlevans,* or champions, are frequently leaders of the religious community as well. The *zurkhaneh* is the place where such men, under the direction of a leader, meet to practice traditional athletic exercises to the vigorous rhythms of the drum of a professional chanter, the *murshed,* who urges the athletes on with verses from the *Shahnameh.*

As a direct outgrowth of *zurkhaneh,* the traditional areas of expertise in Iranian athletics have been wrestling and weight lifting. With emphasis on quickness and strength, Iranian athletes in these traditional areas have held many world championships. Throughout the country wrestling especially has many adherents. At weddings and national celebrations, wrestling is a regular feature of the festivities; and through these contests local and regional champions, both formally and informally recognized, hold their positions and are revered by the community for their prowess.

Horsemanship has been an important area of Iranian skill for centuries. The most noble of all Iranian equestrian activities is the ancient game of polo. Medieval miniatures portray nobles playing this game in idealized rural fields. The Meydan-e-Shah, the vast central square in the city of Esfahan, was originally a polo field constructed by Shah Abbas the Great, a contemporary of Queen Elizabeth I.

The Turkomans in northwestern Iran are perhaps the most skilled horsemen in the country. Originally horse nomads, these people take great pride in the possession, care and racing of horses. The Turkoman town of Pahlavi Dej just west of the Caspian close to the northern Iranian border is the scene of active horse trading and racing at the end of every week. The occasion is accompanied by trading in fine-quality Turkoman carpets and jewelry, making the scene active and colorful.

281

282

283

284

285

286

287

288

289

290

291

292

293

294

295

296

297

298

299

300

301

302

303

In recent decades other athletic activities have captured the Iranian imagination. Soccer, volleyball, basketball and skiing have many adherents, especially in urban areas. As leisure time has increased for the population as a whole, Iranians are learning to enjoy themselves in these new ways.

The Joy of Celebrations

The essence of any civilization is captured in its celebrations, for it is in these festivities that the symbols, ideals and institutions that are cherished most by the people of a nation are brought forth and renewed.

Two celebrations which are especially important for Iranians, and which are occasions for joy, have completely different bases. One, the marriage celebration, has its origin in the realm of the family and its social network. Marriages are occasions which are determined by personal considerations of the families involved, and mark a change in the social state of the two families. Thus the basis for joy at this celebration has its origins in the pleasures derived from the family and social realm. The expression of joy comes in music, food, dance, socializing and traditional performance – all of which may occur during the wedding celebration.

The second important joyful celebration is the Iranian New Year, Now-Ruz. This celebration continues for more than two weeks, from the last Wednesday of the year until the thirteenth day after the new year. During this time many festivities take place. A primary emphasis during Now-Ruz is on nature. Fire, water, earth and air all figure prominently. Social gatherings, athletic activities, food and contact with the outdoors are emphasized. These events are extraordinarily similar throughout the country, and the pleasure that is manifested in the festivities draws from deep cultural wellsprings that reach back to the origins of Iranian civilization.

The high season for wedding celebrations is in the fall after the harvest when food, money and leisure time are plentiful. This time is only avoided when it coincides with the lunar months of Moharram and Safar, which are months of mourning for Shi'a Muslims.

Music, dancing, singing, games and traditional comic theater are all important elements of traditional celebrations. In virtually all tribal and village weddings, local traditional musicians play to accompany dancing and games for a period ranging from three to seven days and nights before the actual wedding or circumcision ceremony, although in recent times there has been a tendency to shorten the time of the celebration.

The piercing sound of the *sorna,* a kind of double reed flute, and the steady beat of the *dohol,* a large drum, signal the people for miles around that a wedding is to take place. Other traditional instruments may be used for dancing. In the cities the clarinet and modern jazz drums have tended to replace these traditional instruments, but the music they play is much the same.

Two forms of dancing are most common throughout Iran. One is the *chupi,* the colorful handkerchief dance, performed in a circle. In some places men and women perform this dance separately, and in others they dance together in the circle. Usually the first person in line holds a colored handkerchief and leads. Another dance which is found throughout Iran is the "stick dance" or *chub-bazi.* This dance has special music associated with it and varies widely throughout the country. In southern and western Iran it usually takes the following form: Two young men encounter each other. One of the dancers holds a stick with which he defends himself, and the other a stick to attack. The defender, after dancing a short while, places one end of his stick on the ground next to his left foot. The attacker holds his stick behind his head with both hands against the back of his neck and dances a circle around the defender. He then whips the stick around with one hand, shouting, and tries to strike the legs of the defender. After this, the two change places.

Guests at weddings are treated no less handsomely than they are on other occasions. They are fed throughout the celebration even if it lasts seven days and nights. Sweets, tea and cigarettes are provided for them at all times. At one point, however, they usually make a cash contribution of their own, which pleases the host, the father of the groom, and sometimes makes him quite wealthy if the number of guests is high and the harvest has been good.

One of the happiest segments of the celebration is the performance of traditional folk theater for the enjoyment of the guests. The performers are the musicians hired for the occasion. Although in some areas this form of theater is so popular that up to four performances are held each day of the wedding, usually the show takes place at night. An open courtyard or square is chosen for the play, and the guests sit around the performing area and on walls and rooftops to watch the show. There is always a danger of someone, overcome with laughter, falling from these heights, so mothers watch carefully over their children in the midst of the hilarity. In cities, where the courtyards of houses often had a shallow pool, or *howz*, a platform was placed over the pool for players to act on. Thus this sort of performance is often known as *ru-howzi* theater, or "theater over the pool." This theatrical form features a clown, often in black-face, who is the principal comedian. The play as a whole is improvisatory and derives its humor from the antics of the clown interacting with his master, mistress, merchants, kings and many other characters. The basic stories are often drawn from Iranian literary classics. In *ru-howzi* theater, music and dance play a major role. Each character has his own special dance and songs. The principal basis for humor is in the use and misuse of language. The clown is continually confusing the speech of the other characters, so that the simplest phrases come out as puns, malapropisms and insults, much to the delight of the spectators.

The clown of traditional folk theater is reminiscent of the perpetual bringer of the tidings of the new year, Haji Firuz. Also dressed in black-face, in a red costume and bearing a tambourine, Haji Firuz parades through the streets during the Now-Ruz period, singing and dancing for the delight of young and old alike.

In the province of Gilan, starting a month before Now-Ruz, special troupes of singers move throughout the province, singing special songs to inform the people of the happy news that the New Year is on the way. In these songs the New Year and the winds of spring are described, and many religious elements are extolled – such as earth, wind, water, light and Mehr, the ancient god of the sun.

At an earlier time many persons would dress as Haji Firuz and march through the streets of the cities bearing torches and singing songs. The streets and shops were decorated with lights and lanterns, and the sounds of the tambourine and the happy songs of Now-Ruz sung in the flickering torchlight gladdened the hearts of many children.

Fire plays another important role in the ceremonies of Now-Ruz, on the last Wednesday of the year, called *Chahr-shambeh Suri.* In the traditional reckoning of time, each day starts at sunset of the previous night. Thus the observance of *Chahr-shambeh Suri* actually begins on Tuesday night. On this night each family takes dried thorns and bushes gathered from the plains and mountains and arranges them in either three, five or seven piles in the house, in the courtyard or in the street. As the sun sets and night falls, men and women, young and old, gather around the piles of tinder and light them. Then they dance around the fires singing songs. One at a time, each family member jumps over the flames and chants verses like the following:

May sadness go and happiness come
May suffering go and blessings come

Ay, Night before Wednesday
*Ay, Key with four teeth**
Grant me my desires

My yellow to you
Your red to me

(*i.e., that can open any lock)

When the fires have died down to ashes, a woman from each family gathers the ashes in a dustpan and carries them away to a nearby street corner or stream and throws them away. She then returns home and raps loudly on the door, telling the family members that she has just come from a wedding and is bringing happiness and blessings for the family. The door is opened, and in this way the family ensures itself of blessings for the coming year.

Iranians, by burning fires at this time, eliminate ugliness and impurity from their lives. In Kordestan children take burning embers to their rooftops and, swinging them around their heads, toss them off into the night. In Sanandaj and surrounding villages, besides lighting fires in each household, the people take an old worn-out broom and set it on fire inside of a broken clay pot. They sprinkle seeds of wild rue on the fire and jump over the flames. Usually a servant in the household, or one of the women if there is no servant, takes the pot and empties the ashes at the nearest crossroads. Then she returns to the household, its purification for the coming year having been accomplished.

The fires of *Chahr-shambeh Suri* are carried over into Now-Ruz in some areas. It is not uncommon in many areas of Iran to see people dancing and singing around fires lit on the roofs of houses on the last night of the old year. Occasionally people explode home-made firecrackers, or throw kerosene-soaked cloth streamers flaming into the night. Rockets and small clay pots filled with gunpowder are set off and the red flames of the fire and the sound of explosions excite the whole neighborhood.

In some rural areas the residents light fires on the tops of hills and mountains. In order to ensure that their animals will bear young and remain free from disease in the coming year, the fires lit on the hills and mountains will be brought to the folds and rekindled there. Likewise, burning embers are brought into the house and storerooms and circulated to bring health, warmth, blessings and kindness to the home.

Now-Ruz is a time when all of the family must be together. The exact second of the change from old to new year is calculated, and at this point all family members congratulate each other, kiss and agree to bury all grievances left over from the past twelve months. Before the family on a table is a ceremonial display consisting of a mirror, a copy of the *Quran,* a goldfish in a bowl, sprouted grains and lentils, occasionally colored eggs, and seven items beginning with the Persian letter *seen,* corresponding to the English "s." Everyone seems to have his own list of "seven *seens,*" but a common grouping is: *serkeh* (vinegar), *senjed* (a kind of sweet, dry, pithy fruit), *sumagh* (crushed sumac berries), *samanou* (a sweet porridge made from sprouted wheat), *sabzi* (edible greens), *seeb* (an apple) and *sekeh* (a coin).

The Now-Ruz holidays officially last for thirteen days. During this time all Iranians try to visit as many of their friends as possible. The first day is reserved for the oldest and most respected members of the family, but after that, one is free to visit all his friends. Everywhere there are tea, sweets and conversation. Everyone traditionally gets new clothes for Now-Ruz, and all who are salaried receive a holiday bonus.

The thirteenth day of Now-Ruz, according to tradition, must be spent out of doors. Consequently, Iranian families leave their homes on that morning with carpets, *gelims* and picnic materials to search out gardens and areas beside streams and under trees. Every family has brought the sprouted wheat and lentils from their Now-Ruz table and they cast them away for good luck.

On this day it is also considered lucky to eat a special thick soup made with noodles. Families take the soup and all the necessary garnishes – fried onions, garlic, dried yogurt, sauce and vinegar – along with them. It is also important to take fresh lettuce to be eaten with vinegar and honey. Of course, a samovar for tea and a water pipe are also necessary, along with drums, tambourines and melody-producing instruments for singing and dancing.

Once the families reach their destination, clustered in small groups under the trees on the banks of streams, they spread their carpets, light their samovars, make wood fires and set their thick noodle soup to heat. While their elders smoke their water pipes, the young people play at their own games – leapfrog, see-saw, swinging, volleyball and many others. Some play with cards or dice, or engage in a game of backgammon or chess.

At noon each family spreads out its food and all eat a substantial meal. Besides the traditional thick noodle soup, there is green herb pilau, fried fish and *kuku,* a fried omelet-like dish thick with chopped greens. The lettuce, vinegar and honey are eaten only in the afternoon as a snack after a siesta of two or three hours.

During the whole day itinerant musicians with monkeys and bears, jugglers, magicians, strong men and the inevitable welcomer of the New Year, Haji Firuz, move from group to group entertaining the picnickers.

306

307

308

309

On the thirteenth of Now-Ruz young girls tie knots in the grass they find on the plains in order to ensure they find husbands during the New Year. A Khorasani verse concerning this day goes as follows:

Thirteen outside
Fourteen inside
Swear by the clucking hen
Next year
In your husband's home
Child at your breast

Some of the principal activities on the thirteenth day of Now-Ruz in the past were polo, horse racing, wrestling and fighting between two bulls. The custom of horse racing and wrestling on this day has still remained active in some parts of Iran, notably Mazandaran, Gilan and the northern part of Khorasan. The people of the Esfarayen area in Khorasan, for example, have wrestling contests every day of the New Year up to the thirteenth. Every village determines its own wrestling champion by that date. On the fourteenth day of the New Year most of the people of the area assemble in the city of Esfarayen with their local champions. These champions wrestle with each other two by two all together in a large square of the city. Eventually a champion (*pahlevan*) for the whole district emerges and is recognized for the next year.

The Now-Ruz holidays capture the Iranians' need to come to terms with nature, the spirit and each other. In music, poetry, socializing and pleasurable activity, the renewal of the cycle that gives rise to the undercurrent of deep, quiet satisfaction is given concrete expression. It is thus fitting that the New Year should begin with a large measure of those small things which seem to produce joy in limited quantities but which ultimately give life itself its primary meaning.

Ali Boloukbashi
William O. Beeman

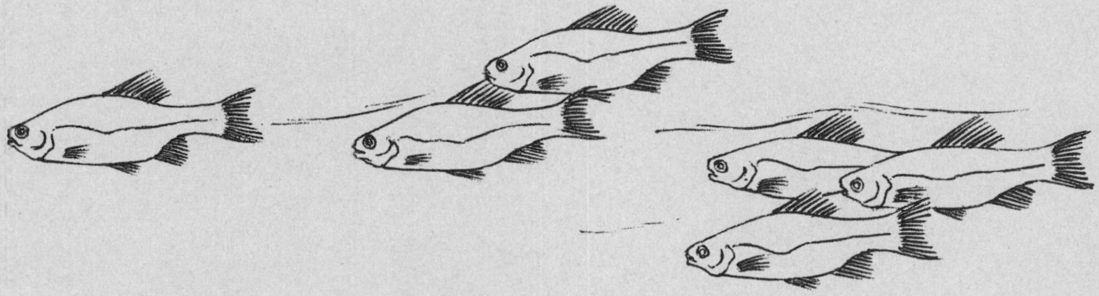

BOOK SIX

SHAHANSHAH

CAPTION FOLDOUT

SHAHANSHAH

312 An intimate moment with Their Imperial Majesties at Niavaran Palace before leaving by helicopter for Rey where ceremonies marking the Fiftieth Anniversary of the Founding of the Pahlavi Dynasty were held on March 21, 1976.

313 The Imperial Guard stand at attention, armor gleaming, during the hour-long ceremony at Rey.

314 The Imperial Guard on horseback proceed from the tomb of Reza Shah the Great along an avenue lined with spectators and guests.

315 His Imperial Majesty delivers the annual Now-Ruz message to the nation in the presence of the Royal Family at Rey.

316-321 Since Achaemenian times, Iranian monarchs have followed the custom of extending a formal *Salaam* or Greeting to the people. During the Now-Ruz *Salaam*, Their Imperial Majesties greet a wide spectrum of Iranian society, including Cabinet Ministers, Members of Parliament, foreign ambassadors accredited to Iran, civic leaders, deans, professors of universities and honor students, heads of religious communities, tribal representatives and many others. Official *Salaams* take place during the year on the occasion of the birthdays of Their Imperial Majesties and on important religious and national holidays.

316 Among the first guests welcomed by Their Imperial Majesties at the Now-Ruz *Salaam* in Golestan Palace are high-ranking members of the Imperial Court, each of whom will receive a specially minted gold coin.

317 The Shahanshah relaxes for a brief moment between receiving groups of well-wishers at his birthday *Salaam*, held at Golestan Palace on October 26.

318 The delegate from the Holy See in his scarlet robes is greeted by the Shahanshah.

319 Foreign ambassadors are presented to Their Imperial Majesties.

320 Honor students from Iranian universities are received by Their Imperial Majesties at Golestan Palace.

321 Their Imperial Majesties retire to a private room in Golestan Palace to receive the respects of Iranian religious leaders.

322 In the glittering mirrored salon of the Golestan Palace, Their Imperial Majesties and Ministers of the Imperial Court and Cabinet pose for a formal portrait in front of the legendary Peacock throne.

323 A rare portrait of the Shahanshah lighting candles at Now-Ruz on the traditional *Haft-Sin* table in Golestan Palace.

324 His Imperial Majesty signing documents on an official visit to Tabriz.

325 Their Imperial Majesties dressed in academic robes attend the annual opening of Tehran University held in the early autumn.

326 The Shahanshah and Shahbanou officially open the Pahlavi Dynasty Museum at the Marble Palace in Tehran.

327 The Shahanshah and Shahbanou show a lively and genuine interest in the inner workings of a tractor during their visit to a Tabriz factory.

328 The Aryamehr Show-Jumping Competition attracted competitors from all over the world. Princess Farahnaz helps her father award prizes to the finalists.

329 The Shahanshah exercises two of the family dogs on the beach at Kish.

330 During the Now-Ruz vacation at Kish Island, official base of operations in the Persian Gulf, the Shahanshah attends to affairs of state.

331 Dancers are congratulated after a state dinner in Niavaran Palace.

332 Their Imperial Majesties pause for tea and watermelon during a visit to the Dasht-e-Moghan agro-industry complex.

333 The Shahanshah is a keen horseman and frequently rides on Kish Island and in the capital.

334 His Imperial Majesty, accompanied by President Giscard d'Estaing of France, walks beneath the Shahyad Monument to the ceremony in which the President was presented with the golden key to the city of Tehran.

335 The Shahanshah, Shahbanou and His Imperial Highness the Crown Prince during a visit to the sacred city of Mashhad. Like millions of Iranian families, Their Imperial Majesties come on pilgrimage to pray in the inner sanctum of the Holy Shrine of Emam Reza (see Plate 102).

JOY OF FAMILY

336 Princess Leila eagerly blows out the candles on her birthday cake in the children's playroom of the Kish Palace while being held by her mother, the Shahbanou. Anxious to see if she succeeds are the Shahanshah, the Crown Prince, Princess Farahnaz and Prince Ali Reza.

337 An avid still and cinematographic photographer, the Crown Prince sets his camera on the beach to capture the sun setting on the Caspian Sea.

338 The Crown Prince ready for takeoff in a Star jet which he pilots himself on trips within Iran. A keen pilot, he first soloed at the age of eleven.

339 The Crown Prince enjoys an afternoon of waterskiing at Nowshahr, the Imperial Family's summer retreat on the Caspian.

340-1 The Crown Prince in dynamic action with his school team at Niavaran Palace.

342 The Crown Prince conducts an experiment before his class at the Reza Pahlavi School which the Royal children and their schoolmates attend.

343 The Crown Prince reviews the troops with Their Imperial Majesties at the Mashhad Airport during an official visit.

344 The Crown Prince at Saadabad Palace wearing his official uniform.

345-6 The Crown Prince in action.

347 Bagh-e-Eram, one of the great garden palaces of the Qajar period, is open to the public. The Shahbanou stays here during her visit to the annual Shiraz Arts Festival held in late August.

348 The mirrored grand staircase at Golestan Palace–a major tourist attraction although the palace is also used to house guests of state and for official court ceremonies.

349 During a state dinner in the gardens of Saadabad Palace, crystal table settings glitter in the candlelight.

350 The fabled Peacock Throne, seat of emperors and kings, stands in

◁ Fireworks over Tehran celebrating the Coronation of Their Majesties

all its gold and turquoise splendor in the Golestan Palace.

351 Symbol of the Negarestan Museum, Tehran.

352 Chandeliers hang from a ceiling of red velvet in the Imperial tent set up at Persepolis to celebrate the 2,500th Anniversary of the Iranian Monarchy. This tent city is now open to visitors.

353 Autumn view of Saadabad Palace. Set in an area of parkland in the cool, quiet foothills of the Alborz Mountains in north Tehran, the palace, built by Reza Shah the Great, is the official summer palace.

354 This white marble bust of Her Imperial Majesty by the Spanish sculptor J. de Avalos stands on the staircase leading to state reception rooms at Saadabad Palace.

355 The gardens of the Private Palace of the Crown Prince at Niavaran ablaze with yellow spring tulips.

356 The Royal Family relax together on Persian carpets beneath an ancient banyan tree on Kish Island. The occasion is *Sizdah-Bedar,* the thirteenth day after Now-Ruz, when Iranian families traditionally leave their homes for a day of picnicking and recreation out of doors.

357 The Royal Family pose for an informal portrait on the Kish Island beach during the Now-Ruz holidays.

358 The Crown Prince lights candles on his birthday cake at a party given by his grandmother, the Queen Mother, who stands between him and his father in her palace at Saadabad.

359 On the Twenty-Eighth of Mordad (August 19) the Crown Prince, Princess Farahnaz and Prince Ali Reza show their delight at a performance of acrobats and magicians during the annual party given by the Queen Mother.

360 A truly Persian tradition–exotic Iranian dishes are enjoyed by the Royal Family and guests who picnic out of doors on the last day of Now-Ruz at Kish.

361 Prince Ali Reza watches an exhibition of waterskiing at Karaj.

362 Relaxing on the weekend with her children, the Shahbanou helps Prince Ali Reza climb a tree to join his older brother the Crown Prince while Princess Leila waits her turn.

363 The Royal children join their parents to welcome President and Mrs. Sadat of Egypt before a state dinner at Niavaran Palace.

364 Every year at Now-Ruz the entire Pahlavi family gather together at Niavaran Palace for an official portrait by court photographers.

SHAHBANOU

365 A detail of the crown of emeralds, rubies, river pearls and diamonds, made to Her Imperial Majesty's own design by Van Cleef and Arpels, was worn by the Shahbanou on the occasion of the Imperial Coronation.

366 The Shahbanou's favorite retreat—her private library and music room at Niavaran Palace. The two-tiered study reflects her many interests. The changing array of paintings, sculpture, gifts and new books are personally supervised from her desk seen on the upper level.

367 Her Imperial Majesty in one of her favorite garden hats.

368 At the summer Nowshahr retreat, the Shahbanou in a moment of contemplation on the pier overlooking the Caspian Sea.

369 In a romantic gown, the Shahbanou takes an evening walk through the upper gardens of Niavaran Palace.

370 The Shahbanou opens the Tenth Annual Shiraz Arts Festival at Naqsh-e-Rostam.

371 Her Imperial Majesty in evening dress embroidered with traditional Persian motifs arrives at 10 Downing Street on a state visit to Great Britain to open the Science Exhibition for the Festival of Islam.

372 Their Imperial Majesties arrive in a gilded state coach for the opening of the Senate building in Tehran.

373 The Shahbanou lights the first candle on the family's Now-Ruz table at Niavaran Palace.

374 At the International Film Festival held at Rudaki Hall in Tehran, the Shahbanou presents the Golden Ibex award to outstanding filmmakers.

375 Her Imperial Majesty's court dress for the Now-Ruz *Salaam* is always designed by Iranian couturiers.

376 The Shahbanou and Crown Prince enjoy the festivities at the birthday celebration for the Queen Mother.

377 The Shahbanou mingles with students at one of the many social centers for young people which she has initiated.

378 Her Imperial Majesty attends the state dinner offered in return by the President of France at Golestan Palace.

379 At Kish the Shahbanou wears a head scarf from Osku, famous for its silk printing in tribal designs.

380 While on an official trip to the Dasht-e-Kavir, the Shahbanou stopped at Birjand to greet local camel herders and watch their thrilling races.

381 The Shahbanou is an eager photographer and keeps albums filled with special memories from her trips.

382 Although they used to travel annually to St. Moritz, Their Imperial Majesties now ski at Dizin in the Alborz Mountains above Tehran where several excellent ski resorts are enjoyed.

383 The Shahbanou visits a leprosarium on the outskirts of Tabriz. Deeply devoted to the control of leprosy, she often visits research and hospital facilities throughout the country.

384 Wearing a worker's peaked cap, the Shahbanou signs the guest book at the Dasht-e-Moghan agricultural complex in the northwestern corner of Iran.

385 Setting a good example for her people, Her Imperial Majesty gives blood at the Iranian National Blood Transfusion Service in Tehran, where later she awarded service medals to the staff.

386 Prince Kambiz, nephew of the Shahbanou, receives a cup and a kiss after an excellent display of waterskiing at the Karaj Water Show.

387 Her Imperial Majesty leads in the revival of the artistic and cultural traditions unique to Iran and helps artists attain an international level of acceptance. After a gala evening in Rudaki Hall, the Shahbanou loves to meet and exchange views with the performers.

MAJESTY

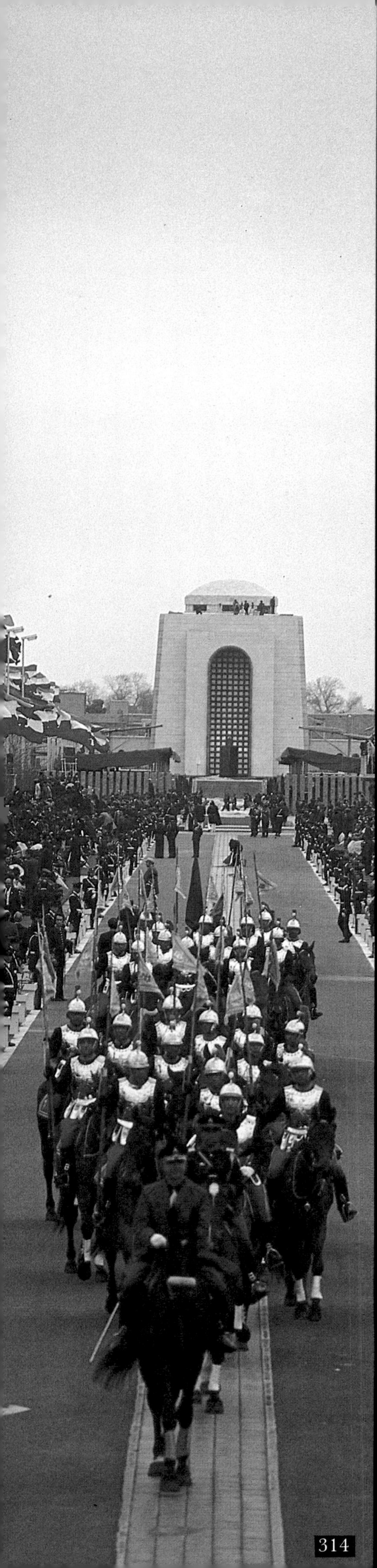

316

317

318

319

320

321

323

324

325

326

327

328

329

330

331

332

333

334

شهنشاه را چون بُوَد پیشه داد   کُند بی گمان هر کس از داد شاد
کنون شاه با داد و بخشایش است   وطن پر ز خوبی و آسایش است
که جاوید هر کس کند آفرین   بدان شاه کآباد دارد زمین
به گیتی نباید که از شهریار   بماند جُز از راستی یادگار
اگر کشور آباد دارد به داد   بماند هم آباد و از داد شاد
خنک شاه با داد یزدان پرست   کز وُ شاد باشد دل زیردست
به داد و به بخشش فزونی کُند   جهان را به دین رهنمونی کند
نگهدارد از دشمنان کشورش   به ابر اندر آرد سر و افسرش

فردوسی

The emperor's justice
radiates joy
his generosity fills the land
with virtue and comfort.
Will his name not live forever
who caused this flourishing?
His heritage is only
his righteousness.
Praise be to a godfearing king
say his people—
may his openhandedness increase.
He will instruct the land
in faith
God will preserve it
from harm
and raise his crown
to the clouds.

Ferdowsi

Overleaf:
Bronze statue of His Imperial Majesty the Shahanshah on horseback, Tehran Aryamehr Stadium (mirror image).

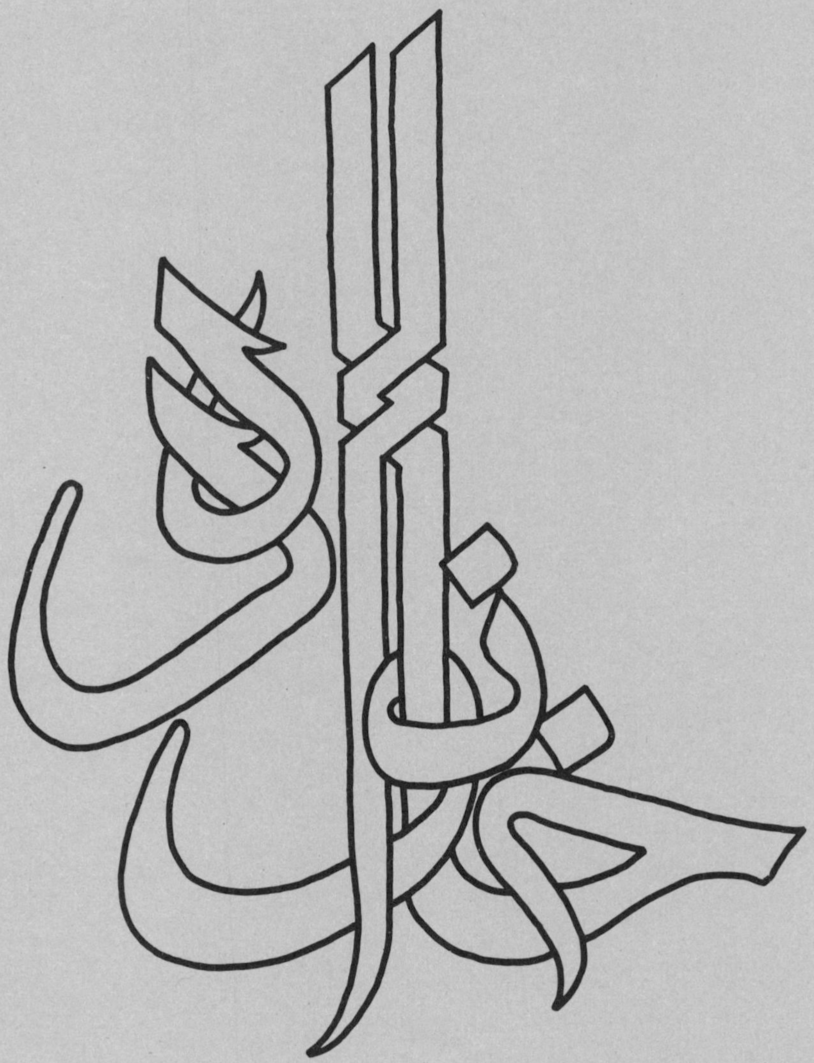

JOY OF FAMILY

337

338

339

340

341

342

343

344

345

346

347

348

349

350

351

352

353

354

355

356

357

358

359

360

361

362

363

به سه چیز باشد زنان را بهی

که باشند زیبای تخت مهی

یکی آنکه با شرم و با خواستست

که جُفتش بدو خانه آراستست

دگر آنکه فرّخ پسر زاید اوُی

ز شوُی خجسته بیفزاید اوُی

سوّم آنکه بالا و رُویش بُود

به پوشیدگی نیز مویش بُود

فردوسی

To be great
to be worthy of the throne
a woman needs
One: modesty and grace
that she might adorn
her husband's home
Two: the birth
of a happy son, to increase
her husband's joy
Three: tallness of stature
a beautiful face, to be robed
in purity and grace.

Ferdowsi

Overleaf:
Her Imperial Majesty the Shahbanou leaves Golestan Palace following the Ceremony of Coronation held on October 26, 1967.

شهبانو

SHAHBANOU

372

373

374

375

376

377

378

379

380

381

382

383

384

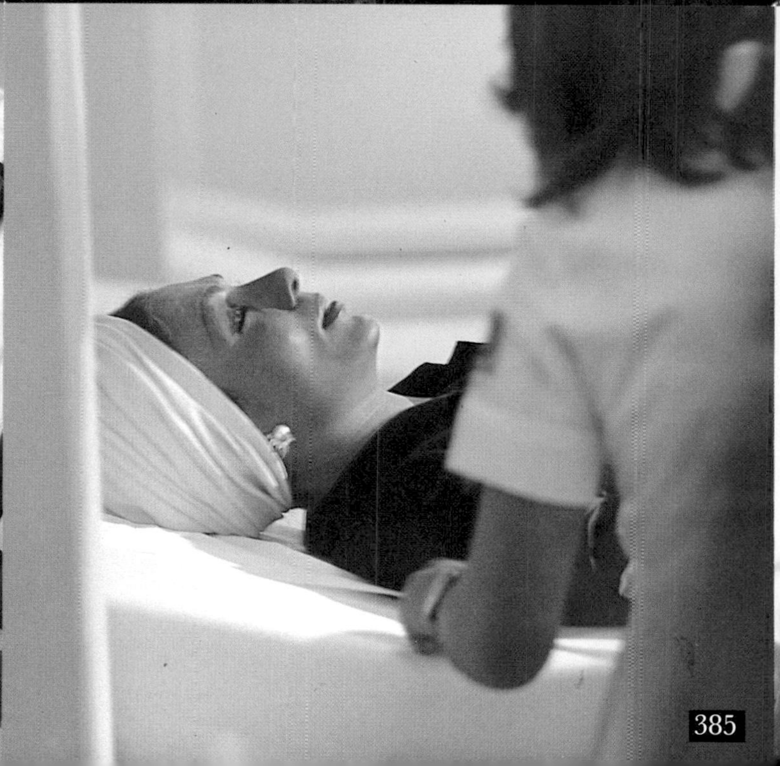
385

386

چاره سازان بیشتر در کار خود بیچاره‌اند

سیل نتواند ز رخ شستن غبار خویش را

وحید

Just as a turbulent flood cannot wash
 the brown mud from its own face . . .
Just so: he who would solve the problems
 of others: helpless.

Vahid

جمع زر هرگز نگردد پیش صاحب همتان

خاک نتواند شدن با باد در یکجای جمع

دوستی با ناتوانان مایهٔ روشندلی است

موم چون با رشته سازد شمع محفل میشود

صائب تبریزی

The Masters of spiritual Resolve
 can never busy themselves after gold
any more than a pure wind and dry dust
 can live together in peace.
Friendship with the helpless: *that's* the way
 to delight the heart;
when string is dipped in wax, it makes
 a candle for everyone.

Sa'eb Tabrizi

همتم بدرقه راه کن ای طایر قدس

که دراز است ره مقصد و من نوسفرم

حافظ

O Phoenix, grant me the Resolve
 for the road I take;
for the way to the Goal is long
 and I have just begun.

Hafez

آب کم جو تشنگی آور بدست

تا که جوشد آبت از بالا و پست

مولانا

Don't be searching always for water;
 Thirst after thirst itself
Till the water beneath your skin starts
 from toe to head—boiling!

Rumi

عمر زاهد همه طی شد به تمنای بهشت

او ندانست که در ترک تمناست بهشت

O so pious he ended his life
 still praying for paradise. Alas
he failed to understand: to give up
 the very begging: *that* is heaven!

پرتو حق است آن معشوق نیست

خالق است آن گوئیا مخلوق نیست

مولانا

TOMORROW

To foresee the destiny of any society is indeed a difficult task. Since social phenomena are so complex and since minor occurrences can have a major impact on the whole, changes cannot be precisely predicted. Nevertheless, this essay will try to make some predictions about the Iran of tomorrow. This task has been made easier by the fact that Iran is a politically stable country, and because the Iranian people have set themselves a target which they are trying to achieve.

Iran need not follow the usual pattern of the industrialized nations, for today technology is available to those who seek it. While the West needed several centuries to reach its present stage of development, Iran can achieve its targets within one or two decades.

Iran aims to continue to develop within the framework of its own traditions, to preserve its culture and to strive to maintain its synthesizing power and resilience. While industrialization has been chosen as the path to follow, Iran recognizes that industrialization is not necessarily the means to attain a utopian society. Iran's most important task will be to achieve the reconciliation of man to himself and to his natural environment. The human being will be considered the most important focal point of the Iran of the future. Each individual will be part of the nation's wealth and all efforts will be directed toward developing his inherent capabilities and toward bringing him happiness and a sense of fulfillment, to the benefit of society at large.

Modern developments have created more possibilities for man and have provided him with more material things, but his needs have also increased correspondingly. The future Iranian society will be aware of these spiraling demands and will try to prevent a growing gap between man's rising expectations and his ability to fulfill them.

As Iran develops, it will become more and more an urban society. But the large city of the future will not be a place which will isolate man and drive him to self-destruction, but a place where he can develop his creative skills and attain his own set goals. Sprawling, polluted, crowded cities will be avoided and man will learn to control his environment for his own benefit. Every member of society will become a participating citizen and contribute to the process of social change. That is why the Empress of Iran proclaims that

> to place the individual in the center of things, the ultimate aim of human activity should be geared toward the achievement of a creative, humanistic world, free from material want.

◁ PREVIOUS SPREAD:
Detail from calligraphic painting of Iranian artist Faramarz Pilaram in the Tehran Museum of Contemporary Art.

The major goals for the future of Iran will not be realized without the participation of the people. This participation will increase the general awareness of existing problems and may result in a greater degree of social maturity among the Iranian people. Everyone will then share the responsibility for shaping the destiny of the nation, and the gap between public officials and the general public will be closed.

To attain this goal, every institution should encourage public participation. In the field of education, formal institutions will become less responsible for the education of the people, and each citizen will become more responsible for his own education and the education of others. Similarly, national defense will not be the task of the armed forces alone, but will be the duty of every citizen. The achievement of justice also demands the full participation of the people. To reach the latter objective, councils comprised of ordinary citizens and invested with official authority to settle disagreements have been set up throughout the country. The number of these Houses of Equity, as they are called, will be gradually increased. To enable the people to shape their own destiny, national councils are being established all over the country, from the smallest remote village to the municipal and provincial level. The Resurgence or Rastakhiz Party (Iran's people united in one political party) will facilitate this participation in both social and political life. It will guarantee the political and national education of the people by establishing party centers throughout the country. It will convene national congresses, set up worker and student organizations, and organize political seminars and dialogue sessions.

The rapid growth of the economy, the increase in foreign exchange and the emergence of technology could produce a situation in which the poor become poorer and the rich richer. In such a society, only the rich would have access to modern conveniences and luxuries. Further differences in income distribution would widen the urban-rural gap and accentuate group differences in which a very limited number of people would have all the advantages, while the lower-income groups would constitute the vast majority. When human aspects of society are sacrificed to materialistic views, violence might result. In order to prevent such a conflict from occurring, efforts will be directed toward harnessing technology, reducing the gap among socio-economic groups and facilitating the emergence of a middle class. In order to realize these objectives, Iranian society will have to combat any form of feudalism, whether administrative or industrial, and encourage indigenous competition among workers.

One such effort in this direction was land reform,

launched to widen the base of social justice, to accelerate the participation of all people in the development of the country, and to serve as an incentive to workers and farmers.

Following the principles of the Revolution of the Shah and the People, another attempt to prevent extreme stratification of Iranian society has been accomplished by the profit-sharing plan, which provides workers a certain percentage of the profits made by industrial concerns. Other principles, added later, provide price controls designed to prevent hoarding. Another scheme aims at selling to the workers 49 percent of all privately owned industrial concerns and 99 percent of state-owned factories. Long-term government loans will be available to workers at concessional interest rates to enable them to purchase their shares. Through the establishment of cooperative stores, offering consumer goods at lower prices to increase the purchasing power of the lower-income groups, Iran intends to provide all of its population with the "vital minimum."

The partial implementation of these measures has already resulted in an increase in the middle-income group in urban areas, according to surveys by the Statistical Center of Iran.

Another way of promoting a progressive and humane society would be to accord higher value to actual work than to capital. There will be no room for timocracy in such a society, as labor will be the source of an individual's wealth and his ascendance in society. Products created by human beings reflect a part of their personalities and they see themselves through their work. An individual's work will become a source of satisfaction to him, thereby reducing alienation. There will be no room for the exploitation of man by man in this culture.

During the last decade, the rise in oil prices has greatly increased the flow of foreign exchange. Demand has outgrown supply everywhere. Major emphasis will be put on production to enable Iran to combat inflation, so that society will not be obliged to devise superfluous rules which attempt to achieve the same objective.

The future will therefore depend on the work of people, work which they owe the society, from which all advantages emanate. In such a humanistic form of capitalism, everything serves the society: science, the arts, literature, natural resources, etc.

In accordance with these beliefs, Iran has nationalized a significant part of its resources. Water, oil, forests, copper and anything else that does not represent the work of man is not to be the property of an individual, but rather of the nation as a whole.

Iranian society, however, will not become a society of consumption and waste. In a world where millions of people go hungry, where food prices are increasing rapidly and where the basic resources for the production of food are either too few or very expensive, no waste will be allowed.

To achieve the goals of the "Great Civilization" and to safeguard the destiny of future generations, the most important guarantees are national unity, strong leadership and social discipline, based on Iranian traditions. Realism will be the main characteristic of Iranian leadership, resulting in a policy that is always one step ahead of the events. Iranian democracy will not necessarily follow outside patterns, for democracy cannot be imported as a consumer good. It is a sociological concept that should be closely connected with all the aspects of a given society and be geared toward its specific personality and traditions. All people will cooperate to achieve national unity and social discipline. The future of Iran will be guaranteed by the combined efforts of the people and the Shah, a leader who emerges as a symbol of the nation. Moreover, national objectives will be a matter close to the hearts of all Iranian citizens and this will eliminate the use of violence for acquiring the benefits of the nation's wealth.

These principles will become the pillars on which the Iran of the future will be built. Our national resources will be of no use if we do not have national unity, strong leadership and social discipline.

Population and Human Resources

One of our major concerns for the future is the growth of population, since this factor will have a tremendous impact on the available food, water, welfare services and quality of life. The population of Iran has been steadily growing and this growth is expected to continue. Iran's population is expected to reach 52.2 million by 1992, an increase of 20 million in less than 20 years. With an annual growth rate of approximately three percent – based on population figures for the decade 1956 to 1966 – it is estimated that Iran's population will reach 62 million during the decade 1991 to 2001, or 2002 at the very latest.

This natural rate of population increase is 24 per 1,000 in urban areas and 35 per 1,000 in rural areas. An annual population growth rate of 2.6 percent is projected for the period 1972 to 1992. At the end of this period the population distribution will be 31 million urban and 22 million rural.

Life expectancy for both sexes has improved steadily and is projected to further improve, as illustrated by the following figures:

	1972-77	1977-82	1982-87	1987-92
Female	52.5	55.0	57.6	60.4
Male	50.0	52.5	56.5	59.0

The population is characterized by a large number of young people. In 1975 about 45 percent of the population was less than 15 years old. The population profile is also undergoing drastic changes by the steady exodus of rural dwellers to the cities, and Iran faces the tremendous task of attempting to bring about an equilibrium in this migration.

Education

The level of economic growth is rightly measured by the level of people's education. The best way to achieve a self-sustained development is to improve education and to develop the intellectual capabilities of each individual, starting as early in life as possible. Believing that education is the best investment any country can make, Iran is currently allocating an unprecedented amount of its financial resources, manpower and facilities for education.

Education will have to undergo drastic changes in the future, however. The first problem to be resolved is the current degree-mania, since this will result in an alienated education dominated by formalistic and administrative views. In future, employers will pay less importance to degrees and more to knowledge. Education will be based less on rote-learning and more on problem-solving. Further, academics often cling to theories and abstractions and live in ivory towers, isolated from the society in which they live and work, thus endangering the whole educational system.

Training programs aimed at giving students some practical experience by sending them to factories have been unsuccessful because the student often feels he is there only to fulfill a degree requirement. This leads to the belief that "productive schools" may be the answer to our present needs. In these schools the students will have to produce for the society at large after acquiring the necessary skills and experience. The teacher will not pursue the student, but vice versa, so that every minute in the educational process will be useful.

The teacher will not force his knowledge upon his students, for this creates indifference, inertia and even resistance. In the era of mass communication where information can be found anywhere, the school should become more than a mere dispenser of facts. It should develop the social maturity of the students to the point where the process of learning is fully understood. The main objective will be to stimulate the educational appetite, to provide methods for acquiring knowledge, to shape the mind of the student by stimulating a scientific spirit and, finally, to encourage self-education. Education will then become closely connected with the realities of life and the expectations of society.

This is not only the goal of Iranian education, but of education *per se.* Before these goals can be realized, however, education must become available to everyone. The first step, to achieve complete literacy in the country, is expected to take place within the next 12 years. In 1956 the literacy rate in the 7-14 age group was only 23.8 percent. This had increased to 58 percent by 1971. According to the 1956 census, only 15.4 percent of the population aged seven or older could read and write elementary Persian. Ten years later this figure had almost doubled to 29.4 percent. In 1968 this rate reached 33.4 percent for the population aged six or over, and by 1971 it had increased to 36.9 percent. In 1975 the literacy rate among persons six years and older was 43 percent (56 percent for males and 30 percent for females).

Based on the above figures, it is believed that during the last 50 years Iranian society has evolved from one in which illiteracy dominated to one in which the ability to read and write has become predominant. Initiatives in the field of education have helped to bring about this improved situation and promise the successful completion of the task that lies ahead. One of these initiatives is the Literacy Corps, a unique group of male and female high school graduates – 20,161 in 1974 – who have been drafted into the army. After receiving their basic military training, they are sent to the rural areas to educate the village children.

Currently education is free for all Iranian children. There are 29,000 primary schools, 3,700 guidance schools, 2,300 secondary schools, 339 vocational schools and 148 institutions of higher education. From 1922 to 1974 the number of primary schools increased more than 42 times and secondary schools more than 49 times. Present school enrollments are as follows: primary schools – 4 million; junior high schools – 1.2 million; high schools – 200,000; vocational schools – 100,000; and teacher training schools – 50,000. In 1922 there was only one university in Iran; by 1936 this number had increased to 10 centers of higher education with a total student population of less than 20,000, as compared to the present 148 with a total student enrollment of 149,000. During the academic year 1975-76, more than 8 million Iranians of all ages, or one-quarter of the total population, attended some educational institution. Another 50,000 Iranians are attending universities and technical schools abroad.

Parallel to the increase in the number of educational institutions, the number of children to be educated is increasing. By 1988 there will be 3,173,000 urban and 3,147,000 rural children in the 6-13 age group. To fulfill their educational needs and at the same time enhance the quality of their education will be a difficult endeavor which needs close attention.

The Iran of tomorrow will witness a revolution in education. One suggestion for reaching this goal would be the use of the mass media in education. This will promote individual learning and provide students with the most up-to-date knowledge. In the future our schools will no longer hold the monopoly in education. Everywhere, even in teahouses, the elements of learning can be found. The school occupies only a limited amount of a student's time and only a limited number of years in his life, but the mass media are capable of delivering a continuous educational process.

Among these radical transformations in education, the role of the teacher will change tremendously as well. The use of films or tapes which can be communicated via TV or radio will free the teacher so that personal contacts can be made with students on the basis of their individual needs.

Agriculture

One of Iran's major goals is the development of a rapid increase in agricultural productivity. As long as a nation cannot provide its citizens with their basic requirements, it will not be truly independent. It is therefore obvious that agriculture is of the utmost importance to the balanced development of the country. By the year 2000 60 million people, with a high per capita income, will have to be fed. To meet the needs of this growing population, agricultural output must be increased.

According to the 1956 census, six million persons, or 31 percent of the population, lived in urban areas. According to the 1966 census, the urban population had increased to 9.8 million, or 38 percent of the total; and in 1971 it was estimated to be 12.4 million, or 41 percent.

The rural population is currently estimated at 55 percent of the total and this proportion is steadily declining (although the absolute number is increasing and is projected to increase from the current estimated 18 million to approximately 20 million by the mid-1980s). Therefore, steps need to be taken to improve the fertility of agricultural lands and to prevent erosion, to develop a more efficient water utilization scheme and an up-to-date system for the marketing of farm products, to obliterate the gap between city and village, and to provide the psycho-sociological and economic motivation to increase farm output.

Although 40 percent of the population is active in the agrarian sector, agriculture constitutes only 10 to 12 percent of the gross domestic value, as compared to 26 percent in 1963. During the period 1962-72 the rate of growth in agriculture was four percent per year and in 1973, approximately six percent.

The implementation of land reform in 1963 marked a turning point in the history of agriculture in Iran. This historical event removed many obstacles for the improvement of agriculture. Before land reform, the total volume of agricultural production amounted to approximately 85 to 87 billion rials per year. During the decade following land reform, it increased by 53 percent. Land reform affected 17,000 villages, covering 8 million hectares and 2.3 million rural families, one-third of whom were landless peasants prior to this event. The emancipation of the peasantry provided the basic elements to increase farm production and established a favorable psycho-sociological framework. Nevertheless, it has become obvious that additional steps need to be taken to bring about an impetus in Iran's agricultural sector. One of the obstacles in reaching this objective is the fact that the villages are widely dispersed over a large area. Iran has about 66,000 village communities scattered all over the country, with 18.5 million population; of this, 14 million are living in 18,000 villages with a population over 250. The remaining 4.5 million live in 48,000 villages with a population under 250.

Isolated villagers, farming small subsistence plots, are widely separated from others with whom they might be able to cooperate. They neither have the means nor the technology to change their traditional methods into a more productive system. If production is to be increased, some consolidation of services and population is necessary, so that sophisticated equipment can be obtained and effectively utilized.

It seems certain that millions of Iranian farmers will have to leave their unproductive villages during the next decade because it will be impossible to provide these remote villages with the basic requirements such as hospitals, schools and economic facilities. To counter this, "village contracts," financed by a cooperative bank or state subsidies, should be developed to facilitate the construction of collective facilities, the renovation of the irrigation network and the allocation of tracts of rangeland. In return, these villages, through the intermediary of a rural cooperative, will tackle the problems of land utilization and consolidation, and institute a reform of water rights. A recently passed law calls for the development of agricultural development poles whose authorities will direct farm corporations and production cooperatives.

Thus, the next few years will witness a massive reconstruction of the rural areas through the media of rural cooperative societies, agribusiness, farm corporations and production cooperatives.

In developing the agricultural sector, use will be made of such modern techniques as drip irrigation, snowpack, cloud seeding and nuclear energy. To control the migration of the rural population to the cities, activities in the rural areas need to become more diversified by the creation of small industries that will lessen seasonal unemployment. Last but not least, attempts will be made to conserve national resources to permit the recycling of national wealth.

Industry and Mining

In order to build a progressive and modern society, Iran will have to make use of the most sophisticated tools that have been invented over the ages. Thus, the path toward the future will be characterized by the acquisition of modern technology.

The following figures give a picture of industrial changes in Iran: The industrial growth rate in Iran has risen sharply, from 5 percent per year in 1962 to well over 20 percent per year in 1974. Industrial production constituted 11.7 percent of the GNP in 1962 and approximately 17 percent in 1974. Currently Iran's total labor force includes about 9.5 million persons, 60 percent of whom are active in industry and the services sector. Manufacturing and mining employ over 2 million, while the services sector employs approximately 3.5 million. Between 1956 and 1972 industrial employment in food and textile industries decreased from 77 to 57 percent of the total labor force. During the same period employment in the metal and machinery industries increased from 5 to 20 percent. Industrial employment has grown 5 percent per annum during recent years. Productivity in the industrial sector, measured by the value added per employed person, has increased 10 percent from 1962 to 1974. Government incentives will encourage the private sector to reinforce the varied nature of Iran's industry. Energy-intensive industries such as aluminum, ferro-alloys, etc. will play an important role in industry as second sector economy. Copper, steel, the automobile industry, petro-chemicals, electronics, the manufacture of electrical equipment and metal smelting will increase rapidly. In order to implement these objectives fully, it will be necessary to emphasize the training of manpower. Paid-on-the-job training must be available to meet the labor requirements of industry and to establish and develop industrial poles. These poles will be situated near the large urban centers and serve ecological and long-term development purposes within the existing infrastructure.

Toward the end of the Sixth Development Plan (1982), the capacity for steel production will exceed 15 million tons, and both the new direct reduction technique as well as the conventional BOF (basic oxygen furnace) technique will be used. Besides the expansion (already underway) of the Aryamehr Steel Works near Esfahan to 1.9 million metric tons, Iran will construct three direct reduction steel works: at Ahvaz, thus creating 3,500 jobs; at Bandar Abbas, creating 9,000 jobs; and at Esfahan, creating 3,500 jobs.

In the petro-chemical field, Iran will gradually emerge as a large exporter of basic petro-chemical building blocks as well as intermediate final products and fertilizers. The objective is to produce 5 to 10 percent of the world's basic petro-chemical needs by 1983 and thereafter to supply 10 percent of the annual growth in world demand.

Iran's natural gas reserves, the largest in the Middle East and possibly the second largest in the world, are estimated at 250 to 600 trillion cubic feet. Yet Iran exported only $130 million worth of natural gas in 1974. During the Fifth Development Plan, $2.5 billion was planned to be invested in the gas industry, leading to an increase in gas exports to $2-$5 billion by 1982. This implies an annual rate of growth in gas exports of between 30 and 45 percent.

Iran's reserves of crude oil are estimated to be between 60 and 85 billion barrels. During the Iranian year 1354 (March 1975 to March 1976), income from oil exports amounted to more than $20 billion. At a production level of 5.5 to 6.5 million barrels per day, this wealth would last at least another thirty years. Because of the fact that the main sources of energy are going to be exhausted sooner or later, and in order to use this wealth to the maximum extent, it is believed that a new world energy consumption attitude is called for. The exhaustion of the oil reserves will radically change the economic picture of Iran and will also exert great influence on world civilization. One means of reducing oil consumption will be to enforce price increases. Iran recognizes a price that compares with the cost of producing alternative commodities that serve similar purposes, such as the energy obtained from coal, shale or tar sands (nuclear or solar energy cannot be compared). This will preserve our petroleum, from which thousands of products are derived, and will establish a just level of income for the oil-exporting countries.

Because of the net value added by the products that can be derived from petroleum, it would also be to the advantage of oil-rich Iran to substitute the export of crude oil with the export of finished products. The initial step in the realization of this objective started with the nationalization of the Abadan refinery. Additional developments are expected to result in an increase in oil-related exports to $25 to $30 billion a year.

Besides oil and gas reserves, Iran is fortunate in having large copper reserves, providing another important source of income. The total copper reserves are estimated to be one billion tons.

These are the industrial characteristics of Iran. They highlight our main purpose: the building of a national technology closely connected with our traditions, habits and national identity. Iranian society will absorb technological elements within the framework of its own culture. And last, but not least, an attempt should be made to master technology. It will have to harmonize with nature and serve the people, and thereby emphasize the rising Iranian humanism.

Economic Growth

In the area of gross national product and per capita income, the trend during the past few years may serve as an indicator for future developments. In 1950 Iran was one of the poorest countries in the world. Seventeen years later, in 1967, Iran's per capita income ranked 56th on a worldwide basis; in 1969 it was 52nd; and by 1973 it had risen to 44th. In 1975 Iran's GNP ranked 19th; and in 1976, 15th.

The evolution of per capita income in Iran is described as follows: In 1972 the GNP per capita was $530; in 1976 and 1977 it reached $1,850 and $2,220. In the *National Spatial Strategy Plan* by Scetiran Consulting Engineers, it is predicted that in 1992 it will reach $3,000; and in 2012, $3.500, at constant 1972 rials. In aggregate terms, during the period of 1962-72 the GNP in Iran increased by an average of 11 percent per year; and during 1973-74, because of the exceptional increase in oil prices, it increased by 50 percent at current prices. In other words, the growth rate of the Iranian economy tripled from 1962-63 to 1972-73, from 5 percent to 15 percent.

The Sixth Development Plan is not yet available, but Iran's revised Fifth Development Plan (1973-78) revealed that total fixed investments amount to approximately $70 billion. A growth rate of 18.4 percent in the industrial and mining sector, of 8 percent in agriculture, and of 5 percent in the services sector is expected, while public outlays (investment plus current expenditures and other payments) during the period covered by the fifth plan are projected to reach $123 billion.

National Defense

The sole purpose of Iran's national defense policy is the maintenance of peace. Its armament and manpower serve a deterrent rather than aggressive army, one which will nevertheless be used without hesitation to assist in the reinforcement of world peace and even to guarantee a complete international disarmament.

Iran therefore continues to spend considerable sums on its defense. The following figures illustrate Iran's concern for national defense and the independence of the country:

Defense Expenditures Since 1962 (in U.S. dollars)

1962	$210 million
1966	$360 million
1970	$820 million
1972	$1.4 billion
1973	$4.8 billion

It is hoped that, in the near future, the world at large will become more aware of the horrors of war, and the arms race, especially the proliferation of nuclear arms, can be averted. The future may bring a world where the law of the jungle has been abolished and where criminal individuals will not be able to kill millions of people by using demagogy or by misusing the concepts of freedom and nationalism. Until that time, reality forces us to remain strong and to secure peace by strength.

The defense of the country will not be a concern of the armed forces alone, however, but of all citizens. The recent social reforms will have a great impact on the implementation of this ideology because a farmer who owns his land, or a factory worker who owns shares in the factory where he works, will do his utmost to defend his property and loved ones.

These are the main philosophies behind the national defense of our country, a country that does not intend to invade another, but whose people are determined to safeguard the sacred land of their ancestors by any means, including their own lives.

Natural Environment

Another major factor in improving the quality of life is the preservation of the natural environment. The real dimension of this problem can be measured by the nostalgia for nature exhibited by the inhabitants of metropolitan areas. Iran will not have gained much by acquiring the advantages of industrialization if the balance of nature is disturbed. Nature is a gift of God, and the preservation of the beauty and resources of our country should bear a religious halo. Information on the present condition of Iran's 18 million hectares of forest land is currently being gathered, and thought is being given to the problems of the cities, which experienced an average growth rate of 5.1 percent during the period from 1966 to 1973. The living environment is deteriorating. To avoid further deterioration, many laws have been passed for the control of water, the decrease of air pollution and the prevention of further erosion of agricultural lands. However, additional steps are to be taken which will permit the regeneration of resources that influence the quality of life and guarantee human survival, and a form of urbanization and agricultural development will be achieved that will harmonize with the natural environment.

Health

As long as poverty exists, especially when accompanied by high mortality rates caused by the lack of medical facilities, we will not achieve the "Great Civilization." Thus, a major objective will be to improve the health of all Iranians, since health is a major prerequisite in raising the quality of life. In order to reach this objective, the seventeenth principle of the Revolution of the Shah and the People emphasizes medical insurance coverage for the whole population, whereas the seventh principle has already initiated the establishment of the Health Corps.

In its struggle against disease, Iran will develop a national health service that is geared toward its specific needs and that takes into account traditional habits, nutrition and climate. Some customs will need to undergo drastic change, and the high birth rate will need to be lowered. Medical services will have to be extended to even the remotest villages by gathering them into development poles where medical facilities can be established. The need for prevention will have to be stressed and a wide meaning will need to be given to this term, ranging from the encouragement of sports to enhancing leisure time activities, to bring about a socialized medical system that will widen the base of social justice and provide equal opportunities. It will also be necessary to provide health education to wipe out nutritional and health care prejudices, to teach people proper health care methods and the adequate use of medicines and medical equipment.

Architecture

The same philosophies are followed in architecture. Iran's rich architectural heritage will be combined with modern technology in the development of a colorful and diversified architectural style. Harmony with the surrounding natural environment will result in the utmost efficiency and comfort. Architectural design will not serve prestige and looks alone; art and technology will be harmoniously blended. Love for beauty will characterize future architectural design, just as it did during the Sasanian and Safavid periods, which marked a climax in the history of Iranian architecture. Iran will continue to follow this tradition.

Another major objective will be the preservation of the architectural splendors of the past. To reach this objective, efforts are already being made to preserve the original structure of the cities of Yazd, Kashan, Tabas, Dezful, etc. Furthermore, Farabi University has been established to enliven national and traditional aspects of architecture, to emphasize its human dimension and to effect a renaissance of architecture in Iran.

Leisure Time

The concept of leisure time has undergone tremendous changes during recent years because of the prolongation of schooling, shorter working hours, and the dissolving of some traditional duties within the family. Other factors which have contributed to the importance of leisure time include the loosening of kinship relations, the rapid exodus of the rural population to the big cities and changing customs and traditions. This trend will continue and leisure time will become an important aspect of Iranian life in the future because correct leisure-time habits will have a great impact on the mental health of the population and the productivity of the labor force, besides enhancing the quality of life. The private sector will be encouraged to provide leisure-time activities and facilities but, in order to prevent profiteering, the government will control and direct private investment; otherwise a desire for personal profits might result in providing improper leisure-time opportunities, which would lead to a general decadence of society.

The mass media will play a massive role in the

leisure-time habits of the Iranian population. Iran now has 100 percent radio coverage, and television coverage is steadily increasing. In 1967 only 2.5 million people were covered by television. This figure increased to 13.5 million by 1972, and 20 million by 1977. These figures represent the technical coverage, which is not necessarily the same as the actual coverage. The discrepancy between these two figures will eventually become negligible, however, because of the disappearance of such factors as the financial inability to purchase a television set and taboos against the watching of television. Moreover, there will be an increase in hours spent in front of the television set because of longer sending times and because of an increasing appetite for watching television programs on the part of the viewers. A research study, undertaken by the Office of Cultural Affairs of the University of Tehran, indicated that there is an increasing demand for more programs among adolescents. The study also noted that internal family problems are resulting from young children wanting to watch more programs than their parents are willing to allow.

Cinemas and theaters are also attracting more people and these new habits will change the structure of leisure time. In 1972 the total number of cinema viewers was 41 million, which shows an increase of 12 percent over 1968. The establishment of additional museums, such as the Negarestan Museum, will be encouraged, as will the opening of more art galleries and the holding of exhibits. However, leisure-time activities will not cater only to the mind. The provision of the necessary facilities for physical exercise will be of equal importance, and sports for the sake of improved physical health will be encouraged for people of all ages and from all walks of life.

Other goals will include improving the tourist infrastructure, increasing the number of Youth Palaces and Houses of Youth, decentralizing leisure-time planning and designing leisure-time schemes that will combat such social ills as addiction, gambling and debauchery. The arts and reading will take on new importance and people will be encouraged to take part in activities that will liberate them from the prerogatives of their daily work. They will find new perspectives and will no longer remain indifferent to the masterpieces of painting and music or the archeological heritage of their nation. Healthy leisure-time activities will enhance the culture of each individual and therefore the richness of Iran's national culture. Each individual will have the freedom to select his own leisure-time activities so that leisure time will not be turned into a time of laziness but into a time of creativity.

The Role of Women

The transformations that are to occur in Iran will exert particular influence on the destiny of women. For centuries, Iranian women have been victims of a socio-economic setting dominated by men. Males had access to decision-making circles and were permitted to take possession of products created by women, especially in the rural areas. This culture bears the impact of a religion influenced by the culture of pre-Islamic Arabs, a culture which was characterized by the humiliation of women and even the burial of female infants. Islam attempted to alter these inhuman conditions by prohibiting the burial of infants and by giving females the right to own property and to participate in public affairs. Nevertheless, polygyny was allowed, divorce was the monopoly of men and, despite the fact that they were granted private property rights, women were considered private property.

From birth on, boys and girls were destined for quite different roles. The son would inherit twice as much as the daughter and was considered the potential heir of the father. He therefore occupied a privileged place and all possible efforts were made to prepare him for the role of assuming economic and social power. He had a wide range of possibilities and freedoms. The girl, on the contrary, was prepared to assume an erotic and even purely biological role. She was to remain at home, preferably bear a large number of children, and was expected not to interfere with the affairs of men. This situation economically paralyzed half the population and deprived the labor market of a large part of its potential labor force. Ethically, it was inhuman to treat half the population according to stereotyped prejudices. Such a state of affairs also had a harmful effect on the quality of the population as a whole since these women, who were treated as inferiors, had to raise and educate the next generation. This situation lasted until 1963, the year the Revolution of the Shah and the People was launched, although one important measure, the imperial decree prohibiting the wearing of the veil, had been taken before that time. Since then, many attempts had been made to liberate women. The first was the granting of female suffrage, which allowed women to elect and be elected to national legislative bodies as well as provincial, district and local councils. Other important measures included the establishment of the Family Protection Law and an amendment to the constitution legalizing the regentship of Shahbanou Farah Pahlavi. From 1963 on, the whole setting changed and, after centuries of exploitation and darkness, the rise of women commenced. Polygyny became conditional to the written consent of the first wife. The Family Protection Law stipulates bilateral divorce and prohibits arbitrary divorces by men. Divorce decisions are made by Family Protection Courts.

One of the factors that played an important role in the liberation of women was the minimum marriage age. In a patriarchal family system, fathers often regarded their daughters as mere instruments to arrange marriages that were politically, socially or economically advantageous, without regard to their own will and even before they reached puberty. According to the new regulations, the minimum age at marriage is 15 for girls and 18 for boys. This change has influenced the whole destiny of women and has facilitated their access to the labor market. Contrary to the earlier provisions of the Civil Code, which obliged women to obtain their husbands' prior approval for employment, the Family Protection Law grants women the right of employment. The following figures demonstrate to some extent the momentum in the evolution in female employment:

Economically Active Population
(percent of population 10 years and over)

Year	Total	Male	Female
1956	47.5	83.9	9.2
1966	46.1	77.4	12.6
1972	42.5	67.8	12.5
1977-78	42.2	69.1	14.1

However, it seems that women's contribution to productivity has not been measured accurately, especially in the rural areas. In the urban areas, the female occupation rate is expected to increase to almost 25 percent by 1992.

One of the most important factors in female employment will be equality of educational opportunity. Education will liberate women from all existing prejudices and will eliminate the gap between men and women in the labor market. Most employed women are currently engaged in manual industry and earn small incomes. The facts have already demonstrated a rapid evolution in the educational field and promise further optimism for the future.

Literacy Rates
(percent of population 7 years and over)

Year	Total	Male	Female
1956	15.4	22.4	8.0
1966	29.4	40.1	17.9
1972	36.9	47.7	25.5

During the period 1956-71, the rate of change in literacy was 2.9 percent greater for urban women than for urban men. But in the rural areas, during the same period, the trend was the opposite. The literacy rate of men over women demonstrated a 13.9 percent increase, with only 8.3 percent of the women being literate in 1971. However, during the period 1961-71 the average annual growth rate in the number of female students at various educational levels was 13 percent for primary schools, 30 percent for high schools, 88 percent for technical and vocational schools and 76 percent for institutions of higher education. It is expected that, by the early 1990s, the female participation rate will reach 100 percent at primary schools, 95 percent at guidance schools, 90 percent at secondary schools and about 10 percent at institutions of higher education.

The Iranian woman will face a different situation and destiny by the early years of the third millennium. With this objective in mind, the Iranian Women's Organization was created to promote the status of women throughout the country and Farah University was established to assist them in the educational field. In the years to come, there will be no need for Iranian women to imitate men because they will no longer be humiliated as women. The gap between men and women will be eliminated from birth on through the education of the family and the influence of the mass media.

Conclusion

These are the main goals of the Iranian people for a future characterized by the struggle of the nation against any form of man's alienation from nature and society. Iran will also demonstrate a strong determination to diminish the "cultural gap," and to combat the sort of overspecialization that results in fragmentation of human beings. Progress will not be a mere quantitative or economic phenomenon. The human dimension will be the most important aspect of every situation and life in general. Human life was indeed sacred in ancient Iran, and in the coming national renaissance man will be the focus of all action taken by society. His equilibrium will be guaranteed by society, he will be considered the unfading wealth of the country, and the maximum development of his capabilities will be the main objective of the society.

There are no perfect formulas for economic growth, freedom and social justice, and not all of today's opinions will be beneficial to tomorrow's development. Problems are part of life and their solution will bring ideals and aims to the people. Therefore, no generation will be sacrificed for a vague utopian future and no stage of life will be ruined to achieve a few moments of great happiness.

The path toward the future will lead us to all sorts of dilemmas, the first of which are the extremes of materialism and spiritualism. Iran will not be a purely spiritualistic society, and Iranians will have to sense their material needs and strive to solve the problems of the world without disturbing the constant equilibrium between aspirations and possibilities, a disturbance which would bring frustrations and hamper the integrity of life.

Iran will not become a rootless society given totally to so-called modernism by stimulating ever-increasing needs in individuals, but neither can we permit the loss of traditions that have been sacred over the ages. The Iran of tomorrow will have to adapt constantly to ever-changing conditions, but this will have to take place within the context of its traditions. The children of Iran will be aware of their traditions and be proud of them, so that the national identity will be secured.

A major asset will be the work of the people and the wealth obtained from national resources. A capitalistic society emphasizing excessive competition uproots altruism. Iran will moderate this sense of competition so that the people, from their childhood on, will not consider each other as rivals or enemies, but will learn to love one another. Therefore, the implementation of a "humanistic culture" and the encouragement of a religion in which the utmost ideal is the happiness of others will be major objectives of the nation. This emphasis on altruism has a very long tradition in Iran's culture.

Amid these dilemmas and along with the decision to meet the challenges of the third millennium, the best results will be obtained by drawing upon the Iranian culture which has proven itself resilient over the ages. While Iran will move toward becoming a highly industrialized society, it will do so without experiencing many of the negative aspects of the process. In modern industrialized societies, man knows much about space and the oceans, but he is a stranger to his neighbors. Man lives among crowds but is lonely. Man works hard, but under the inhuman conditions that prevail in most large cities he loses his identity and dignity. His actions seem to be directed at destroying his natural environment, endangering the equilibrium of the ecological system and, accordingly, his own life. Mass production obstructs the view of the worker, producer and creator of his own products, so that he will lose the sense of satisfaction he had during the period when giant cities and gigantic factories had not yet replaced small workshops. Exaggerated utilitarianism and an excessive tendency toward wasteful consumption diminish any hopes for a better future. Therefore, using the practical and philosophical experiences of others, Iranian ways to solve the problems of Iran will have to be found amid the pessimism that presently rules our world.

Agriculture will indeed have to meet the ever-increasing demands of an increasing number of people. All our means will be put at the disposal of agriculture in order to achieve improved farm output: the Literacy Corps, the Health and Extension Corps, rural cooperative societies, production cooperatives, agribusiness, agricultural development poles, farm corporations, etc.

Women will also witness radical transformations of their destiny in the years to come. In the future, the participation of women in the political and economic life of our country will mobilize half of our population, and the emancipation of women will prepare the whole nation to meet the challenges of the third millennium.

In the educational field especially, revolutionary means will be used to reach these objectives. Science for the sake of science, with a "fundamentalism" far from being vital and realistic and that isolates the scientific community, will not be tolerated. We will witness the birth and expansion of apprenticeship and university workshops in which students first study the theoretical framework and then, while continuing their education, begin to produce for the benefit of society.

The emergence of a new Iranian society will bring new ideas and aspirations. In a world where about 800 million people are barely surviving, one country alone cannot live in abundance and prosperity. Nations will have to learn to live together and share experiences to pave the path toward true interdependence that implies mutual respect for each other's dignity, sovereignty and independence. To implement this objective, it will be Iran's policy to secure cooperation with all nations, on a bilateral basis and in multilateral settings. Thus, foreign trade, economic cooperation and foreign aid will be put at the service of these aims.

These are the main goals to lead an ancient people to a better future, goals which emanate from a very long history and which Iran will continue to follow for the survival and happiness of its people. It is hoped that Iranian culture will be presented as something original, because of its resilience, synthesizing power and harmony. In a world plagued by hunger, misery, disparity, ignorance and disease, the voice of this civilization will echo humanism and the emancipation of man.

Bagher Saroukhani

VISION

The vision of future Iran emanating from the creative ferment of the Iran of today is one of a society once again attaining greatness. With half the population less than one generation old and with an ancient heritage to build upon, the nation is at once more than 2,500 years mature and less than twenty years young. This duality expresses itself in an ever-widening interaction with all parts of the globe, complemented by a renewed sense of cultural roots.

Eagerness for a modern and progressive life in Iran is coupled with a concern that, in achieving the new millennium, the essence of the civilization may be lost. The nation's future may well be fashioned into an authentic continuum from the past, however, by once again reasserting that unique Iranian ability to assimilate what is foreign and remold it into something genuinely Iranian.

The vision of the Iran of tomorrow may be seen in outline in projects planned for the future. The large variety of these projects shows that Iran is making efforts on all fronts, with no one sector emphasized at the expense of another.

Thus, while industrialization races ahead, agriculture is not neglected. The Land Reform of 1952 is proceeding a step further, toward cooperative farming units with associated agro-industries. The scheme aims to utilize the land more efficiently and husband the nation's scarcest resource, water, by bringing together small, unproductive villages into planned rural towns.

No longer isolated and fearing the harsh conditions of the arid Iranian Plateau, the new agriculturalist will work in partnership with nature to make the surface of the land more productive. At the same time, the geologist, aided by satellite surveys, will continue to coax from the land her subterranean riches—copper, natural gas and whatever other treasures lie hidden there.

The environment, with its rugged terrain and difficult climate which gave birth, by contrast, to the walled and strictly geometrical Persian garden, need no longer be considered hostile. It is now seen as something to be protected through environmental parks and extensive wildlife preserves.

In the field of energy, Iran's pursuance of the leading edge of technology is evidence of an earnest attitude of conservation and efficient utilization. There is an acute awareness that the supply of oil is limited, that there is little flowing water for such a vast land and growing population, and that even the recently discovered natural gas fields must eventually be depleted. Thus, the nation has planned and already begun the establishment of nuclear power stations and has initiated research into ways of harnessing the energy of the endless sun which parches the desert wastes.

Development projects directed toward the natural elements are complemented by programs concerned with the growth of society and the individual. Cultural centers for the visual and performing arts, centers for the intellectual development of youth, and centers of higher education are being established throughout the country. Some of the latter, such as Jondishapur University in Ahvaz, revive ancient seats of learning; others, such as Hamedan's Bu Ali Sina University, will concentrate on uniquely Iranian applications of modern knowledge; still others, such as Reza Shah Kabir Graduate University in the north, will fill specific gaps in the country's educational fabric, at the same time providing the basis for new communities.

Highly specialized institutions are being designed to incorporate the most sophisticated techniques. The Imperial Medical Center of Iran, for example, will utilize extensive communications media on an international scale for education, research and medical services.

Iran's rapid growth in industry and population is resulting in urban migration and development of urban facilities on a scale destined to change the face of the nation. But special efforts are being made to improve the conditions of life for those who still live in rural areas. The provision of medical, educational and social services is one aspect of this improvement. Another, and even more basic one, is ensuring the safety of life and limb in the face of devastating natural disasters such as earthquakes. Experimental work is being done to create inexpensive earthquake-resistant housing systems which are related to traditional rural forms, methods and life.

Attention is being directed simultaneously to rural areas and to towns and cities of every size. The center of activity in Iran, however, is destined to remain its capital, Tehran, with its future government center, Shahestan Pahlavi. While continuing decentralization of government aims to reinvest each region with a greater degree of autonomy and self-motivation, Tehran's role as the commercial hub of the nation remains assured. Its place as an international center

◁ PREVIOUS SPREAD:
Model for the Iran Museum of Modern Arts in Shiraz, designed by Alvar Aalto.

among the world's cities is growing, and will be efficiently served by the ultra-modern Tehran International Airport. Tehran's own growth in relation to the overall development of the nation will therefore play a decisive role in Iran's urbanization process.

This process appears to be taking on a unique multi-directional approach, one which acknowledges both the attraction of cities and ties to ancestral lands. On the one hand, the establishment of industrial development poles and agricultural centers—a comprehensive scheme which is in the first stages of implementation—is intended to distribute the future urban population more evenly throughout the country. These industrial poles offer opportunities to guide the development of existing towns of medium size as they grow into major cities.

Large-scale cooperative farming and agro-industries are expected to create further opportunities to consolidate scattered villages into a planned network of viable rural communities. These communities would offer the amenities of urban life, but remain less than major city size. They must be able to accommodate a population which still has a strong element of tradition, and anticipate the rising expectations of the young.

On the other hand, among Iran's more than 60,000 villages are many whose inhabitants have such an attachment to the land that, in spite of isolation and an austere life, they wish to remain where they are. Rather than insisting that these people migrate to the cities, Iran is developing ways of bringing to them the advantages offered by rapid industrialization. This is being done through a coupling of the most advanced technology with the concept of mobility, which has historic roots among Iran's ancient tribes.

Already, tribal schools travel with nomadic herdsmen and their families and mobile libraries bring the written word to remote corners. A rural health network is being tested which progresses from the village "health house" with a para-medical resident to urban medical facilities serving the region. In addition, recent undertakings in solar energy research and in the development of educational radio and television via satellite together promise a higher standard of physical comfort, energy, communication and education to the most isolated sectors of the country.

Iran's high incidence of sunshine and scattered villages provide an ideal situation for the use of solar energy for heating, cooling, the pumping of water and the generation of electricity. With this electric power, each village can have access to education programs broadcast nationwide via satellite and stemming from an academic complex planned near the Caspian Sea. From this new college town will issue the programs for Educational Radio and Television and for the Free University which will ultimately reach four hundred centers throughout Iran. The Reza Shah Kabir University of Graduate Studies in the same community will supply many of the teachers as well as professors for other universities. This interaction of high technology, small village and new town illustrates the multi-directional approach which Iran is using for its regional development and national growth.

In the field of architectural design, Iran possesses an ancient tradition of excellence; the nation now has a unique opportunity to create a significant, contemporary architecture. The process of industrialization has resulted in a growing middle class which seeks a modern rather than traditional life. Burgeoning urban areas require a whole new stock of buildings, from dwellings to social institutions. Industrialization has brought about the manufacture and importation of all types of building materials and techniques, and it is providing the economic mechanism to finance large amounts of construction. These are the practical conditions prevailing; certain ingredients for a productive aesthetic condition exist as well.

The long and well-documented history of classic Iranian architecture is itself a rich heritage from which new forms may be derived. This tradition of creative design can be traced in actual examples from the Achaemenian Empire to the Qajar Dynasty in the nineteenth century. At that time, imitation of European styles and motifs became a dominant concern and the continuity of indigenous architectural development was broken, an instance of the severance of cultural roots. However, the hiatus, which lasted beyond the occupation by foreign powers during World War II and the later beginnings of industrialization, has now left the aesthetic ground free.

There is a group of talented young architects in Iran today who are developing a new design philosophy stemming from a conviction that there is no need to imitate either the past or the building styles already produced by other nations. They believe that design solutions must grow directly out of the cultural background to satisfy the requirements of the nation's future. Indeed, many of the world's most respected architects and planners agree that Iran at this moment has an unparalleled opportunity to learn from and avoid the mistakes of those countries which have already passed well beyond the industrial revolution. It can create something entirely new without the constraints of insurmountable financial limitations or overburdening tradition.

It cannot be predicted whether a leader will emerge from this group to guide the development of the country's architecture upon such a new path. Certain fertile conditions exist, but there are obstacles as well. The very situation of rapid growth itself creates the classic problem of architects being so busy actually producing that they too easily accept ready solutions and have little time for creative thought.

There is also the temptation to design "tourist architecture"—to apply standard motifs in a pastiche attempt to "Persianize" modern forms. At the opposite extreme is the danger of being too fond of all things foreign. The nation's construction demand makes it particularly vulnerable to imported systems which can quickly fill a need but may not be suitable for Iran's conditions or the people's requirements.

Although there is certainly a place for the work of foreign architects in Iran, one must realize that for the most part they are here only temporarily and their interest is most often limited to the project in hand. There are a few who can nevertheless give Iran examples of high-quality modern architecture to stand alongside others anywhere in the world—as France's Le Corbusier did in India, as the American Louis Kahn did in Bangladesh, as Finland's Aalto did in the United States and was doing in Iran upon his death. Today there are internationally known architects from around the globe making their marks in Iran, such as Kenzo Tange and I. M. Pei, to name but two, from the far east and the far west. Indeed, the interchange of ideas brought about by such contacts with the new and the foreign is necessary for growth, and Iran has historically thrived on just such conditions.

In one respect, the distinctive assimilating and synthesizing approach of the creative Iranian mind is already at work not only among graduates of universities here, but also among young architects and planners who have received their training abroad and have recently returned to their homeland. Combined with professional knowledge and expertise gained in foreign places and a skill with foreign styles, one finds in them a renewed and genuine appreciation of their culture and its values. This has resulted in a growing concern with developing Iranian solutions to building programs from a single dwelling to an entire town. And equally as important, there is the conviction that this can be done now.

For the future, it is this kind of concern and the attempt to express it in actual projects which will assure the quality of Iranian architecture. It is both impossible and hardly important to arrive at "final solutions" to modern Iranian design, for the society, particularly because it is predominantly young, will continue developing in new directions with new requirements. In the long run, it is not the container which is of first importance, but the contents: it is not the visual perfection of the city and its buildings which is the primary goal, but the quality of life of the inhabitants.

In addition to providing comfort and a high physical standard of living, the country's architects and planners are also addressing themselves to the strengthening of those values intrinsic to the culture. The design of urban spaces, for example, can foster or destroy the personal one-to-one relationship so basic to Iranian social intercourse from manners to business dealings. Housing policy can reinforce or weaken the strong extended family structure and the traditional commitment to neighborliness. Architectural design can illustrate the concept of teamwork that accompanies the management of industrialization, while still reflecting the value of that individuality so basic to the Iranian character. The architecture of the future can symbolize the ideals, the goals, the essence of the society.

What has already been planned embodies a vision of Iran tomorrow as a major world center linking East and West in a modern version of the ancient Silk Route which once passed through her borders. It envisions a well-rounded society which concerns itself with culture as well as technology, with philosophy as well as commerce, with the quality of life as well as the quantity of production.

The elements of greatness are there—in the land and in the people.

E. Nader Khalili
Moira Moser-Khalili
Editors of *Vision*

Miniature from the *Shahnameh* ordered by Shah Esmail II showing Ferdowsi approaching the three court poets of Ghazna, A.D. 1576-77 (Reza Abbasi Culture and Arts Center, Tehran). ▷

PARDISAN

The Mandala Collaborative/
Wallace, McHarg, Roberts and Todd,
Architects and Planners

Pardisan is a total environmental park in the image of the Persian garden, a paradise in the desert. It is the unique conception of Iran's Department of the Environment and is designed to bring all the organizations traditionally concerned with nature – zoos, botanical gardens, museums of natural history, etc. – under the aegis of one institution. Situated on 300 hectares on the west side of Tehran at the foot of the Alborz Mountains, Pardisan will present the visitor with the cosmos, the environments of the world, and the environments of Iran in a series of bioclimatically faithful open-air and enclosed settings combining animal and plant life, physical and geological settings. All of Pardisan may be traversed by monorail, and particular areas more leisurely explored on foot.

The park's activities will focus on conservation, research, education and recreation. It will be concerned with the subject of adaptation in order to assure survival and success of interdependent creatures – plants, animals, men and institutions. It will endeavor to illustrate the man-environment relationship and sequences of environmental cause and effect.

Presented from the Iranian cultural viewpoint, the aim of Pardisan is "to induce such changes in the existing values of society as to demonstrate that the final aim of development must not be technological achievement solely, but the preservation and enhancement of environmental quality for the greatest good of all mankind by means of technological achievement in its broadest sense."

Flamingos at Lake Rezaiyyeh.

Shah Abbas Caravanserai, near Siahkuh on the northern edge of the Dasht-e-Kavir Desert.

One of the many indigenous plants that will be on view in Pardisan.

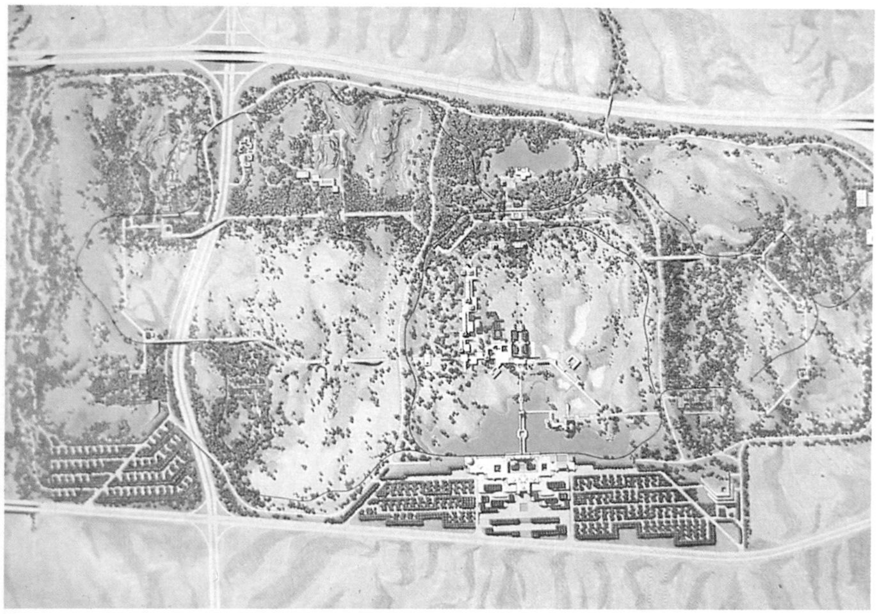

△ Master plan for Pardisan ▽ Detail

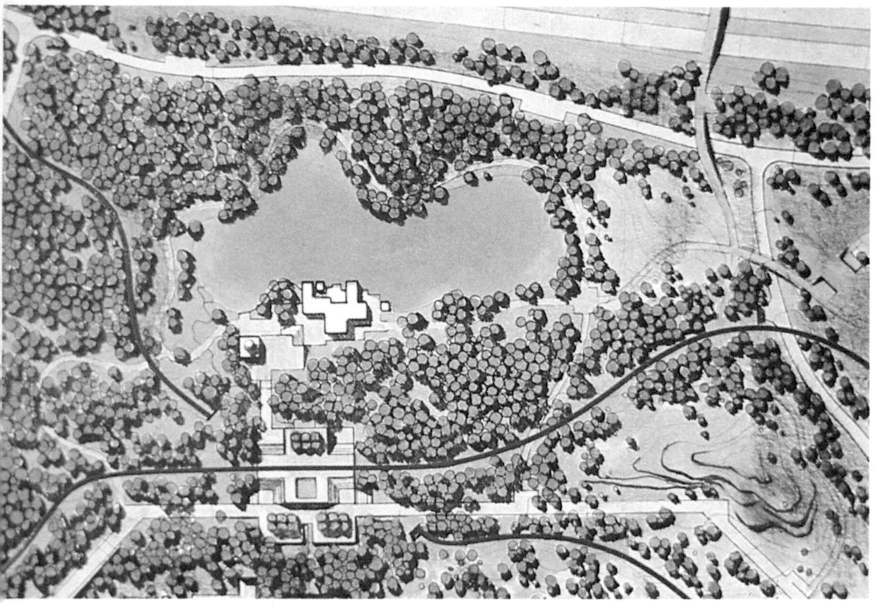

An oasis of peace and green at Birjand, north of the Dasht-e-Lut.

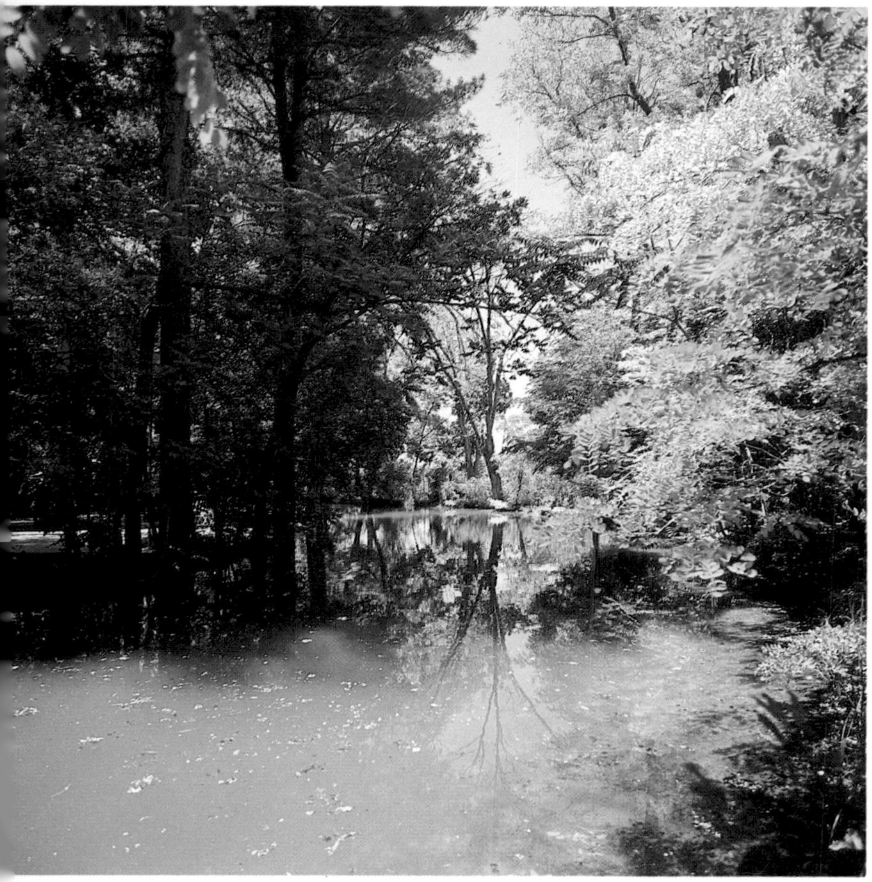

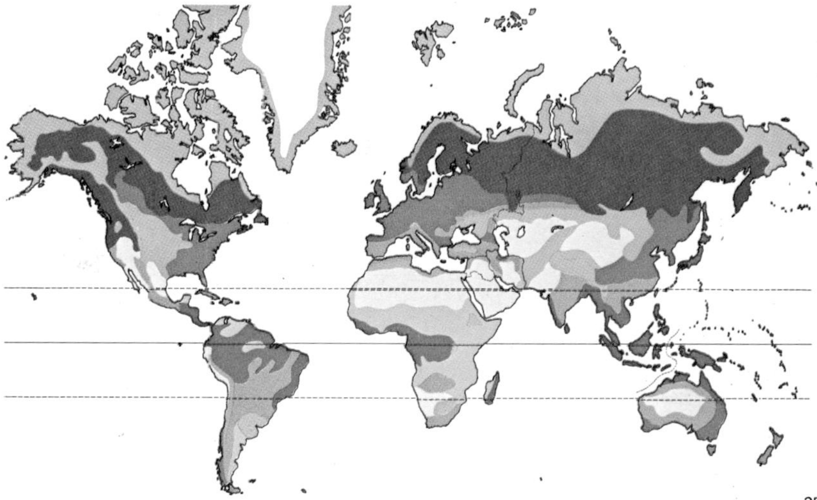

35

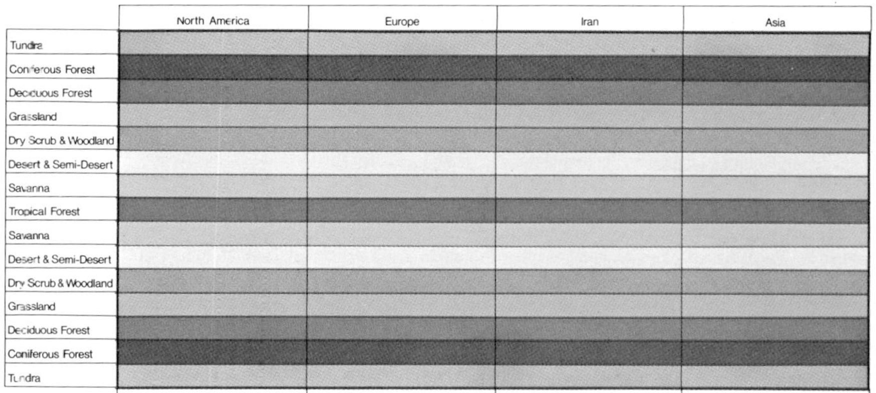

36

BIOCLIMATIC ZONES

The six geographic regions of the world - North America, South America, Europe, Africa, Asia and Oceania - are each represented in Pardisan with their appropriate mix of the eight bioclimatic zones - tundra, coniferous forest, deciduous forest, grassland, dry scrub and woodland, desert, savanna and tropical forest. Each of these zones is shown in Pardisan as a combination of ecosystems sharing major environmental features and similarities in animal communities and vegetation structure. The location of the geographic regions within Pardisan corresponds to their north-south, east-west relationships in the world with Iran at the center. The selected world bioclimatic zones are analogous to the full complement of Iranian bioclimatic zones presented, from Persian Gulf marshes to desert plateau, from mountain valley to Caspian littoral.

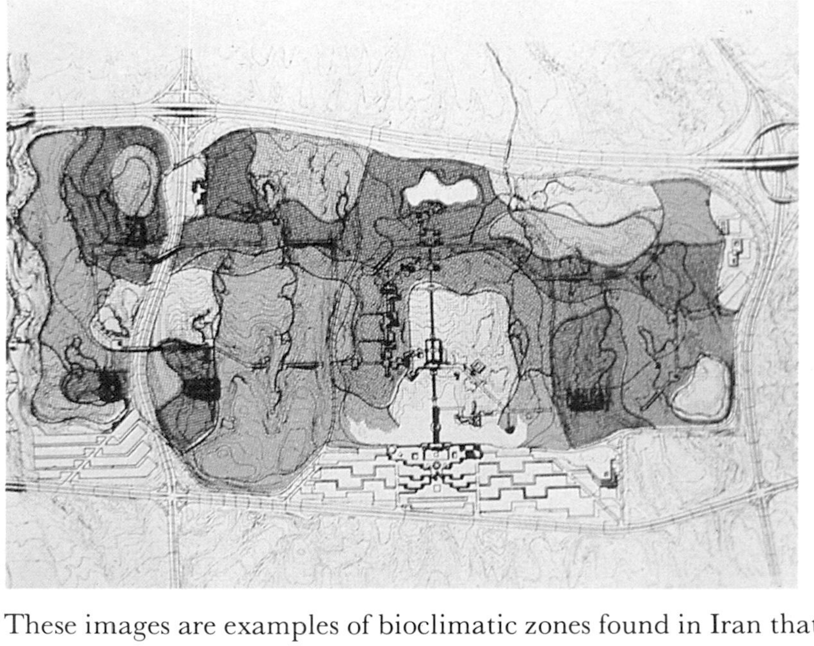

◁ These images are examples of bioclimatic zones found in Iran that will be replicated in Pardisan.

TEHRAN CENTER FOR THE PERFORMANCE OF MUSIC

Concert hall ceiling interior

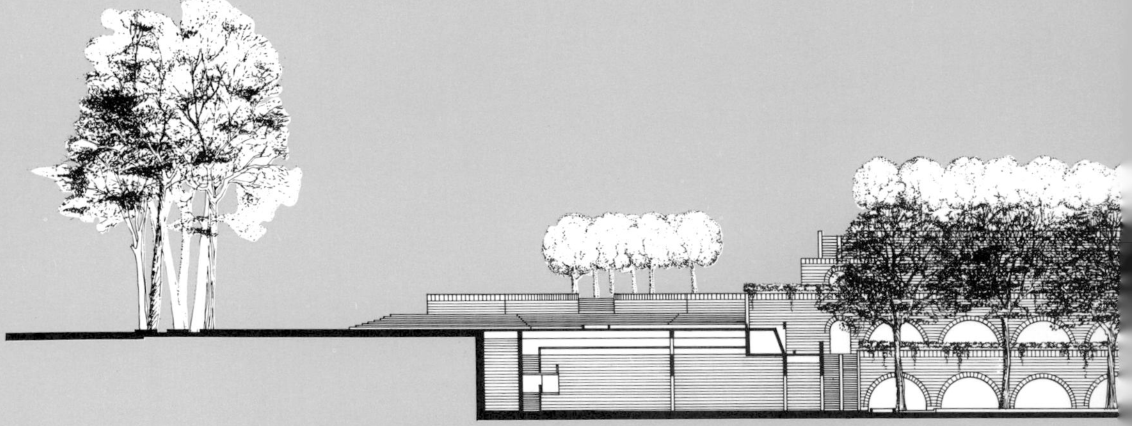

Section through sunken garden court and concert hall

The Tehran Center for the Performance of Music is strongly grounded in the philosophy of "place making," using the Persian garden concept to link the green spaces surrounding the site into what becomes effectively a new urban garden park. A concentric series of spaces - public lobbies, restaurant, lounges and offices surrounded by practice halls, recital hall and main concert hall - are organized around an enclosed sunken garden court which is spatially reminiscent of the sunken garden of Kashan's Agha Mosque. The areas above these spaces in turn become terraced, rooftop gardens with a broad, shaded plaza linking water- and tree-lined Pahlavi Avenue with a wooded campus behind the site.

The modulated ceiling surfaces of the main concert hall are acoustically effective and, within the eccentric volume, a modern derivation of the molded plasterwork of traditional Iranian domes and apses. The complex, of reinforced concrete sheathed in clay masonry, contains spaces for the performance of music ranging from the individual voice to traditional Iranian instruments, to chamber music orchestras, experimental music groups, symphony orchestras and choirs.

The Mandala Collaborative Architects/Planners

Section through theater and multi-level meeting hall

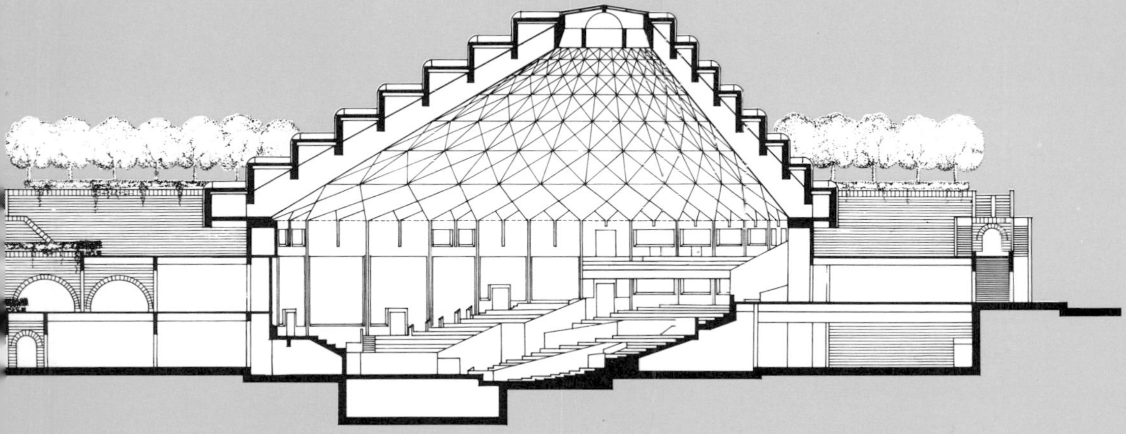

Concert hall roof exterior

NEGARESTAN CULTURAL CENTER

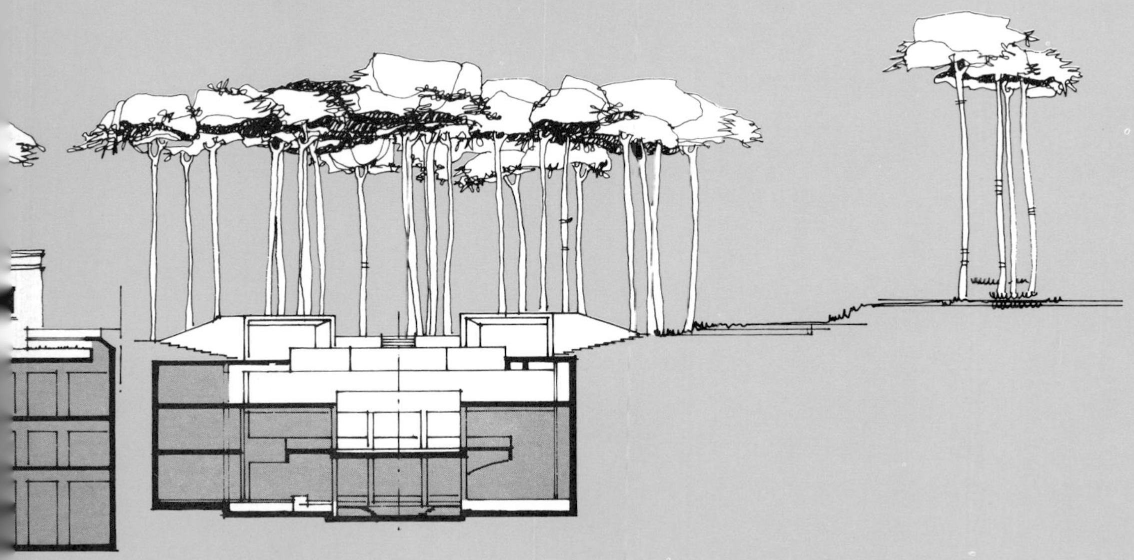

Unobtrusively tucked beneath the grounds of the Marble Palace, once the residence of Reza Shah Pahlavi, the Negarestan Cultural Center simultaneously completes a total cultural complex in the midst of Tehran and preserves the wooded green space so vital to this busy urban area. Theater, studios, workshops, library, bookstore, exhibit halls and office areas have all been carefully located underground in such a configuration that the gardens and stately pine trees remain and continue to dominate the scene. The octagonal pattern of the skylit foyer roof at ground level becomes a major landscape element on axis with both the Pahlavi and Negarestan Museums, while the form and location of the theater below are echoed in the open-air amphitheater above.

Also underground, identified only by its wedge-shaped light scoops at garden level and its octagonal sunken courtyard, is a multi-level meeting hall. As the traditional Iranian tea-house was once a cultural center, so this area can function as a restaurant, with the architecture and materials designed together to create a traditional volume of space.

The strong geometric pattern of brick, tile and wood, the pools, vaults, domes and skylights of the complex have been combined with contemporary concrete technology in such a way that the visual strength of the structural system reinforces the pervasive feeling of traditional Iranian architecture.

Manouchehr Iranpour, Architect

Symbolic of Iran's urban future, Shahestan Pahlavi will stand on nearly five million square meters of open land in the heart of Iran's capital, Tehran. It will be a new city center of distinctive civil and ceremonial spaces, balanced with open areas, pedestrian precincts and vehicular access, and with cultural and business functions. Within the central spine running north-south through the sloping site, ministries will be mixed with commercial uses; entertainment and restaurant facilities will occupy the lower floors of private office blocks to encourage continuous day and night activity. The Shahanshah Boulevard, the main vehicular and pedestrian route along the central spine, will be flanked with a stepped linear park with cascading water courses; while below the boulevard will run the first link of Tehran's metro system, connecting to other parts of the city and to the new international airport south of the city.

Proceeding northward and uphill along the central spine, where building heights are controlled to preserve major views, the Shahanshah Boulevard terminates in the Shah Nation Square, the ceremonial and symbolic center of Shahestan Pahlavi and one of the largest urban spaces in the world, exceeding in size even the Meydan-e-Shah of Esfahan. North of the square a cultural precinct of museums, facilities for the performing arts, and libraries, including the Pahlavi National Library, will overlook the Shahbanou Park.

More than a third of Shahestan Pahlavi will be open space - plazas, formal parks, and gardens within the denser, central section and larger, more natural green spaces on the surrounding ridge and valley system. Here, three residential areas of mid- and low-rise housing with related social and community facilities will bring Shahestan Pahlavi's total population to 50,000.

Detail showing Shah Nation Square in model

MASTER PLAN

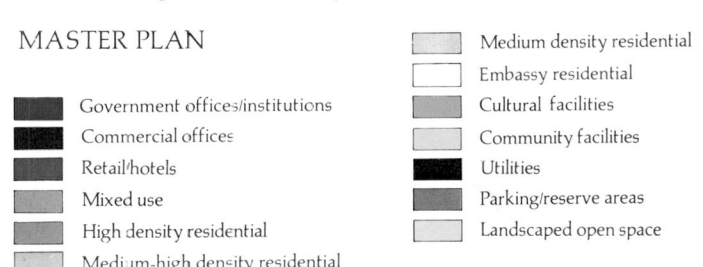

- Government offices/institutions
- Commercial offices
- Retail/hotels
- Mixed use
- High density residential
- Medium-high density residential
- Medium density residential
- Embassy residential
- Cultural facilities
- Community facilities
- Utilities
- Parking/reserve areas
- Landscaped open space

▽

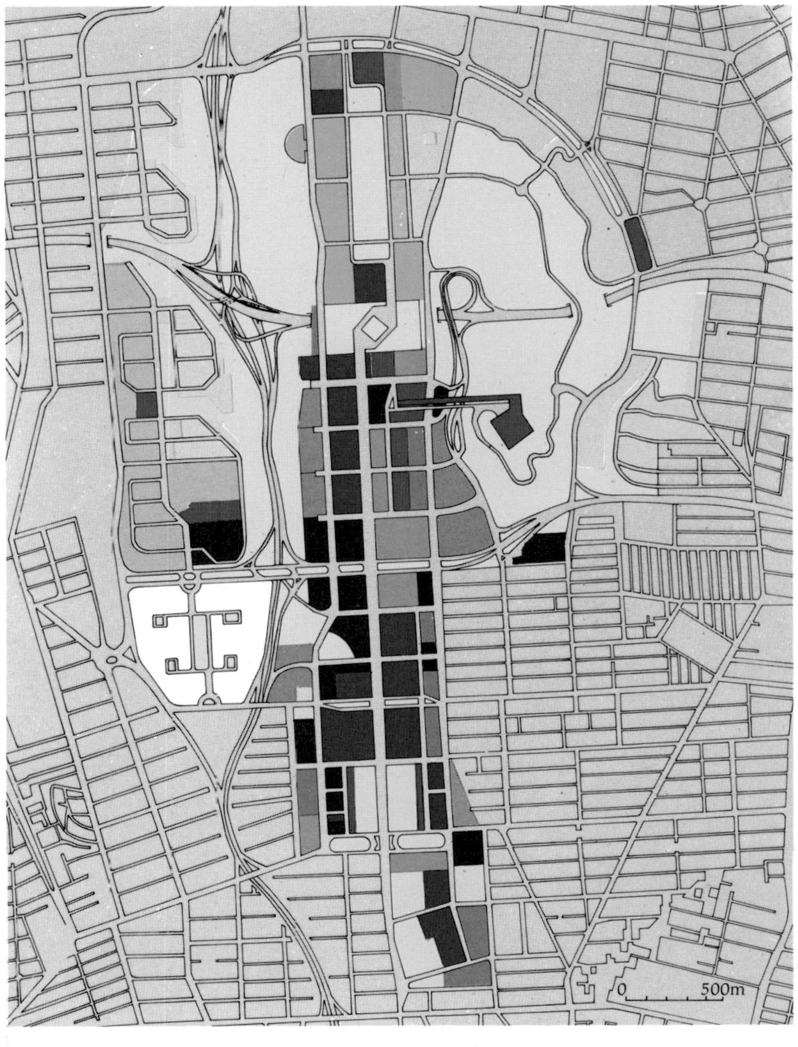

Drawing by Mark Osborn

IMPERIAL MEDICAL CENTER OF IRAN

William L. Periera Associates, Architects

A comprehensive center incorporating patient care, health sciences education, and research, IMCI is designed to overcome the nation's dependence on imported biomedical technology. It will serve not only the people of Iran, but a larger geographic area extending beyond the frontiers of the country as well. Its educational components include graduate and undergraduate schools of medicine, nursing, dentistry, allied health sciences, health planning and management and an institute of continuing health sciences education. There is also a center for basic biomedical and clinical research with laboratory facilities, a 600-bed hospital, outpatient and ancillary facilities. The comprehensive Biomedical Information Center housing the Pahlavi Medical Library will include direct computerized participation in the international Medical Literature Analysis and Retrieval System, allowing a constant exchange with the world scientific community. Architecturally, IMCI is a contemporary response to the heritage of Iran, reinterpreting the traditional elements of space, water, light, gardens, vaulted ceilings and faceted mirror surfaces to create a complex at once functional and distinctive.

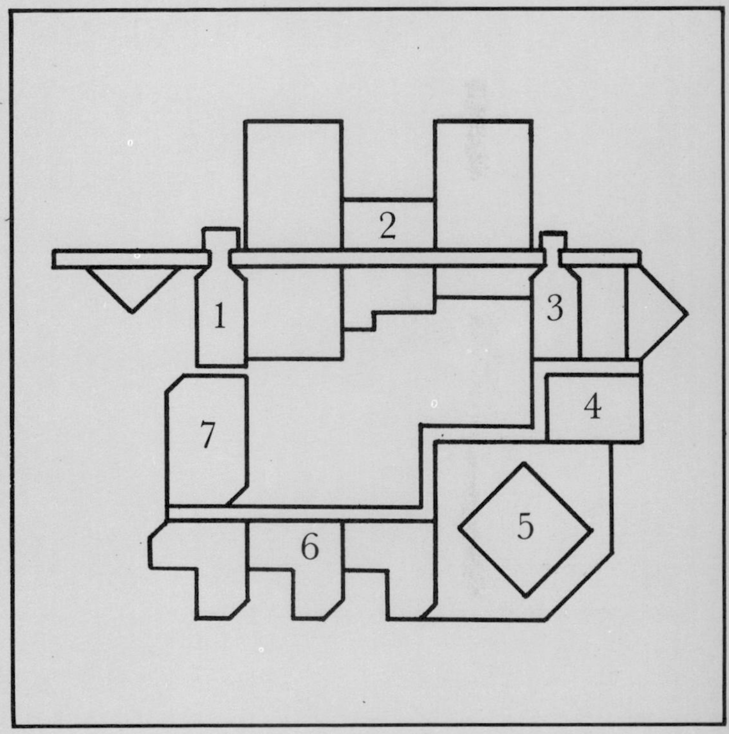

Master Plan

1. Inpatient Tower—600-bed hospital
2. Ancillary and Supporting Services
3. Outpatient Tower—Medical Offices
4. Conference Center
5. Pahlavi Medical Library and Biomedical Communication Center
6. Basic Sciences and Allied Health
7. Research—Medical School

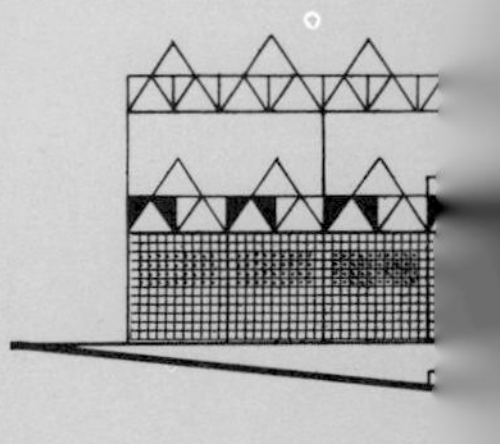

LEFT: Main concourse with vaulted ceiling.

Overall rendering of the Imperial Medical Center with the Pahlavi Medical Library and Biomedical Communication Center in the foreground.

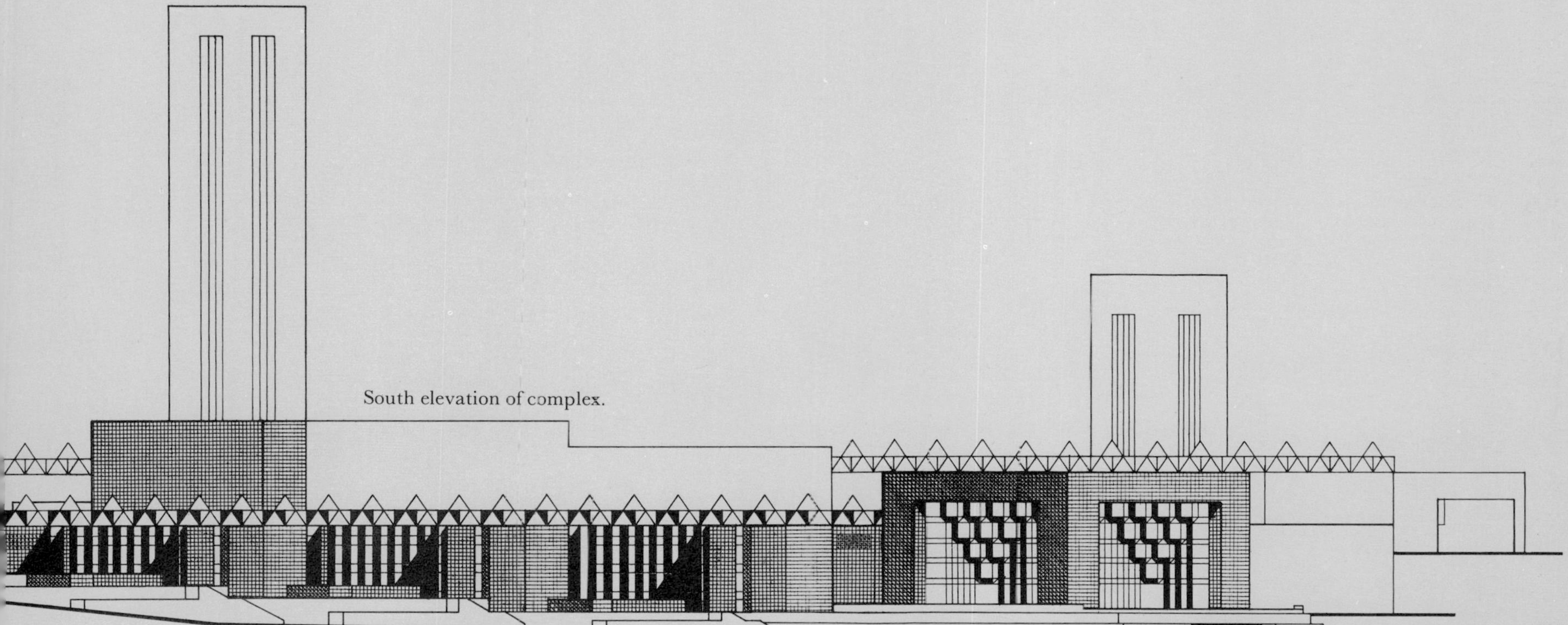

South elevation of complex.

FOUNTAINS AND MEYDANS

"Water is light," goes the Persian saying, and on the hot, arid Iranian Plateau there is nothing quite so delightful as the sound of falling water. The parks and *meydans* of cities all over the nation are dotted with fountains sparkling in the sun by day and illuminated with color by night. The *meydans,* squares most often located at the center and at the entrance of each city, are themselves tiny parks, green oases embellished with any combination of sculpture, flowers, trees and water that gives respite to the urban citizen.

Counterclockwise from left to right: Illuminated fountains at night, Ahvaz meydan; An adjustable plastic sculpture designed for a fountain by M. Vaziri; Grand staircase of the Shahanshahs at Park Shahanshahi, Tehran, with sculpted heads of Iran's ancient rulers by Parviz Tanavoli; Garden path and fountain among the trees joining Her Imperial Majesty's Special Bureau, to the Niavaran Cultural Center, Tehran; "Metal Bird," fountain in Tajrish meydan by Reza Keikavousi, Tehran; Fountains of Park Shahanshahi seen from Pahlavi Boulevard; "Water Helix," sculpture by Karl Schlamminger in the courtyard of Behshahr Industries Headquarters, Tehran.

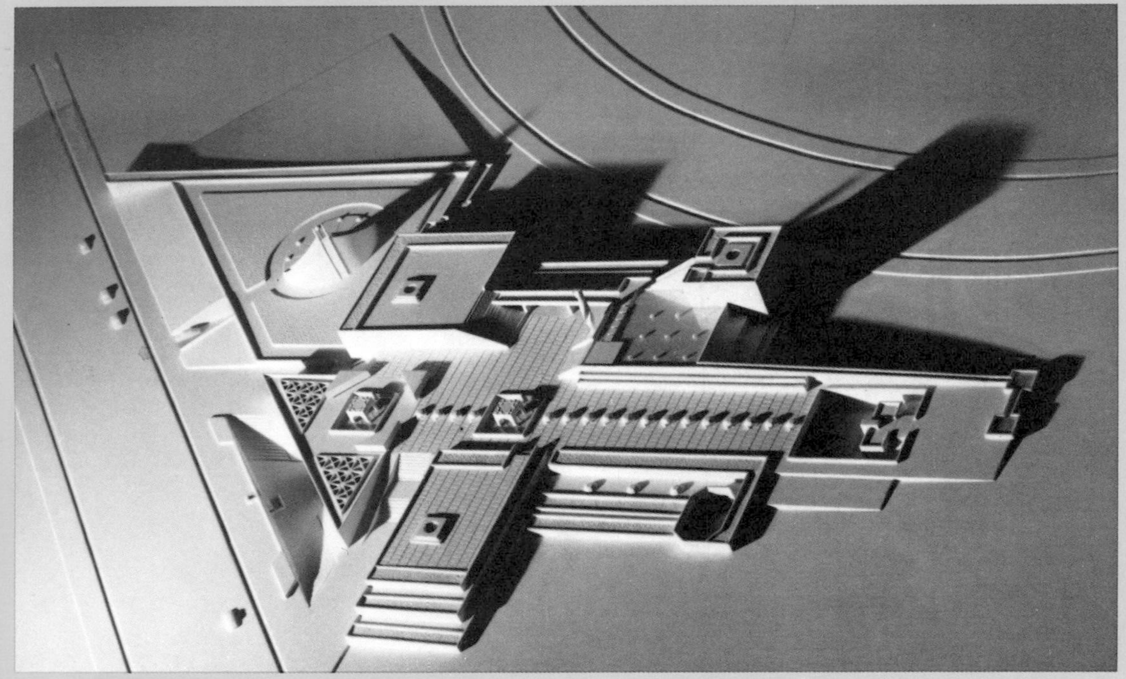

THE CREATIVE ARTS CENTER

Tehran's main facility of the Institute for the Intellectual Development of Children and Young Adults, the Creative Arts Center, will provide extensive opportunities for Iranian children to develop their creative talents. A complex of workshops, exhibit spaces, theaters, libraries, a restaurant and special areas will familiarize them with the possibilities available in various fields. The 20,000 square meters will include facilities for film making, puppeteering, drama, music, photography, printing, ceramics and the fine arts.

Adjacent to Farah Park, the complex maintains a low profile and makes extensive use of rooftop green spaces and plazas, becoming itself a garden which visually brings the park to the street.

The Mandala Collaborative Architects/Planners

INSTITUTE FOR THE INTELLECTUAL DEVELOPMENT OF CHILDREN AND YOUNG ADULTS

The headquarters building for the Institute for the Intellectual Development of Children and Young Adults, whose centers and libraries operate throughout Iran, will be located along the northernmost boundary of Farahzad, the new urban sector in west Tehran. The complex includes six office towers approached through linking courtyards, a 700-seat auditorium which functions in conjunction with recording and film animation studios, extensive book storage facilities and subterranean parking. The deep valley on the site has been utilized to avoid the sense of a tall, overpowering structure, and emphasis has been placed on pedestrian movement through the arrangement of plazas and courtyards.

D.A.Z., Architects & Planners

TABRIZ CULTURAL CENTER

With a sensitive regard for the social and historical background of Azarbayejan province in which it is located, the Tabriz Cultural Center is designed around a large *meydan* (traditional Iranian square or plaza) which will be filled with daily pedestrian movement, bringing constant liveliness to the complex. Musical and theatrical programs will take place in this *meydan,* protected from the weather by a translucent dome of classic geometrical design. The surrounding spaces will house a variety of activities – performance halls for 200 to 1,200 people, a library, an exhibit hall, restaurant, teahouse, studios, workshops and an audio-visual hall presenting the history and life of Azarbayejan.

Amanat and Associates Consulting Architects

IRAN MUSEUM OF MODERN ARTS, SHIRAZ

The Museum of Modern Arts, designed in 1969 by the great Finnish architect Alvar Aalto shortly before his death, rises like an inevitable brick and stone outcropping atop a hill overlooking the city of Shiraz. Nearly 3,000 square meters of exhibit space within the elegant structure are complemented by lecture halls, a library and a walled sculpture garden as well as cafeteria and administrative facilities.

The segmented form, completely sheathed in brick masonry, contains an open but divisible exhibit floor which gathers its illumination directly from the sky through glazed and louvered roof surfaces. Aalto identified three aspects of the Iranian sun: glare, heat and light. With his design, he declared, "I am stopping the glare, barring the heat, but capturing the light for my building so that you can still see the blue sky of Shiraz."

Alvar Aalto, Architect
Manouchehr Iranpour, Supervising Architect

TRADITIONAL CALLIGRAPHY

Siah-Mashq is a variation of Nasta'liq calligraphy consisting of a superimposition of lines and words without regard to continuity or meaning; the antithesis of the literary aspect of calligraphy.

Mirza Qolam Reza Esfahani, one of the finest Siah-Mashq calligraphers of the nineteenth century, attained freedom through severe self-discipline, creating an abstract expression, a pure and dynamic art. In this calligraphic style, content is unimportant because the forms themselves testify to the intrinsic value of the work (see right). The delicate choice of brown ink, the almost unimaginable purity of line in circular and elongated letters, the facsimile of letters repeated. All of these components contribute to an image endowed with affection, love, finesse and a faith that no longer exists.

A. Behzad Golpayegani
B. Nasrollah Afjei
C. Reza Mafi
D. Hosein Zenderudi ▼

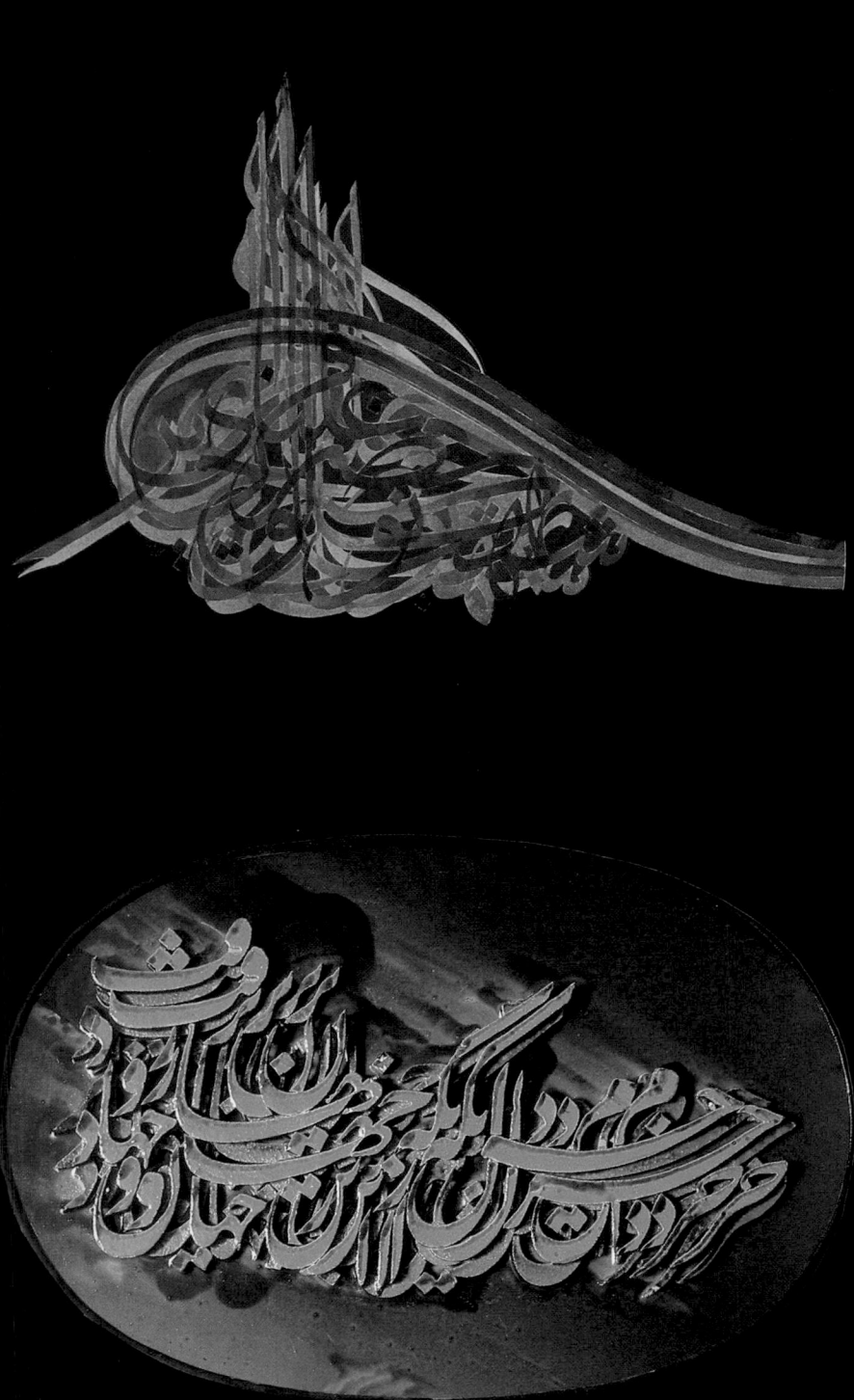

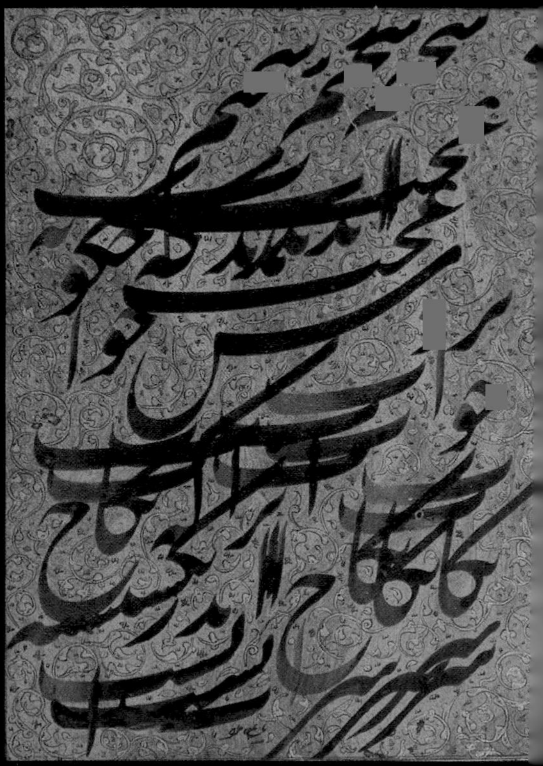

E. Jalil Rasuli

CONTEMPORARY CALLIGRAPHIC ARTISTS

The works of Iran's modern calligraphic artists will be among the collections exhibited in the new Museum. Representative of only a single facet of the many-sided evolution of contemporary Iranian art, these painters form one of the groups exploring vernacular motifs in a strikingly new manner.

After the coming of Islam, much of the dynamism of an older, figurative Iranian art found new expression in elaborate calligraphic ornamentation. Raised to a grand scale, the Word became part of the built environment, adorning the tiled entranceway, ivans, domes and minarets. Today's calligraphic artists abstract the words in order to seek new forms and shades of meaning in the chromatic scales of the letters themselves.

▶ F. Faramarz Pilaram

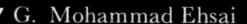

▼ G. Mohammad Ehsai

TEHRAN INTERNATIONAL AIRPORT

With Iran rapidly becoming the hub of airline routes across the Middle East, Tippetts-Abbett-McCarthy-Stratton of New York and Abdol Aziz Farmanfarmaian and Associates of Tehran have joined together to develop a major airport facility for the nation comparable to the largest in the world. It is to be located 35 kilometers southwest of Tehran on 12,000 hectares of land between two major freeways which, along with a future high-speed rapid transit link, will provide direct access from the capital.

In the initial stage, one domestic and one international module totaling 36 gates will be constructed. By the year 2000, the series of five terminal modules and four runways in dual parallel configuration, with just over 100 loading/parking positions, will be capable of handling an annual traffic load of 12,000,000 international passengers, 14,900,000 domestic passengers and 620,000 metric tons of cargo.

Terminal modules straddle a central spine road and transit system connecting the two freeways to Tehran. This spine also allows for inter-airport circulation and for under-terminal parking with direct vertical check-in and baggage claim. The airfield provides for the most advanced Air Traffic Control procedures. In addition to the terminals, hangars and cargo areas, a residential town is planned for airport employees.

TAMS-AFFA, Consulting Engineers and Architects

LEFT: First Phase domestic and international terminal modules.
ABOVE: Space frame roof structure of typical terminal.
BELOW: Bird's-eye view of model.

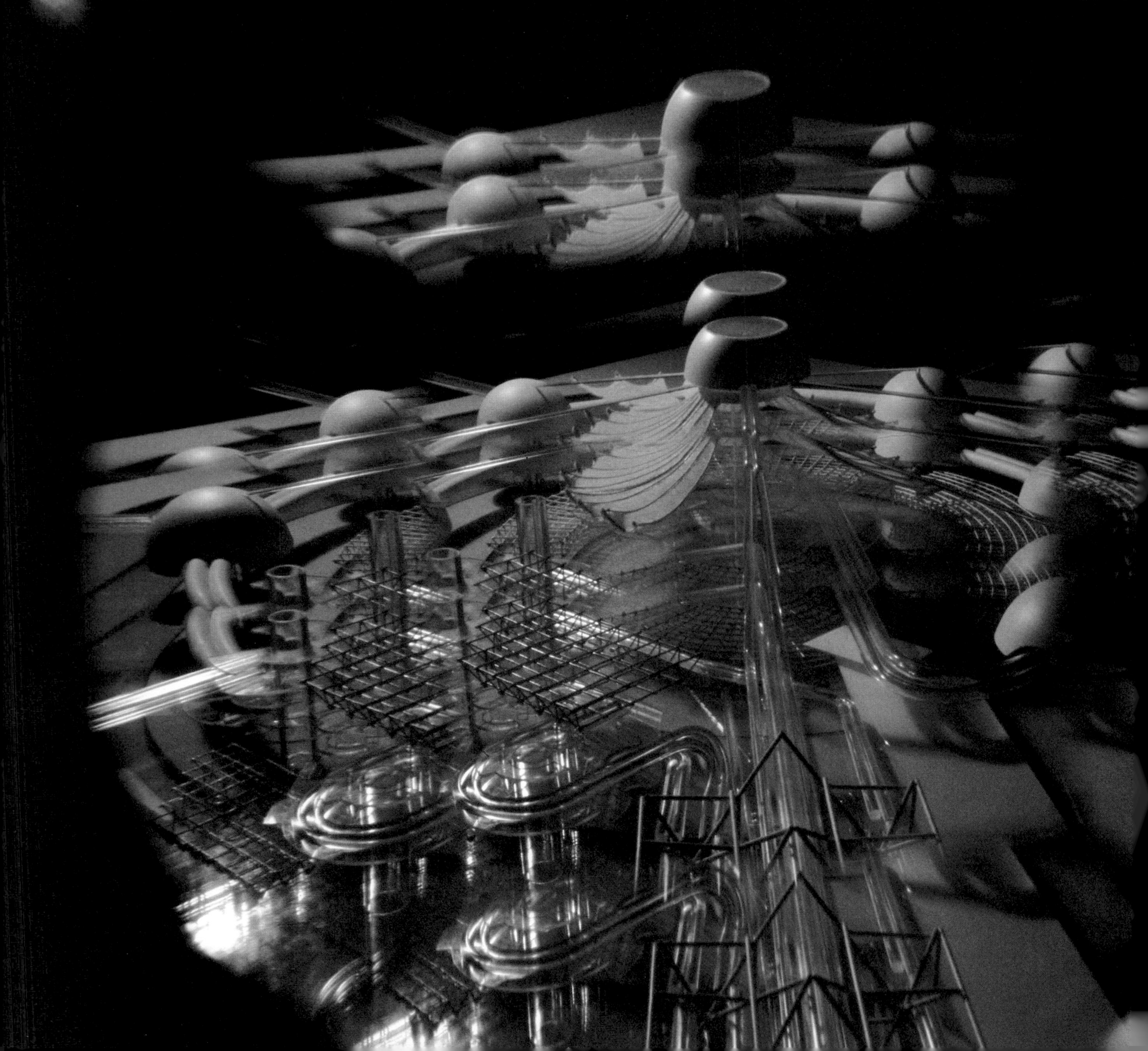

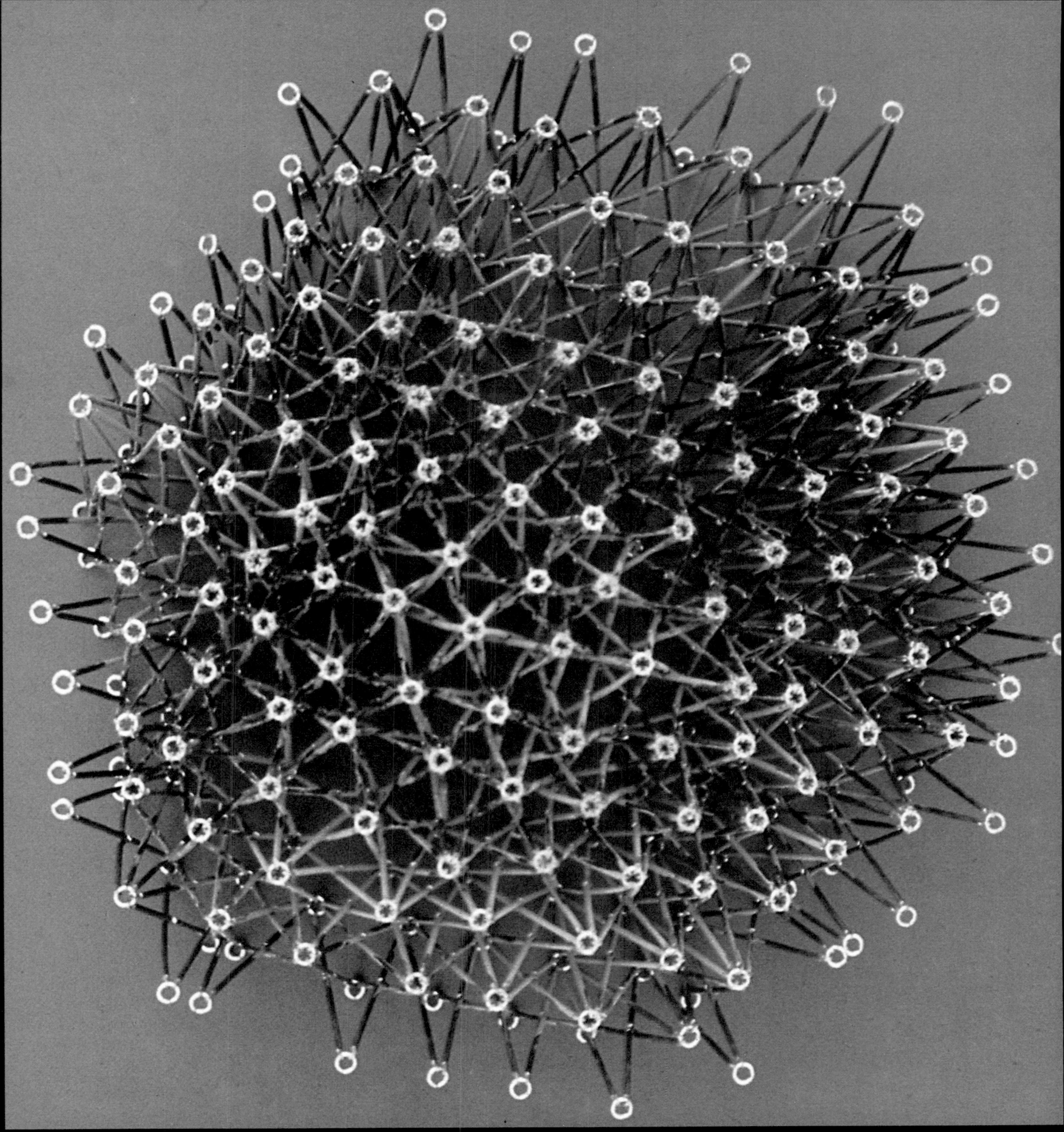

STUDENT PROJECTS FOR A FUTURISTIC CITY

The thesis project "Man and Social Groups" by Ahmad Ta'eb embodies a futuristic vision of the world and all men in a prototype urban environment designed for the province of Khuzestan. Its goals are maximum use of technology and automation to meet the needs of modern man, maximum closeness to and relationship with nature, and maximum freedom to move about and to work.

The thesis project "A Study on Structural Shells" by F. Shahmoradi and M. R. Ehterami combines a sensitiveness to Iran's heritage with an understanding of present urban problems to create a vision of the future which can be realized with contemporary technology.

These futuristic studies are an outgrowth of a conviction that rapid growth and changes in technology have given a universal dimension to the problems of urbanization so that the future must be planned today.

Professor Mehdi Kowsar, Advisor
University of Tehran

Kenzo Tange and URTEC, Architect/ Mir-Djalali and Detail Consulting Co., Associate Architects

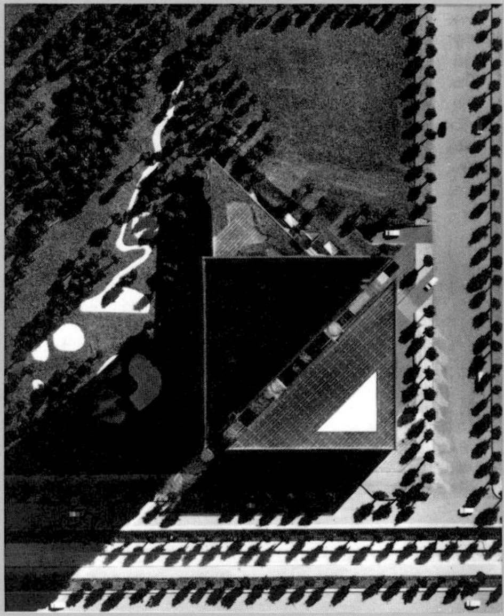

HOTEL TEHRAN

The 30-story, 700-room Hotel Tehran, to be housed in a triangular tower at the southeast corner of Farah Park in downtown Tehran, presents itself as a pure glass prism of strict geometric form. The reflective structure is oriented to take maximum advantage of views of the Alborz Mountains on the north, to integrate with the tree-filled park on the west, and to open up the intersection visually. The 7.5-meter-tall lobby sheathed in transparent glass affords unobstructed views of park, sky and mountains while banquet and conference facilities are located underground. The triangular form and reflective façade of the hotel together are intended to soften the impact of such a massive corner structure and enable it to harmonize with the park and surrounding environment. A Japanese-style garden with waterfall on the north is another deliberate attempt to unify the hotel landscape with Farah Park and to create an atmosphere that suggests an oasis.

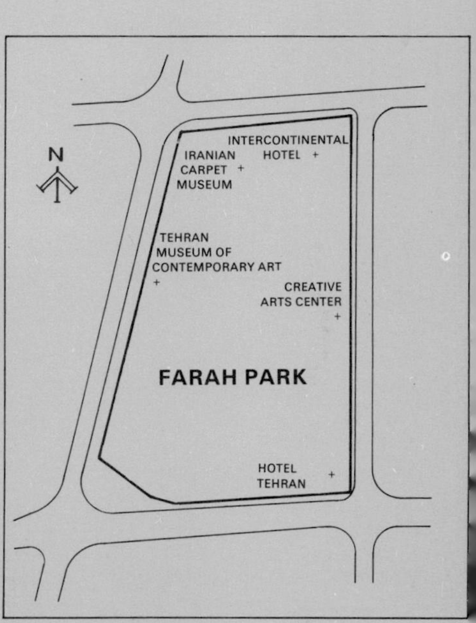

INDUSTRIAL CREDIT BANK

The new headquarters for the Industrial Credit Bank will be situated in downtown Tehran creating, with the nearby Rudaki Opera House, a sophisticated urban space at a focal point in the north-south street system. The 27-story office tower uses the traditional Iranian notched-square motif to provide maximum natural light for each floor and translates this into a sophisticated structural system. The lower office/commercial structure, with skylit interior wintergarden, wraps protectively around two sides of the 7,000-square-meter site and transforms the intermediate plaza into a modern version of a traditional walled courtyard. This plaza, from which both buildings gain entrance, is further enhanced by a water tower fountain and a small grove of trees. The façades of glass and aluminum recall traditional Iranian motifs while the reflective exterior acts to minimize the mass of the buildings. A restaurant and a café opening onto the plaza, a lower-level concourse of shops and the subterranean parking will serve patrons of the Rudaki Opera House as well as the project itself, bringing activity to the area both day and night.

Sazeh Consultants/
I. M. Pei & Partners, Architects

KISH ISLAND

Kish Island in the Persian Gulf was for centuries a pirate stronghold, hostile in aspect with few trees and little water. Now it is being developed into a luxury resort and a free port of entry, inviting those who have sought their vacations elsewhere in the past to winter along its sunny beaches. Visitors arrive by air - the airport will accommodate even the Concorde SST. On Kish they will find royal residences, private villas, exclusive hotels and restaurants, a casino, clubs, a civic center and a small bazaar all nestled among the 25,000 trees which now dot the 8 by 14 kilometer island. Private automobiles are prohibited, and a myriad of outdoor sports are available - a marina, bridle trails, an 18-hole golf course.

The architectural theme throughout the island is contemporary, with the predominant element being angular form. The symbolic decorative element, used extensively, is the Pahlavi arch. However, the spirit of traditional building has been preserved in the local village, completely rebuilt in its original form on a new site, and a number of ruins on the island have been retained as thematic links with the past.

Kish Island Development Organization

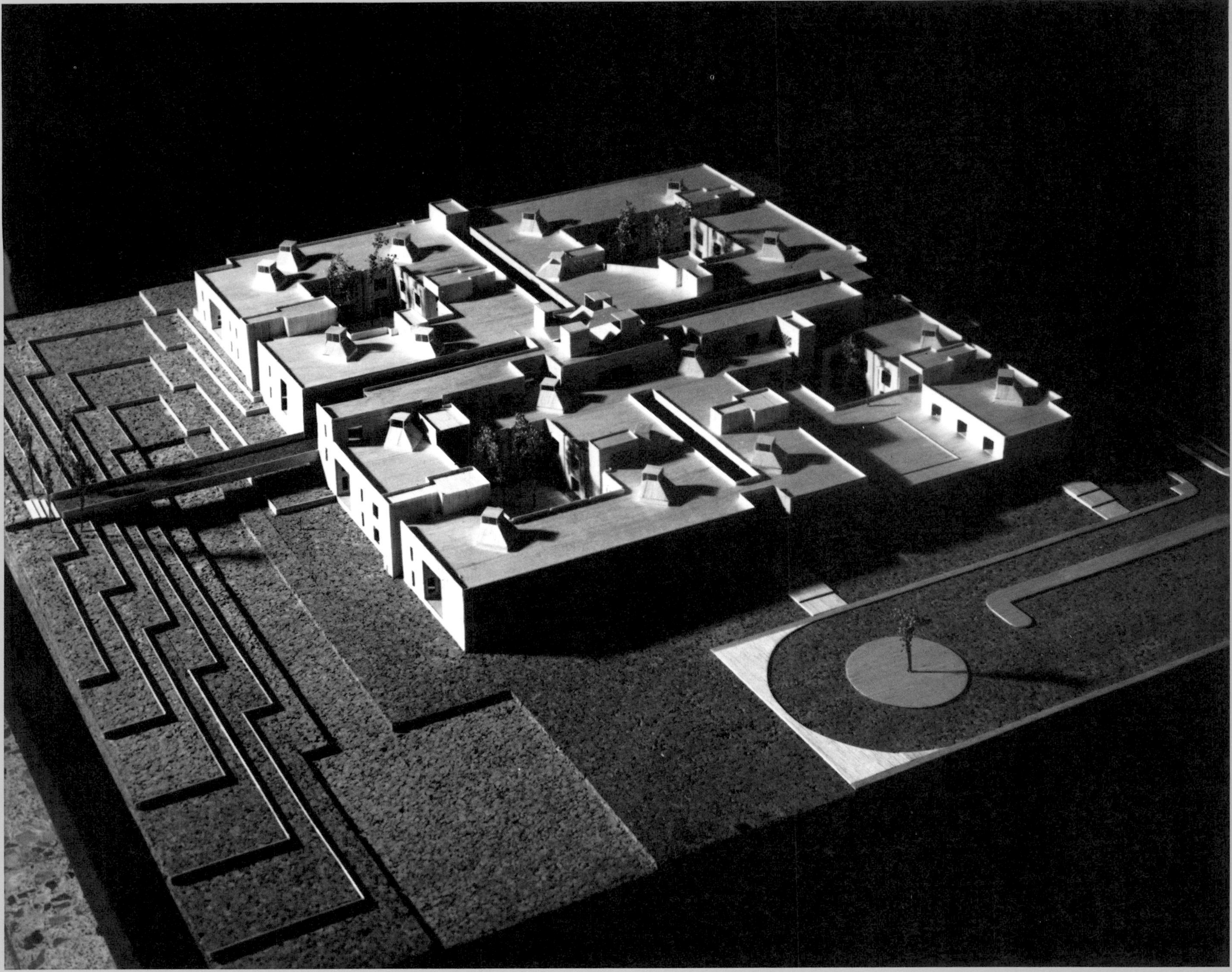

BU ALI SINA UNIVERSITY

Bu Ali Sina University, designed for an enrollment of 5,000 students, is situated on 172 hectares at the foothills of the Zagros and Alvand mountains and overlooks the city of Hamedan, near the site of ancient Ecbatana. The university's goal is to establish a multiple relationship between students, faculty and the culturally rich city in order to graduate students who have an understanding of self, others and the environment. With such a background, and with training in the fields of education, health, agriculture or the environment, they will be specially suited for an important role in the evolution and development of Iranian society and culture.

In keeping with the objectives of the university, the architecture of the campus itself fully utilizes the existing tree-lined streams, fields and other natural features as part of the total learning environment. In addition, cultural awareness is incorporated into the building designs and forms, which are inspired by the heritage of Iranian architecture.

The Mandala Collaborative/
Georges Candilis Architects and Planners

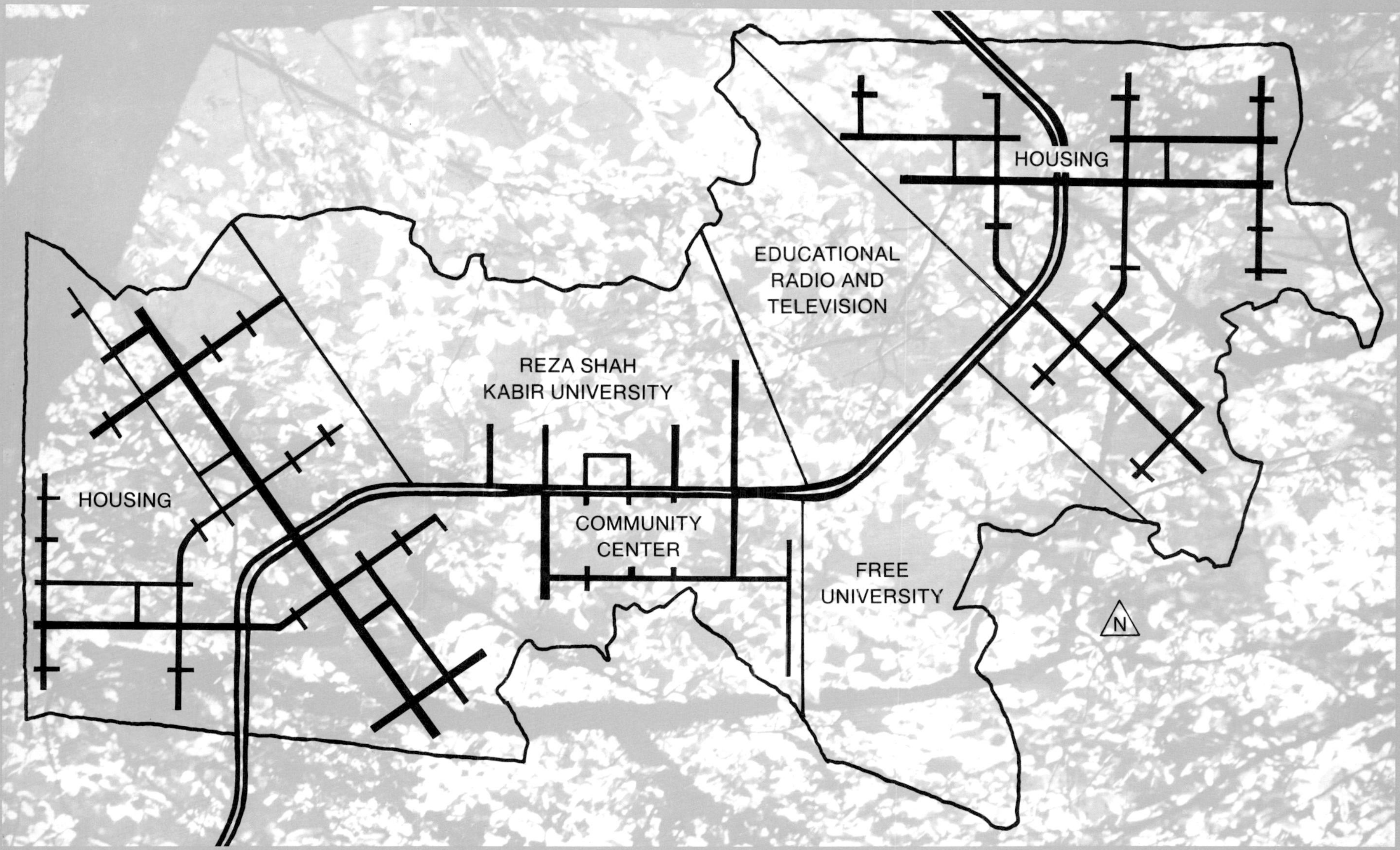

In the midst of the forested Caspian littoral of Mazandaran Province, on 800 hectares of land, a new education-based community is to be created which will contain three interacting but separate organizations: Reza Shah Kabir University, the Free University of Iran, and Educational Radio and Television of Iran. Together they are expected to generate a new town of 50,000 inhabitants in approximately fifteen years' time, significantly stimulating the economy of the region.

REZA SHAH KABIR UNIVERSITY

Near the birthplace of Iran's late leader, Reza Shah the Great, Reza Shah Kabir University will be Iran's first school of graduate studies. RSKU is designed to meet the demand of the nation's university system for qualified faculty, to offer research facilities, and to provide an international orientation. The eventual 500 yearly graduate students will reduce Iran's dependence on foreign universities for the training of university faculty and will increase the research capability of the nation. The university's main thrust will revolve around the sciences, social sciences and humanities, and research, with the first of three development phases to begin in 1980.

FREE UNIVERSITY OF IRAN

One hundred hectares of the site will be allocated to the Free University, which will use various media to disseminate its educational programs to some 400 centers throughout Iran. With a concept of higher education based on the open learning system, the Free University will use self-instructional material comprised of books, cassettes, television programs and practice kits. Local and regional centers for study and reference have been located throughout the country to cover a maximum potential student population within one hour's commuting distance. Designed to fill national needs for skilled personnel, the first programs will begin in 1978 with instruction in the teaching and paramedical fields. Courses will be added or deleted periodically according to the overall needs of the country. The majority of lecturers for the multi-media courses will be graduate students from neighboring Reza Shah Kabir University, and many of the programs will be recorded and transmitted by the neighboring Educational Radio and Television complex.

EDUCATIONAL RADIO AND TELEVISION

Working in collaboration with both the Free University and Reza Shah Kabir University, the Educational Radio and Television center will comprise the third unit of this academic community. ERT will expand its involvement with multi-media educational systems at the secondary school level designed to meet Iran's rising demand for education. By making education both public and ubiquitous through the use of the latest technology, ERT can overcome the lack of teachers and school facilities which limit the effectiveness of traditional teaching methods. Broadcasts on national and local channels, already used as teaching aids in the classroom, will be further developed into a new learning concept based on creative thinking and an understanding of the social context of the lessons taught. In addition, ERT will devote itself to training instructors to use the broadcasts as teaching aids, organizing listening groups in areas removed from school facilities, and pursuing further research in the field.

Harvard University Site Planning Task Force

These will also cater, where appropriate, to the needs of the old town which, with more than seventy existing places of worship, will fulfill most of the new town's religious needs.

This apportioning of urban facilities between old and new settlements will encourage stronger interaction between the traditional community of traders and agriculturalists and the new town neighborhoods of young families. Thus, there will be a firm grounding in age-old Iranian traditions and a commitment to modernity within the new planned environment, allowing for a natural response to the future dynamics of growth.

D.A.Z., Architects & Planners

LEFT ABOVE: Aerial view of old Shushtar and Karun River with new town site beyond.

BELOW: Map of region.

RIGHT: Model of Shushtar New Town.

SHUSHTAR NEW TOWN

Situated across the Karun River north of the existing town of Shushtar in Khuzestan Province, Shushtar New Town is planned initially to house the employees of the nearby Karun sugarcane industry development. It is designed to complement rather than compete with the architectural form and social functions of the old town so that the two may develop together into a city of a quarter million by the turn of the century.

Originally a pre-Islamic settlement and still containing archeological sites, old Shustar is now a typical Iranian Islamic town. Its physical form is organic and dense with a precise movement pattern and a definitive architecture of mud brick. Taking its cue from the character of its neighbor, Shushtar New Town places a strong emphasis on pedestrian movement and courtyard housing, creating the network of small open spaces so essential in the region's hot, arid climate.

Major environmental features such as cliffs, mounds and the river itself have been incorporated into the new town plan, delineating neighborhoods and determining the location of parks and water recreation spaces. Urban facilities such as a civic center, schools and health centers will be provided.

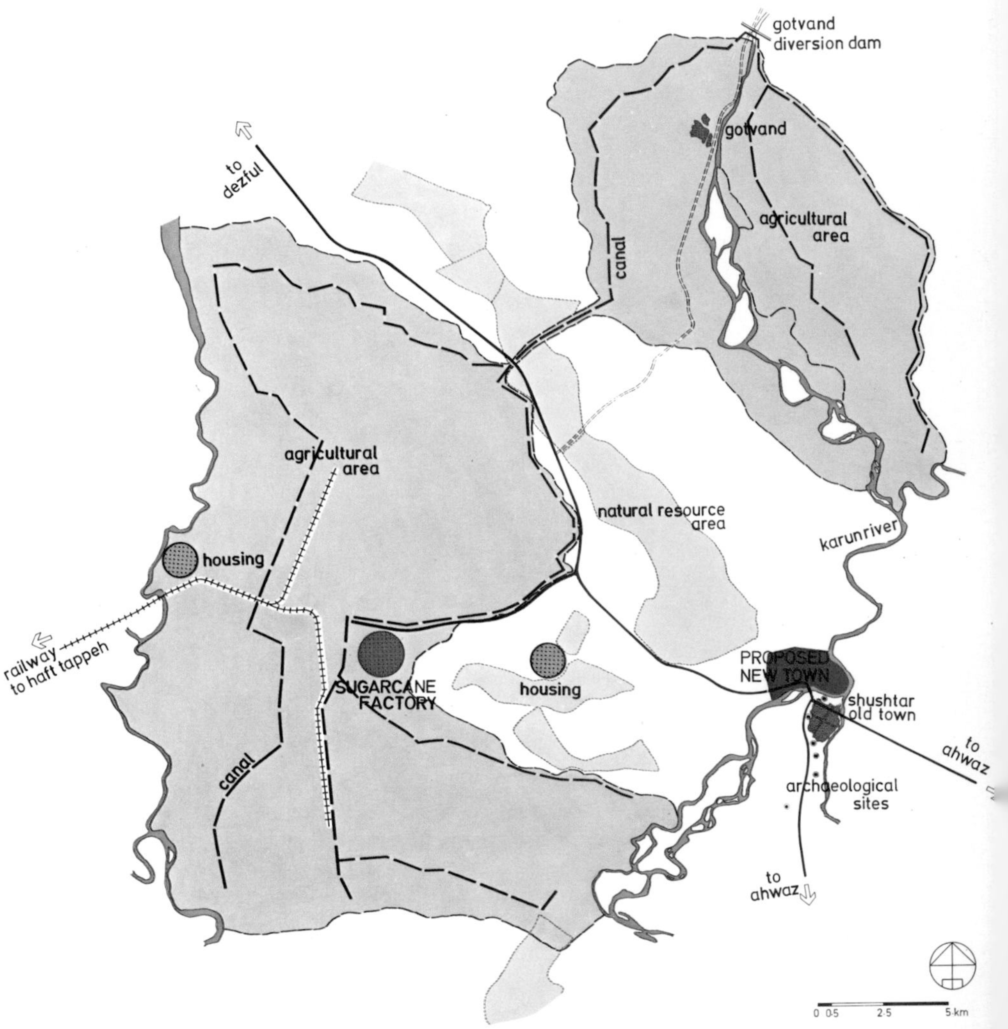

FARAHZAD

Farahzad lies on eleven million square meters of the Alborz foothills directly in line with the planned westward growth of Tehran. As a major new urban sector, already under construction, Farahzad will have 2,300 single-family dwellings and 18,000 apartment units in six complexes, each designed by an Iranian or foreign company. In addition to schools, local shopping centers and commercial areas, the development will include Iran's first regional shopping center, with a mosque, an 800-room hotel and a high-rise office tower.

The separate developments will be tied together with green spaces, which will contain parks, pedestrian circulation safe from vehicles, playgrounds, tennis courts, outdoor amphitheaters on the gentle slopes and other recreational facilities. Each residential side street will open onto these green spaces, which will account for one-third of the total area. The community's semi-treated waste water will be used to maintain the foliage, the first major system of this type to be employed in Iran.

LEFT BOTTOM CORNER: Iranzamin School.
Major projects, *from left to right:* Zomorod Apartments, Arya Towers, Tehran Taj Apartments, Regional Shopping Center, Franco-Iranian Apartments, Mahestan Apartments, Golestan-e-Farahzad Apartments.

West Tehran Development Organization

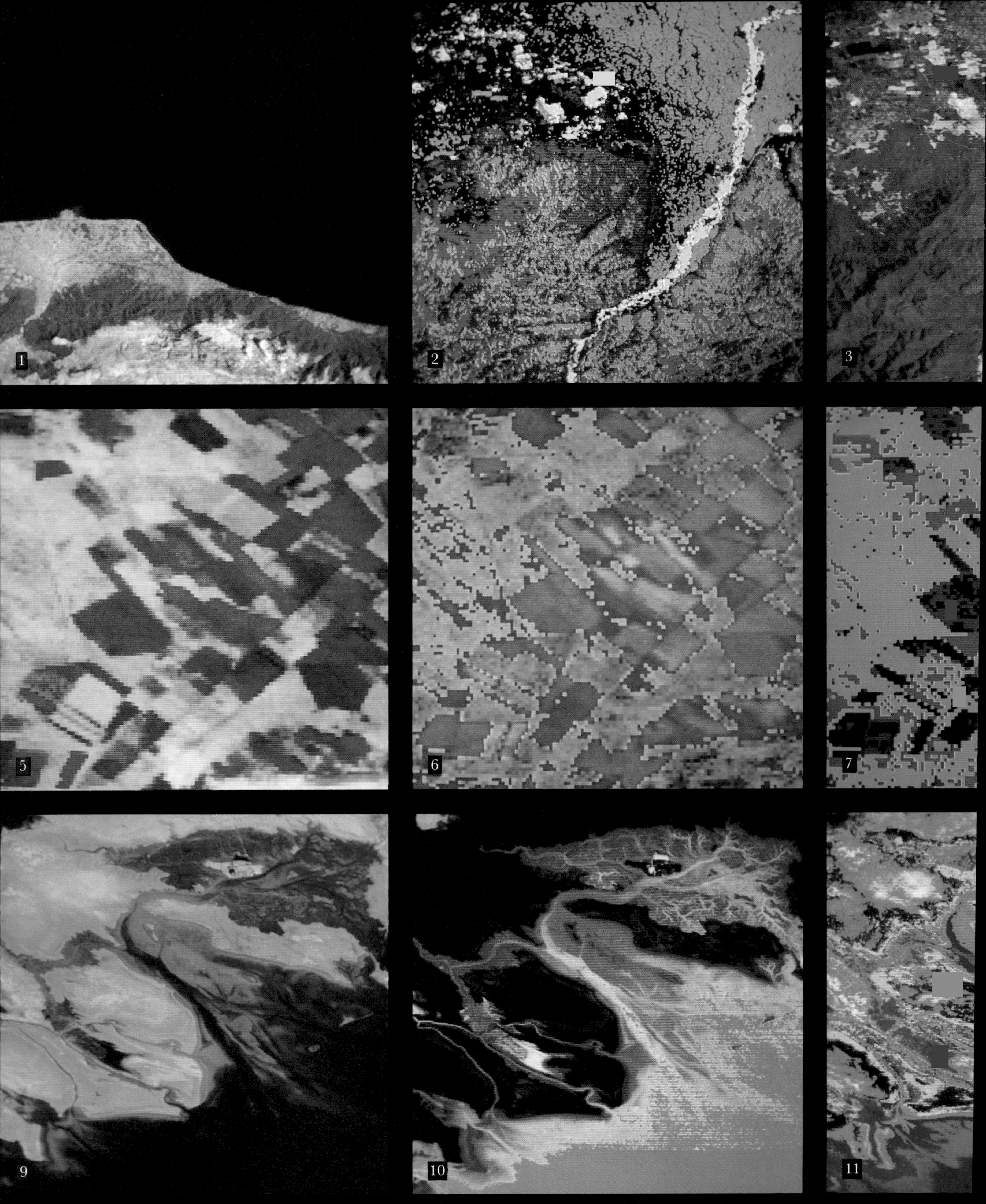
1
2
3
5
6
7
9
10
11

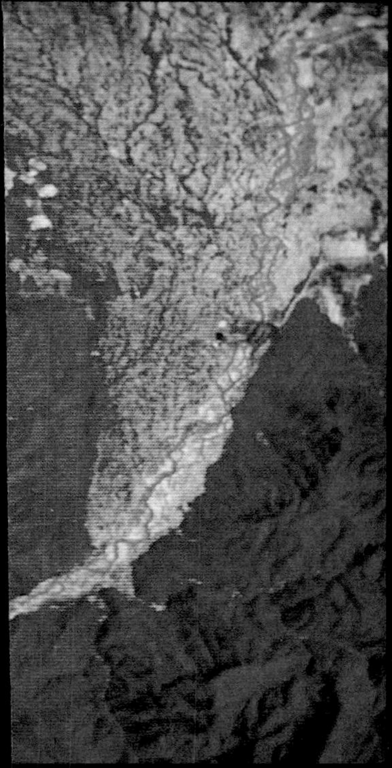

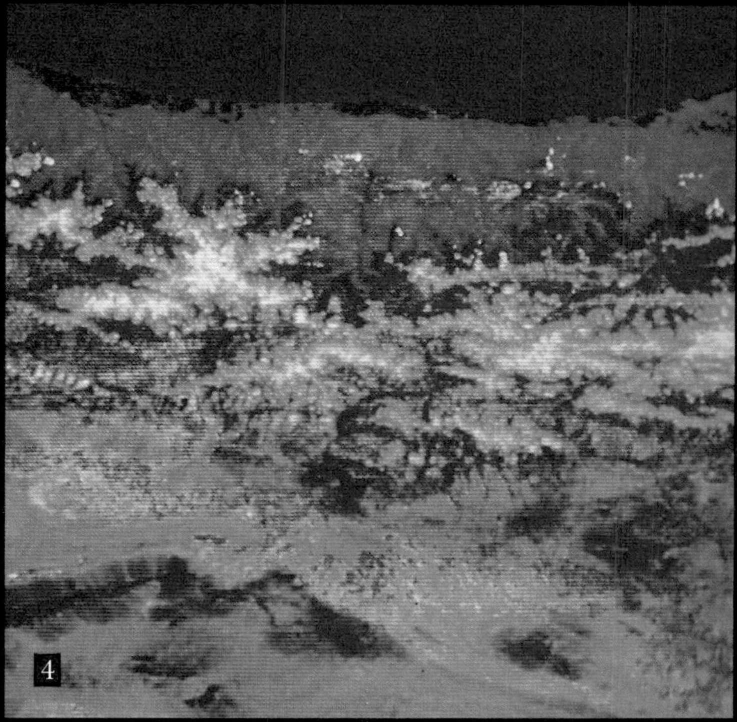

4

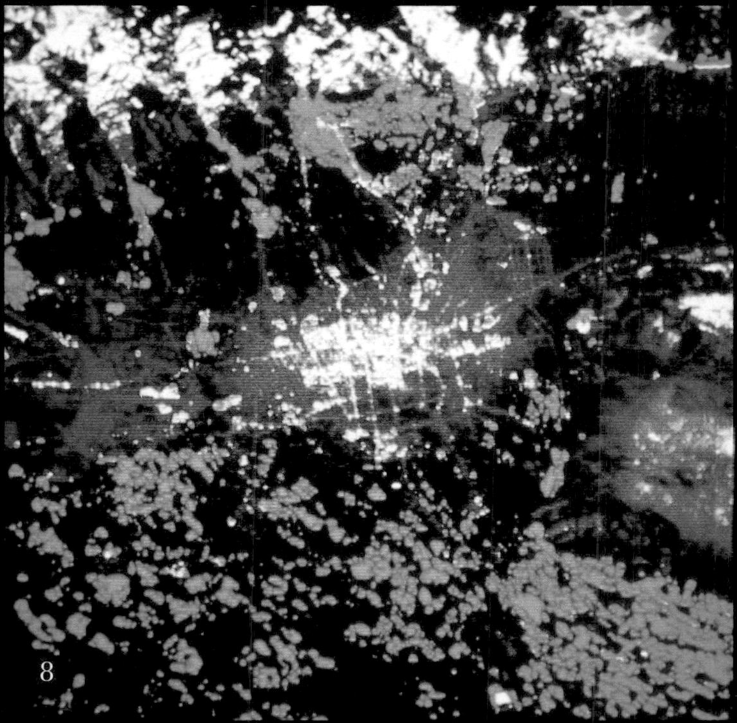

8

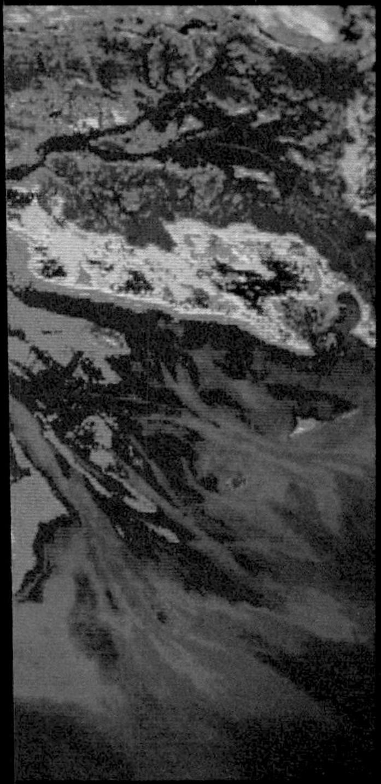

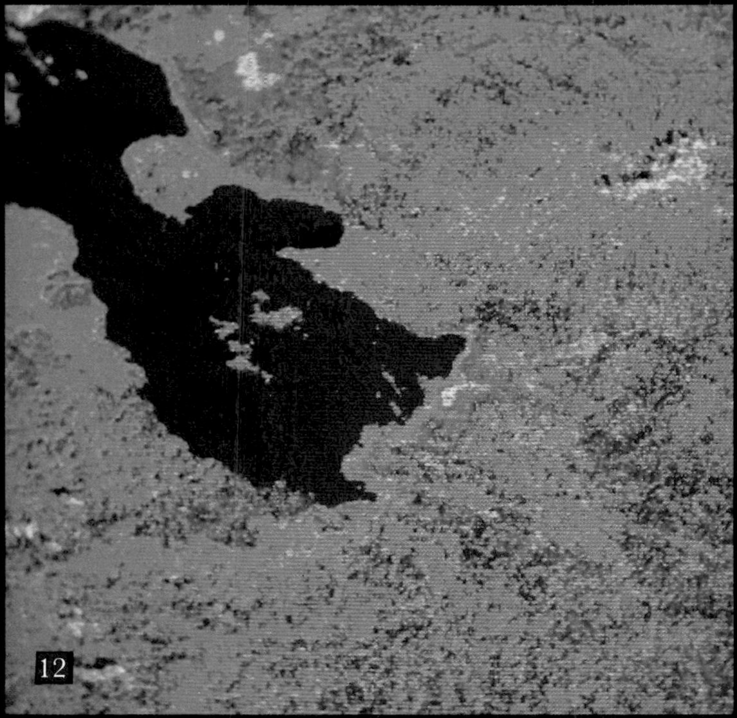

12

AGRICULTURE– A TOTAL APPROACH

Earth Resources Satellite (ERTS-1) photographs taken periodically over Iran, combined with infrared aerial photography and ground truth (field data) measurements, are currently supplying data to a sophisticated computerized crop forecasting and production estimating system at the Ministry of Agriculture and Natural Resources. As Iran's population and the demand for food increase in the future, the nation's limited arable land and lack of water will make it imperative that the best strategy be found for allocating land use between agricultural crops, pasture grasses and forest lands. Regional cropping patterns derived from the combination of remote sensing data, computer models and demand forecasting will be designed to give the optimum balanced national yield of animal protein, vegetable protein and calories for the total population.

The coordination of agricultural activities throughout the country will then be accomplished through the development of agricultural products in each region according to expected yields and available water supplies and through the development of agricultural poles in twenty areas of the country where irrigation networks are being established. The emphasis will continue to be placed on increasing productivity per acre through the use of intensive methods of cultivation, mechanization and irrigation, through a more effective integration of animal and crop husbandry, and through the further development of large-scale farm corporations and agro-industrial units.

The computer equipment which has processed this data, spanning the year 1976, was designed by Mohammad Ali Sharifi, a brilliant young Iranian engineer.

1	Gilan area (180 km x 180 km); color composite of landsat-2 data.
2 & 3	Two studies of Rasht area (40 km x 40 km); enhanced color composite and tree-type classification of forest.
4	Caspian area (180 km x 180 km); enhanced color composite.
5, 6 & 7	Three studies of area south of Qazvin (10 km x 10 km); color composite of agricultural area, vegetable separation and computer identification of growing crops.
8	City of Tehran (40 km x 40 km); computer enhancement.
9, 10 & 11	Three studies of Bandar-e-Shahpur (80 km x 80 km); color composite, computer analysis for water quality, and computer analysis for soil classification and depth of water.
12	Eastern zone of Lake Rezaiyyeh (180 km x 180 km); color enhancement of landsat-2 data.

Ministry of Agriculture and Natural Resources

ARYAMEHR

مسجد آریامهر

Sardar Afkhami & Partners/
Consulting Architects

ISLAMIC CENTER

The Aryamehr Islamic Center is designed to satisfy a spiritual need and at the same time to respect the religious, cultural and national heritage of Iran. Neither a repetition of the past nor an imitation of conventional modern design, it is composed of unusual forms and spaces which together signify the unique aspects of a House of God.

Low structures surrounding the dominant main mosque and ceremonial hall contain a library and museum, a research and discussion hall, guest house and offices, and a mausoleum. Five minarets are placed to integrate the various forms and elements into a single composition while at the same time symbolizing the five saints and the five basic tenets of Islam. The whole is designed for the role of a religious center which will take its historical place as the symbol of an era.

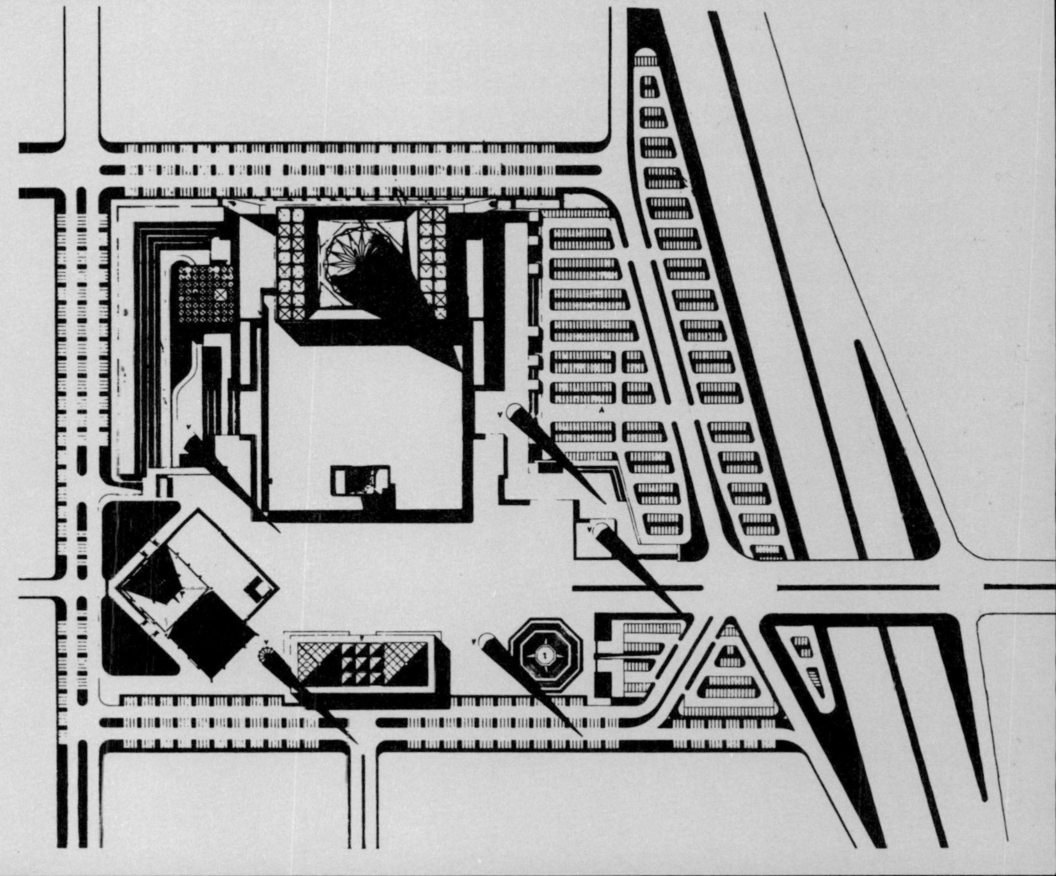

water
air
fire

"Geltaftan" is a composite name made up of two Persian words—"Gel," meaning clay, and "taftan," meaning firing, burning or baking.

In arid regions, there exists a need for low-cost, earthquake-resistant, self-help rural housing. To respond to this need, several factors must be considered: minimal cost, limited range of naturally available building materials, simple construction procedures, traditionally acceptable building forms and, of crucial importance, resistance to earthquake.

Geltaftan is a simple, breakthrough concept still in the process of development. It was created from the four classic elements which are universally available even on the simplest level: earth, water, air and fire. Each module can be thought of as a "one-brick house" or a "giant hollow brick." The modules may be glazed in an artistic fashion, becoming mammoth ceramics of the villages. Although designed for self-help, the modules can be manufactured in a simple casting and firing assembly system for a development or town of any size. Heating and cooling for the houses are supplied naturally through a solar windtower—cooling through wind sieves and heating by a solar panel.

باد
AIR

آتش
FIRE

آب
WATER

خاک
EARTH

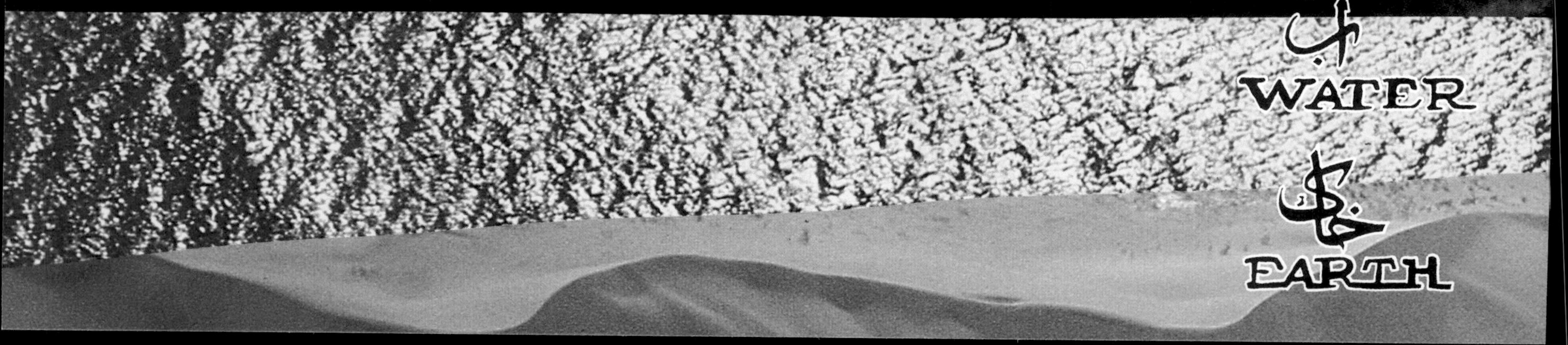

a giant glazed hollow brick at human scale
a true integration of the ceramic arts into architecture

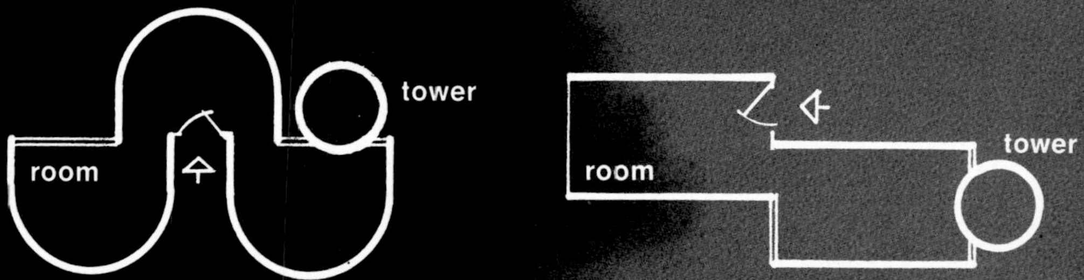

apse grouping-plan

vault grouping-plan

method:
1. spread a layer of sand on solid ground.
2. construct a vault, a dome, a form of clay.
3. burn the structure in the fire till it fuses into unity.
4. glaze inside and out and burn again.
....a shelter ready for living

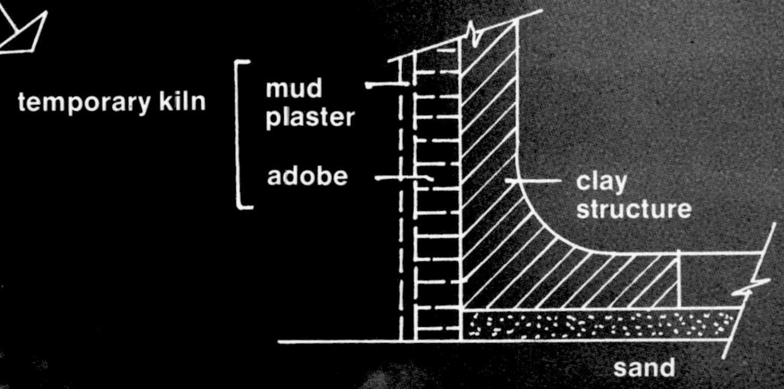

e. nader khalili
architect

ENVIRONMENTAL PRESERVATION

Charged with the preservation of natural ecosystems in the rural environments of Iran, the Department of the Environment has established a network of 134 national parks, wildlife refuges, protected areas and nature monuments throughout the country. This network is the most comprehensive in southwest Asia. In keeping with the concept that the key to wildlife protection is habitat protection, the floral and faunal resources are maintained in as natural a condition as possible. In addition, programs to improve conditions for reproduction and survival of natural wildlife populations are being implemented. Thus, rare and vanishing species such as the Persian fallow deer have a chance to survive, the environment is protected, and gene pools of plants and animals of potential value to mankind are preserved.

These national parks and reserves are also a valuable source of outdoor recreation space for Iran's increasingly urban population. With this in mind, master plans have been prepared for the management and selective development of national parks to preserve and interpret outstanding examples of Iran's natural heritage for the enjoyment and education of the people in such a way that the resource will remain unimpaired for future generations. Mohammad Reza Shah National Park in northern Iran will be the first of these to be developed. Visitor activities, administration, research and management facilities will all be planned with the primary objective of protecting the great variety of natural communities which the park contains and its rich, largely undisturbed fauna.

Department of the Environment

PEREGRINE FALCON
Falco peregrinus

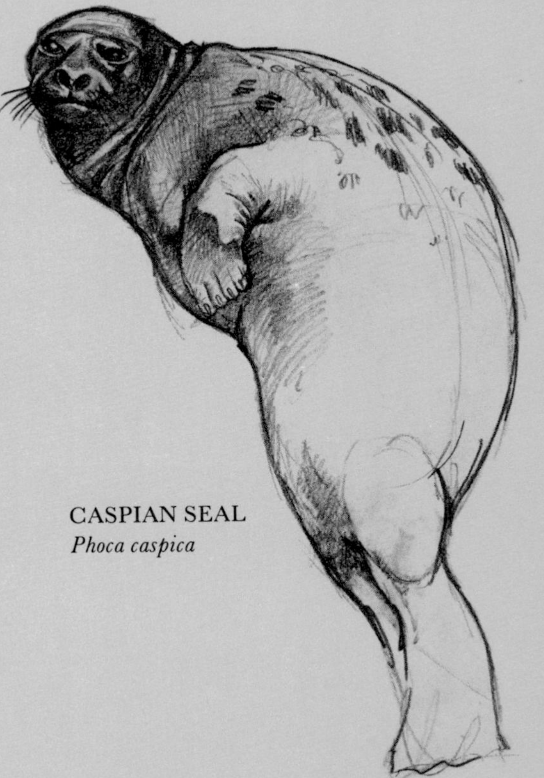

CASPIAN SEAL
Phoca caspica

WHITE PELICAN
Pelecanus onocrotalus

PERSIAN IBEX
Capra aegagrus

LONG-EARED HEDGEHOG
Erinaceus Europaeus

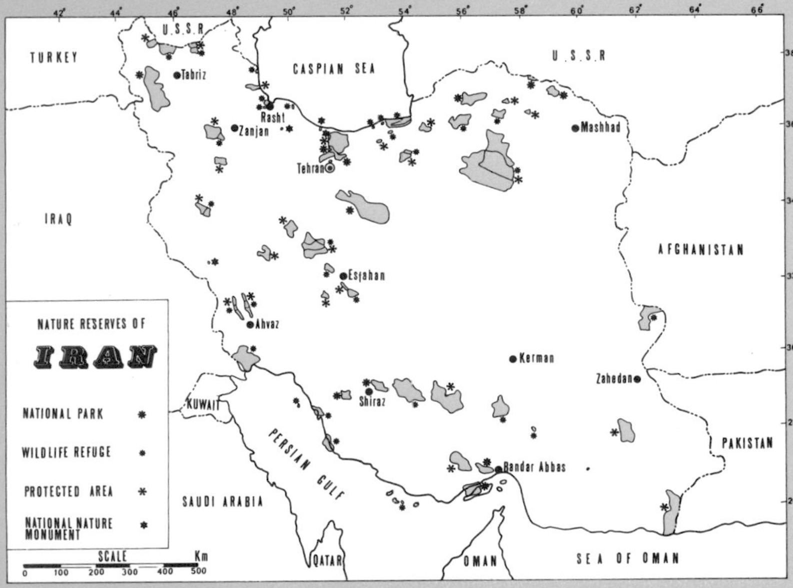

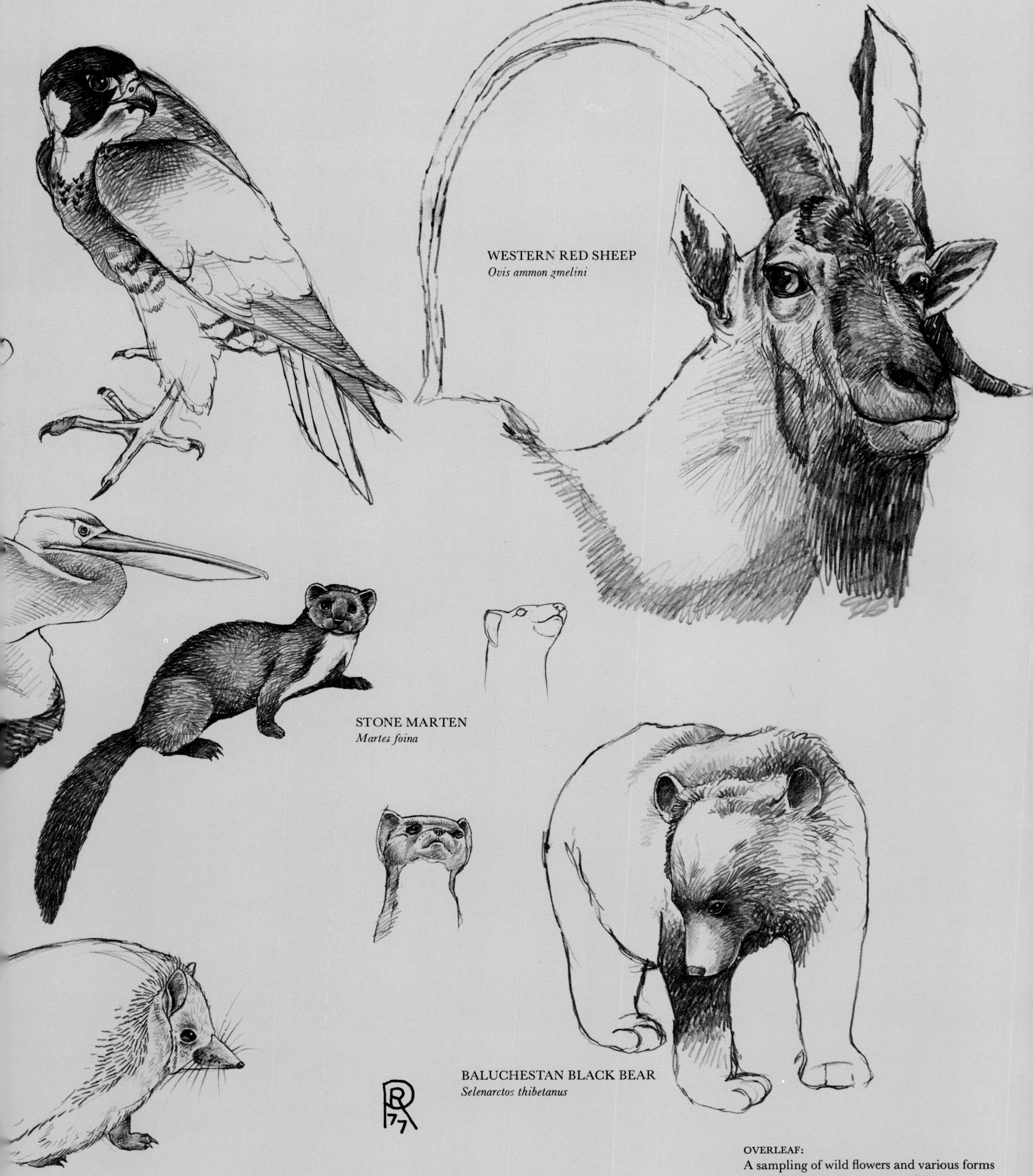

WESTERN RED SHEEP
Ovis ammon zmelini

STONE MARTEN
Martes foina

BALUCHESTAN BLACK BEAR
Selenarctos thibetanus

OVERLEAF:
A sampling of wild flowers and various forms of vegetation from all corners of Iran. ▷

گفتار اندر رزم اسفندیار با سیمرغ

NOTES TO THE PLATES

by Mitchell Crites

1 IMPERIAL YACHT, KISH ISLAND

The Pahlavi flag and crest were photographed on His Imperial Majesty's yacht, *Kish,* anchored off the island of the same name in the Persian Gulf. Kish Island has for a number of years served as a base of operations and vacation resort. The Royal Family also visit the island during the Now-Ruz celebrations at the end of March and early April.

2 FOUNTAINS, SHAHYAD MONUMENT, TEHRAN

In the Persian language, the word "Shahyad" means the memory of the Shah. The first major monument encountered by the tourist entering Tehran from Mehrabad International Airport is this impressive one inaugurated on October 16, 1971, for the 2,500th Anniversary of the Iranian Monarchy. This mirror image shows the graceful fountains leading up to the tower. The area surrounding the Shahyad Monument has been beautifully landscaped and the entire area has become a tourist and recreation center for both Iranian and foreign visitors (see Plate 25).

3 SHAHYAD MONUMENT, TEHRAN

The grandeur of the Shahyad Monument, designed by a young Iranian architect, Hossein Amanat, is captured here in a different view showing the tiled underside of the soaring arches. It is under this exact spot that visiting foreign dignitaries are formally presented with the keys to the city of Tehran.

4 DANCERS, SHAHYAD MONUMENT, TEHRAN

Wearing colorful tribal costumes, dancers welcome a delegation of state visitors arriving at Mehrabad International Airport.

5 SULPHUR, KHARK ISLAND

Khark Island in the Persian Gulf, where giant supertankers are loaded with oil, is a key link in Iran's vast petroleum industry (see Plates 166, 190). Also located on the island is the Khark Petrochemical Complex which produces from gas more than 700 tons of sulphur daily. The sulphur, red in liquid form, becomes the brilliant yellow shown here after drying. A tractor collects the dry sulphur which is then exported to world markets.

6, ASADABAD SATELLITE STATION, NEAR HAMEDAN

7 The Asadabad Satellite Station located near Hamedan links Iran via satellite to the rest of the world. Asadabad I, the first station, was opened in 1968 and connected Iran via satellite with Europe and the United States. In 1976 Asadabad II was completed, providing communication with a satellite fixed over the Indian Ocean. These stations provide international telephone, telegraph and television communication within Iran and beyond its borders. Sixty percent of the rural areas of Iran also receive communication through this system. Pictured here are two views of one of the largest receiving discs at Asadabad. Plate 6 shows the faceted underside of the huge disc while Plate 7 reveals the smooth, curving outerface.

8 GAS FLARING, AHVAZ

Natural gas flares illuminate the horizon day and night at Ahvaz, a petroleum center in southwestern Iran. Soon the energy dissipated through flaring will be constructively channeled into giant petrochemical plants now being built at Bandar-e-Shapur and other sites where vital petrochemical products will be produced for Iranian and international consumption.

9 BIRTHDAY OF HIS IMPERIAL MAJESTY, TEHRAN

Hundreds of thousands of Iranians gathered together around Tehran on October 26, 1976, to celebrate the fifty-seventh birthday of His Imperial Majesty the Shahanshah. The most spectacular celebration took place in Tehran's Aryamehr Stadium and was attended by the Royal Family. Following several hours of massed stadium gymnastics and parades, a brilliant display of fireworks climaxed the festivities while pattern cards across the stadium spelt out the nation's gratitude to His Imperial Majesty.

10 PALEOLITHIC REMAINS, TEHRAN

This dramatic collection of early human and animal remains was discovered during recent surveys and excavations conducted by the Iran National Museum of Natural History in East Azarbayejan. The newly founded museum is actively engaged in a program of excavations, scientific research and public exhibitions.

◁ Miniature depicting Esfandiyar and the Simorgh, from the *Shahnameh,* dated A.D. 1648. (Reproduced by permission of P. & D. Colnaghi & Co. Ltd., London)

Dr. Hind Sadek-Kooros, the director of the museum, eloquently expresses its aims and aspirations: "In planning educational exhibits it shall be our aim to stimulate in the museum visitor the same interest and enthusiasm that we as scientists and curators have for natural history phenomena and some of the concern we feel for their protection and preservation. As the National Museum of Natural History, we must not neglect to bring to the public a sense of awareness of environmental problems, a realization that humankind evolved not in a vacuum but in a natural environment of animals, plants, rocks and minerals, air and sunshine, whose protection and preservation must become the concern of every man, woman and child alive today. I for one know no better way of teaching a child to love and protect than by teaching him to understand, to look and see the great natural beauty of our world, and to understand how and why ecosystems can be destroyed.

"We do not plan for a finished museum or a static one. We do not see our National Museum of Natural History as being isolated from the public and national aspirations or detached from the very soil of Iran. Rather, we see this museum as an integral part of the development and growth of the nation and of Iran's new, larger role in the world today."

11 EXCAVATIONS AT SHUSH, KHUZESTAN

The French Archeological Mission began excavating at Shush (Susa) in 1884 and built the large castle seen in the background to protect the archeologists and workers from local bandits. Shush was an important Elamite center and later became a capital of the Achaemenian Empire. The deep cut in the central mound seen here exposes habitation levels extending back in time more than six thousand years. Because of its excavations, archeological museum and nearby tomb of the Prophet Daniel, the town of Shush has become a popular tourist attraction in the province of Khuzestan.

12 LORESTAN BRONZES, TEHRAN

These exquisite bronze horse harnesses date from the eighth to the seventh centuries B.C. The wild goat head decoration on top of the ring is flanked by crouching lions creeping up on either side. Discoveries of bronze vessels and implements in the early part of this century in the region of Lorestan around Kermanshah in western Iran brought attention to a well-developed style of art which spans a period from about 2600 B.C. to A.D. 800. These bronze harnesses are part of the private collection of Her Imperial Majesty the Shahbanou.

13 GANJ NAMEH, HAMEDAN

These well-preserved rock-cut inscriptions record the victories of two Achaemenian kings, Darius I (524-485 B.C.) and Xerxes I (486-465 B.C.). The inscriptions were traditionally called Ganj Nameh or the Treasure Book from the belief of local people that their undeciphered message held clues to the location of a lost treasure. Ganj Nameh is located beside a beautiful waterfall on the lower slopes of Mount Alvand, about five kilometers southwest of Hamedan, ancient Ecbatana, the summer capital of the Achaemenian rulers.

14 STONE CAPITAL, IRAN BASTAN MUSEUM

This imposing human-headed capital, a guardian figure, came from the Tripylon building at Persepolis, ceremonial center of the Achaemenian Empire, and now forms part of a collection of outstanding art and archeological treasures that can be viewed at the Iran Bastan Museum in Tehran.

15 HERCULES VASE, TEHRAN

This gilded silver vase stands 17.8 centimeters high and dates from the mid-third century A.D., although the theme is supposed to depict four of the twelve labors of Hercules. Hercules is shown here slaying the lion of Nemea, whose skin he thereafter wore, and capturing an ibex. Two other tasks not seen in the photograph are the capture of the wild boar of Mount Erymanthus and the bringing up of the triple-headed dog Cerebrus from the underworld. The vase is part of the superb collection of the recently opened Reza Abbasi Culture and Arts Center in Tehran.

16 BRONZE STATUE OF A PARTHIAN PRINCE

This larger-than-life bronze statue of a Parthian prince was discovered at a temple at Shami near Malamir in southwest Iran. This fine example of the art of the Parthian Dynasty is part of the permanent collection of the Iran Bastan Museum in Tehran.

17 TAQ-E-BOSTAN RELIEF, KERMANSHAH

Nestled in a stone grotto at Taq-e-Bostan near Kermanshah in western Iran is a remarkable series of stone reliefs showing scenes from the court life of Sasanian kings. Seen here is an imperial hunt which is a constantly recurring theme in the art of both the Parthian and Sasanian dynasties. This relief was photographed in January and appears even more striking temporarily stained by the seepage of winter rains.

18 GLASSWARE MUSEUM, TEHRAN

These four examples of ceramic ware are from the collection of the Glassware Museum in Tehran. They date from the eleventh and twelfth centuries A.D. and exemplify the brilliant quality of ceramics produced in those centuries especially at the city of Neyshabur. The collection, numbering nearly one thousand items, dates back to as early as 5000 B.C. and covers almost all the archeology of Iran up to the nineteenth century A.D. The Glassware Museum is housed in a residential complex built in Tehran in 1915, and its inauguration is expected to occur in the autumn of 1978.

19 KHARRAQAN TOMB TOWERS

The Saljuq architects were masters of brick decoration, and some of the finest and most intricate patterns have been preserved on two tomb towers at Kharraqan, northeast of Hamedan. The two octagonal towers are covered with complex geometric patterns in raised brick and date from the second half of the eleventh century A.D.

20 LUSTER MEHRAB, IRAN BASTAN MUSEUM

In the fourteenth century the technique of polychrome underglaze painting was introduced in Iran. This fragment of a luster-ware *mehrab* or prayer niche comes from the Jame Mosque at Qom and was probably executed in Kashan, a desert city famous for the manufacture of luster-ware tile.

21 IRANIAN CARPET MUSEUM, TEHRAN

This exquisite lion medallion center comes from a superb silk brocade carpet dating from the sixteenth century. It is part of a large collection of carpets from all periods acquired by the Shahbanou which will soon be on public display in the recently constructed Iranian Carpet Museum located in Tehran's Farah Park.

22 NADER SHAH JEQQEH, CROWN JEWELS, TEHRAN

This opulent jeweled *jeqqeh* or headdress ornament is thought to have been worn by Nader Shah, the great eighteenth-century ruler of the Afsharid Dynasty. On entering Delhi in 1739, the Mughal Emperor presented to Nader Shah the royal treasures, which he brought to Iran. Much of these found their way into the Crown Jewels Collection which can be seen by the public at the Melli Bank in central Tehran. The *jeqqeh* is over five inches in height and the central stone is a magnificent round emerald weighing about sixty-five karats.

23 DOWLATABAD GARDENS, YAZD

Spectacular examples of the architecture of the Zand Dynasty are not limited to the Zand capital at Shiraz but survive in provincial centers as well, as shown by this beautiful stucco ceiling from the Dowlatabad Gardens in Yazd. The graceful pavilion and formal gardens have recently been carefully restored to their original splendor by the Ministry of Culture and Art. The gardens date from the Zand period and were built by Mohammad Taghi Khan Yazdi.

24 QAJAR MIRROR BOX, NEGARESTAN MUSEUM, TEHRAN

This lovely lacquer-ware mirror box signed by Mohammad Reza Emami and dated 1265 A.H./A.D. 1840 is part of an impressive collection of eighteenth- and nineteenth-century Iranian art housed in Tehran's Negarestan Museum, a former palace of the Queen Mother. The Negarestan's attractive exhibition rooms and varied collection of paintings, jewelry and other minor arts of the Qajar period make it one of the most beautiful and important museums in the country.

25 SIXTH OF BAHMAN MUSEUM, SHAHYAD MONUMENT, TEHRAN

Among the most fascinating tourist attractions in Tehran is the Sixth of Bahman Museum located under one corner of the Shahyad Monument. Seen here is the staircase of the vast cinerama hall opened in January 1977, where the audience is seated and enjoys a moving audio-visual display in several languages which traces the history of Iran from the founding of the Achaemenian Empire to the present (see Plate 98). The museum, library and audio-visual complex were created and designed by a Czech artist, Jaroslav Fric, and this complex is the largest of its kind in the world.

26 BALUCHESTAN LANDSCAPE, AERIAL VIEW

Although arid and barren, the Baluchestan landscape in the southeast of Iran, with its unusual geological formations, is often bizarre and dramatic.

27-32 IRANIAN LANDSCAPE

27 — Mount Ararat, the legendary site of Noah's Ark and sacred to Iran's large Armenian population, dominates the northwestern border with Turkey near Maku.

28 — Rice paddies ready for spring planting along the Tajan River Valley near Sari.

29 — Aerial view of surface salt deposits in the Dasht-e-Kavir desert of eastern Iran.

30 — Snow blankets crumbling mud walls on the plain of Soltaniyyeh, a fourteenth-century Mongol capital. The magnificent tomb tower of the fourteenth-century Mongol ruler, Oljaitu Khodabandeh, can be seen in the distance.

31 — Spring flowers bloom in fields beneath the snow-covered peak of Mount Sahand in East Azarbayejan.

32 — Mount Taftan, the highest mountain in the province of Sistan-Baluchestan and an active volcano, soars 4,043 meters. Smoke can always be seen issuing from the eight-meter-wide upper cone and mineral waters stream from the mountain's base. Mount Taftan is located 256 kilometers southwest of Zahedan, the provincial capital, and forty kilometers east of Khash, a nearby small town.

33-38 IRANIAN LANDSCAPE

33 — A snowbound village with terraced tree farms in the Alborz Mountains north of Tehran.

34 — Mount Damavand, Iran's highest mountain, rises majestically over winter fields near Varamin.

35 — Aerial view of feathery trees being cultivated at a farm near Karaj.

36 — Mist covers a mountain pass leading from Tehran to the Caspian Sea through the Alborz chain.

37 — Weird and colorful geological formations hint at buried mineral riches on the coast of Hormoz Island in the Persian Gulf. During the fifteenth and sixteenth centuries, Hormoz was an important Portuguese fort and trading center fabled as the Pearl of the Orient.

38 — View of Kandovan, a troglodyte village situated nineteen kilometers south of Osku in East Azarbayejan. The local population of 742 lives in natural caves, subsisting through farming and animal husbandry.

39 EROSION PATTERN ON THE KHUZESTAN PLAIN

Erosion patterns on the vast Khuzestan Plain frequently offer a startling view from the air, resembling the structural formation of a forest fern. During Sasanian times, Khuzestan was a rich agricultural area and through the recent construction of new dams and the introduction of modern agro-industry, together with its oil and mineral resources, the province has become green and prosperous once again.

40-42 FLOWERING TREES AND PLANTS OF IRAN

40 — These autumn-blossoming flowers, known as sternbergia, are protected and cultivated at the Aryamehr Botanical Gardens near Tehran. This important botanical institute is engaged in a program of horticultural development and research and consists of an herbarium and garden covering 145 hectares. Botanists have selected and studied over 20,000 Iranian and foreign dried plant specimens. Plans include the construction of cultivated areas representing the typical flora of Iran as well as foreign plants from other temperate regions of the world.

41 — One of the many varieties of flowers native to Iran is the tulip seen here in a formal garden in north Tehran. Wild tulips bloom in the countryside during the spring, and botanists conjecture that tulip bulbs made their way to Europe in the baggage of merchant caravans traveling the Silk Route from the first century A.D. onwards.

42 — The Judas tree owes its name to the tradition that the disciple Judas hanged himself from its branches after betraying Christ. These flowering trees color the landscape in late spring along a quiet country road leading from Tehran to the village of Lashgarak.

43-44 PELICAN OF TABAS AND WILD THISTLE

43 — The famous pelican of Tabas, a desert city in the heart of the Dasht-e-Kavir, suddenly appeared some years ago in the Golshan Gardens. He lived a solitary life until recently when a mate was found to share his flowering oasis. The Golshan Gardens and handsome pavilion date from the late Zand and early Qajar periods.

44 — Wild thistle, surviving extreme summer heat, blooms alongside the cracked stone walls of the monumental platform at Persepolis.

45 ALPINE MEADOWS, ALBORZ MOUNTAINS

The Iranian upland along the Alborz Mountains is an important section of the Alpine-Himalayan system. This picturesque terrain was once more heavily forested, and just a few hundred meters lower thick stands of trees can still be found, including the oriental beech, oak, hornbeam, maple, ash, elm and the coniferous yew.

46 CLAY POTS, LALEJIN VILLAGE

Lalejin, located a few kilometers from Hamedan, is a village where the ancient tradition of pottery-making has remained intact and has even been able to flourish in the face of modern factory competition. Many of the glazed and painted vessels from Lalejin are sold in the Central Handicrafts stores in Tehran where other examples of Iranian crafts are available, having also been revived through the efforts of dedicated specialists.

47-56 IMAGES OF INDUSTRY AND TRANSPORTATION

47 — A golden crown and fifty golden orbs, symbol of the Fiftieth Year of the Pahlavi Dynasty at the Tehran International Exhibition Grounds.

48 — Oil storage tank painted with Persian numerals at the Shiraz National Iranian Oil Company refinery (see Plate 163).

49 — Painted steel pipes at the Tehran Trade Fair.

50 — General Motors of Iran display, Tehran Trade Fair.

51 — A monstrous tractor loads harvested sugarcane on its way to the sugar refinery at Haft Tappeh in Khuzestan (see Plates 91 and 160).

52 — Specialized forestry machinery used in lifting heavy logs at the Gilan Forest Products Complex near Bandar-e-Pahlavi (see Plate 72).

53 — Twisted and twirled iron forms, Tehran Trade Fair.

54 — Freshly dyed red and green wool hanging on wooden beams in underground chambers at the desert city of Yazd.

55 — Tanks and boilers at the Pars Paper Company, Haft Tappeh.

56 — Modern warehouse facilities at the Karun Sugarcane Project at Shushtar.

57-66 INDUSTRY AND TRANSPORTATION

57 — Coiled springs of heavy machinery in a Caspian development project.

58 — Stacked aluminum pots in the Shiraz Bazaar.

59 — Brass rice cookers awaiting final assembly at the Esfahan Taj Company.

60 — A giant ring symbolizing the wheel of Iranian progress at the Pahlavi Dynasty Exhibition, Tehran.

61 — Steam shovel at Sarcheshmeh Copper Mines near Kerman removing tons of surface earth to expose the rich copper ore beneath (see Plates 67 and 133).

62 — Steel rods in the foundation of the water desalination plant being built at the Bushehr Atomic Energy Reactor (see Plates 171-172).

63 — Polished motorcycles for sale in a Dezful store window.

64 — Colorful decals decorate this truck parked at the Tehran fruit and vegetable market.

65 — Lar Valley Tunnel road pierced by shafts of light, northeast of Tehran.

66 — Glistening silver rails at the Ahvaz Train Station, linking the southwest corner of Iran to the nation's capital.

67 SMOKESTACKS, SARCHESHMEH COPPER MINE, KERMAN PROVINCE

The Sarcheshmeh copper deposits near Kerman are the

largest known in Iran, containing some 450 million tons of 1.2 percent copper. Iran's total copper resources are now believed to be more than 850 million tons. Before the deposits can be reached at Sarcheshmeh, forty-one million tons of top soil will have to be removed. The Sarcheshmeh complex is expected to be in operation soon (see Plates 61 and 133). Copper presently ranks second only to oil as Iran's richest natural resource. The two 185-meter smokestacks being painted here will ultimately connect to the smelting plant. Copper reserves in Iran are managed through the National Iranian Copper Industries.

68 STACKED WATER PIPES NEAR SHIRAZ

The agriculturally rich Marvdasht Plain near the ancient Achaemenian sites of Persepolis and Naqsh-e-Rostam is being irrigated through the water resources dammed by the Dariush Kabir Dam. These water pipes will be welded together to form part of a vast irrigation network which also includes open canals.

69 KRUPP STEEL COIL, TEHRAN PARK

Steel plays a prominent role in the wide range of products and services which Krupp exports to all parts of the world. This coil of cold-rolled steel strip was photographed at the Tehran Park-e-Shafagh, a delightful urban park designed by Kamran Diba. Car bodies and refrigerators are among the many products manufactured from this material. In 1974 Iran acquired an interest in Fried. Krupp Hüttenwerke AG, the company which encompasses all the Krupp steel interests. This was followed by Iran's acquisition of a 25.01 percent interest in the equity capital of Fried. Krupp GmbH, the parent company of the Krupp group. In addition to major orders for the supply of steel, Krupp's activities in Iran encompass the planning and construction of industrial plants such as cement works, plants for the iron and steel industry, seawater desalination plant, sugar factories and diesel power stations.

70-71 ARYA CEMENT PLANT, ESFAHAN

The Arya Cement Plant is a gigantic enterprise presently being constructed on a barren plain thirty-five kilometers southwest of Esfahan. When completed, the plant will produce 10,000 tons of cement daily to be used primarily for Iran's domestic needs.

72 GILAN FOREST PRODUCTS COMPLEX, NEAR BANDAR-E-PAHLAVI

The Gilan Forest Products Complex is one of the world's largest new projects and involves major Canadian cooperation in project construction and care and reforestation of the precious Caspian forest (see Plates 45 and 52). Several Canadian companies are working in Iran with the Iran Wood and Paper Inc. and the Mazandaran Wood and Paper Inc. The complex includes the development of a complete forestry utilization program including the inventory of existing forests, nurseries, plantations, logging roads and harvesting. The project also includes the construction of a 500-ton-per-day kraft pulp and paper mill, a large sawmill, a plywood plant and a townsite.

73 SAND DUNE FIXATION, AHVAZ

In the drier areas of Iran, sand and soil stabilization is essential to agricultural development. The Ministry of Agriculture and Natural Resources has tackled this problem in an effective and original way by stabilizing vast areas of unstable dune through the spraying of a bitumen-based mulch. Giant tanks mounted on sleds are pulled over the sand by track-laying vehicles and the mulch is sprayed from jet guns in a ten-to-fifteen-meter swath. After stabilization, various kinds of grasses, trees and shrubs are planted. Thanks to this program, chronic dust storms which once afflicted the city of Ahvaz have become a thing of the past. The Ministry has expanded this program with similar success in many other parts of Iran.

74 GRAPE HARVEST, WEST AZARBAYEJAN

These grapes were photographed at the Pakdis Winery at Rezaiyyeh in northwestern Iran before being crushed and transformed into one of the many Pakdis products: champagne, table wines, vodka, port, sherry, grape juice, as well as industrial alcohol. Pakdis bottles 6,000,000 items a year and is the largest wine producer in Iran, competing successfully in the international market.

75-86 AGRICULTURAL PRODUCE OF IRAN

75 — Back-lighted sheep graze at the Pars Meat Packing Plant near Shiraz.

76 — Tall stand of trees at a farm near Shahrud.

77 — Tractors at the Dasht-e-Morghab agro-industry complex in Fars Province.

78 — Watermelons at the bustling Tabriz fruit and vegetable bazaar.

79 — Woven palm frond basket at Khash, Baluchestan, used to collect fresh dates, a major agricultural product in this dry but oasis-dotted region.

80 — Aerial view of cultivated vegetables and fruit trees in Gilan.

81 — Date palm oasis and furrowed land ready for cultivation near Iranshahr in Baluchestan, one of the hottest areas of Iran.

82 — Orange trees at the lush oasis of Jiroft, south of Bam.

83 — Sliced melon advertises the quality of a vegetable vendor's wares in the Rezaiyyeh bazaar.

84 — Date palm blossoms with the male flower wrapped around the female flower which ensures conception. Photographed at Nagor, Baluchestan.

85 — Wheat fields, dotted with blue cornflowers, stretch across the horizon at the agro-industrial complex at Dasht-e-Morghab in Fars Province.

86 — A cornucopia filled with the riches of the land—a decorative fantasy created for a banquet at the Tehran Hilton Hotel.

87-95 AGRICULTURE IN IRAN

87 — Banana blossoms in a tropical garden, Ahvaz.

88 — Fruit of the banana tree in the Tis Gardens, an exper-

imental horticultural station near Chahbahar on the Persian Gulf.

89 — White-flowering tea bushes at Lahijan on the Caspian coast.

90 — Plaster statue from a fountain at Fumen, a small town in the province of Gilan, showing a woman holding up brown tobacco leaves.

91 — After being burnt to remove dead leaves, sugarcane is harvested by hand at Haft Tappeh (see Plates 51 and 160).

92 — Reddish-green pistachios nearly ripe for picking in a Tayyebat shrine garden.

93 — Lemon blossoms in a Behshahr garden in Mazandaran.

94 — Golden pears from a Rezaiyyeh orchard.

95 — Ripe cherries from a private orchard along the Shahanshahi Parkway in Tehran.

96 MINISTRY OF AGRICULTURE AND RURAL DEVELOPMENT, TEHRAN

The imposing building of the Ministry of Agriculture and Rural Development in central Tehran is a twenty-two-story concrete structure completed in 1975. The bronze statue at the entrance was cast in Italy by the Iranian sculptor, Dariush Sani, and represents the Iranian farmer. Large agro-industrial projects as well as modern scientific research are coordinated in the ground floor of the Ministry utilizing the latest computer programming.

97 GULL OVER MOUNT DAMAVAND

Mount Damavand, the highest mountain in Iran, stands 5,772 meters high and can easily be glimpsed on a clear day from Tehran seventy-one kilometers away. The peak of Damavand casts an extraordinary shadow on the atmosphere at sunrise even on a cloudless day, and at the time of the summer solstice its perfect pyramid shadow points to Tehran, which may account for the ancient and continuing habitation of the area beginning with a probably Achaemenian or even earlier settlement at Rey. Here a land gull is soaring above the sacred, snow-capped mountain peak.

98 SIXTH OF BAHMAN MUSEUM, SHAHYAD MONUMENT

This striking exhibit is part of the marvelous Sixth of Bahman Museum located under the Shahyad Monument where a series of dramatic audio-visual presentations trace the history and dynamic cultural and economic growth of Iran (see Plate 25).

99 BIRDS IN FLIGHT, PERSIAN GULF

These birds were captured on film at early morning near the small boat-building village of Bandar-e-Lengeh along the Persian Gulf coast.

100 AHVAZ MICROWAVE STATION

The Ahvaz Microwave Station situated on a high peak is part of the Ministry of Post, Telephone and Telegraph. The station provides microwave telephone and telex communication between Ahvaz, Esfahan and other parts of Iran.

101 LAKE REZAIYYEH

This view of Lake Rezaiyyeh at sunset was taken from Kabedun Island, the largest island in the lake which also serves as an important natural wildlife preserve for the hundreds of thousands of birds which make this area their home.

102 CLOUDY SKY ALONG A COUNTRY ROAD

Motorbike riders stop for a chat along this ancient "Road of Kings" which runs from Tehran through the desert to Mashhad. Wind and a possible storm threatens near the small historic town of Shahrud.

103 HELICOPTER EXHIBITION, TEHRAN

This rear view of an advanced model helicopter was displayed at the Pahlavi Dynasty Exhibition held in Tehran in August 1976, where all branches of the Iranian Armed Forces exhibited their latest hardware.

104-107 AVIATION IN IRAN

104 — Two members of the Imperial Iranian Special Forces in free fall during a parachute jump at Bandar-e-Pahlavi. The Special Forces group is part of the Imperial Iranian Army.

105 — Major Khalili of the Golden Crown Acrojet Team photographed inside his F-5 aircraft at Tabriz prior to a dazzling display of aerial acrobatics.

106 — Sophisticated control board of an Iran Air 747 Jet, Tehran.

107 — About two dozen parachutists, part of the Imperial Iranian Special Forces, drop to the ground in an amazing mass jump at Bandar-e-Pahlavi. Like the Acrojet Team, these men also perform at various national and military holidays and are dropped from a C-130 Air Force plane.

108-110 AVIATION IN IRAN

108 — A pilot of the Imperial Iranian Air Force sits ready for take-off in his helicopter.

109 — F-4 fighter pilot photographed inside his jet at Tehran.

110 — Parachutists of the Imperial Iranian Special Forces, a branch of the army, land on the grass after a massed jump at Bandar-e-Pahlavi.

111 "IN SKYSPACE," SCULPTURE OF RICHARD LIPPOLD, KISH ISLAND

Perhaps the words of the renowned American artist, Richard Lippold, best express the brilliant sculpture he has created on Kish Island: "As though made from fragments of the blue sky itself, caught in golden shafts of the sun's rays, the flying forms of this work suggest the movement of the inhabitants of the air: birds, clouds, airplanes, rockets, traveling in all directions, like flocks of migrants passing across our vision in the vast spaces above our upraised eyes."

112 GOLDEN CROWN ACROJET TEAM, TABRIZ

Since its establishment in 1958, the Golden Crown Acrojet

Team of the Imperial Iranian Air Force has continued to perform extraordinary feats of aerobatic precision. The Acrojet Team was photographed in a formation of six F-5 planes in the airspace over Tabriz.

113-115 IRAN AIR 747 JET, TEHRAN

Iran Air has become one of the fastest-growing airlines in the world and now has regular flights to twenty-four countries connecting twenty-six capitals and major cities with Tehran, and is among the very few major world airlines with a flawless record. These three views of an enormous Iran Air 747 Jet, which is named "Pars," were taken at Tehran's Mehrabad International Airport. The bottom photograph shows the "Homa" symbol seen on all Iran Air planes. The Homa is an ancient bird of Iranian mythology, symbolic of royalty and good fortune.

116 NATIONAL IRANIAN RADIO AND TELEVISION, TEHRAN

This photograph was taken through a modern sculpture entitled "Palm Grove" created by the Finnish artist, Eila Hiltunen, who also designed the Sibelius Monument in Helsinki. The work of art was given by Her Imperial Majesty to the Shahanshahi Park. Although only recently landscaped, the new Shahanshahi Park in north Tehran has become extremely popular with the city's residents. Above the park stands the impressive complex of National Iranian Radio and Television (NIRT). Radio was started in Iran in 1940 and television introduced in 1966. The two were joined in the highly successful and imaginative National Radio and Television in 1971. NIRT now has twenty-four radio and television stations and 287 relay stations with broadcasts in Persian and other international languages. NIRT regularly receives programs relayed from around the world via satellites suspended over the Atlantic and Indian Oceans.

117-120 ACTIVITIES OF NIRT IN IRAN

117 — The National Iranian Radio and Television station in Bandar Abbas boasts a distinctive style of architecture designed by Mohandes Darvish who was also the architect for the Tehran NIRT complex. The stone buildings echo the forms of local water reservoirs found along the Persian Gulf coast.

118 — Members of the Pars National Ballet perform in tribal dress at the Tehran NIRT studios. This excellent ballet company under the direction of Abdollah Nazemi provides an important contribution to the cultural broadcasts of NIRT.

119 — In an international mood, a famous Turkish singer, Emil Sayin, photographed during her musical spectacular in the NIRT studios, Tehran, at which she sang many Iranian songs.

120 — Again dancers of the Pars National Ballet performing impromptu on the lawn of the NIRT grounds in Tehran.

121-124 NATIONAL IRANIAN RADIO AND TELEVISION

121 — Night-time view of the main NIRT administration building in Tehran.

122 — The Shahbanou visits the NIRT studios in Tehran to view and tape portions of a special documentary created by NIRT on a day in Her Imperial Majesty's life.

123 — Amir Abbas Hoveyda, then Prime Minister of Iran, delivers his annual Now-Ruz message to the nation from the Tehran NIRT studios.

124 — NIRT television and sound crews broadcasting live the impressive festivities of the Fiftieth Anniversary of the Pahlavi Dynasty celebrated at Rey before the tomb of Reza Shah on March 21, 1976.

125 FLAGS AT THE INTERNATIONAL EXHIBITION GROUNDS, TEHRAN

Flags of contributing nations at the International Exhibition Grounds in Tehran where major trade fairs and international expositions are held. One of the most successful exhibitions was that mounted for the Fiftieth Anniversary of the Pahlavi Dynasty in the late summer of 1976 when over one million people attended.

126 MOSQUE, KISH ISLAND

One of the most serene spots on Kish Island is Safin village where life still revolves around the ageless rhythms of the sea. Here a small boy stops for a moment in the central prayer hall of the old mosque silhouetted against the water with the mainland of Iran in the hazy distance.

127 WATER LILIES, BANDAR-E-PAHLAVI

A naturalist's paradise, the *Mordab* or Still Waters which lie behind Bandar-e-Pahlavi on the Caspian Sea teem with plant, animal and aquatic life. The famous pink water lilies of the *Mordab (Nelumbium caspicum)* bloom in the late summer.

128 WATER SPRAY, SHAH ABBAS THE GREAT DAM, ESFAHAN

Although the dam is not pictured here, this elemental spray of water was photographed from a motor launch at the Shah Abbas the Great Dam in Esfahan Province. This thick arch dam stands ninety-five meters high and channels the power of the Zayandeh Rud River which flows through the city of Esfahan.

129 GOLDFISH STALL, TEHRAN STREET

Each year at the time of Now-Ruz, small goldfish stalls appear on street corners in all parts of Iran (see Plate 307). The *Haft-Sin* table, a ritual for each Iranian family, requires the presence of one or more of these brilliant golden fish. This tradition is celebrated differently in various parts of the country. In Shiraz the custom of setting a table with items beginning with the letter *"Mim"* or "M" is practiced, and it is possible that the tradition of the fish or *mahi* as it is known in Persia may be a legacy of an earlier time when the *Haft-Mim* table was an ordinary event.

130 ASTROLABE OF SHAH ABBAS II

This extraordinarily precise astrolabe was made for Shah Abbas II in 1057 A.H./A.D. 1647-48 and helped Iranian navigators chart their sea voyages. It was lent by the Museum of the History of Science at Oxford to the Science Exhibition held in the summer of 1976 as part of the Festival of Islam in London. Many precious treasures were loaned for this exhibition from Iran and other countries, and Her Majesty the Shahbanou officially opened the Science Exhibition at the Victoria and Albert Museum.

131 BANDAR-E-MAHSHAHR PORT

Bandar-e-Mahshahr is one of the largest petrochemical plants in Iran and is situated east of Ahvaz on the Persian Gulf coast. A complex system of pipes feeds the ships waiting in the harbor with various petrochemical products.

132 KHORRAMSHAHR PORT

The Khorramshahr Port is Iran's most active shipping center. Congestion which blocked many of Iran's ports and harbors a few years ago has been cleared and more than 5,000,000 tons of imports pass through Khorramshahr annually.

133 SARCHESHMEH RESERVOIR, KERMAN

Looking like an enormous space-age stadium, the water reservoir at the Sarcheshmeh Copper Complex near Kerman is lined with a special plastic material to prevent seepage and evaporation and to facilitate regulation of the water (see Plates 61 and 67). Water will be brought to Sarcheshmeh from Khatunabad forty-five kilometers to the west. Intertwined within the reservoir dam is a massive water distribution system which will provide the 60,000 cubic meters of water required daily by the Sarcheshmeh plant and another 10,000 cubic meters for domestic purposes. The scale can be judged by the small Giacometti-like figures of workmen on the far bank of the reservoir. The stark black tower in the foreground of the picture regulates the overflow.

134-139 CHANNELS OF WATER IN IRAN

134 – Aerial view of *qanats,* underground water courses, used to irrigate desert areas of Iran, photographed in the Dasht-e-Kavir near Varamin.

135 – The Shahbanou Farah Dam at Manjil provides hydro-electric power and water for irrigation to the province of Gilan. A handsome statue of Her Majesty after whom the dam is named stands on an artificial island above the main dam.

136 – The turquoise green Dez River photographed at Dezful from the main bridge fording the river.

137 – Mohammad Reza Shah Pahlavi Dam at Dez from the air. This striking dam has a capacity of 3,350 million cubic meters of water and supplies hydro-electric power and water for irrigation to the entire province of Khuzestan.

138 – The Farahnaz Pahlavi Dam at Latiyan channels the energy of the Jajerud River in central Iran.

139 – Aerial view of a small river in Baluchestan where many of the rivers in this dry province are being funneled into local dams to provide needed irrigation.

140 DARIUSH KABIR DAM, FARS PROVINCE

The Dariush Kabir Dam, built on the site of an ancient Achaemenian dam, has been named after a great king of the same dynasty. This rock-fill dam has a capacity of 993 million cubic meters and irrigates 76,000 hectares of land across the agriculturally rich Marvdasht Valley.

141 REZA SHAH KABIR DAM, KHUZESTAN

The Reza Shah Kabir Dam is an enormous rock-fill dam harnessing the considerable power of the Karun River in northern Khuzestan. The dam is an important link in Iran's growing need for hydroelectric power and a major source for irrigation in the area.

142-146 COMMERCIAL FISHING IN IRAN

142 – The annual catch of the Persian Gulf or Southern Fisheries averages about 20,000 tons, of which 1,300 tons contains some of the finest shrimp available anywhere in the world. This shrimp boat unloading its catch was photographed at the Fisheries' headquarters in Bushehr. Shrimp can be found from August until April, but are especially abundant during the autumn months.

143 – Caspian Sea sturgeon being washed down with hoses at the Bandar-e-Shah Caviar Factory. Iran's production of superb caviar now reaches almost 200 tons annually.

144 – Fresh Persian Gulf shrimp iced and ready for packing, Bushehr Persian Gulf Fisheries.

145 – A Persian Gulf lobster caught off the coast of Kish Island. Over fifty different species of marine life are found in the Persian Gulf and the Sea of Oman. The five main commercial varieties are tuna, mackerel, king mackerel, shrimp and the spiny lobster.

146 – Local fishermen pull in their nets on the Caspian coast near Bandar-e-Pahlavi in late October.

147-151 IMPERIAL IRANIAN NAVY

147 – Ships of the Iranian Navy docked in the Bandar Abbas naval port, headquarters for the Persian Gulf fleet.

148 – A destroyer crew at their battle stations go through combat maneuvers.

149 – Harmonious contrast between the old and the new—a wooden dhow seen for centuries in the waters of the Persian Gulf, and a modern destroyer of the Imperial Iranian Navy.

150 – Aerial view of the Bandar Abbas Beach Club where Navy officers and enlisted men relax.

151 – Insignia of the Imperial Iranian Navy ship, the *Artemis*, with a crown, anchor and two spear-bearing Achaemenian guards.

152-154 DEVELOPMENT IN THE PERSIAN GULF

152 – Several offshore production platforms are located near Khark Island in the Persian Gulf. The platform seen here stands in the Ardeshir oil field. After

separating out the non-usable gas, the production platform pumps the crude oil to the Iran Pan American export terminal at Khark Island where the oil is shipped to world markets.

153 — As part of their protective force in the Persian Gulf, the Imperial Iranian Navy maintains the modern hovercraft, a multi-purpose vehicle capable of hovering above the land or water.

154 — Working day and night, heavy equipment dredges the harbor at the Bushehr Atomic Energy Plant to facilitate the movement of heavy machinery by sea to the plant area (see Plates 171 and 172).

155 MICHELANGELO, BANDAR ABBAS

More than eight hundred officers and enlisted men of the Imperial Iranian Navy live on board the 275-meter-long *Michelangelo* docked at Bandar Abbas in the Persian Gulf. The great ocean liner purchased by Iran from Italy also serves the Iranian Navy as a major recreational resource for this part of the Persian Gulf.

156 ACHAEMENIAN SHIP

This life-size reproduction of an Achaemenian sailing vessel was prepared by the Imperial Iranian Navy for a military exhibition held in Tehran to commemorate the Fiftieth Year of the Founding of the Pahlavi Dynasty.

157 POTTERY KILN, CASPIAN VILLAGE

This alchemy, old as time, still flourishes as a village industry. Here a simple terra-cotta vessel is fired in a kiln outside the thatched home of a traditional and gifted potter in the village of Lareh-Sara near Bandar-e-Pahlavi (see Plate 304).

158 TORCHES AT NAQSH-E-ROSTAM

The Tenth Annual Shiraz Arts Festival was opened on a summer evening in 1976 at the appropriate site of Naqsh-e-Rostam with a performance by a troupe of Indonesian dancers (see Plate 159). At the conclusion of their moving performance, two dancers climbed on ropes from the base of the great stone cliff to the upper tombs, pulling behind them a torch which was extinguished in the highest tomb, dramatically recalling the days when fire was worshiped across the Persian Empire.

159 INDONESIAN DANCERS AT NAQSH-E-ROSTAM

A group of talented Indonesian village dancers under the direction of Sardono Kusumo inaugurated the Tenth Annual Arts Festival held at Shiraz. Reenacting ancient rites, the dancers gathered in a circle around a blazing fire embodying the Divine Spark, as the sacred flames of Naqsh-e-Rostam themselves once did. The Shiraz Festival has become an important focal point for artistic and cultural exchange between traditional and modern artists from east and west.

160 HAFT TAPPEH SUGARCANE PROJECT, KHUZESTAN

Sugarcane is one of the few crops that is burnt before harvesting. The burning removes much of the dead leaves and trash but does not damage the stalk, allowing the workers to cut the cane more easily (see Plates 51 and 91).

161 GAS FLARES, AHVAZ

Gas burn-offs around Ahvaz and other petroleum centers will soon be a thing of the past when the natural gas will be transformed into petrochemicals or shipped through pipelines to several of Iran's neighbors (see Plate 8).

162 SOUND AND LIGHT, PERSEPOLIS

Under the stars during the warm months of the year tourists and local people gather for this dramatic pageant at Persepolis, recreating the past of this ancient ritual capital—the legendary center for spiritual energy revered by the Achaemenian kings.

163 STORAGE TANKS, SHIRAZ NIOC REFINERY

These impressive symbols of the twentieth century are as sculptural as any contemporary art form. They contain oil products stored prior to being shipped to various domestic and international markets (see Plate 48). The refined products at the National Iranian Oil Company's Shiraz Refinery include gasoline, aviation fuel, bitumen, gas oil, fuel oil, aviation spirits, kerosene and liquid gas.

164 ABADAN NIOC REFINERY FLARE

The first oil refinery in Iran was built at Abadan in 1912. Due to its strategic location on the Persian Gulf, Abadan remains a major commercial and petroleum center in southwestern Iran.

165-170 STEEL, OIL AND PETROCHEMICALS

165 — Evening panorama of the Shiraz Chemical Fertilizer Plant opened in 1963, the first petrochemical plant in Iran.

166 — Khark Island, a small coral island situated forty miles off the mainland in the northwestern Persian Gulf, is the single most important link in Iran's oil trade with the world. These 48-inch pipes, extending across mountainous terrain and underwater, carry crude oil to waiting tankers docked at the sea island and T-jetties offshore (see Plate 5).

167 — Production unit at Ahvaz where poisonous gas is burnt off and separated gas sent on to Bid Boland and other pumping stations.

168 — View of the main cutting room of the Aryamehr Steel Mill in Esfahan with sparks flying. The Aryamehr mill was completed in 1972 and produces approximately two million tons of steel annually.

169 — Factory worker at the Ahvaz Pipe Mill, a subsidiary of NIOC. The mill was established in 1967 and manufactures line pipe specially designed for the pumping of gas and oil.

170 — Aerial view of Khark Island showing the tank farm where reserves of about twenty million barrels of oil can be stored. The tank farm is located on an elevated hill in the southern section of the island, enabling crude oil loading to be effected by gravity flow (see Plate 5).

171, 172 BUSHEHR ATOMIC ENERGY PLANT

Photographed by day and night, this enormous atomic

energy plant is being constructed near the Persian Gulf city of Bushehr. With the cooperation and support of West Germany, Iran is building two reactors, each with a capacity of 1,200 megawatts, expected to be operational in 1981. Their function will be to produce electricity through nuclear power to support the growing energy needs of Iran. Outside work is almost suspended during the excessive heat of day on the Gulf but continues unabated through the cooler night (see Plate 154).

173 KERMANSHAH NIOC REFINERY

Flares of the Kermanshah NIOC Refinery in western Iran turn the nearby Gharasu into a river of gold. The original refinery was built in 1936 during the reign of Reza Shah the Great and expanded in 1972.

174 OIL-DRILLING RIG, AHVAZ

All aspects of the petroleum industry, including exploration, refining and shipping abroad, can be found in the dynamic industrial city of Ahvaz, the capital of Khuzestan, with a growing population of 300,000.

175 SOLAR ENERGY DEVICE, MATERIALS AND ENERGY RESEARCH CENTER, TEHRAN

The Materials and Energy Research Center located in Tehran is an affiliate of Aryamehr University and is the leader in the development of solar energy in Iran. Chief consultant to the Ministry of Energy and Power, the Center was opened in 1975 and carries on a varied program of research into alternate technologies and new sources of energy. The glowing parabolic metal dish concentrator seen here was developed at the Materials and Energy Research Center for high temperature solar energy application. (This was chosen as the subject for the jacket of the book.) On this small scale the device could boil water and cook a villager's meal, and similar units are already being used by the Iranian army. By increasing its size, larger units of about fifty square meters could have significant industrial application. Recognizing the diminishing nature of petroleum resources, many research and educational institutions in Iran, through the guidance and support of the Shahanshah, have embarked on ambitious programs for the development of solar energy within the country.

176 SPIRIT OF LIGHT, NEAR GANJ NAMEH

The smoky light of a local charcoal-maker's fire filters through the branches of a small tree, symbolizing the eternal light of the spirit, and brings to mind the Quranic verse "God is the Light of the heavens and the earth" (*Quran*, XXIV, 35).

177 EBRAHIM KHAN MADRESEH, KERMAN

The recently restored Madreseh of Ebrahim Khan in Kerman was built as a theological college in the early eighteenth century. The pastel-painted tiles decorating its inner walls complement the exquisite inner gardens and are a fitting place for this solitary young man to perform his late-afternoon prayers.

178 THE HOLY SHRINE OF EMAM REZA, MASHHAD

The shrines of Emam Reza at Mashhad and of Hazrat-e-Masumeh at Qom annually draw hundreds of thousands of pilgrims. Emam Reza was the eighth of twelve Shi'ite Emams and his resting place is constantly being restored and beautified by the shrine foundation through donations of the faithful (see Plate 190). In the background the tiled dome of one of the most serenely beautiful mosques in Iran, the Gowhar Shad Mosque, rises above the courtyard built between 1405 and 1418 by the wife of the Timurid monarch, Shah Rokh.

179 TAZIEH EXHIBITION AT SHIRAZ

Elaborately wrought heavy metal ritual standards known as *alams* are carried in procession during the mourning month of Moharram to commemorate the deaths of Emam Hoseyn and his followers at Karbela in A.D. 680. This *alam* topped by ostrich feathers was part of an unusual exhibition of the regalia of the *tazieh* mounted during the Tenth Annual Shiraz Arts Festival, when several performances of the traditional passion play and an international symposium dealing with the history and origins of the *tazieh* took place (see Plate 180).

180 TAZIEH OF HAZRAT ABBAS, SHIRAZ

The first *tazieh* performed at the Tenth Annual Shiraz Arts Festival and attended by the Shahbanou in the Hoseyniyyeh Moshir recalled the murder of Hazrat Abbas, brother of Emam Hoseyn, whose hands were severed during the battle. The audience surrounding a circular stage in the middle of the hall was deeply moved by the anguished suffering portrayed by the traditional actors.

181 FIRE SANCTUARY AT YAZD

This rare photograph shows a Zoroastrian priest feeding the sacred fire which burns eternally within the Fire Sanctuary at Yazd, an important Zoroastrian center in Iran. This priest or *dastur* came from Bombay where many Zoroastrians or Parsis have made their home.

182-185 EXPRESSIONS OF THE ARMENIAN FAITH

182 – The church of Saint Thaddeus, also known as Qara Kilise or the Black Church, is a sacred pilgrimage center for Iran's large Armenian population who annually visit the church in the late summer. Qara Kilise, located near Maku on the Turkish border, is presently under restoration, as are the other early Armenian churches in Iran including the remote church of Saint Stephanos on the Russian border. The original construction at Qara Kilise dates from about the tenth century.

183 – This impressive portrait of Archmandrite Mesrob Ashjian, spiritual leader of the Armenian Diocese of Iran and India, was taken during the performance of the Holy Mass inside the Old Savior's Cathedral in New Jolfa, a suburb of Esfahan. New Jolfa has remained an important commercial and ritual center of the Armenian community since the days of Shah Abbas when the ruler moved many Armenians from the original Jolfa on the present northern border of Iran to Esfahan.

184 – An overall view of the Old Savior's Cathedral built

in 1606-1654 during the Holy Mass. The church, designed on an Armenian plan, is an important museum of early seventeenth-century art containing Dutch paintings and Iranian tile work. A museum has been constructed within the cathedral compound where the general public can view old manuscripts, liturgical vestments, miniatures and other relics of the rich Armenian past.

185 — Detail from the stone carvings on the Qara Kilise church depicting a traditional tree-of-life motif.

186 ANCIENT TORAH, TOMB OF ESTHER AT HAMEDAN

This carefully preserved *Torah* is given a place of honor inside the cave-like tomb believed to house the remains of the Biblical Queen Esther, who married the Achaemenian King Artaxerxes, and her foster father Mordecai at Hamedan. The present building is probably of Islamic date but the ancient stone foundations hint at a much earlier origin. There has been a small Jewish colony in Hamedan at least since Sasanian times.

187 TRIBAL TENT SCHOOLS, NEAR SHIRAZ

For many years the education of Iran's large tribal population was a major problem until the remarkable efforts of Dr. Mohammad Bahman-Begui focused on the issue through the establishment of the Tribal Education Center in Shiraz. Dr. Bahman-Begui took education to the tribes as they moved on their winter to summer migrations in the form of tent schools. After graduating from the tent school, many tribal students continue their education at the tribal high school in Shiraz. Pictured here are girl students of the Qashqai tribe performing a joyful dance as a welcome to visitors. The white tents of the school are pitched near the summer grazing grounds of the tribe in Fars Province southwest of Shiraz (see Plate 246).

188 QAZVIN MUSEUM

The Qazvin Museum is housed inside a sixteenth-century palace built by the Safavid ruler, Shah Tahmasb. The museum's collection includes glass and brass ware as well as several superb painted wooden doors, a specialty of the Qazvin area.

189 STORYTELLER, CARAVANSERAI MOSHIR, SHIRAZ

Much of the grand Shiraz Vakil Bazaar dates from the Zand period, and in the heart of the bazaar can be found the charming Caravanserai Moshir which has been restored and turned into restaurants and shops catering to the many tourists who frequent Shiraz. Inside the main Caravanserai restaurant, this flamboyant story and fortune teller delights the guests with tales of past and future glory, reciting verses from the great epic poem of Ferdowsi, the *Shahnameh*.

190 SHRINE OF EMAM REZA, MASHHAD

During the last few years extensive reconstruction and development has taken place in the congested area around the central shrine (see Plate 178). This aerial view of the shrine shows the newly cleared and landscaped area surrounding the shrine where a modern arcaded bazaar will house many of the displaced shopkeepers and serve the needs of the numerous pilgrims journeying to Mashhad.

191-196 REVIVAL AND RESTORATION

191 — The Tehran Rug Society sponsors exhibitions as well as research and publication projects in its concern for the revival and understanding of this traditional craft. These salt bags, on exhibition in Tehran, were used by tribes to carry their necessary supplies of salt during long migrations. They range in date from fifteen to ninety years of age.

192 — A skilled workman restores the upper brick and tile dome of the Hamman or Bath of Khosro Agha in Esfahan. The large bath dating from the Safavid period stands opposite the Chehel Sotun Palace.

193 — Mirror and stucco ceiling from a nineteenth-century house in Tabas soon to be restored and opened to the public.

194 — The image of an Achaemenian in a modern bronze sculpture by the Iranian artist, Ardeshir Arjang, stands inside the central salon at the Darius Hotel, Persepolis.

195 — This unusual modern statue at the Tehran Aryamehr Sports Complex depicts the legendary story of the battle between the hero Rostam and the White Div or Demon (see Plate 222). It was executed by an extraordinarily gifted Iranian artist, Tavakkol Esmaili, popularly known as Masht Esmail, who is concerned with expressing in art the traditional folk roots of Iran but in a startlingly modern idiom.

196 — Inaugurated in October 1977, the First Festival of Popular Traditions held in Esfahan successfully achieved its aim of bringing together a rich variety of traditional art forms and performers, including a performance of the Iranian passion play or *tazieh*, comic theater, acrobats, magicians, storytellers, musicians (see Plate 200) and many others. The festival, which will be an annual event, is co-sponsored by the Festival of Arts Office, an affiliate of NIRT, and the Farah Pahlavi Foundation as well as by the Office of Anthropology of the Ministry of Culture and Art. Seen here is a wandering darvish from Esfahan, one of many invited to the festival. These religious mendicants wander throughout Iran telling fortunes, reciting and writing prayers for the sick and performing other ritual functions.

197-202 REVIVAL AND RESTORATION

197 — The annual Tus Festival held in mid-summer attracts ever more visitors who delight in the performances of traditional wrestling, storytelling, plays, music and dance. This production of the play *Siavush and Sudabeh* was presented at the 1976 festival and was adapted from a story in the *Shahnameh* composed by the great Iranian epic poet Ferdowsi whose tomb is at Tus. The play rehearsal was photographed in the back gardens of the Bagh-e-Ferdows, a magnificent Qajar summer palace in Tehran that has been restored and is now used for cultural events and exhibitions.

198 — Two young musicians dressed in Safavid costumes play at a state dinner at Niavaran Palace.

199 – The excellent dance troupe of the Ministry of Culture and Art seen here dressed in Safavid period costumes inspired by a wall painting from the Chehel Sotun Palace in Esfahan. The dancers often perform for state guests and in public.

200 – Seated on the raised porch of the beautiful Chehel Sotun, a restored Safavid palace in Esfahan, these Kermanshah musicians sang and played on *tanburs*, a traditional stringed instrument, several times during the First Annual Festival of Popular Traditions in Esfahan (see Plate 196). The group sang *madh*, a form of eulogy, and songs of praise for Hazrat Ali as well as *ghazals* from the *Divan-e-Shams.*

201 – The Imperial Iranian Academy of Philosophy was founded in the spring of 1974 under the patronage of Her Imperial Majesty the Shahbanou. The Academy is concerned with the teaching and exchange of traditional philosophies and has a serious publication program. A group of students and visitors relax around a fountain in one of the Academy's meeting rooms.

202 – This impressive modern dome, designed by the Iranian architect, Hushang Seihoun, and completed in 1951, covers the tomb of Ebn-e-Sina (Avicenna), the great Iranian philosopher and physician who was buried in Hamedan in 1037. Adjoining the resting place of this great scholar and thinker is a museum and library containing many of his precious works.

203 RESTORATION OF HASHT BEHESHT, ESFAHAN

Skilled restorers and art historians have been busy during the last several years preserving the buildings and original urban fabric of the historic Safavid capital of Esfahan. Italian experts working on the monuments have at the same time trained young Iranian students concerned with the preservation of their country's rich heritage. A young workman is seen here preserving the delicate stucco and mirror decoration inside the Hasht Behesht, the Palace of Eight Paradises, built by Shah Soleyman about 1670, situated in one of the loveliest and most tranquil gardens in the city.

204 MODERN SCULPTURE OUTSIDE THE CITY THEATER, TEHRAN

This startling photograph harmonizes the creative works of two of Iran's leading architects and artists, Parviz Tanavoli and Ali Sardar-Afkhami. Tanavoli's bronze sculpture of "Farhad the Mountain Carver" depicts the legend of the humble stone carver, Farhad, who, in order to win the hand of Shirin, the queen, was commanded by the king to cut his way through a mountain. As he reached the other side, the king sent a false message saying Shirin had died, and the heartbroken Farhad threw himself off the cliff.

Tanavoli's sculpture stands beside what is thought by many to be the most beautiful contemporary building in Tehran, the City Theater. In this graceful structure completed in 1973, the architect, Ali Sardar-Afkhami, has successfully merged the traditional with the modern, especially in the subtle surface treatment of tile and brick.

205 SHAH ABBAS HOTEL, ESFAHAN

Located in the center of Esfahan, the Shah Abbas Hotel is one of Iran's finest luxury hotels. It is actually a restored Safavid caravanserai built in the early eighteenth century by the mother of Shah Soltan Hoseyn, the last of the Safavid rulers. In the background the tiled dome and minarets of the Mother of the Shah Madreseh rise above the great courtyard of the romantic caravanserai.

206 AERIAL VIEW OF SHAHYAD CIRCLE, TEHRAN

View from a helicopter of the recently re-landscaped Shahyad Circle with cool green spaces inside the strong organic design (see Plate 2). Eisenhower Avenue stretches off in the upper part of the photograph.

207-215 DAILY LIFE IN IRAN

207 – Young boys selling fruit in the covered Tehran fruit and vegetable bazaar.

208 – A banquet table arranged at Rudaki Hall, Tehran.

209 – Visitors are serenaded by a local band at Shahanshahi Park in Tehran on a crowded Friday afternoon.

210 – Reflection of a tree falls across a cloth shop window dappling the faces of chador-draped mannequins.

211 – Golden chains hang in a bazaar window in Yazd. High-quality gold-working still remains an active and profitable craft in Iran.

212 – A *naqqal* or traditional storyteller mesmerizes visitors to the Keramat Teahouse in Shiraz. Taking a break from their jobs or just relaxing, people come to this quaint teahouse to chat, gossip, listen to gripping tales from the *Shahnameh* and, of course, to drink tea.

213 – Glittering chandelier and furniture store in Tehran.

214 – A fruit-juice stall caters to the thirst of hot Tehranis during the summer. Pomegranates and watermelon are favorites.

215 – This gigantic crystal chandelier hangs in the Pars Department Store in central Tehran. Specially constructed for the store, the chandelier weighs almost ten tons.

216-221 DAILY LIFE IN IRAN

216 – Opening session of the Rastakhiz or Resurgence Party held at the Aryamehr Stadium in Tehran in October 1976. Fifty thousand local chapters and a growing membership of seven million registered members help the Rastakhiz Party effectively serve as a two-way channel transmitting the views of the people to the government and carrying education in official policy and national aims back to the people.

217 – Aerial view of Ecbatana, a vast urban housing development being created in west Tehran.

218 – Elegantly dressed wives of foreign diplomats grace an evening embassy party in Tehran.

219 – Exterior view of the Senate building in Tehran designed by the Iranian architect, Heydar Ghiai.

220 — View of the Etelaat presses in Tehran, a publishing giant with daily, weekly, monthly and yearly publications in four languages and an international readership of more than four million.

221 — Inside the Hyatt Regency Hotel on the Caspian Sea near Chalus—a luxury seaside hotel sponsored by Bank Omran of Iran.

222-228 STADIUM EVENTS

222 — Aerial view of the 100,000-seat Aryamehr Stadium in Tehran, part of a vast recreational and sports complex designed by the Iranian architectural firm of Aziz Farmanfarmaian.

223 — Ultra-modern Farah Stadium designed by the Iranian architect, Mohandes Darvish, completed in 1975, Tehran.

224-227 — Colorful gymnasts celebrate the birthday of the Shahanshah at Aryamehr Stadium on October 26, 1976, Tehran.

228 — At the same birthday celebrations for His Imperial Majesty, workers from the Paykan Automobile Factory present an ingenious precision drill in which they assemble Paykan cars in front of the spectators and drive away waving from the field after only five minutes. Paykan is the leading automotive manufacturer in Iran and its cars and other products are exported to many European and Asian countries.

229-232 DEVELOPING TEHRAN

229 — The University of Tehran, with a long-standing tradition of academic excellence, was established in 1934 under the direction of Reza Shah the Great. The university has an enrollment of 17,931 students and offers fifty-six bachelor degrees, eighty-six masters and twenty-four doctorates in various fields. This photograph shows the central Tehran University campus with its striking mosque designed by Aziz Farmanfarmaian.

230 — The new luxury Hyatt Hotel under construction in northwest Tehran will help fill the ever-growing need for first-class accommodation in the nation's capital as tourism within and to Iran expands rapidly. The international Hyatt chain also runs two other excellent hotels within Iran, one on the Caspian Sea coast (see Plate 221) and another in Mashhad, the capital of the province of Khorasan.

231 — This helicopter view shows the open spaces available to rapidly expanding west Tehran. Exciting new housing developments, an environmental park, medical center and other projects are planned for this area in the immediate future.

232 — The handsome new headquarters of the Rastakhiz Party is located in north Tehran on Aryamehr Avenue. The building contains a helicopter pad on the roof as well as conference and office facilities for more than five thousand party members and guests. The architecture, created by two Iranian architects, Iraj Parvin and Nik Khesal, is an interesting blend of traditional and modern and is especially noted for its distinctive brickwork created by local artisans and masons.

233-239 TEHRAN MUSEUM OF CONTEMPORARY ART

A vision of the future becomes manifest, the Tehran Museum of Contemporary Art reflects Iran's present cultural duality in combining traditional architectural elements with the most advanced principles of contemporary design. The bold, copper-clad light catchers diffusing the Iranian sky's bright illumination throughout the concrete structures are inspired by the desert home's *badgir* (wind tower) and the roofscapes of indigenous architecture. Similarly, in its programs of both Iranian and international art, architecture and design, the museum recognizes a unique mandate to link the latest developments in contemporary art with Iran's own artistic heritage. The striking museum building was constructed by DAZ Consultants, Architects and Planners, a Tehran-based firm, and inaugurated at a gala celebration in October 1977.

240 NIAVARAN CHILDREN CENTER, TEHRAN

The Niavaran Children Center and Camp was built to provide a place where less privileged children could come during vacation periods and participate in educational, cultural and recreational programs. This center and another at Shahsavar on the Caspian coast function under the Farah Pahlavi Socio-Educational Association which supervises many child-care and social services. The Niavaran Center was designed by Ali Sardar-Afkhami and completed in 1967. Its contemporary architecture, which incorporated for the first time in Iran the use of brick sun screens, blends harmoniously into the hilly Niavaran landscape.

241-245 IMPERIAL MILITARY FORCES OF IRAN

241 — Members of the Iranian Imperial Army Special Forces (A.B.N. Men) parading on Azarbayejan Day. This important national holiday commemorates the 21st of Azar, December 12, 1946, when advanced units of the Iranian army arrived in Tabriz to liberate the province. Azarbayejan Day was celebrated in Tehran on December 13, 1976, by a grand parade in which all units of the Imperial Military Forces of Iran as well as the police and gendarmerie participated.

242 — Flag of the Officers School carried in the Azarbayejan Day Parade.

243 — Parading frogmen, part of the Iranian Imperial Armed Forces.

244 — Tanks in impressive formation. Azarbayejan Day Parade in Tehran.

245 — Cadets at the Officers School in Tehran parade at the Coronation of Their Imperial Majesties held in Tehran on October 26, 1967.

246-253 TRANSFORMATION AND SERVICE IN IRAN

246 — Tribal students escaping the summer heat study inside white tents in Fars Province. These remarkable

young people rank among the best in Iran and many continue their higher education through government scholarships (see Plate 187).

247 — Young children draw pictures with colored chalk at the entrance to the Shiraz Institute for the Intellectual Development of Children and Young Adults, to welcome the Shahbanou who often visits the institutes around Iran.

248 — Students of the School for the Blind in Esfahan learn not only to read and write but excel at handicrafts and vocational training as well. In this photograph a teacher instructs one of the advanced students, a brilliant young man who has entered Esfahan University and is studying mathematics, a field seldom explored by the blind.

249 — One of the most effective new social service organizations transforming Iran is the Institute for the Intellectual Development of Children and Young Adults. These institutes with a core library are actually comprehensive cultural centers offering young people a variety of educational, artistic and recreational experiences. Through its more than one hundred fixed centers and mobile libraries, the Institute has attracted almost 800,000 members and rapidly continues to grow. The students photographed here were participating in a drawing and painting class at the center in Esfahan.

250 — Students at Esfahan University relax in the cool of the campus rose garden, a habit common to many Iranians who often study late into the evening reciting their lessons under the lights of city streets and in quiet parks.

251 — Students of Tehran University use a sophisticated microscope in the laboratory for Cytology and Electronic Microscopy, part of the International Institute for Biochemistry and Biophysics.

252 — This highly sophisticated coronary by-pass operation was performed by an Iranian surgical team at the American Hospital in Tehran. Several hospitals in Iran, including the Queen Mother's Heart Hospital in Tehran, offer advanced treatment for heart and related diseases.

253 — As part of the transformation of Iranian society realized through the White Revolution of 1962, health corps units have been sent all across Iran to administer to the needs of the many villages in rural areas. Many local social service and educational institutions have also sponsored their own health care projects. In an innovative pilot project, the Department of Community Medicine at Pahlavi University in Shiraz has developed a program to train auxiliary health workers selected from local young people. These health workers return to their villages where they are able to treat less severe illnesses as well as give instruction in community development, sanitation and family planning (see Plate 255). In this photograph, a doctor and a student at the Marvdasht Clinic near Persepolis listen to a patient's heartbeat through a double stethoscope.

254-261 TRANSFORMATION AND SERVICE

254 — A young girl of Esfahan reads one of the many delightful children's books created by the Institute for the Intellectual Development of Children and Young Adults. The institute's films and books have received many prestigious international awards.

255 — A health worker instructs a local woman in the village of Mozaffari how to care for her small child hanging in a hammock. This program is part of the Kavar Health Project, an innovative experiment in rural health care begun in Fars Province (see Plate 253).

256 — Display of the latest blood clinic equipment at the Pahlavi Dynasty Exhibition.

257 — Worker in the Atabak Henna Factory in Yazd packing by hand the green henna powder used in the ancient and popular tradition of dyeing hair a brilliant red.

258 — This ready-made clothing factory in Zahedan is run by the Imperial Organization for Social Services under the direction of Princess Ashraf. This organization gives two sets of clothing free to every student in Zahedan annually.

259 — Modern bread factory in Zahedan where three to four tons of bread are baked daily and sold in the city.

260 — Yek-o-Yek Canning Factory at the Dasht-e-Morghab agro-industry complex formed in 1967 in Fars Province to provide high-quality conserved food products. This project is only a small part of the far-reaching work of the Ministry of Agriculture and Natural Resources.

261 — A health worker dispenses medicine to villagers from a mobile van, another useful service of the Kavar Health Project south of Shiraz (see Plate 253).

262-266 MODERN ARCHITECTURE IN IRAN

262 — Damavand College, established in 1968 as an outgrowth of Presbyterian mission schools, is a private liberal arts college for women located in Tehran. It is fully accredited to grant the A.B. degree in a four-year inter-cultural program in the liberal arts and also the M.A. degree in education. The impressive new campus buildings have been designed by the Frank Lloyd Wright Associated Architects and additional buildings are in the planning stage.

263 — A spring rainbow arches over two of Iran's finest new architectural creations—the Ministry of Agriculture and Rural Development (see Plate 96) and the Saman Buildings, a twin apartment and office complex in central Tehran.

264 — The Iran Center for Management Studies located in Tehran is an independent non-profit educational institution that provides training at the graduate level for future managerial and leadership positions in business, government and other organizations. This aerial view of the Center shows some of the striking

architecture, contemporary and yet traditional, that has come to exemplify the work of one of Iran's leading young architects, Nader Ardalan.

265 ARSHAM FOUNDATION, KERMAN

The Arsham Higher Technical Teachers Training College provides quality education in vocational studies and engineering to the young people of Kerman and southeastern Iran. The college is funded by the philanthropic Arsham Foundation which has built and sponsored a number of social and educational institutions during the last decade. Three hundred students attend the college which opened a few years ago and enrollment is expected to expand to three thousand within the next couple of years. The college grants a Bachelor of Science degree in several fields of engineering as well as pursuing imaginative research into solar and other alternate sources of energy. The striking architecture of the campus was designed by the Yazdi architect, Haerizadeh. The central administration building and library of the college is seen here illuminated at night.

266 HOME OF ALI SARDAR-AFKHAMI, TEHRAN

This contemporary home built by the prominent Iranian architect, Ali Sardar-Afkhami, for his family in northeast Tehran, though acutely aware of the traditional Iranian sense of shelter, boldly conforms to the new dimensions of today's architecture.

267 OUTDOOR BANQUET IN A TEHRAN GARDEN

This impression of banquet tables laden with food was taken at a lavish dinner in the carpeted garden of a home in Niavaran. Traditional Persian cuisine is rich and delicious, with many regional variations.

268-273 A MONTAGE OF ENTERTAINMENT

268 — Bronze sculpture by the Iranian artist, Bahman Mohasses, of a flutist piping, at the entrance to the City Theater, Tehran (see Plate 204).

269 — The internationally acclaimed Bejart troupe from Belgium present a dance drama, *Eleogabalus*, at the 1976 Shiraz Arts Festival.

270 — The Tehran Symphony rehearses in Rudaki Hall under the direction of Farhad Meshkat, one of Iran's leading musicians, composers and directors. Rudaki Hall, named after a tenth-century Iranian poet and musician, is the center of Iran's rich cultural life, hosting many performances of music, dance, drama and opera.

271 — Performance of an original opera, *Samandar*, commissioned by the Ministry of Culture and Art to open the autumn 1976 season at Rudaki Hall.

272 — Asghar Bahari, a specialist in Asian and Iranian music, plays the *kamancheh* while Hosein Ghavami sings at the Tehran studios of National Iranian Radio and Television (NIRT).

273 — Reza Shajarian, a singer of classical Iranian music, performs on television.

274-279 A MONTAGE OF ENTERTAINMENT

274 — One of the most popular singers in Iran, the fabulous Haideh, performing on Kish Island at the Palace of the Crown Prince.

275 — Brilliantly costumed dancers, sponsored by the Ministry of Culture and Art, entertain after a state dinner in the gardens of Saadabad Palace.

276 — The National University choir sings at the school's annual graduation exercises in Tehran.

277 — Abdol Vahab Shahidi, a master of the *ud,* a traditional Persian stringed instrument, plays and sings at an NIRT musical evening.

278 — During the annual Shiraz Arts Festival, Iranian and foreign musicians perform each evening at midnight under the torch-lit dome of the Hafeziyyeh, tomb of the great Iranian poet, Hafez.

279 — Gougoosh in concert, a delightful singer and versatile performer loved and enjoyed in her country.

280 FLUTE PLAYER

A young villager playing his flute for his wife, mother and child in the cool of a green grove near his home in a rural area of Fars Province. This freshwater spring is considered a sacred place by the local villagers. Its waters flow on to irrigate the large agro-industry project at Dasht-e-Morghab in the Pasargad Valley, famed for the tomb of Cyrus the Great and other historical monuments.

281-287 THE PLEASURE OF SPORT

281 — Motorcyclists leaping across the open spaces of Shahestan Pahlavi, soon to be developed as the cultural and commercial center of Tehran. Motorcycling has recently become a major recreational sport and several racing matches are held each year.

282 — A horse and rider suspended in mid-air rehearsing before the Aryamehr International Show-Jumping Competition held at the Indoor Sports Hall of Aryamehr Stadium, November 1976. Sponsored by the *Kayhan* newspaper, the competition was attended by jumpers and horse enthusiasts from all over the world (see Plate 328).

283 — An Iranian athlete competing in the international weight-lifting competitions held at the Weightlifting Hall at Tehran's Aryamehr Sports Complex on November 13, 1976. Iranian weightlifters have won many medals at the Olympics and other international events.

284 — During the warmer months of the year, more than 100,000 Iranians enjoy mountain climbing. At Darband, in north Tehran, many weekend climbers begin their ascent of Towchal, a peak in the Alborz chain above Tehran, at this bronze statue of a mountain climber cast by Lal Mohavedi a quarter of a century ago.

285 — Water acrobatics held at the Second International Festival of Water Skiing on the Amir Kabir Dam at Karaj, north of Tehran (see Plate 386).

286 — Champion wrestlers practice at the Amjadiyyeh Stadium in Tehran in a free-style match. Various ancient and traditional regional styles of wrestling remain popular. Iranian wrestlers have won many international matches.

287 — A young diver competes at the Aryamehr Stadium Diving Pool. Diving is rapidly gaining many fans through the sponsorship and support of the Iranian Swimming Federation.

288-295 JOY OF DAILY LIFE

288 — A young man hands out traditional water pipes to guests at the Four Seasons Teahouse in Shiraz.

289 — Sitting on his father's scales, a Rezaiyyeh boy gobbles delicious local grapes.

290 — Poster for the Eleventh Annual Shiraz Festival of Arts designed by the distinguished Iranian artist, Qobad Shiva.

291 — Small boys splashing in an irrigation canal to escape the summer heat.

292 — The people of Baluchestan Province in southeastern Iran seem to compete with each other as to who can wear the most colorful costumes. Here three young Baluchi boys, wearing colored pajama-like outfits, share a bicycle.

293 — A cheerful balloon seller warmed by gas flares at the picnic grounds at Ahvaz.

294 — Dressed in their finest, these little girls of Azarbayejan wait eagerly to present their bouquets to Their Imperial Majesties.

295 — An offering of flowers for the Shahbanou from a Birjandi girl in her charming local dress.

296-303 JOY OF DAILY LIFE

296 — International guests, members of the diplomatic corps and prominent Iranians mingle on the steps of the Senate building in Tehran after the annual opening of this important legislative body (see Plate 219).

297 — Women in their traditional costume represent their tribes during a reception for foreign visitors in Tehran.

298 — International guests and their Iranian hosts enjoy themselves at the Tiare, the penthouse Polynesian restaurant at the Intercontinental Hotel in Tehran.

299 — Portrait of a mounted escort, member of the Imperial Horse Guard.

300 — This handsome young Iranian guides visitors through the Pahlavi Dynasty Museum recently installed in the Marble Palace, Tehran.

301 — An elfin beauty, this little girl proudly displays her tribal dress on a Zahedan street.

302 — Guests in formal dress arrive for the Coronation of Their Imperial Majesties at Golestan Palace in 1967 (see pages 300-301).

303 — Iranians are keen travelers and show a deep interest in their own historic places. Here tribal visitors ascend the monumental staircase at Persepolis.

304 LAREH-SARA VILLAGE, GILAN

The wife and family of the village potter mentioned earlier relax at the end of the day on the porch of their charming thatched-roof home with its traditional wooden architecture, in the Caspian province of Gilan (see Plate 157).

305 MOTHER AND CHILD

Framed by flowering fruit trees, this village woman proudly holds her child in the garden of the family home, enclosed by high mud walls, near Shahrud in northeastern Iran.

306-309 RITUALS OF NOW-RUZ

306 — During the Now-Ruz holidays, a special mixture of fruits and nuts called *ajil* is prepared, using raisins, dried mulberries, shelled almonds, hazelnuts, pistachios, peaches, pears, sugar-filled plums, cardamom and baslogh, a special Persian sweet. On the night of *Chahar-Shanbeh-Suri,* small children eat the *ajil* while their mothers and grandmothers tell them stories.

307 — The people of Esfahan buying goldfish for their Now-Ruz table.

308 — A traditional *Haft-Sin* table set with the seven items beginning with the letter "S" or "*Sin*."

309 — This charming scene of a traditional Iranian family gathered around the *Haft-Sin* was painted by Ostad Hoseyn Sheykh, a student of the great master, Kamal-ol-Molk. In this detail, one of the elders of the family examines his watch to announce the exact beginning of the New Year. The painting is part of the collection of the Iran Bastan Museum in Tehran.

310 HAJI FIRUZ, ZAHEDAN

A young student from a local Zahedan school, dressed in the costume and traditional blackface of Haji Firuz, sings and dances with great vitality and enthusiasm as he jumps over the fire lighted on the evening of *Chahar-Shanbeh-Suri.*

311 YOUNG BOY WITH A HORSE

During the Now-Ruz holidays, visitors to Ahvaz go to picnic near the warmth of the open gas flares (see Plate 293). This young boy, his face illuminated by the flames, earns a little extra money by allowing the city folk to ride his horse.

THE AUTHORS

Editorial Staff

Shahrokh Amirarjomand, *Editorial Director*
Vice Chancellor and Associate Professor,
Tehran University

Mohamad Moghdam, *Editor-in-chief*
Professor Emeritus and former Vice Chancellor,
Tehran University
Former Deputy Minister of Science and Higher Education
A Glimpse of History/page 30

Jacquiline Rudolph Touba, *Editor*
Associate Professor and Head of the Comparative Sociology Section, Institute for Social Studies and Research, Tehran University

Shahram Khial, *Assistant to the Editorial Director*
Assistant Director for International Relations, Tehran University

The Authors

Hossein Ali Anvari
Associate Professor, Aryamehr University
Former Deputy Minister of Information and Tourism
Space, Sound and Time/page 114

Laleh Bakhtiar
Author and Managing Director of the Hamdami Foundation
The Divine Secret/page 167
Spirit/page 197
Revival of Tradition/page 214

William O. Beeman
Assistant Professor, Brown University, Providence, Rhode Island
Research Advisor, Center for Performing Traditions, Tehran
And a Time for Pleasure/page 252

Ali Bolоukbashi
Assistant Director, Center for Iranian Anthropology, Ministry of Culture and Art
And a Time for Pleasure/page 252

Mitchell Crites
Archeologist and Teacher in Delhi
Notes to the Plates/page 369

Mohammad Hassan Ganji
Professor Emeritus, Tehran University
Rector of Amir Shokat-el-Molk Alam Institute of Higher Education, Birjand
Contour and Profile/page 67
Patterns of Industry/page 82
Dawn, Day and Dusk/page 103

Reza Hashemian
Associate Professor and Head of the Electronic and Computer Department, Aryamehr University
Assistant, Material and Energy Research Center, Tehran
Energy Revealed/page 176

Amir Abbas Hoveyda
Minister of Court
Prime Minister of Iran (1964-1977)
Iran—The Eternal Land/page 16

E. Nader Khalili
Moira Moser-Khalili
Members of the American Institute of Architects
Architects and Critics
Editors of *Vision*/page 324

Nader Afshar Naderi
Associate Professor, Tehran University
Head of the Institute for Rural Studies
Transformation/page 228

Said Nejand
Associate Professor, Tehran University
Director of the Institute of Hydro Sciences and Water Technology of Iran
Gift from Heaven/page 133
Channels of Power/page 144

Bagher Saroukhani
Associate Professor and Director of the Department of Cultural Affairs, Tehran University
Tomorrow/page 314

Peter Lamborn Wilson
Poet, writer and editor of *Sophia Perennis,* journal of the Imperial Iranian Academy of Philosophy, Tehran
Poetry translations

The calligraphy in this book was created by one of Iran's leading calligraphic artists, Nasrollah Afjei, who trained with Ostad Hossein Mirkhani. Mr. Afjei's work has been exhibited in many international galleries and cultural festivals.

ACKNOWLEDGMENTS

To complete this companion volume to *Persia–Bridge of Turquoise*, my encounter with Iran continued for another three years. During the twenty-two visits I made to Iran and the journeys within the country, there were changes on every level of the Imperial Court, the government and the ministries. Many new cultural foundations and educational institutions were inaugurated.

Were I to mention the countless individuals from every walk of life who assisted and encouraged me during the long research and preparation involved in the work, the list would be so long as to be encyclopedic. Instead, I should like to record my debt of gratitude to the following: The Imperial Court, the Ministries of Information and Tourism, Agriculture and Natural Resources, Science and Higher Education, Health and Welfare, Arts and Culture and the Plan and Budget Organization, the Special Bureau of Her Imperial Majesty and the Shahbanou Farah Foundation.

I feel a personal obligation to thank certain Iranians who devoted much time and effort to the completion of this book: Dr. Shahrokh Amirarjomand, who personally directed and edited the text in close collaboration with Dr. Mohamad Moghdam and the many contributors. The authors must be complimented on the sensitive execution of their individual tasks. I thank Shahram Khial for his invaluable administrative assistance, and Jahangir Beheshti, my technical assistant, for his dedicated interest and support. My many friends in the Ministry of Information and Tourism in Tehran who planned the trips and the complex itineraries will always be remembered, as well as their representatives in Rome and London.

Both in Iran and in my Rome studio, Mitchell Crites dedicated himself to the task of informing the reader through his careful research, resulting in the notes to the plates and captions for this book.

In my studio on the Tiber, Trisha Mitchell and Sallie Marcucci assisted in the recording and selection from over fifty thousand images and in all stages of design in preparation for press. Coordination of the studio throughout the project was ably handled by Judy Allen. Bruno Cioci was entirely responsible for my laboratory preparation of the monotones, and Franco Bugionovi assisted with the creation of the line engravings. For editorial comments, I thank my friends Dame Freya Stark and Sylvia Matheson, and for special assistance, in Toronto, T. Cuyler Young Jr and Roger M. Savory; in London, Lady Duff Assheton Smith.

Special care to the processing of the Agfachrome film was given by the Agfa laboratory in Tehran, which I used exclusively for my Hasselblad, and the professional color laboratory Autenticolor in Rome was responsible for the development and interpretation of all Kodak products which I used in the Nikon cameras.

One volume can only be a sketch, never a complete portrait of Iran in transition. Many omissions are inevitable. I can only invite Iranians, foreign travelers and armchair readers to evaluate for themselves the adventure and excitement that was mine as a guest while in this remarkable country.

Roloff Beny
Rome

Acknowledgments to A Glimpse of History

The introductory historical survey is based mainly on the following works with the kind permission of the publishers. The compiler alone is responsible for some new interpretations and for the thread of thought running through the essay.

Z. Behruz, *Taqvim o tarikh dar Iran* (*Calendar and History in Iran*), Tehran, 1951.
M. A. R. Colledge, *The Parthians*, Thames and Hudson, London, 1967.
W. Culican, *The Medes and Persians*, Thames and Hudson, London, 1965.
Jean-Louis Huot, *Persia I*, Nagel, Geneva, 1965.
V. G. Lukonin, *Persia II*, Nagel, Geneva, 1967.
P. Sykes, *A History of Persia*, vol. II, Macmillan and Company, London, 1963.

We are most grateful for permission from Penguin Books Ltd. to quote from R. Ghirshman, *Iran*, 1954, pages 289–318 and 314–349.

M. Moghdam

Note on Transliteration

In transliterating proper names, the contemporary Persian pronunciation has been followed throughout, and to avoid inconveniences in printing, diacritical marks have been omitted.

INDEX TO THE PLATES

Note: Folios in parentheses relate to the plates; all other folios indicate page numbers.

INDEX TO VISION

The Projects

The Architects and Planners

Design and photographs
Roloff Beny, O.C., LL.D., RCA.

Cameras
Hasselblad and Nikon

Film
Agfachrome 50S and 50L
Kodachrome 25 and 64

Typefaces
Display: Eve Light filmset by Techni-Process
Text: Baskerville filmset by Howarth & Smith
Toronto, Canada.

Paper
Text: Cartridge specially dyed fen green
Illustration: Ascot Matt Art

Colour separations
Adroit Photo Litho Limited, Birmingham, England.

Printing
Balding + Mansell Limited, Wisbech, England.

Binding
Webb Son and Co. Limited, Ferndale, Wales.

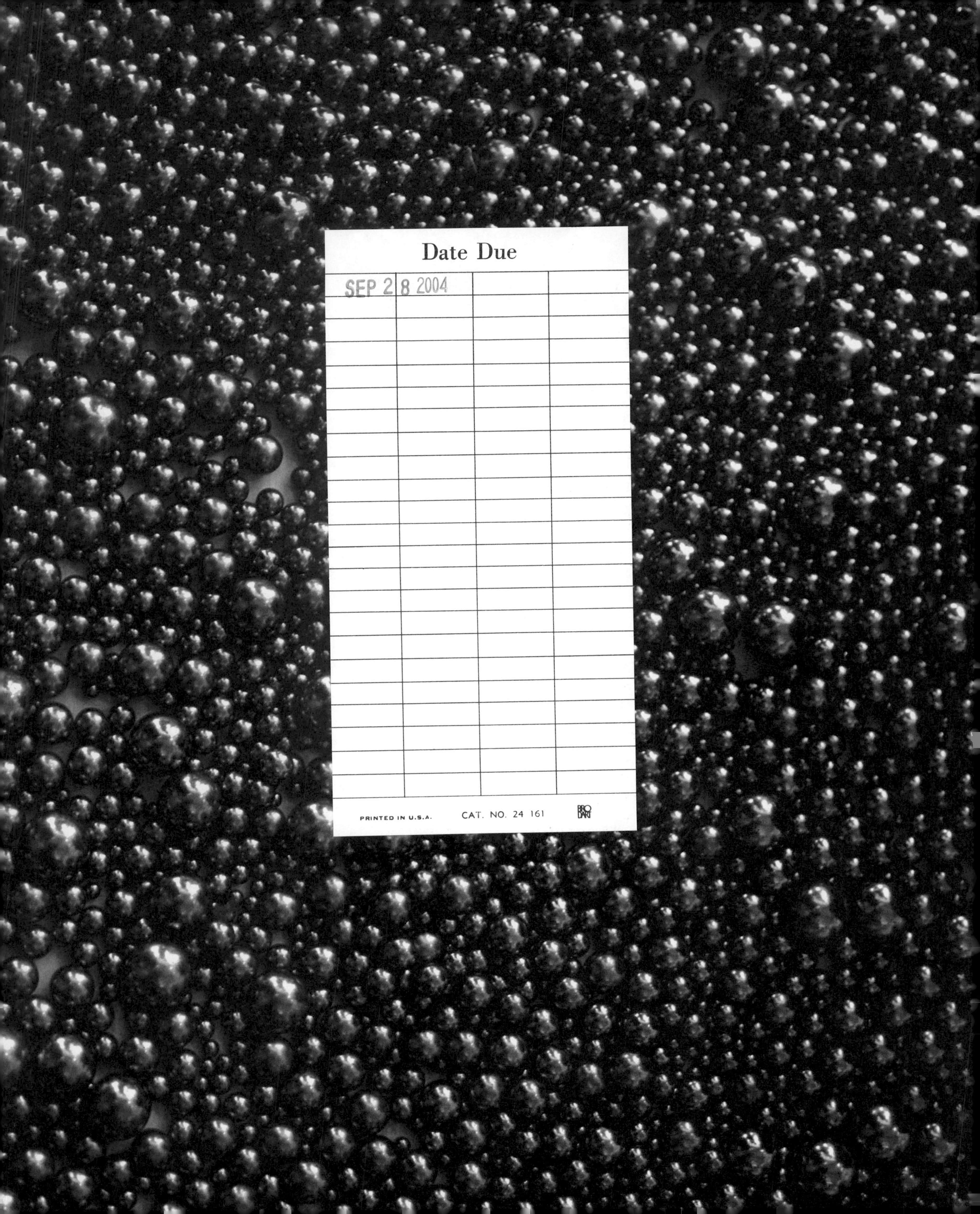